The Making of Middle English, 1765–1910

✛

David Matthews

Medieval Cultures
Volume 18

University of Minnesota Press
Minneapolis
London

The University of Minnesota Press gratefully acknowledges permission to reprint the following. Portions of chapter 3 originally appeared as " 'Quaint Inglis': Walter Scott and the Rise of Middle English Studies," *Studies in Medievalism*, vol. 7 (1995): 33–48. Portions of chapter 5 originally appeared as "The Deadly Poison of Democracy," *Parergon*, vol. 17 (January 1998). Portions of chapter 7 originally appeared as "Speaking to Chaucer: The Poet and the Nineteenth-Century Academy," *Studies in Medievalism*, vol. 9 (1997): 5–25.

Published by the University of Minnesota Press
111 Third Avenue South, Suite 290
Minneapolis, MN 55401-2520
http://www.upress.umn.edu

Library of Congress Cataloging-in-Publication Data
Matthews, David, 1963–
    The making of Middle English, 1765–1910 / David Matthews.
        p.   cm. — (Medieval cultures ; v. 18)
    Includes bibliographical references (p.   ) and index.
    ISBN 0-8166-3185-9 (alk. paper). — ISBN 0-8166-3186-7 (pbk. : alk. paper)
    1. English philology — Middle English, 1100–1500 — Historiography.
2. English philology — Middle English, 1100–1500 — Study and teaching —
History.   3. English literature — Middle English, 1100–1500 — History
and criticism — Theory, etc.   4. Great Britain — History — Medieval
period, 1066–1485 — Historiography.   5. Medievalism — Great Britain —
History.   I. Title.   II. Series.
PE515.M38   1999
427'.02'09033 — dc21   98-53478

AEJ–611/

The Making of Middle
English, 1765–1910

MEDIEVAL CULTURES

SERIES EDITORS
Rita Copeland
Barbara A. Hanawalt
David Wallace

*Sponsored by the Center for Medieval Studies
at the University of Minnesota*

Volumes in the series study the diversity of medieval cultural histories and practices, including such interrelated issues as gender, class, and social hierarchies; race and ethnicity; geographical relations; definitions of political space; discourses of authority and dissent; educational institutions; canonical and non-canonical literatures; and technologies of textual and visual literacies.

VOLUME 18
David Matthews
The Making of Middle English, 1765–1910

VOLUME 17
Jeffrey Jerome Cohen
Of Giants: Sex, Monsters, and the Middle Ages

VOLUME 16
Edited by Barbara A. Hanawalt and David Wallace
Medieval Crime and Social Control

VOLUME 15
Kathryn Kerby-Fulton and Denise L. Despres
*Iconography and the Professional Reader: The Politics of Book Production
in the Douce "Piers Plowman"*

VOLUME 14
Edited by Marilynn Desmond
Christine de Pizan and the Categories of Difference

VOLUME 13
Alfred Thomas
Anne's Bohemia: Czech Literature and Society, 1310–1420

VOLUME 12
Edited by F. R. P. Akehurst and Stephanie Cain Van D'Elden
The Stranger in Medieval Society

VOLUME 11
Edited by Karma Lochrie, Peggy McCracken, and James A. Schultz
Constructing Medieval Sexuality

For other books in the series, see p. 232

To Noel King

Contents

✣

Preface   ix

Introduction   xiii

Abbreviations   xxxvii

Part I: Patronage and the Antiquarian Self   1

1. "Barbarous Productions": The Making of Thomas Percy   3

2. Turning the World Upside Down: The Unmaking of
   Joseph Ritson   25

3. The Last Minstrel: Walter Scott and the Decade of Romance   54

4. Turtle Soup and Texts: From the Roxburghe Club to the
   Camden Society   85

Part II: Nationalism and the Selling of Middle English   111

5. "The Deadly Poison of Democracy": Frederic Madden,
   Scholar-Knight   113

6. "Go-a-head-itiveness": Frederick Furnivall and Early English   138

7. "Wise and Gentle Speech": From the Chaucer Society to
   the Universities   162

Conclusion   187

Notes   199

Index   223

Preface

❖

Working through *Sir Gawain and the Green Knight* some years ago as undergraduates at the University of Adelaide in South Australia, a fellow student and I came to the line "Towres telded bytwene, trochet ful þik." George Turner, leading the seminar, stopped us and asked us where the nearest example of such an architectural feature might be found. The question left us both perplexed. Not only did we not know the answer, the question itself seemed obscure. There are no medieval castles in Australia; the text was not about the things we knew, and its very otherness was the reason we had gone on to the advanced course in Middle English. What was the nearest bit of England, where such things are to be found? Was that what we were being asked? Altogether the question seemed to be one of those tricks in which the literature and history of the Old World abound. The answer to the question seemed likely to be sneakily unstraightforward, and the person who answered it likely to be caught, just like Gawain. We kept quiet.

The answer was that the nearest *towre trochet ful þik* was about two hundred yards away, on top of the Mitchell Building, a Gothic-revival pile then serving as the university's main administration block. The University of Adelaide, like the universities of Melbourne and Sydney that preceded it, is a nineteenth-century establishment that directly imitated the example of the universities of Oxford and Cambridge. All three began with neo-Gothic buildings, and Sydney and Melbourne have at their centers quadrangles imitative of the English models on which they were based. The architecture reflected the pedagogical assumptions that were also based firmly on the Oxbridge model. It was overwhelmingly the tendency, well into the twentieth century, to appoint Englishmen at the highest levels in English departments, or at least an English-educated Australian (usually an Oxonian).[1] Although at the time I am recalling, the battles over the inclusion of Australian literature in the work of such departments was largely won, and at both South Australian universities there were courses in what was then called Commonwealth Literature, English was still very evidently a colonial subject, speaking from a distant point of origin to its scattered subjects living in the shadows of ersatz dreaming spires.

Colonial Gothic is doubly displaced—temporally and geographically—and so signals the more forcefully its otherness. The early Australian universities were conceived in this longing for the other, and it is not surprising that they were intensely interested in the Middle Ages and medieval literature. The University of Melbourne, for example, subscribed to the Early English Text Society's publications in 1864, the year the society began. It still subscribes, and it may well be that the library of this university is the only continuous subscriber through the society's 130 years and more of existence.

It was because of this that I first encountered the subject of this book, or much of it, neatly laid out in hundreds of EETS volumes in the University of Melbourne's Baillieu Library. What might seem the oddity of an Australian publishing in the United States on the discipline of Middle English is in fact quite straightforward. There would be few places in the world where such tradition would be so lovingly preserved. The great deposit libraries can afford to be complacent about such series; the Melbourne library had to subscribe, keep up that subscription, and, in the early days, bind the books itself. I grew up and was educated in a culture that demonstrated its valuation of Englishness and the medieval in this way.

This is only the story of how I came to this topic, not the story told in this book. The dissemination of Middle English to America, Australia, and India would make a fascinating topic. It is a story that remains to be told. This book is simply an account of Middle English in Britain in what I have designated its formative stages. The book comes from the margins, conventionally defined, perhaps because it only appears to be a story from those margins. In England, Middle English (indeed, the discipline of English itself) is a less obvious subject because it is simply *there*. A Gothic cathedral is a real Gothic cathedral, a neo-Gothic building not an imperialist imposition but (like the Houses of Parliament at Westminster) a legitimate gesture to a heritage owned by the British. English literature is simply literature. Perhaps it is from the outside that the story becomes visible. In the 1980s, for example, a number of scholars whose work and concerns were obviously outside the political assumptions of traditional English began to tell the story of English in politically motivated ways. My education led me, as it happened at a very early age, to an appreciation of medieval literature, but even that deep appreciation could not smooth over the rift that seemed to divide me from this culture deriving from elsewhere.

This book had its origins with a consideration of the relations between the work of Thomas Percy and Frederic Madden, and the realization that if I wanted to know more about Middle English in this period I was going to have to find it out for myself. There were moments when I envisaged coverage of the entire project of postmedieval Middle English, from Caxton and the sixteenth-century printers onward. This somewhat immodest aim proved impossibly large in the kind of detail I have tried to supply. In any case, as I discovered, there were already several initiatives under way in different aspects of the study of Middle English. As I was finishing this project, Charlotte Brewer's book on the editing of *Piers Plowman* appeared; James Simpson is working on medieval studies in the Tudor period; and there has been, generally, a new interest in the medievalist antiquarians of the nineteenth century. This book is not a study of "medievalism" — the postmedieval reception of the Middle Ages — as such. Although the discipline of Middle English is, of course, a part of the overall revival in study of the Middle Ages, it is distinct, even if it must at times be picked out from the broader strand of medievalism in the period. The scope of the book is simply what I hope to demonstrate is the formative phase of Middle English, from 1765 and the publication of Percy's *Reliques* to the early years of this century, and the establishment of Middle English in the British universities. Along the way, it tries to engage with what seem to be some of the most pressing debates in discussions of the discipline at present: the nature of editing and the politics of editing; the perceived marginalization of Middle English studies; the relation of Middle English studies to the wider, nonacademic world; and, finally, the implications of such genealogical exercises as this one for current practices of teaching and criticism.

The earliest ideas from which this book arose were provoked by Stephen Knight, discussed with Michael Connor and Stephanie Trigg, and given an airing at a conference at Deakin University, Victoria, Australia, organized by Kevin Hart and Ian Reid. I am grateful to all of them. The road testing since then has been extensive: I am particularly grateful to the organizers of the international congresses at Kalamazoo (1993); the University of Leeds (1994, 1995, 1997, and 1998); and the Arizona Center for Medieval and Renaissance Studies (1997), Tempe; to Kathleen Verduin and Leslie Workman of the International Conference on Medievalism at Kalamazoo College (1996); and to everyone who commented. I am grateful to the patient audiences in English departments and schools at the University of Sydney, Macquarie University (New South Wales), the University of New South Wales, the University of Leeds, and the University of Wales, Cardiff, and especially to my colleagues at the University of Newcastle who remained attentive and helpful through serial paper-giving. The Research Management Committee of the University of Newcastle made the research possible with several generous grants, and a period of leave granted by the university made most of the writing possible. As the air miles mounted, I was helped and (very importantly) housed by many friends and those who became friends: Patricia Erasmus, Susan Haynes, Allen Frantzen and George Paterson, and Carmen Callil. At a crucial stage, the support and friendship of Bernhard Klein, Sue Wiseman, and Steve Barnett made the writing of the book a much less lonely experience than it might have been.
   Of those who have read and commented on parts of the work, my especial thanks go to Ruth Evans, whose encouragement and expert help

over the years have been vital. James Simpson read chapter 1; Graham Tulloch put out some Walter Scott spotfires; the anonymous readers at *Parergon* helped improve chapter 5; and the two readers who read the manuscript for the University of Minnesota Press made dozens of helpful suggestions, many of which find their way into the final version. At home, Geraldine Barnes, Margaret Clunies Ross, Clare Forster, Mark Gauntlett, Peter Holbrook, Roslyn Jolly and Simon Petch, Jenna Mead, Brian Matthews and Jane Arms, Marea Mitchell, Julian Pefanis, Barbara Pertzel, John Potts, Terry Ryan, Imre Salusinszky, Edward Scheer, and Rosalind Smith all encouraged me and kept me going, while Noel King contributed to the book in more ways than I could now enumerate.

The work could not have been carried out without the patience of the staff at the Bodleian Library (especially Timothy Rogers); Cambridge University Library; Fisher Library; Huntington Library; Houghton Library; the library at King's College, London; the Thomas Fisher Rare Book Library; and, above all, the staff in the North Library of the British Library.

Parts of chapter 5 appeared in *Parergon*, and early versions of chapters 3 and 7 in *Studies in Medievalism* 7 (1995): 33–48 and 9 (1997): 5–25; I am grateful to the editors of those journals for permission to reuse material.

Finally, I am especially grateful to all at the University of Minnesota Press who made the final stages so smooth: Lisa Freeman, William Murphy, Robin A. Moir, Laura Westlund, and Anne Running, and the series editors, David Wallace, Rita Copeland, and Barbara A. Hanawalt.

Introduction

❖

"We Are Dreadfully Real": Forgetting Middle English

Beside me I have an old and long disused edition of a Middle English poem. It is bound in blue buckram; on the spine are several abbreviations. To anyone with more than a passing acquaintance with the field of Middle English literature, the notation "E.E.T.S. E.S. 4 1868" readily identifies the volume as number 4 in the Early English Text Society's Extra Series. The book has been rebound and retrimmed by a library, whose call number, "WOLF PR 1119.E5 P.M.C.," also appears on the spine. Stamps on the pages tell me that P.M.C. stands for the Pennsylvania Military College in Chester, Pennsylvania. Inside the front cover is a book plate with the Greek motto τὰ διδακτὰ μανθάνω (ta didakta manthano) and the name of Lieutenant William J. Wolfgram, English Reference Library, Pennsylvania Military College. The surname, presumably, explains part of the volume's call number, which perhaps implies that Lieutenant Wolfgram bequeathed or donated this book to the library of the college he worked in.

A few pages beyond the book plate, there is the original binding of this EETS edition, with the rather lurid purple paper used in the days before EETS editions were casebound. This is adorned with an engraved picture of the seal of an English town, Grimsby, and features various pieces of information. In ornate script, imitative of black letter, the title is given as *The Lay of Havelok the Dane*. It is edited by the Reverend Walter W. Skeat and formerly edited for the Roxburghe Club by Sir F. Madden, now published for the Early English Text Society by Kegan Paul, Trench, Trübner & Co. in Charing Cross Road at a price of ten shillings. It was first published in 1868 and reprinted in 1891, 1893, and 1903.

Beyond this information, there lie several pages of promotional material relating to the Early English Text Society, the sort of thing we would now expect to see in a publisher's catalog rather than as prefatory material to an actual book. Then, beyond this, the scholarship begins: the reader comes to Skeat's comprehensive preface, which is based in part on the introduction Madden had written in 1828; a list of corrections and emendations; and then the poem itself, edited from the unique copy in MS Laud Misc. 108, in the Bodleian Library.

This text—not the edition but this single book—is a microcosmic moment in the material history of the study of Middle English. This is a multistranded history. On the one hand, there is the history of the romance, *Havelok,* itself, which in the modern period begins with Frederic Madden's accidental discovery of the text in the Bodleian Library in 1826. His edition of it was produced under the patronage of the bibliophile second Earl Spencer for the Roxburghe Club in 1828. Reediting it, Skeat paid explicit tribute to Madden's work, but also projected the text into new forms of circulation: the open, democratically minded format of the EETS, which aimed its books at an educated middle class, as opposed to the tightly controlled Roxburghe Club, which reserved its texts for an aristocratic and gentlemanly few.

Individual copies of a book within a print run, on the other hand, have their own histories. My copy of Skeat's *Havelok* (bought for fifteen dollars by mail order from an antiquarian bookseller in Philadelphia) has been differentiated by its original owner, marked with the signs of his purpose in owning it. As the bookplate motto ("I learn the lessons") and its eventual place in a scholarly library suggest, this book was valued as an object of scholarly inquiry. That much seems obvious; perhaps the romance of Havelok also offered lessons that spoke directly to an army officer or the clientele of a military college library. Although that is speculative, the book's presence in Pennsylvania in the early years of the century does testify to the extremely successful export of the fledgling subject of Middle English to the East Coast of the United States in the later nineteenth century, through the combined efforts of Frederick Furnivall, the director of the EETS, and Francis Child at Harvard University.

It is possible to go further in the construction of such a history by drawing on a combination of different forms of knowledge: biographical information about Skeat himself, research into the Early English Text Society, and research into the nature of the scholarly circles within which such books were produced. Why, for example, was the edition not reprinted between 1868 and 1891, but then reprinted three times from 1891 to 1903? Probably because Furnivall wildly overestimated demand and printed too many copies in the 1860s, but then had to cater to increased demand in the 1890s, when this kind of material was beginning to be taught in universities and schools.

Why did Skeat call this poem the "Lay" of Havelok the Dane, for example, when Madden had labeled it *The Ancient English Romance of Havelok the Dane?* Skeat would never have called it "ancient" because he worked with a more refined model of medieval chronology, informed by a knowledge of comparative philology, than had existed in the 1820s. The apparent generic shift of the poem to a "lay" was probably because the French version of the Havelok story was known as the "Lai d'Havelok le Danois," under which title it was edited by Francisque Michel in Paris in 1833. In other respects, Skeat retained aspects of Madden's scholarship. The by then notoriously crusty Madden was grateful for this gesture, and he was a man whose good opinion was well worth cultivating so that he would continue to permit the EETS to reedit texts he had first edited. So Skeat worked within a network of scholarship and—equally important—gentlemanliness.

This is only one copy of one text, and although *Havelok* once held a much more central place in Middle English studies (when, in Madden's edition, it was one of only a few available texts), its importance cannot be exaggerated. Nevertheless, it is in such microhistories—of the text in the manuscript, the text in its editions, the circulation of the text, the transmission of editions, the social and scholarly placement of editors—that a larger history of the study of Middle English, such as I aim to trace here, can be found. Yet Middle English studies has shown little interest until recently in its material history. There is in fact built into scholarship of Middle English (more so, perhaps, than in other areas of the study of English literature) a notion of authority that often has the effect of effacing the prior critical history of a text. We work with such concepts as the "authoritative edition" and "authoritative criticism." These are powerful: if a new edition of a Middle English text is available (and new editions usually claim to be newly authoritative), scholars might look, for comparison, at the preceding edition and perhaps the one before that, but earlier editions can be entirely forgotten.

It is only in a few cases that scholars bother with what was said in Middle English editions in the nineteenth century and earlier. When they do, it is usually because the text in question has not been edited since or, more rarely, because, like Madden's edition of the two manuscripts of Laȝamon's *Brut*, the work still commands respect. Certainly, few editors of the nineteenth century brought Madden's care and expertise to their editions, which might therefore be better forgotten. But Middle English studies can be very forgetful indeed. Modern editions of *Piers Plowman* often make no reference to the sixteenth-century editions of the B-text. A recent and authoritative edition of *Confessio Amantis* does not record the dates of the early editions by Thomas Berthelette. It is true that there is a relative wealth of material on Chaucer scholarship through the centuries,[1] but it is balanced by a great paucity in almost every other respect.

This is because editions of Middle English texts are far more interested in manuscripts and their history. No one would publish an edition without an account of the manuscript. Yet the long, often rich history of textual transmission since the invention of print is increasingly neglected. The manuscript retains an unquestioned status as originary source of a text. No matter how problematically it does so, the manuscript is thought to put us in contact with an original, medieval text. The printed text, on the other hand, more often impedes our access to that text, by corrupting it or by presenting it badly edited or framed by poor scholarship.

However true it often is that early editions involve wild departures from the manuscripts, something is lost when they are ignored. New discoveries and new approaches can produce a newly authoritative text and newly authoritative commentaries, even of such a worked-over author as Chaucer. What can be missed, though, is the point that the prior authority could once have been precisely as "authoritative" as we now perceive modern authorities to be. Authority ceaselessly reinvents itself, but a condition of its doing so is a forgetting that there was any prior authority. And so authority creates a continuist narrative of scholarship, in which it is assumed that literary history is always on the improve and that nobody has done it as well as we are doing it now.

Modern scholarship has no use for the conclusions of one of the first great literary historians, Thomas Warton. If the compendious *History of English Poetry* has any value today, it is principally as narrative, as literature itself, not as scholarship. Yet modern scholarship espouses, at least implicitly, the same basic attitude to history that Warton did. He assumed that his own era was the most advanced that there had ever been. For him it was a given that he wrote "[i]n an age advanced to the highest degree of refinement" and from a viewpoint that allowed "a tacit comparison of the infinite disproportion between the feeble efforts of remote ages, and our present improvements in knowledge" (*HEP*, 1:i). Modern scholarship, in Middle English studies at least, operates with exactly similar assumptions. We do not carry on a dialogue with nineteenth- and eighteenth-century scholars of Middle English because they have nothing to tell us. Norman Cantor, for example, repudiates the work of the romantic nineteenth-century medievalists because, although they reversed the prevailing view of the Middle Ages, they "lacked the scholarship, the learning and instruments of research, to go beyond the most superficial kind of inquiry into the medieval past. Both the Renaissance denigration of the Middle Ages and the romantic acclamation of medieval culture were almost exclusively based on mere ideological projections."[2] This conviction of the superiority of medieval studies in our century over that of the nineteenth only spells out explicitly an attitude implicit throughout modern scholarship.

Perhaps it does not matter that we efface the prior history of editions. Perhaps it is as well to get rid of much of the voluminous nineteenth-century commentary, little of which could help the student of today. Perhaps what matters is producing as authoritative a text as possible of a given author's work, so that readers can be put in touch, through it, with the medieval literature that forms the object of our study. But I have assumed that it does matter. I have assumed that we are always engaged in a dialogue with the object of our study, and one side of that dialogue is modern scholarship. Our own historical situatedness is as important as respect for the historical character of our object of study. In turn, our situatedness is produced by a lineage or genealogy of scholarship for which we should also have respect, instead of, as we tend to do, instantly forgetting it, indeed actually effacing it, by omission.

It is not that there is a need to *revive* romantic or eighteenth-century scholarship. Scholarship cannot be egalitarian in this way; scholars must discriminate, make choices, and, indeed, say that this is right and that is wrong. But this is not the same as forgetting and belittling. There is something alarming in Cantor's formulation: what is "mere" about an ideological projection? Are we free, now, from ideological projections? (The material in his book *Inventing the Middle Ages* would hardly suggest so.) There is a belittling here of a scholarship that might have been wrong, in our current view, but that, in fact, was greatly influential, not just on scholars, but also on the lives of ordinary people.

In *Dombey and Son* (by the generally antimedievalist Dickens), Mrs. Skewton rhapsodizes about the Middle Ages — "Such charming times! . . . So full of Faith! So vigorous and forcible! So picturesque! So perfectly removed from commonplace!" — in a way that makes it hard to avoid the implication that the author is satirizing this vapid romantic vision, particularly when the litany is capped with the memorable complaint: "We are dreadfully real, Mr Carker . . . are we not?"[3]

We *are* dreadfully real. We are always dreadfully real, whoever "we" happen to be at a given time. But our reality must not be allowed to efface the importance of prior realities. In this book, which aims to begin a material history of the study of Middle English literature, I try to stress the competing realities that such study produced. The scope of the book is what can be called, because of the volume of output at least, the most important formative period for Middle English studies, the period in which an increasingly romantic scholarship discovered and constructed the subject, between 1765 and 1910. The first date is significant as that of the first edition of Thomas Percy's *Reliques of Ancient English Poetry*; the second, the year when Frederick Furnivall died, is rather more symbolic, but coincides with the period in which Middle English entered the old English universities and the paradigm of romantic and largely amateur scholarship was fundamentally altered.

In undertaking such a material history, what I chiefly examine here is both the materiality of the books produced in the period and the impact of the lives and approaches of the scholars who produced them. Attention paid to the materiality of books involves the kind of scrutiny I began to give to Skeat's edition of *Havelok* above. This entails looking not simply (or even principally) at the actual medieval text as it has been edited from the manuscript, but at everything that surrounds that text: the scholarship — in introduction, notes, apparatus, glossary — along with anything else that might have made its way into the text, such as promotional material, lists of subscribers, owner's annotations, and the like.

I see this as an approach already well under way in manuscript studies. Seth Lerer, for example, deliberately works against conventional no-

tions of authoritative manuscripts by the scrutiny he gives to "bad" manuscripts of Chaucer's work and other poetry, looking at what they imply
for authorship and readership.[4] Many of the chapters in Ralph Hanna's
Pursuing History are also relevant here.[5] The approach is explicitly theorized by Lee Patterson and Stephen G. Nichols in their special issue of
South Atlantic Quarterly, entitled "Commentary as Cultural Artifact."[6]
The premise of the issue is the inclusion, as the object of critical scrutiny,
not simply of the text a manuscript contains, but the contexts as well:
the glosses, illustrations, illuminations, marginal doodles, and scribblings;
what we might know about manuscript history and ownership; and so
on. These facets constitute what Nichols calls, in his article "Commentary and/as Image" (965–92), "the manuscript matrix," a term indicating
"the historical fact that medieval texts were written in a manuscript
format which is both multimedia in form and temporally open-ended"
(991 n. 12).

Despite the focus on manuscripts, Nichols's article and Patterson's
introduction to the issue (787–91) seem to offer a way forward for the
study of old printed texts as well. The differences between the edited
texts of the first two editions of *Sir Gawain and the Green Knight,* to
take an example, are minimal. But the surrounding scholarly material
constructs the texts in entirely different ways. For Madden in 1839, *Sir
Gawain* was a Scottish poem of the late fourteenth century; for Richard
Morris in 1864 it was an English poem of the early fourteenth century,
and the differences multiply from there. This kind of scrutiny of early
editions is not designed to replace or substitute for study of the manuscript or to compensate for the relative paucity of contexts for and in (in
this case) MS Cotton Nero A.x. To borrow Nichols's own phrase, what I
am proposing here is effectively the study of a "supplement" to the manuscript tradition.[7] The concern would be not with the supposed accuracy or otherwise with which the editors had recreated an authorial *Sir
Gawain,* but with the way in which each edition supplemented the manuscript, prior editions, and other existing scholarship.

In later work, however, Nichols specifically repudiates the application
of his concept to printed texts. In his essay "Philology and Its Discontents," he writes that his own practice is distinguished from that of
Jerome McGann by "the fundamental difference between print technology and manuscript reproduction":

> Print technology is copy technology. Manuscript propagation may be
> viewed as a means of copying pre-existing texts, and that is the way
> text editing and textual studies have regarded manuscripts. This is
> a reductive view—based on the empirical or functional observation
> that since manuscripts were to provide copies of works for reading,
> they must have been *copies.* A reproduction may indeed be a copy,

but a copy with a difference—a difference born of the intervention of an author, someone who sees and reports (reproduces) what is seen, transposing it into his own dialect, and so forth. It is this difference that makes the manuscript a space of representation, a space of supplementation, and not simply a copy.[8]

While I respect Nichols's broader conclusion and believe that his refocusing of attention on areas of the manuscript traditionally neglected is long overdue, this decisive removal of printed texts from the "space of supplementation" seems to me methodologically flawed. Print technology does not, as is sometimes assumed, simply deliver a socially and politically inert product, a copy. It can only be imagined to do so if the text is thought of as existing not so much in a material realization as in the ideal text that the author intended. But as Tim William Machan argues, "since readers' access to a work is only through a particular realization, for practical purposes it is impossible to differentiate readers' responses to a work from their responses to particular material realizations of that work. Moreover, documentary realizations themselves—in their size, color, layout, typeface, illustration, and construction—are thought to signify as complexly as literary texts."[9]

Nichols's fundamental distinction between manuscript and printed texts is based on horizontal and vertical text relations. When a manuscript is produced, it copies a preexisting text, and itself can be copied, to produce a series of texts that can be imagined as having a vertical relation to one another (as stemmatic diagrams suggest). Print technology, on the other hand, because it is a copy technology, produces texts not only in this vertical relation, but in a horizontal one as well. The 130 or so copies of Frederic Madden's 1839 text, *Syr Gawayne,* for example, can be imagined in horizontal relation to one another—as exact copies of one another—and in vertical relation to the manuscript, and to the next edition, Morris's 1864 text.

It is difficult to see why the "horizontality" of such a text should of itself exclude print technology from an analysis of commentary as cultural artifact. The criterion separating the copy technology from the manuscript is simply the uniqueness that the latter results in, and this, while important, should not automatically privilege a text (however much it might inflate its value on a market). In any case, the "horizontal" texts— what might be considered "allotexts"—in practice quickly begin to be differentiated from one another. They are marked by their social circulation, just as any manuscript is. Owners put their names in them, libraries put shelf marks on them and stamp them against theft, editors inscribe them to friends, and generations of readers mark them and write in the margins. These might be routine markings of the text, or they might, as in the last case, be unlicensed, but they nevertheless inscribe the text with the marks of its own individual history.[10] Aspects of that history, such as the application of *Havelok* in Pennsylvania Military College, may remain unknowable, but it is history nonetheless, and some of it is recoverable and relevant.

Another good reason for attention to printed editions is particularly pertinent to the early production of Middle English texts. Nineteenth-century editions of Middle English were often produced and circulated in a mode much more reminiscent of manuscript production than of the mass distribution enabled by modern copy technology. An extreme example is provided by Edward V. Utterson's edition of *Robert of Sicily*, published by him under the title of *Kyng Roberd of Cysylle* in 1839. This elegant little book of twenty-seven pages was produced by Utterson anonymously in a run of only thirty copies, of which none were offered for sale. It seems that he gave the copies away as gifts; this was certainly the case with the copy in the British Library, which once belonged to the Bodleian librarian Philip Bliss and is inscribed to Bliss from "his friend the Editor." Bliss, or someone else, has gone through the book very carefully with a pencil, noting errors, querying readings, drawing a line through the *z*s Utterson has used for yoghs, and putting in thorns where Utterson has *th*.[11]

Utterson's *Robert*, then, far from entering the typical mode of production and distribution that print technology allowed, was circulated privately with no profit motive in view. Nor, apparently, was there any motive of scholarly aggrandizement, as Utterson's name appears nowhere in the book. The possibilities allowed by a copy technology are here deliberately ignored in favor of a form of circulation akin to that of a manuscript culture.

Although this represents an extreme example, the mode is by no means uncommon in the production of Middle English texts at the time. The Roxburghe Club, for example, which dominated Middle English editions for several years after its founding in 1812, rarely produced more than sixty copies in a print run, all of which were restricted to club members. This remained typical among other clubs that followed the Roxburghe's model. The books were circulated, therefore, among a limited, privileged audience in very small numbers; they were venerated, and they gained their particular cultural cachet not from the name of the editor and the indication of his labor, but from the name of the society representing the rich capital investors who had made their production possible. Sometimes, as when a young and impoverished Frederic Madden edited *Havelok* for Earl Spencer and the Roxburghe Club, the clubs created a situation reminiscent of the medieval relation of great lords to humble monastic transcribers.

Obviously there is limited usefulness in pushing this analogy too far, interestingly divergent from most modern conceptions of book production though the early club books were. To forget the diversity possible in a print culture, however, and to assume the existence solely of multiple allotexts is to forget the social status of the printed text—to coalesce a whole tradition of printed editions into one homogenized notion of "text." *Sir Gawain*, then, would become a text that appears in an important and interesting manuscript, Cotton Nero A.x, but that, for study purposes, needs to be looked at only in the authoritative edition of J. R. R. Tolkien and E. V. Gordon, revised by Norman Davis. The printed tradition is just a set of variants, some right, some wrong. It is therefore dehistoricized and only the manuscript is historical and social. And yet there is something ironically perverse in this, especially in the case of *Sir Gawain*, because we know almost nothing about the history of Nero A.x outside of the modern period, while the interesting data concerning the printed tradition are readily available.

I have, then, treated the printed tradition of Middle English as a fruitful area of study, as commentary, in Nichols's sense. To do this, as I see it, is to apply his notion of "material philology" to Middle English editions, but in a way that does not privilege manuscript culture over copy technology.[12] It is, after all, through print that almost every reader has approached *Sir Gawain* or any other Middle English poem. There is a tendency, inherent in the idea of the "authoritative" or "scholarly" text, to treat an edition as transparent, to forget that an edition is a material intervention in a text. The "new philology" of recent years has so far always come back to editing as a central concern, which would therefore suggest that a recentering of early *editions* in the field of analysis is due. As David F. Hult puts it, recalling a simple but significant point, "it is important to keep in mind that editing is not simply prior to interpretation, it is consubstantial with it."[13] It is in any case particularly important, in the case of Middle English studies, that attention be paid to the contexts surrounding the printed editions. In the almost complete absence of work on Middle English in the universities before the 1870s, Middle English studies, such as it was, was conducted in editions of texts.[14] The study of "commentary" in them is crucial to an account of what constituted the early study of Middle English.

The Self and Ideology: Remembering English Studies

In whatever way an inquiry such as I have outlined is framed, it necessarily exhibits its debts to a lineage of accounts of the broader phenomenon of "the Rise of English." The more obviously genealogical work, entailing an analysis of ideology, by Chris Baldick and Terry Eagleton, comes to mind here, as, in the sphere of medieval studies, does Allen Frantzen's work on Anglo-Saxon studies, Lee Patterson's on Chaucer studies, and Theresa Coletti's on the Records of Early English Drama project.[15]

Each of these writers, in different ways, has argued for the importance of a deliberate remembering of English studies' ideological past, the kind of remembering I am proposing for Middle English.

This kind of work, as is now well known, has implicated the study of English in various ideologies, particularly those of nationalism, class, and gender. There are reasons, however, to be wary of the ideological grand narrative in relation to Middle English. Unlike "English" per se or the venerable subject of Anglo-Saxon, Middle English only belatedly comes into visibility as an object. It was not even constituted as "Middle English" until the 1870s, and the moment of its being so constituted—as I will show in the next section—was also the moment in which it joined English studies as a whole; its definition, in other words, was rapidly followed by a loss of disciplinary autonomy. Before these late-nineteenth-century transformations took place, Middle English was almost entirely the preserve of the few, not because of a high cultural valuation (as was the case with classical studies), but because of its insignificance in the eyes of the many. Even after Middle English was connected to an increasingly officialized English in the later nineteenth century and so linked to the mass education movement, the market of interested people (as figures given in chapter 6 will show) remained very small. The ideological *impact* of this form of study, then, must be thought of as negligible, however rich the actual texts can be shown to be in ideological assumptions.

My approach here, particularly with Middle English in the period before the establishment of the EETS in 1864, is to look at the texts as local examples of a politics that has its place at the base of an ascending model that takes in much broader, hegemonic forms of power, capable of influencing a nation. "[T]he important thing," writes Michel Foucault, "is not to attempt some kind of deduction of power starting from its centre and aimed at the discovery of the extent to which it permeates into the base.... One must rather conduct an *ascending* analysis of power, starting, that is, from its infinitesimal mechanisms, which each have their own history, their own trajectory, their own techniques and tactics, and then see how these mechanisms of power have been... invested, colonised, utilised, involuted, transformed, displaced, extended etc., by ever more general mechanisms and by forms of global domination."[16] The texts examined here were sometimes printed in runs of as few as thirty copies and circulated in small groups. They were often a long way from the center, and I treat them here as infinitesimal mechanisms, each with its own small history.

The consideration of scholarly selfhood, and its relation to the scholar's work, has also involved recourse to a rather different account of English. Deliberately setting himself against the tradition he sees as exemplified by Baldick, Eagleton, and others, Ian Hunter has described the rise of English not as an ideology, but as the development of a technology of the self. Using some of Foucault's later ideas to propound a view of English as a means of self-formation through ethical-aesthetic education, Hunter sees English studies as having its origins in the school in the late eighteenth century and as being deployed in a more broad-based way in the move to mass education in the nineteenth century. The growth of English studies is a process, taking place from the late eighteenth century to the early twentieth, "in which the reading and criticism of literature lost their function as the aesthetico-ethical practice of a minority caste, and acquired a new deployment and function as an arm of the emergent governmental educational apparatus."[17]

Hunter's account is avowedly a genealogy in the Foucauldian sense, aiming to trace the conditions of emergence of modern literary education. But he does not pursue the idea, which he identifies with the work of Eagleton, Baldick, and other British critics on the left, that English was an ideology that fundamentally repressed individuals: "English is not an ideology.... English exists neither as a set of ideas or representations, nor as the little theatre where the 'formation of the subject' is staged through the narcissistic relation to its ideal image. Rather it exists as the autonomous and irreducible ensemble of ethical techniques and pedagogical practices and relations whose hybrid form we have described."[18] English, in this account, is obviously a technology of the self in that (in Foucault's own description) it "permit[s] individuals to effect by their own means, or with the help of others, a certain number of operations on their own bodies and souls, thoughts, conduct, and way of being, so as to transform themselves in order to attain a certain state of happiness, purity, wisdom, perfection, or immortality."[19] On this basis, Hunter argues that English, "a hybrid ethical technology formed when a specialised practice of aesthetic self cultivation was deployed inside a pedagogical system dedicated to the moral regulation of the population," far from repressing subjectivities, actually *creates* possibilities for selfhood.[20]

The use of literature and literary study as a technology of the self is a characteristic of Middle English from the 1760s, despite the separation I have mentioned between Middle English and the study of postmedieval English.[21] The first section of this book, "Patronage and the Antiquarian Self," is concerned with a phase of Middle English study in which the antiquarian self is shaped and projected by the literature. The typical model—certainly the model of the most successful scholars—involves a connection between the literature promoted by the scholar and the scholar's advancement through aesthetic work on the self, a form of work usually deployed in the furtherance of aristocratic patronage.

Like English, in Hunter's description, Middle English studies, too, gradually became less the property of a minority caste and more the object of a mass education program from around the middle of the nineteenth century. In this guise, Middle English literature was promoted among the working class and middle class as a moral technology, deriving much force from the fact that it was for its main promoter, Frederick Furnivall, a substitute for the missionary religious faith he had lost when his Christian Socialism gave way to agnosticism in the 1850s and 1860s. At the same time, as Middle English texts became increasingly public property, the potential nationalist value of this early literature began to emerge as the prime justification for study. Middle English needed a selling point, and Furnivall found it in duty to England's national heritage. The reading of Middle English now became or was projected as a technology of the self that helped fashion better Englishmen and -women, not simply through their moral improvement, but through the service they did to their nation by reading, and helping to pay for the cost of producing, the country's early literature. This phase is dealt with in the book's second section, "Nationalism and the Selling of Middle English."

"It is not a political analysis of English that we need today," Hunter writes, "but one capable of situating English as one technology of the self amongst others."[22] As my earlier remarks make clear, ultimately I have resisted Hunter's severing of his own form of description from that of the political critics. The narrative of Middle English seems to me to require description of an ideological element. In the shift from the deployment of Middle English studies as an essentially privatized means of aesthetic self-transformation to its reformulation as an arm of governmentally sanctioned education, Middle English studies at all stages had a political dimension, demanding a political description. This is not to suggest that Middle English must be reimagined as a technology that repressed individuals, but that a moral technology can coexist with an ideological technology.

One of the key facets of Middle English in its early phases was that it commanded little official or general attention. For the most part it was not successful men, men already in fixed social stations, who involved themselves in this barely known subject, but men who wanted to get somewhere, to *be* successful. The self-transformations of such men as Thomas Percy and Walter Scott, as chapters 1 and 3 argue, involved class mobility and material improvement, and are therefore social and political as well as aesthetic transformations. Chapter 2 considers the reverse case of the political radical Joseph Ritson, who did not try to advance himself or achieve patronage through his editions, and whose spectacular failure as a scholar can be directly linked to precisely his failure to fashion the self via the literature he studied.

In this phase, then, Middle English was deployed in a privatized way as a technology of the self. Percy's *Reliques of Ancient English Poetry* was a widely successful work in the last third of the eighteenth century, but the most dramatic recorded effect it had was on Percy's own self and career. Many other early editions were circulated in closely controlled ways, so that the literature remained more the preserve of an elite coterie than a public property. Furthermore, as the most influential scholars based their self-reinvention on aristocratic patronage, a medieval literature was produced and constructed that was in accord with perceived aristocratic values.[23] Overwhelmingly, the genre of romance became the object of study because of the positive envisionings of aristocracy in literary chivalry.

Chapter 4 shows how this model of aristocratic patronage was formalized by the Roxburghe Club in the early years of the nineteenth century, and then began to break up with the advent of such subscription societies as the Camden Society. Chapter 5 discusses Frederic Madden's career as a phase of transition. When he began editing texts in the 1820s and 1830s, it was still possible to link such work to private ambitions and aristocratic patronage. By the end of his career in the 1860s this had changed, and a new political phase of Middle English had begun with the increased emphasis on nationalism.

Before the middle of the nineteenth century, there was only sporadic interest in Middle English literature as national heritage. For many English scholars, what was most interesting about Middle English was its strangeness, its difference, and they could consequently see little obvious connection with their own culture. Nor were they always particularly keen to connect the literature of this barbarous, superstitious, and Catholic era with their own England. The overtly nationalist moment in the early phase of Middle English studies comes therefore from Walter Scott, who made much of what he thought was the Scottishness of the romance of *Sir Tristrem* and its supposed (Scottish) author, Thomas of Erceldoune.

Nevertheless, the key justifications for study of these texts were the ways in which they displayed the stages of the English language and their depiction of the "manners and customs of our ancestors," to use the basic, much repeated formula. By the middle of the nineteenth century, there was less emphasis on the barbarism of medieval literature (partly because comparative philology allowed a greater understanding of how early languages worked), and the full potential for these contentions began to be explored. Middle English in this guise, particularly in the hands of Furnivall, began to take its place as part of a search for Englishness, which chapter 6 describes.

Finally, as chapter 7 argues, the study of Chaucer and the study of other Middle English began to merge as one discipline. Chaucer studies, as this chapter proposes, had a history very different from that of the rest of Middle English. There is an almost complete separation between antiquarian work on Chaucer and other Middle English up until the edition of *The Canterbury Tales* produced in 1847–51 by Thomas Wright, who was also a prolific editor of other Middle English texts. The fusion signaled in Wright's career continued with the combination of Chaucerian work and broader medieval work that occurred when the Early English Text and Chaucer Societies were founded by Furnivall in 1864 and 1868.

Middle English studies, now all but governed by the tireless Furnivall, progressed steadily toward the academy. The EETS was unquestionably the flagship of the emerging discipline. As the discipline was disseminated in the later nineteenth century, it moved outward from London. German scholars increasingly contributed to editions and criticism, and the subject was successfully exported to Australia, India, and especially the United States. But the EETS remained central through this phase. The Middle English element of English studies was critical in the entry of English studies into Oxford and Cambridge because of the well-developed methodology of philology, which could be used to counter claims that there was nothing to say about literature; that criticism was, in the historian E. A. Freeman's famous words, "mere chatter about Shelley."[24] It is not surprising that the first lectureship in English at Cambridge was created partly at the urging of a medievalist (Skeat) and filled by another, Israel Gollancz.

It is Middle English as sanctioned by the academy in the late nineteenth and early twentieth centuries that became accepted and that we have inherited. Essentially, we see "Middle English" as a subject much as Skeat, Henry Bradshaw, and Gollancz did. But this term, which seems inertly descriptive on university syllabuses today, was only arrived at after a long development, which involved many competing ways of looking at the English Middle Ages. A middle is often a less certain category than the two other things it serves to keep apart. The middle in English is a relatively recent invention, and even when scholars began agreeing that there was one, they did not agree on where exactly it occurred. So there was no sense, before the 1870s at the earliest, that the period between the Conquest and the Renaissance (whenever that began) was linguistically coherent, and in these conditions of uncertainty, different ideologies could stake different claims. What was at issue was no less than Englishness, what it might be said to be and where it might be said to have begun.

The Sense of a Middle

It was only after the decisive yoking of Chaucer and other Middle English that the term "Middle English," in its current sense, began to be regularly used. Strictly speaking, there was no discipline of Middle English before 1868, at the earliest. But its growth, in the last third of the nineteenth century, was rapid. Middle English, the term and the concept it denoted, though still not everywhere popular, had emerged as an ideological coherence too useful to be ignored any longer as the eccentric pursuit of the dry antiquarian few.

In contrast with twentieth-century medieval studies, the antiquarian scholars tended to be concerned not so much with where the Middle Ages ended and modernity began as with the ways in which the Middle

Ages could be divided up and the origins of English could be distinguished. Despite what comparative philology, from the 1830s, had taught them about linguistic change, they still tended to identify the emergence of "English" with a particular moment: for some, this moment was a literary event; for others, it was political; for others still, "English" had to be traced right back to the Anglo-Saxon of Alfred. Inevitably, as the issue of language became more and more bound up with ideas about nationalism, this ideological coherence was resolved as an element of nationalist thinking, so that Middle English took its place in a set of disciplines with nationalist motivations.

For a long time, the antiquarians could distinguish no such entity as "Middle English" at all. Instead they concentrated on what they thought of as different versions of Saxon, and looked for the point at which this became genuine "English." In his *Thesaurus* of 1703, George Hickes referred to "Dano-Saxon," spoken in the north of England after the Viking incursions, and "Norman-Saxon." Hickes called the language spoken by the English population after the Conquest "Semi-Saxon": "*Semi-Saxonicam* autem eam docti nominant, quòd medius quasi sermo, vel pene medius esset, inter puriorem *Anglo-Saxonicum*, & *Anglicanum* illum, qui majoribus nostris ante centum & quinquaginta annos vernaculus erat."[25] Rather than seeing the Conquest as a decisive break between linguistic phases, then, Hickes describes a transitional linguistic stage, one that separates the Anglo-Saxon of the pre-Conquest period and English as it is now known. Contrasting with the typical modern view of the English Middle Ages as essentially bipartite linguistically, Hickes gives a tripartite view of the Middle Ages, with English proper succeeding a phase of Semi-Saxon.

With similar terminology, Thomas Warton used the terms "Danish Saxon," which he maintained succeeded "Saxon" after the invasions of the Vikings, and "Norman Saxon," which obtained from the Conquest into the reign of Henry II (*HEP*, 1:1–2). Like many writers, Warton could only conceive of change in a language as occurring when it mingled with, or was contaminated by, other languages, rather than as involving any internal alteration. Warton does not specify what follows "Norman Saxon," but from later references it appears that he sees English as we know it as constituting the next phase, beginning in the reign of Henry II. English, for Warton, came about through a process in which the language loses "much of its antient barbarism and obscurity" to approach "more nearly to the dialect of modern times" (1:43). For John Pinkerton a few years later, "the Saxon language remained almost pure" till the mid–twelfth century, while "The *Ormulum* . . . is Saxon fermenting into English."[26] The third edition of the *Encyclopaedia Britannica*, published in 1797, stated that "the ancient British language was in a manner extirpated by the Romans, Danes, and Saxons, and succeeded by the Saxon, and after that the Saxon blended with the Norman French."[27]

In 1819, Jacob Grimm introduced Old, Middle, and Modern as terms describing the morphological shifts in time of West Germanic languages, and provided a model conceiving of internal change to replace the model of linguistic "contamination" or "fermentation." However, in an oddity that would affect the study of English language and literature for many years, Grimm retained the then current German term, *Angelsächsisch*, rather than replacing it with *Altenglisch*. He instead introduced *Altenglisch* to describe the linguistic phase immediately following *Angelsächsisch*, and *Mittelenglisch* to describe what follows that.[28] The result was that in the nineteenth century, "old English" actually meant what we would now call "early Middle English" and instead of the current bipartite notion, another complicated tripartite scheme was employed. Often, in fact, it was more complicated even than this, given that the English followers of comparative philology tended also to retain the earlier term, "Semi-Saxon," which was revived by philologists in the 1830s, now with specific reference to a handful of texts. The result was a relatively complicated linguistic map of medieval English, which allowed different conceptualizations of where exactly English began and different arguments about whether it owed its true character to Germanic or Gallic elements.

For Benjamin Thorpe, in his *Analecta Anglo-Saxonica* (1834), "Semi-Saxon" referred to that phase of English "in which the vocabulary is still free from foreign terms, but the grammatical construction nearly subverted."[29] As with Hickes, it was a transitional phase; the resultant dialect was represented in Laʒamon's *Brut* and the *Ormulum*. Notably, Thorpe's book was specifically designed as an anthology of extracts of Anglo-Saxon literature for students, so the inclusion of this "Semi-Saxon" material related the *Brut* and the *Ormulum* more closely to Anglo-Saxon than to Middle English. Making a further distinction, Thorpe stated that "Orm's dialect merits, if any, to be called Dano-Saxon: his name also betrays a Scandinavian descent" (x), comments suggesting flux rather than certainty in scholarly conceptions of the century and a half after the Conquest.

Most scholars remained in fact less concerned with labeling the phases of medieval English than with the point of origin of English proper. "Nothing can be more difficult, except by an arbitrary line, than to determine the commencement of the English language," wrote Henry Hallam in his *Introduction to the Literature of Europe* (1837–39), "not so much, as in those of the continent, because we are in want of materials, but rather from an opposite reason, the possibility of tracing a very gradual succession of verbal changes that ended in a change of denomination."[30] The introduction of the term "Semi-Saxon," Hallam felt, by "the best masters of our ancient language . . . to cover every thing from 1150 to 1250" (1:58 n) was indicative of the difficulty. Hallam's conclusion was that English emerged around the mid–thirteenth century: "Some metrical lives of saints, apparently written not far from the year 1250, may be deemed English; but the first specimen of it that bears a precise date is a proclamation of Henry III" (1:60–61).

Probably the most generally influential text on language in England in the middle years of the century was R. G. Latham's *The English Language,* first published in 1841 and revised and reprinted many times thereafter. Latham, an avowed follower of Grimm and Rasmus Rask, insisted that the classifying of a language must be governed by its structure, not its conformity to one or another date, and argued against the notion that external influence was the main agent of linguistic change. Distinguishing the shift from Saxon to Semi-Saxon was, then, a matter of studying the loss of grammatical inflections.[31] In explaining the transition of English, Latham, too, found it useful to employ the term "Semi-Saxon," again principally because he wanted to define when English proper began: "At a given period, then, the Anglo-Saxon of the standard, and (if the expression may be used) classical authors, such as Cædmon, Alfred, Ælfric, &c. &c. had undergone such a change as to induce the scholars of the present age to denominate it, not Saxon, but *Semi*-Saxon. It had ceased to be genuine Saxon, but had not yet become English" (62). A small number of works could be placed in the Semi-Saxon canon, including the *Peterborough Chronicle* and the *Brut* (62). The *Ormulum,* just as for Thorpe, was in a more liminal position, for "although [it is] in many points English rather than Saxon, [it] retains the Dual Number of the Anglo-Saxon Pronouns" (62–63). Latham established Semi-Saxon more precisely than previous writers by listing the various morphological changes that in his view characterized it.

Latham argued that further linguistic changes then produced "Old English," here in a very specialized usage even narrower than Grimm's *Altenglisch.* Latham dated this first appearance of English as such to the reign of Henry III and, like Hallam, proposed that Henry III's 1258 proclamation to the people of Huntingdonshire "currently passes for the earliest specimen of English" (64). Despite Latham's more philologically informed judgment, he, too, associates the emergence of English with a moment that is political as much as it is linguistic: English is seen as springing into being with a regal proclamation about liberty and individual rights. The proclamation, a rare thirteenth-century example of the use of English in an official document, was often seen in the nineteenth century as a key moment; for the *Saturday Review* in 1869, it was "our one native oasis in a howling wilderness of French and Latin."[32]

For Latham, this "Old English" continued until the reign of Edward III, when further linguistic changes brought the transition to what he calls Middle English. "In Chaucer and Mandeville," Latham suggested, "and perhaps in all the writers of the reign of Edward III, we have a transition from the Old to the Middle English" (67). Finally, the transition to New or Modern English occurs during the reign of Queen Elizabeth, when the verb plural in *-en* disappears. Latham was misled into this conclusion by noticing that Spenser uses the plural in *-en* "continually" (67), but apparently failing to see that the poet was working in a consciously archaic language.

Latham's division of medieval English was soon adopted by editors of Middle English texts in the 1840s, men who had at least some knowledge of comparative philology. Before the 1840s, it had been the norm simply to refer to these texts as "ancient," as Thomas Percy did, indiscriminately, in his *Reliques of Ancient English Poetry*; Joseph Ritson, in his *Ancient Engleish Metrical Romanceës*; and Frederic Madden, as we have seen, when he edited *The Ancient English Romance of Havelok the Dane*. But Madden took the side of the philologists in the debates of the 1830s and broadened his understanding of philology. In his edition of Laȝamon's *Brut*, which appeared in 1847, Madden called his text "a Poetical Semi-Saxon Paraphrase of the Brut of Wace," and endorsed the opinion of "A recent and sound critic" (Latham), reiterating his proposal that what determined the shift to Semi-Saxon from Anglo-Saxon was not a particular date, but the disappearance of grammatical forms.[33] Nevertheless, like Latham and almost every other writer, Madden could not resist providing a chronological table, in which he proposed "Semi-Saxon" as obtaining from 1100–1230; "Early English," 1230–1330; "Middle English," 1330–1500; and "Later English," 1500–1600 (1:vi).

The combined influence of Latham and Madden is evident in several midcentury editions. James Morton, for example, editing the *Ancrene Riwle* for the Camden Society in 1852, claimed it as a Semi-Saxon text and said that this linguistic phase was "the first of the various stages through which [the language] had to pass before it arrived at the copiousness and elegance of the present English."[34] Generally, medieval English was parceled out into four distinct phases, in Anglo-Saxon, Semi-Saxon, Old or Early English, and Middle English, sometimes with a fifth phase, Later English, as a buffer between medieval and Modern English. At the same time, German grammars, though far more technically detailed, presented a similar picture. For C. Friedrich Koch in 1863, Laȝamon's *Brut* and the *Ormulum* belonged to the period of "New Anglo-Saxon," continuing the persistent nineteenth-century tradition of linking these works more closely to what preceded them than to what followed.[35] This was reflected in Robert Meadows White's meticulous edition of the *Ormulum* that appeared in 1852; White discussed the work entirely in the context of Ango-Saxon studies, devoting the first sixty pages of his preface to this topic before turning to Orm's work.[36]

A shift is evident in the 1870s, a decade in which several rival books on the language appeared after thirty years' dominance by Latham's text and in which more simplified conceptions began to be formulated. Semi-Saxon had disappeared from T. L. Kington Oliphant's *The Sources of Standard English* (1873), in which he discusses both the *Brut* and *Ancrene*

Riwle in terms of their dialect and analyzes their preservation of Anglo-Saxon forms, without labeling them Semi-Saxon. Oliphant laid out English with Old English from 680 to 1120, Middle English from 1120 to 1300, and New English from 1303.[37] The precision of this last date is explained as the time when "Robert of Brunne... began to compile the Handlyng Synne, the work which, more clearly than any former one, foreshadowed the road that English literature was to tread from that time forward" (182). Once again, philological rigor gives way to the need to define a precise origin for true English, this time in the work of the "Lincolnshire bard" who "may be called the patriarch of the New English, much as Cædmon was of the Old English six hundred years earlier" (183). "English" proper finds its origin this time in a patriarchalized literary moment.

In 1874, Henry Sweet cleared away all these fine distinctions and asserted a simple model of Old, Middle, and Modern English.[38] This was soon reflected in editions of texts. In the introduction to the 1879 reprint of Madden and Josiah Forshall's edition of Wycliffe's New Testament, Walter Skeat wrote:

> The chief stages of the English language are three, viz. Anglo-Saxon, from the earliest times of which we have records to about A.D. 1150; Middle-English, from that time to about A.D. 1500; and modern English, later than the fifteenth century. The Anglo-Saxon is almost free from admixture with Norman-French; the Middle-English is remarkable for the numerous Norman-French words which are so mixed up with it as to form an essential part of the vocabulary; the modern English is marked by a still larger increase in its vocabulary.[39]

Here, finally, is Middle English in its contemporary guise. This model gradually became the accepted vision of the English medieval linguistic map, and in its essentials is what is accepted today. But it was not uncontested; around the same time as Skeat's pronouncement, the ninth edition of the *Encyclopaedia Britannica* included an entry on English written by the lexicographer James Murray in which the old and the new schemes coexisted:

> In its widest sense, the name [English] is now conveniently used to comprehend the language of the English people from their settlement in Britain to the present day, the various stages through which it has passed being distinguished as Old, Middle, and New or Modern English. In works yet recent, and even in some still current, the name *English* is confined to the third, or at most extended to the second and third of these stages, since the language assumed in the main the vocabulary and grammatical forms which it now presents,

the oldest or inflected stage being treated as a separate language, under the title of *Anglo-Saxon,* while the transition period which connects the two has been called *Semi-Saxon.*[40]

Here, again, the old wariness about the extent of the Englishness of Anglo-Saxon is evident. Murray's model is at once unwieldily complex and improbably pat. Old English or Anglo-Saxon is assigned to the period up to 1100, Transition Old English or "Semi-Saxon" to 1100–1200, Early Middle English or "Early English" to 1200–1300, Late Middle English to 1300–1400, Transition Middle English to 1400–1485, Early Modern English to 1485–1611, and Modern English from 1611 onward.[41] Comparative philology was by Murray's time a commonplace; yet again, however, its lessons give way to the need to identify the emergence of English with decisive political and literary moments, in this case those of 1485 and 1611. Although the simpler dual scheme of Old and Middle English was increasingly the norm in the later nineteenth century, Murray's entry was reused as late as the eleventh edition of the encyclopedia, in 1911.

In the course of these terminological developments, one of the problems that confronted scholars looking for the beginning of English was the fact that the slightest research showed that the language had always been known as "English." King Alfred had translated Bede *on Englisce,* as Latham noted.[42] Madden stated that "the language was always called *English* by those who wrote in it, in every century downwards, from the earliest period of Anglo-Saxon literature to the time of Dunbar and Lyndsay."[43] In fact, despite the dominance of the terms "Anglo-Saxon" and "Saxon," some writers throughout the nineteenth century dismissed them, wanting "English" or "Old English" not as synonyms, but replacements. Joseph Bosworth wrote in 1864, "Instead of Anglo-Saxon, I prefer calling it, as Alfred & Ælfric <u>always</u> did, <u>Englisc</u>."[44] Another writer on language said rather prematurely in 1872 that the terms "Saxon" and "Anglo-Saxon" had been abandoned, because the language and people of England "have been always *English*;—which is, and can be, the only reason why they are *English* now."[45]

To use the term "English" in the way these writers proposed was to invoke continuity with the nation's Germanic origins. The use, by historians (and E. A. Freeman in particular) of "English" in this fashion in the later nineteenth century must be recognized, Clare A. Simmons argues, as a polemical act.[46] An opposing, anti-Germanic, view was often held by those who maintained that English emerged with literary self-consciousness. This was seen to have derived from a *shedding* of Germanic origins, in favor of the refining French speech. So Oliphant, who had found the origin of English in *Handlyng Synne* because it shows "the road that English literature was to tread from that time forward," claimed that what distinguished Mannyng's work in comparison with that of his

predecessors was that "it contains a most scanty proportion of those Teutonic words that were soon to drop out of speech, and a most copious
proportion of French words."[47]

The increasing acceptability in the later nineteenth century of the
Saxon origins of the English nation denoted by such phenomena as the
cult of Alfred no doubt aided acceptance of the simplified philological
scheme of Old, Middle, and Modern English in the 1870s.[48] This scheme
allowed no hedging over the Germanness in the English language, and
implied continuity rather than the presence of some decisive rupture out
of which a truer English grew. At the same time, a coherent notion of
Middle English literary culture—newly enabled by the coherence of the
linguistic concept—was established. Skeat, and other scholars such as
Henry Bradshaw and Frederick Furnivall, made Middle English attractive
to an era of belletristic criticism, which required authors and in which
nationalist pride in literature was increasingly at stake. If everything after the Conquest was Middle English, then the less well regarded material could ride on the back of the canonical authors in the newly coherent Middle English literary scene.

One of the most important men behind the EETS and Chaucer Society,
despite the fact that he wrote so little himself, was Bradshaw, the Cambridge librarian. In 1868, Bradshaw wrote to Furnivall with suggestions
for how the late-fourteenth-century literary scene might be constructed:

> Trevisa's Bartholomeus. I don't know why you all fight shy of it.
> If you want standard English, a halfway halting place between Old
> & Middle (early) and later Middle and Modern English—go to the
> reign of Richard 2 when London became the centre of English life.
> Here you have two voluminous poets Gower & Chaucer—neither
> of them provincial—the English Bible, the English Cyclopedia
> (Bartholomeus) and the then English modern & ancient Universal
> History (Polychronicon). Here is a literature in itself. I only wish I
> could see good & pure texts of this series in a portable and cheap
> form. They w^d form a pivot round which to work, & all the provin-
> cial books would have their standing points easily settled.[49]

This is a strong statement for a canonical basis for the study of Middle
English. At this crucial time, with the EETS in its fourth year and the
Chaucer Society about to be established, Bradshaw offers a vision of how
Middle English literature—still a fragmentary thing—could be made to
coalesce around a core of texts that most observers would agree to be
literary. Bradshaw's statement is, first, author-based, a fundamental requirement for an era of belletristic criticism that tended to be baffled by
texts without authors. Second, Bradshaw aims to establish a canon, and
one of the criteria for that canon is centrality as opposed to provinciality.

The attractive aspects of Chaucer and Gower are not simply their volu-minousness, but their metropolitan character. Bradshaw's concern is to locate provincial texts in relation to those produced in the metropolis.

This construction is familiar to us because it is what has become Middle English literature. It took its place because of the successful ac-tivities of Furnivall and his circle, which, if they did not quite lead Middle English into the universities, prepared it, as a subject, to be adopted by academe. The success of this construction derives not just from a greater *philological* certainty about what Middle English was, but a strength-ened sense of the literary value of late medieval texts (which in effect meant the perceived *similarity* of the literary scene to that of the pre-sent time), around which "Middle English," as something ideologically coherent, could be constructed.

"Middle English," then, was a surprisingly problematic and uncertain category until the 1870s. Nobody "professed" Middle English until the 1890s — Skeat, who did so much to establish it, was a professor of Anglo-Saxon. In theory, this lack of an official construction meant that through-out eighteenth- and nineteenth-century scholarship, there was room for conjecture, speculation, and a variety of widely differing formations for the study of Middle English texts. Furthermore, before the 1870s at the earliest, any antiquarian could have his say without having an institu-tional position. Unlike the study of Anglo-Saxon, which had been official-ized as early as the sixteenth century,[50] or English studies proper, which emerged from the school system, Middle English evolved in a much looser way, with little supervision from authorities. Middle English, po-tentially, existed in the public sphere in a way that no other element of the study of English did.

Yet, as some of the remarks already made imply, such a notion must be immediately qualified. Middle English in the late eighteenth and early nineteenth centuries was in fact tightly controlled by narrow interests. Later, however, the possibilities of a public sphere seemed to emerge, with the establishment of the subscription societies. Tied to no official institution, costing only a guinea a year, a society such as the EETS ap-pears to offer a genuine enfranchisement, to educated people at least, in Middle English studies. For a while, as the statistics concerning EETS membership show, this potential appears to have been realized. The so-ciety's initial subscriber base consisted not so much of academics as of ordinary middle-class men (and, very occasionally, women) in a range of professions.

In fact, the moment of the emergence of Middle English into a public sphere is the moment of its decisive linking to a particular political pro-gram. Deciding, no doubt correctly, that Middle English needed a selling point, Furnivall tied it to nationalism and patriotism, which had ramifi-cations for the texts edited, the way in which they were presented to the public, and the way in which they were taught. It was very much as Furnivall had fashioned it that Middle English entered the old universities, as a key element of English studies, in the 1890s. Does Terry Eagleton's argument, that criticism committed "political suicide" when it ensured its continuance by entering the academy, hold good here?[51] Or had Middle English been politically neutered even earlier, when it was taken up by Furnivall and his circle? Is the brief moment when Middle English appears to be a thriving public property, in the 1860s, an illusion of scholarship in the public sphere? And what, finally, are the ramifications of these considerations, and this history, for medieval studies now? These questions I will consider in the conclusion of this material history.

Abbreviations

Add MS   Additional manuscript
BL   British Library
Bod Lib   Bodleian Library
Camb UL   Cambridge University Library
DNB   Sir Leslie Stephen and Sir Sidney Lee, eds., *Dictionary of National Biography*, 66 vols. (London, 1885–1901)
EETS, e.s. Early English Text Society, Extra Series
EETS, o.s. Early English Text Society, Original Series
Eg MS   Egerton manuscript
HEP   Thomas Warton, *The History of English Poetry*, 3 vols. (London and Oxford, 1774–81)
HuntL   Huntington Library
MS Harl   Harleian manuscript

Note: The antiquarians did not have a set of uniform titles for Middle English texts. For ease of reference, I have in general used the titles of individual works as they are given in *A Manual of the Writings in Middle English*, ed. Albert E. Hartung, 9 vols. (New Haven: Connecticut Academy of Arts and Sciences, 1967–93), or, in the case of Chaucer, in *The Riverside Chaucer*, ed. Larry D. Benson, 3rd ed. (Oxford: Oxford University Press, 1988). However, it has sometimes been appropriate to use earlier titles given by the antiquarians.

PART I

✢

Patronage and the Antiquarian Self

"Barbarous Productions"
The Making of Thomas Percy

1765

On the fifth of June, 1835, in the Royal Hotel in Pisa, Italy, a young man styling himself Baron Eunice de la Batut died of hard living. The baron—also known as Henry James Hungerford or Henry James Dickinson—was not yet thirty years old, and left no wife and no heirs. The fortune he had inherited five years before on the death of an uncle, and which had supported his life of pseudoaristocratic leisure, gambling, and drinking, consequently became subject to an unusual clause in this uncle's will. The money was bequeathed to the government of the United States of America, for the purpose of founding in Washington "an establishment for the increase and diffusion of knowledge among men."[1] On 17 December 1835, U.S. president Andrew Jackson was informed of a bequest by an unknown Englishman. Debates began in Congress over how to deal with it, enlivened by strenuous objections to acceptance from members of Congress who believed that the unknown foreigner was trying to immortalize his name through endowment of an institution.[2]

But John Quincy Adams, representative from Massachusetts, successfully argued for acceptance. In doing so, he presented to Congress the results of his researches into the obscure identity of the benefactor—Hungerford's uncle—a man named James Smithson. Smithson, Adams discovered, had been the illegitimate son of a great English aristocrat in the time of George III, Hugh Percy, earl and later first duke of Northumberland. The duke, however, was a Percy only by marriage; he had been born a commoner with the name of Smithson and in 1740 had married Elizabeth Percy, a descendant of the family famous in the Border ballads and in Shakespeare's Henry plays. When her older brother died young, Elizabeth Percy became heiress to the Percy titles, and Hugh Smithson inherited them, as her husband, in 1750, when he also changed his name to Percy. His son James Smithson, the result of an affair with a woman named Elizabeth Macie, was born Jacques Louis Macie in Paris in 1765. He was apparently spurned by his father and barred from a career in England. He was well off, thanks to money probably inherited from his mother, and made a successful career for himself as an amateur chemist.

It is not known why, in 1801, he changed his name to his father's by then long-disused surname of Smithson.[3]

Adams was enormously excited by these associations. He did not establish *why* Smithson had provided for the money to go to Washington, but he was intrigued by the way in which the romantic Percy tradition had the potential to be turned to new purposes in the United States. Adams thought that Smithson would be a benefactor of mankind if his educational institution were established. Contrasting Smithson's past lineage with this imagined future veneration, Adams made this ornate statement in his speech summarizing the case for acceptance:

> [R]enowned as is the name of Percy in the historical annals of England, resounding as it does from the summit of the Cheviot hills, to the ears of our children, in the ballad of Chevy Chase, with the classical commentary of Addison; freshened and renovated in our memory as it has recently been from the purest fountain of poetical inspiration, in the loftier strain of Alnwick Castle, tuned by a bard of our own native land; doubly immortalized as it is in the deathless dramas of Shakespear; "confident against the world in arms," as it may have been in ages long past, and may still be in the virtues of its present possessors by inheritance; let the trust of James Smithson to the United States of America, be faithfully executed by their Representatives in Congress; let the result accomplish his object, "the increase and diffusion of knowledge among men," and a wreath of more unfading verdure shall entwine itself in the lapse of future ages around the name of SMITHSON, than the united hands of tradition, history, and poetry have braided around the name of Percy through the long perspective in ages past of a thousand years.[4]

Adams here provided for the doubts of those who did not wish a foreigner to immortalize his name. For all the fame of the name of Percy, it is "a wreath of *more* unfading verdure" that the name of Smithson will garner if his will be carried out, and that wreath will have been earned by a benefactor of mankind, one who would be immortalized not because he was rich or famous, but because of his democratic ambition to enrich others at his own expense. Congress was swayed, and a suit in Chancery was initiated to recover the money, which converted into more than half a million dollars. Several years later, after yet more protracted wrangling in Congress over its purpose, the Smithsonian Institution was opened in 1846.

It remains a historical irony that this great institution, a byword for history in the United States, should have been endowed accidentally. It is hard to detect any real intent in Smithson's will to immortalize himself by the establishment of an institution; he left all his money to his nephew and to his nephew's heirs, and could hardly have expected that

4

the nephew would be dead before the age of thirty without issue. Smithson had never visited America, but, rejected as he was by an aristocratic father, he seems in turn to have rejected monarchies and favored republics and their causes. But that his considerable fortune should have reached America owed less to a grand beneficent vision than it did to the fact that four thousand pounds a year, in the 1830s, allowed a man a life of fatal dissolution.[5]

The main actors in this story are engaged in a more or less pragmatic work on the self that involves drawing on the capital—symbolic and cultural—deriving from literary and historical tradition. Each such act involves the individual's carving out of a social place for himself, using tradition to establish origins, origins that in turn can fuel further traditions. Hugh Smithson, by origin an obscure country baronet, adopted the Percy name and titles in 1750, enthusiastically renovated the near-moribund Percy estates, and became one of the most notable aristocrats of his day. Jacques Macie, when he was naturalized as the Englishman James Macie, had his path to any public career in Britain blocked (probably by his natural father).[6] But with access to a substantial fortune and the educational capital of an Oxford degree, he was able to make his way, as a celebrated amateur chemist, the respected colleague of Humphry Davy, Joseph Banks, and Henry Cavendish, and the youngest-ever member of the Royal Society.[7] His adoption of the name Smithson invoked the connection with his father, yet obscured it at the same time. Even Henry Hungerford, with his invented title as the baron de la Batut, attempted to attach to his fortune the aristocratic lineage he seems to have thought it required.[8]

The case of James Smithson shows the limitations of economic capital in perpetuating the memory of one's self. It shows what money cannot buy: Smithson could never reinsert himself into the lineage of the ancient Percys, and despite perpetuating his name in the Smithsonian Institution, he is himself largely forgotten. But his father, Hugh Smithson, made much more from an alliance of economic and symbolic capital. Building on the considerable symbolic capital that came with the Percy name, Hugh restored, by astute management of the Percy estates, the family's social brilliance and historical associations. As an anonymous obituarist in the *Gentleman's Magazine* shrewdly wrote, commemorating the magnificence of the duke's establishment, he "was a very conspicuous instance of what great things may be done by common care, working upon large property."[9]

Pierre Bourdieu, discussing cultural capital, proposes that "[a]ristocracies are essentialist."[10] Those who hold "educationally uncertified capital" have to keep proving themselves "because they *are* only what they *do*," while "the holders of titles of cultural nobility...only have to be what they are."[11] His remark refers more to the symbolic "aristocracies" of academe than to nobilities of blood but nevertheless stands in the case of Hugh Smithson and the Percys. Hugh Smithson assumed the essential authority deriving from lineage, and denied this lineage to his illegitimate son, leaving James a cultural, and literal, commoner.

It was, however, a third man involved with the Percy name at this time who performed the most comprehensive self-invention and attendant accumulation of symbolic capital. He managed to give himself the Percy name, insert himself into the family lineage, and fashion a successful career. Unlike James Smithson, he began with no economic capital. His achievements were made solely on the basis of educational and symbolic capital, the latter based on the manipulation of literary tradition. To tell the story of this man is also, almost incidentally, to tell the story of the beginning of the modern study of Middle English.

As Elizabeth Macie fled England and her affair with the earl of Northumberland in 1765 to Paris where she gave birth to the future James Smithson, this man was making his way into the Northumberland household. Thomas Piercy was born at Bridgnorth in Shropshire in 1729, the son of a grocer. As a young man, Piercy showed an aptitude for learning and literature; he wrote poetry and pursued literary studies, and eventually received an exhibition from his school to go to Oxford. There he took a B.A. and an M.A., and entered the church. At some point in the 1750s, by which time he was a country curate, Piercy retrieved a tattered manuscript of ballads and romances from the house of a friend, where the maids were using it, half a page at a time, to light the parlor fire. The Percy Folio, as it became known, was the major inspiration for his best-known literary production, *The Reliques of Ancient English Poetry*, which first appeared in 1765.

Around the time he found the manuscript, the young antiquarian began styling himself "Percy" and established, via a genealogy he traced himself, his descent from a younger son of the second earl of Northumberland, who lived in the early fifteenth century. The discovery of the manuscript and the name change appear to have happened at around the same time, which strongly suggests that the manuscript, which contains several ballads about the medieval Percys, played a role in the beginnings of Percy's self-transformation.[12]

The full ramifications of Percy's name change and genealogy represent a classic wish-fulfillment fantasy of noble origins. Percy's genealogy, as John Nichols later pointed out in *Illustrations of the Literary History of the Eighteenth Century*, did not just mean he was descended from the earls of Northumberland, it meant that he *was* the earl of Northumberland.[13] But Percy, a tactful careerist, did not pursue this invented claim to the title, which at the time was being so ably revived by the former Hugh Smithson. What he did do played upon the myth of origins in a more subtle, and much surer, way. In an era of bardic invention, Percy took a step further than James Macpherson, Thomas Chatterton, and John

Pinkerton, each of whom invented bards and then recovered their literary output.[14] Thomas Percy invented himself.

In doing so, it can also be said, he invented or helped to invent the study of Middle English. The term "Middle English" did not exist in Percy's time; most of the texts in the *Reliques* were not Middle English, and those that were had been greatly altered by their editor. But the *Reliques* represented the beginning of modern scholarly discussion on Middle English, even if it was generically restricted to ballad and romance. In his scholarly essay on metrical romances, prefixed to the third volume, Percy published the first bibliography of Middle English romance,[15] and his "Essay on the Ancient English Minstrels" provided a controversial but highly influential theory about medieval textual production.[16] For the second edition of the *Reliques* (1767), Percy greatly expanded this essay, augmenting it with twenty-three pages of notes, containing copious quotations from Latin, French, and English sources. In the same year his publisher, Dodsley, put all four essays of the *Reliques* together as a book, which, as Bertram Davis points out, was "the most comprehensive and authoritative literary history that Percy's contemporaries could turn to until Thomas Warton published his *History of English Poetry* about a decade later."[17]

When Warton began publishing his history in 1774, Middle English had become a scholarly topic for discussion. It was unorganized, largely extramural (with Warton the exception), and generically narrow, but the outlines of a discipline concerning itself with the literature that came between the Anglo-Saxons and Spenser were becoming visible. Before the 1760s—with the major exception of the work of Chaucer—almost the entirety of Middle English literature lay undiscovered and ignored. Middle English lacked the compelling ideological appeal that, as Allen Frantzen has shown, the Tudors and Stuarts found in Anglo-Saxon literature.[18] It did not appeal, as Anne Hudson notes, to the religious reformers, and it was irrelevant to a literary education still dominated by the classics.[19] Contemporary standards of criticism were governed by a notion of taste that demanded that poetry conform to absolute, rather than historical, standards, and in these conditions, the later medieval literature was regarded as primitive and barbaric.

Middle English consequently became the preserve of antiquarian scholars who tended not to be attached to universities, though they might have university educations. Where Middle English was concerned, they were self-taught. Some were dilettantes of means, such as Thomas Tyrwhitt or George Ellis, but more often they were of the lower middle class, at best, and found employment either in the church or the law, Percy, Joseph Ritson, and Walter Scott being eminent examples. As these examples also show, this kind of antiquarianism was often provincial rather than metropolitan, as Marilyn Butler points out.[20] Antiquarianism, as Philippa

Levine has noted, was "a largely amateur sport" because of the lack of opportunities to make it a professional occupation, and this was particularly true for those antiquarians who worked on Middle English.[21] The antiquarian subbranch of Middle English, then, potentially existed in an ideologically free-floating way, in the spaces between universities, upper-class education, and other state-sanctioned ways of organizing disciplines. It belonged to the public sphere, and unlike the study of either postmedieval or Anglo-Saxon literature, was in theory appropriable from all kinds of politically diverse positions. Another consequence was scholarly freedom, in the absence of a monitored training. If the would-be antiquarian had no real idea how to edit a text, this did not matter; he could edit it as he wished.[22] If he had no deep knowledge of the medieval context, he could speculate on the basis of a few facts and be unlikely to face serious correction.

In practice, the price of amateurism was that most antiquarians, because they tended not to be in Warton's luxurious position of a professorship at Oxford University, had to sell their texts to contribute to their livelihood. As the general public would not buy the raw data of ancient literature and culture, scholars had to make their material appealing. The resultant dilemma was a recurrent one for eighteenth- and early nineteenth-century antiquarians: the problem of the reconciliation of the man of taste with the rigorous antiquarian scholar.[23] The very otherness of the ancient text that made it worth recovering was that which made it unacceptable to a broad public. But the more the scholar polished the material to make it acceptable to modernity, the less authentically antique it became. This dilemma tended to place at the heart of antiquarian study the persona of the scholar himself or herself. The purer antiquarian, such as Thomas Hearne, was widely condemned as tasteless, while fame came to such a man of taste as Percy. Readers were not judging the inherent value of the material itself, but the taste and discretion of the person who made it suitable—or otherwise—for the modern public.

Preserving the balance between the two demands usually involved not just work on the text by the editor, but a work on the self inspired by the text. In this respect, the study of Middle English, although not closely related to the broader discipline of English before the 1870s, can be seen as a technology of the self, as Ian Hunter describes it.[24] The antiquarian editor became crucially linked to the work he produced and to that work's success or failure. Through his researches into an obscure and scarcely understood disciplinary area, he developed a cultural authority and—as the example of Thomas Percy shows—could alter aspects of his persona and his material circumstances thereby. The success and authority of the work could accrue symbolic capital for the editor, which might then be deployed in practical ways.

My aim in this chapter is to trace two inventions: Thomas Percy's invention of himself and the invention of Middle English that underpinned it. The use of Middle English literature as a technology of the self in these processes is allied to something more explicitly political. Despite the apparently utopian possibilities for a discipline about which no one cared enough to bring it under official control, what in practice happened was that the kinds of scholars who came to Middle English usually lacked economic capital and sought to accrue it through a prior accumulation of symbolic capital. The demands placed as a result on the nascent study overwhelmed it, ensuring that it would be, for some time to come, the tool of a politically conservative self-fashioning.

Editing the Middle Ages

> This very curious Old Manuscript in it's present mutilated state, but unbound and sadly torn, &c., I rescued from destruction, and begged at the hands of my worthy friend Humphrey Pitt Esq., then living at Shiffnal in Shropshire....I saw it lying dirty on the floor under a Bureau in yᵉ Parlour: being used by the maids to light the fire.[25]

There is no reason to doubt Percy's well-known account of his discovery of the manuscript that inspired him to antiquarianism. Nevertheless, it is not surprising that a rival antiquarian would imply that there was no manuscript at all. There is something of the attractive fiction of origins about this account, even if it is not quite as romantic as the story Thomas Chatterton would concoct a few years later about the imagined fifteenth-century monk, Thomas Rowley, nor as dramatic as James Macpherson's "discovery" of the Erse fragments by "Ossian" he had begun publishing in 1759. But this tattered, unattractive (and decidedly nonmedieval) manuscript would take on a profound significance in medieval studies for many decades to come because of the founding status of the *Reliques*.

In compiling what would become the *Reliques*, Percy was at first assisted by the poet William Shenstone, but he continued alone after Shenstone's death early in 1763.[26] In the later eighteenth century, there were no firm protocols for the editing and translating of early English texts. At one end of a spectrum, there was the sheer fabrication of Chatterton or the more complicated mélange put together by Macpherson; at the other, there would be, by the 1780s, the insistence on fidelity to the manuscripts practiced by the antiquarian Joseph Ritson. The evil of the former was by no means universally admitted, while the merits of the latter were rarely recognized. Thomas Warton might have conceded that Chatterton's Rowley poems were forged, but that did not stop him from acclaiming their author as "a prodigy of genius" who "would have proved the first of English poets, had he reached a maturer age." On the other hand, as Bertrand Bronson points out, *The British Critic*'s review of one of Ritson's scrupulous editions in 1797 condemned his work in such a way as to suggest that "[t]he great fault is that the editor has given his ballads almost literally as he found them!"[27]

It was Shenstone, more than Percy, who conceived a rough form of editorial theory, advising Percy at the outset that he did not object to what he called "*Improvements*" to the poems "unless you were plainly to *contradict* Antiquity." The alteration "of a *word or two*" did not need to be noted, but "where a whole *Line* or *More* is alter'd, it may be proper enough to give some Intimation of it."[28] Shenstone thought that such alterations could be signaled by italics, which would "have the appearance of a modern *Toe* or *Finger*" added to an old statue. But the readers should be left to think that such additions "were owing to *Gaps*, rather than to *faulty Passages*."[29] In several cases, Percy was more candid about the defects of the folio than Shenstone advised him to be, admitting that several poems were mutilated in the manuscript and required editorial repairs.

Allowing himself considerable editorial license, Percy was accordingly able to edit his ballads into conformity with the vision he developed of the Middle Ages. About a quarter of the first edition of the *Reliques* consisted of poems drawn from the Percy Folio, and these were altered, sometimes dramatically, for their appearance in the anthology. The vandalizing maids provided some excuse for this, but they alone cannot be held accountable: at stake was a vision of history. Percy went much further than filling in the torn-out half pages; as Joseph Donatelli notes, *reliques* is an apt term for what "Percy seems to have conceived of ... as mere vestiges of complete narratives."[30] Percy rewrote, expanded, and conflated. As has been well known since the publication of the actual manuscript in 1867–68, and more particularly since Walter Jackson Bate's 1944 article on the subject, Percy's alterations could be so extensive as to bring about a complete generic shift. Most notoriously, perhaps, this occurred in "Sir Cauline," when the original ending, and Sir Cauline's reunion with his love and their marriage, was rewritten into Gothic tragedy, in which Sir Cauline dies of his wounds after killing a giant and his despairing lady expires over his corpse.[31]

Working in the absence of well-developed protocols for editing, Percy dealt with his poems in a way more obviously authorial than editorial. Donatelli has made the provocative argument that in reconstituting the ballads, "Percy composed in a manner similar to that of the medieval minstrels," seeing himself not "as an 'editor' of these ballads in the modern sense of the word, but ... as a latter-day minstrel."[32] This suggests that one of Percy's major achievements in the *Reliques* was to historicize *himself* as a poet, rather than his texts as poetry. Instead of bringing them, objectively, as productions of the past into his own modern era, he participated in precisely the kind of piecing together now thought to have characterized medieval ballad production; he rewrote the poems, and did so in a process that reinvented them for his time. Less overtly, but ultimately more successfully, Percy actually achieved what Macpherson, Pinkerton with his "Hardyknute" forgery, and Chatterton set out to do, by working like a medieval poet and emulating medieval literary production. It is at this point that Percy's practice as an editor and shaper of views on the Middle Ages and Middle English literature touched on, and crossed over into, his own practices of the self.

Percy had originally proposed to dedicate the anthology to Shenstone. But in March 1764, late in the process of editing, he wrote to his namesake (and supposed relative), Countess Elizabeth Percy, wife of Hugh, earl of Northumberland, requesting that she allow him to dedicate the anthology to her. She accepted, and Percy made some last-minute editorial changes to the substantially complete collection.[33] He purged some of the more bawdy poems and brought a new gentility to others by the changing of such expletives as "Jesus God!" to "Out alas!" In a much more sweeping transformation, he exchanged the contents of volumes 1 and 3, which was done so late in the printing process that the footers throughout both volumes are incorrect, volume 1 bearing those for volume 3, and vice versa. It would seem that Percy felt so strongly about the change that he made it even at the cost of introducing a glaring error.

This change may have been made because Percy felt that it was important to spare the countess finding, in what was originally to have been the anthology's opening poem, a stanza on Queen Guenevere describing her as "a bitch and a witch, / And whore bold."[34] But the more obvious reason for the switch was the way in which it privileged the Percy ballads: the two versions of the Border ballads of "Chevy Chace," "The Battle of Otterbourne," Skelton's "Elegy on Henry, fourth Earl of Northumberland," as well as such later ballads as "The Rising in the North" and "Northumberland Betrayed by Douglas." The anthology had originally buried the Percy material in the last volume, in part at least because Shenstone doubted the appeal to the public of such poems as "The Battle of Otterbourne."[35]

Now, with the privileging of this material, the *Reliques* became an encomium to the Percys. Comparison of manuscript originals with Percy's versions shows, furthermore, how he adjusted the poems to make them more suited to this role. The ballad "The Rising in the North," for example, is not consistently flattering to the Northumberland concerned, the seventh earl, who, with the earl of Westmoreland, had risen against Queen Elizabeth in 1569, aiming to restore Catholicism. Percy wrote that the manuscript versions of the ballad that he had consulted (one of which is in the folio) "contained considerable variations, out of which such readings were chosen as seemed most poetical and consonant to history" (R, 1:251). Consonance with history meant a systematic white-washing of unfavorable references to the rebels as they appear in the folio manuscript version, to present a far more attractive view of Northumberland and Westmoreland than appears there.

In the first stanza of "The Rising in the North," Percy's version in the *Reliques* introduces "a noble earle, / The noblest earle in the north countrìe" (R, 1:250), who, in the folio, is a "noble Erle" who commits a "treason against the crowne," which Percy leaves tactfully unmentioned.[36] Percy's earl complains, "Mine enemies prevail so fast, / That at the court I may not bee" (R, 1:251), where the folio has: "my treason is knowen well enoughe; / att the court I must not bee" (*BPFM*, 2:211, lines 23–24). Percy's rebels, outnumbered, make an expedient departure from their stronghold at the end of the poem—"though they were brave and bold, / Against soe many could not stay"—leaving their ally Norton to die pathetically and tragically with his sons: "alas! for ruth! / Thy reverend lockes thee could not save, / Nor them their faire and blooming youthe" (R, 1:256). The folio original gives a rather different view:

> but the halfe moone [Northumberland] is fled & gone,
> & the Dun bull [Westmoreland] vanished awaye;
> & ffrancis Nortton & his 8 sonnes
> are ffled away most cowardlye.
> (*BPFM*, 2:216, lines 155–58)

The newly privileged Northumberland ballads were given further prominence in the elaborate dedication to the *Reliques*, ostensibly written by Percy, but in fact penned by his friend Samuel Johnson. Here it was proposed that the poems "now return to your LADYSHIP by a kind of hereditary right" (R, 1:vii). What goes unspoken here is Thomas Percy's own "hereditary right," as invented by him, to this historical material and its heritage. The dedication is further demonstrative of Percy's great tact in that it is addressed to the countess, rather than the main power behind the Percy name, the earl. For the earl—the former Hugh Smithson—had no blood relation at all to the balladic forebears from whom his wife and titles were descended. The countess was the key to both men's claims on the medieval name.[37]

At this time, it must be remembered, Percy was no more than a country vicar and apprentice antiquarian. Dedicating the *Reliques* to Countess Percy was a brilliant career maneuver, one bringing rapid material and social improvement. The year following the publication of the *Reliques*, the earl was created first duke of Northumberland by George III. Thomas Percy, having secured the attention of the family with the *Reliques*, was invited to the Northumberland household as tutor to the younger son in the months before he left for the University of Edinburgh and was later asked to write a history of the family. His original appointment was extended when he became chaplain to the Northumberlands, and he remained with the family in this capacity until 1769, when he was appointed one of the King's Chaplains. He later became dean of Carlisle, and, in 1782, bishop of Dromore. He remained, while they were alive, the friend of his former patrons, and a habitué of their various households.

Written as it was late in the process of production of the *Reliques,* the dedication to Countess Percy functions as a kind of abstract of many of the broad ideas about the Middle Ages presented in the anthology overall. It presents in microcosm Percy's ideas about medieval literature and also foreshadows his own expectations of the effect the literature, when offered to his noble patron, might have on his own career and selfhood. The dedication subtly balances the claims of the various Percys—real, balladic, and invented—on their historical heritage. Percy—I will keep to the fiction of his authorship, as the views expressed are clearly his—began with a standard self-deprecatory claim on patronage:

> Those writers, who solicit the protection of the noble and the great, are often exposed to censure by the impropriety of their addresses: a remark that will perhaps be too readily applied to him, who having nothing better to offer than the rude songs of ancient minstrels, aspires to the patronage of the Countess of NORTHUMBERLAND, and hopes that the barbarous productions of unpolished ages can obtain the approbation or the notice of her, who adorns courts by her presence, and diffuses elegance by her example. (1:v–vi)

The presentation of the Middle Ages and its literature as "barbarous" and "unpolished" is, in this context, both the hyperbolic modesty of the literary supplicant and the very real attitude of eighteenth-century criticism to medieval literature. Percy went on to offer the ballads "not as labours of art, but as effusions of nature, shewing the first efforts of ancient genius, and exhibiting the customs and opinions of remote ages" (1:vi). In these few lines, the fundamentals of literary criticism of medieval writing, such as it was, are encapsulated. The poems in the *Reliques,* like most of the Middle English literature editors would encounter after Percy, could scarcely be considered "art," though they had some aesthetic value as an indication of the early state of literature. As Tim William Machan notes, only Chaucer, among Middle English writers, could be considered an "auctor," and the dominant note among editors of writing other than Chaucer's was one of apology.[38] Ancient texts were best studied for the pictures of "customs and opinions" they provided, as the material for a positivist historicism in which questions of literary value were largely bypassed. Lawrence Lipking has remarked, specifically of Percy's contemporaries William Warburton and Thomas Warton: "As a picture of life...early English poetry needed to be studied only for the customs and relics it described. The effect on the historian is once more to view the poem as source material for some other kind of study. Insofar as poems deal with antiquities, they claim our interest in the strange and quaint, not in art."[39]

The "strange and quaint" could in themselves form an aesthetic category in the eighteenth century; Ronald Paulson, discussing Addison's "aesthetics of the Strange," refers to the "secondariness" of the texts of the superstitious Middle Ages, whereby the eighteenth-century reader brings an enlightened perspective to the superstitions of the past.[40] "Superstition becomes an aesthetic object," Paulson writes, "when belief is replaced by curiosity" (68), and we see this in the repeated use of the term "curious" by Percy and others as a term that often stands in justification of the study of medieval literature (Percy's Folio manuscript, notably, was "very curious").

But there is nevertheless a fundamental displacement at the heart of this early scholarship, which Lipking describes. Warburton thought the chivalric romances to be "pictures of life and manners," and Richard Hurd, author of *Letters on Chivalry and Romance* (1762), perpetuated "the notion that 'Gothic' poets, even at their most outlandish, were describing the romantic life they saw around them."[41] So late-eighteenth-century scholarship did not, and apparently could not, describe the literature it wanted to study through the use of a literary-critical vocabulary as we now understand it; no formal approach of any extent was available, and the main approach open was historicist. It involved the search for the "customs and relics" described in the work, and these were usually to be found in what was considered "strange and quaint," or "curious."

This produces a bifurcation in the work of the early medievalists: they tended to regard the old texts with which they worked as important and interesting, but at the same time as almost entirely lacking in literary merit, simply because they did not (of course) conform to late-eighteenth-century notions of taste. Writing about medieval literature, scholars are continually insisting on the great historical merit of their material, while at the same time apologizing for its barbarity and absence of literariness.

This form of literary study, then, relied on a fundamental alienation, a concession, before a word was written, that the literature under study was not valuable for the same reason that either the classics or literature since the Renaissance was valuable; one did not read medieval ballads for the same reason one read Shakespeare or Homer. In practice, no doubt, there were many readers who did take as much pleasure in the ballads as in anything else, but this response was rarely transferred to authoritative literary commentary. Machan argues strongly that this was built into textual criticism of Middle English: "If Middle English textual criticism was informed by the principles of textual criticism in general, then one of the informing principles was that works of the Middle Ages were inherently and variously inferior to those of the Antique or the Renaissance. Hence, there could be little artistic or moral reason to devote a great deal of attention to the editorial theory and practice of these works" (48). The "ancient" literature, then, was distanced several times over; not literary in the accepted sense, linguistically barbarous, its main interest lay in the "strange and quaint." The paradox of the study of medieval literature was that "ancient" texts were always hypostatized in a distant, irretrievably other, historical past, from which the editor and reader had to pluck the familiar, that which would speak to their own age.

To be made to perform their historicist function in this way, medieval texts had to be approached as *reflections* of medieval society and its practices. Obviously problematic in the case of most medieval texts, this was especially difficult with the apparently ahistorical and fanciful romances. As Arthur Johnston writes, romance in the seventeenth and eighteenth centuries denoted narratives

> in which the author had given free rein to his imagination in the invention of marvellous beings and wonderful happenings. The writer's judgement was held to have been in abeyance, otherwise he would have seen that his stories were full of impossibilities.... Romance was synonymous with magic, with the incredible and the impossible, with the abandoning of accounts of plain matter of fact, in actions and characters.[42]

This perception had to be negotiated by scholars wanting romance to be taken seriously. Percy's response was to advance what amounts to a theory of how to read the romances in historicist fashion, and in this he was aided by the important work of his predecessor, Richard Hurd. Hurd did not really know a great deal about romance and was not remotely the scholar Percy was. In the popular *Letters on Chivalry and Romance* he told his reader that although he had taken information from "the *old Romances*," he would not "make a merit with you in having perused these barbarous volumes my self," nor would he "impose the ungrateful task," for the "knowledge may be obtained at a cheaper rate."[43] He meant that it could be found in the work of J. B. de la Curne Sainte-Palaye, though he did not name him. However, as Johnston notes, Hurd "had the ability to present his material in a very attractive manner," and this ensured his popularity.[44]

Hurd's thesis was that romance arose as the expression of the social reality of chivalry, and chivalry in turn arose from the feudal system.[45] The relative baronial power and freedom allowed under feudalism led to a "state of war," and the consequent prominence of arms "gave rise to that military institution, which we know by the name of CHIVALRY" (8). Jousting and tournaments followed naturally: "You see, then, my notion is, that Chivalry was no absurd and freakish institution, but the natural and even sober effect of the feudal policy" (10). Combined with the respect that the knights accorded to women, this martial state of affairs caused the phenomenon of chivalry, which was then expressed in the romances.

Hurd explained some of the unrealisms of romance by claiming the fabulous figures of the genre to be expressive exaggerations: giants, for example, represented "oppressive feudal Lords" (28). Much can be attributed to the superstition of the age: monsters, dragons, and serpents, for example, which appeared because of "the vulgar belief of enchantments" as well as their reported role in "Eastern tradition" (30). Later, stories of strange beasts in the New World would account for this credulity (31). Magic, too, could be explained. The charms and enchantments of female characters were "often metaphorical . . . expressing only the blandishments of the sex, by which they either seconded the designs of their Lords, or were enabled to carry on designs for themselves" (33).

This approach enabled a recovery of romance in its imagined realist function as documentary evidence of medieval practices. Percy quoted Hurd, approvingly, early in his essay "On the Ancient Metrical Romances." Rather more learnedly than Hurd, though with the same end in view, Percy discussed the origins of poetry with the bards and skalds, who "are thought to have performed the functions of the historian pretty faithfully."[46] In later, literate societies, when history could be recorded in prose, the bardic songs became "more amusing, than useful," their function more "to entertain and delight," so that the poets began to embellish their stories "and set off their recitals with such marvelous fictions, as were calculated to captivate gross and ignorant minds" (3:ii–iii). For these reasons, supernatural figures entered poetry, "uncorrected by art" (3:iii), and so romance developed and the functions of historian and poet diverged (3:v). Nevertheless, "the minstrels still retained so much of their original institution, as frequently to make true events the subject of their songs" (3:v). Percy then argued for the importance of skaldic figures among the Anglo-Saxons and the Scandinavians and for the descent of the later medieval minstrels from these figures.[47]

The divide between orality and literacy is, for Percy, the divide between poetry and history. He expresses a nostalgia for orality and a lost congruence between poetry and history — poetry's ability, in other words, to be both purely reflective of reality *and* poetic. In the later Middle Ages, the visible sign of this prelapsarian congruence was the minstrels, the inheritors of the role of the early bards. Through his arguments for their origin and their role in the Middle Ages, Percy implies that the minstrels retained some of the priestly aura of their pagan past. Appropriately, they have a special class location: without being *of* the aristocracy, they are nevertheless favored by the aristocrats, whose martial ideology they promote. The minstrels' artistic production and the interests of the aristocracy are unified, and the balladeers create a place in the social hierarchy through their repeated utterance of the aristocracy's dominant ideology.

Figure 1. Percy's minstrel. On the frontispiece of the second edition of the *Reliques* (1767) a minstrel entertains two knights and other gentry. Cherubs strewing petals are a mysterious touch. By permission of the Rare Book and Special Collections Library, University of Sydney.

Percy concludes that many of the romances "contain a considerable portion of poetic merit, and throw great light on the manners and opinions of former times." Despite their use "of the exploded fictions of Chivalry, [they] frequently display great descriptive and inventive powers in the Bards, who composed them" (3:8). "Poetic merit" here might sound like a fragment of literary-critical discourse, but it is not followed up, other than in Percy's suggesting that the romances compare well with Gower's "tedious allegories" or Lydgate's "dull and prolix legends" (3:ix). The principal point is historical; by Percy, too, the romances are recovered for the kind of documentary realism that will make them historical and validate the reading of them.

The dedication to the *Reliques* exhibits the directly practical applications of such a historicism. Percy proposed the importance to the present-day Percys of the history of their illustrious ancestors, and concluded by introducing the agent of these records of the past:

> By such Bards, MADAM, as I am now introducing to your presence, was the infancy of genius nurtured and advanced, by such were the minds of unlettered warriors softened and enlarged, by such was the memory of illustrious actions preserved and propagated, by such were the heroic deeds of the Earls of NORTHUMBERLAND sung at festivals in the hall of ALNWICK: and those songs, which the bounty of your ancestors rewarded, now return to your LADYSHIP by a kind of hereditary right; and, I flatter myself, will find such reception, as is usually shewn to poets and historians, by those whose consciousness of merit makes it their interest to be long remembered. (*R*, 1: vii–viii)

For all the glory of the deeds of ancient nobles, another figure, the bard, was required in the Middle Ages to record those deeds and remind the nobles of what they ought to be and do. There is, then, an essential complementarity between nobles and minstrels, and without it the nobles are not entirely complete, cannot have a full sense of themselves.

It is in the scholarly centerpiece of the *Reliques,* the "Essay on the Ancient Minstrels of England," that these arguments receive their fullest treatment. The argument was originally very simple: first, medieval poems, Percy proposes, must have had their (single) authors; second, these authors collectively formed a special, cherished class of men in medieval England. They were poets, not mere reciters, who composed their own material, and they were favored and patronized by aristocrats and kings (1:xv). Furthermore — in echo of the essay on romances — these minstrels were the "genuine successors" to the skalds and bards of the early Germanic and Celtic tribes, figures whose "skill was considered as something divine, their persons were deemed sacred. . . . they were every where loaded with honours and rewards" (1:xv). When Percy revised the essay for the second edition of the *Reliques,* he added to this picture: the minstrels were, he wrote, "extremely popular and acceptable" because of their arts, and, "so long as the spirit of chivalry subsisted, they were protected and caressed, because their songs tended to do honour to the ruling passion of the times, and to encourage and foment a martial spirit."[48]

Although this exaltation of the minstrels had its critics, the idea of a caste of bardic author-performers was influential in much thought about Middle English literature well into the nineteenth century. Percy responded to early criticism by doing more research and bolstering his case, and in doing so persuaded a major detractor, Samuel Pegge, of the justness of his position. Pegge, who had read a paper critical of Percy's ideas about the minstrels to the Society of Antiquaries, was persuaded by the heavily annotated revision of the essay that appeared in the 1767 edition of the *Reliques.*[49] What no critic perceived, however, was the degree to which in writing about the minstrels, Percy was writing about himself. Frederick Furnivall, a century after the first appearance of the *Reliques,* would cast an amused eye on Percy's social aspirations,[50] but he saw no connection between Percy and his minstrels. It was evident enough to one friend who wrote to Percy in 1765. Edward Blakeway congratulated Percy on his "promotion," in the year before Percy left for the Alnwick seat of his "noble patron":

> The sight of the Castle of Alnwick will most agreeably call to your remembrance your venerable and now highly to be esteemed friends, the ancient British bards. But I trust that the ingenious critic and illustrator will profit more by his labour than they did by their poetic rhapsodies. All they could hope for was present subsistence, and a slight portion of future fame: in the latter I doubt not you will share more abundantly, and as to the more substantial rewards of genius, I am confident you may depend on the princely disposition of your Lord.[51]

These were cannily prophetic words. The connections between aristocratic patronage, bardic labor, and the Middle Ages were later played upon by Percy in his own ballad composition, *The Hermit of Warkworth,* published in 1771. Warkworth was one of the Percy titles, and an actual hermitage near the village of Warkworth, not far from Alnwick, could still be visited in Percy's day. Percy's poem was popular, though it has the dubious distinction of having inspired Johnson to an improvised mockery of its meter: "I put my hat upon my head, / And walk'd into the Strand, / And there I met another man / Who's hat was in his hand." But it is competent enough, and its narrative is a further repositioning of its author in an imaginary relation to the medieval Percys, occasioned by the concrete relations of patronage to the Percys by which he had continued to benefit.

The poem is set in the early fifteenth century, and opens with the hermit lying awake in the hermitage of Warkworth during a storm. He hears a female voice and, on investigating, discovers, separately, a young woman and a man. He reunites them and harbors them in the hermitage; the youth asks him who is the lord of the lands they are in, and the hermit tells how the "rightful lord" is banished: ten years ago Hotspur lost his life fighting Henry Bolingbroke, and his son was sent away to Scotland.[52] "And now the PERCY name, so long / Our northern pride and boast, / Lies hid, alas! beneath a cloud; / Their honours reft and lost" (6). The realm has fallen into decay and is raided frequently by the Scots. The young man then reveals that he is Hotspur's son, another Henry Percy, heir to the earldom, returned from Scotland; the hermit weeps and "Pour'd blessings on his head" (8). Henry Percy then tells how, while living in the earl of Westmoreland's house, he has fallen in love with the earl's daughter, Eleanor, the young woman with whom he has now eloped.

The following day, the pair are married by a friar, who then goes to Raby Castle to seek their reconciliation with Eleanor's father. Exploring the hermitage, Eleanor and Henry find a tomb, "On which a young and beauteous Maid / In goodly sculpture shone" (17). They ask the hermit who she is; he weeps and sighs, but then commences a story. It concerns Henry's grandfather (first earl of Northumberland, the wily lord of Shakespeare's *Henry IV* plays) and his friend, Sir Bertram. Sir Bertram loved the daughter of an "old Northumbrian chief" (19), "But she with studied fond delays / Defers the blissful hour; / And loves to try his constancy, / And prove her maiden power" (19). Lord Percy holds a feast at Alnwick, at which minstrels tell of "The great atchievements of thy race" (20), at the conclusion of which the crowd "Applaud the masters' song, / And deeds of arms and war became / The theme of every tongue" (22).

At this point, a damsel enters the hall, carrying a helm from Sir Bertram's beloved and the message that she will be his bride "When thou hast prov'd this maiden gift / Where sharpest blows are try'd" (23). Percy and Bertram then ride in Tiviotdale with their retainers, where they are met in force by Douglas. Bertram assails the enemy first, alone, doing great deeds before a blow cleaves his helmet and he falls. Percy and his men join him and after a mighty battle, "The Scots reluctant yield" (27), and Bertram is taken away to Warkworth, having proven himself.

In the third fit of the poem, Bertram recovers from his wounds and rides with his brother to his lady, only to find that she had ridden out to him several days before and has not been seen since. Grief-stricken, Bertram goes in search of her, convinced she has been abducted by Scots. He and his brother separate on the search, both disguising themselves. Bertram dresses as a palmer and sometimes in the guise of a minstrel. Eventually he discovers the castle where his lady is confined; there, despite moving the porter's heart with the power of his sweet playing, he is refused admission. On the third night of lingering by the castle, he approaches it, only to see his bride escaping, via a rope ladder, with a "sturdy youth / In highland garb y-clad" (37). Overcome with jealousy, Bertram attacks the youth and kills him; Isabel, seeing through his disguise at the sound of his voice, interposes herself, crying that the youth is in fact his brother, only to receive a misdirected, fatal blow from Bertram. At this point the hermit who is telling the tale, overcome, speaks in the first person. He, of course, was Sir Bertram. After the death of his lover and brother, he was left to regret his deeds and to become "humble BENEDICT," living in penitence in the hermitage, where he has carved the tomb of Isabel, visited occasionally by his old friend, Earl Percy, and his son, Hotspur, both of whom he has now outlived. "But thou," he tells young Percy, "the honours of thy race, / Lov'd youth, shalt now restore; / And raise again the PERCY name / More glorious than before" (45). The young couple go to Scotland; they are reconciled with Eleanor's father, and then Eleanor, who is aunt to Henry V, intercedes for her husband, who has the Percy lands restored to him by the king. Henry Percy and Eleanor live happily ever after, and the poem ends.

But not quite. Percy—inevitably—has more to say, supplying from a chronicle some historical justification for his depiction of Henry Percy and his future wife, Eleanor. Henry, Hotspur's son, did indeed marry Eleanor, daughter of the earl of Westmoreland, and later received back from Henry V the Northumberland titles and lands, forfeited when his grandfather was attainted in the reign of Henry IV. Henry and Eleanor, Percy relates, had nine sons, the eldest of whom, another Henry, succeeded as third earl of Northumberland.

The poem works on many levels as a narrative of patronage and self-fashioning. As a composition by someone no longer of the Northumberland household, it could be seen as a simple gesture of gratitude. It also imaginatively furthers the vision of the minstrel familiar from the *Reliques:* the minstrels at Earl Percy's Alnwick feast, for example, are fomenting a martial spirit, doing honor to the deeds of the Percys and, like Thomas Percy himself, continually reminding their aristocratic masters of the family's glorious past. The poem of course locates itself on the territory, and around the time, of the great Percy ballads. The romance motif of the helmet given by Isabel, which provokes Northumberland to ride in Tiviotdale, implicitly provides the motive that is lacking for Percy's aggressive riding in Cheviot in "Chevy Chase."

Less obvious connections lie beneath the surface. Among the things Percy does not mention is the fact that the historical Eleanor, represented in the poem as a "dear maid" (14) who blushes, "o'erpower'd" by "sweet surprise," when Henry asks her to marry him (13), was in fact already a widow by the time she met Henry. She had been married to a son of the earl of Gloucester, Richard le Despenser. But to have mentioned this would have disrupted the poem's generic enclosing of the tragic tale of Bertram and Isabel with the optimistic romance of the young lovers Henry and Eleanor. In Thomas Percy's footnote, the poem ends with history. But not too much of it: the depiction of Henry and Eleanor is not about the realities of medieval marriages, but the restoration of the Northumberland fortunes through a felicitous marriage, as Hugh and Elizabeth, Percy's patrons, would later restore the house through their union.

Also submerged in the historical footnote is another interesting figure, Ralph Percy, a younger son of the poem's Henry. It was this younger son from whom Thomas Percy traced his noble lineage. So the poem in this regard was also about Percy's dormant, but never forgotten, genealogical link with his aristocratic patrons. Like Sir Bertram, the noble knight who so easily and convincingly slips into the role of a minstrel in the poem, the minstrel Thomas Percy had similar, if inverse and imaginary, powers of adaptation. Neither footnote nor poem makes anything of Ralph Percy; that connection lies unspoken, and the overt function of the poem is as an offering by the Northumberlands' priest-minstrel, Thomas Percy, of their own history to them. It is the minstrel's function to do this, and in return, he is cherished by his noble patrons. Percy was by no means the only person to seek the patronage or good opinion of the Northumberlands through poetry,[53] but he alone was able to remake himself as a minstrel so successfully as to reinvent, through his "barbarous productions," that "spirit of chivalry" that would ensure that he was "protected and caressed."

Imagining the Middle Ages

As Thomas Percy's career in the church progressed toward his ultimate preferment as bishop of Dromore, he distanced himself from his activities as ballad editor. By 1778 at the latest he was representing the ballads as the forgivable distractions of youth.[54] The fourth and last edition of the *Reliques* in Percy's lifetime appeared in 1794 under the nominal editorship of his nephew, though it is generally thought to have been principally Percy's own production. His literary activity generally slowed later in his life, no doubt in part because of the professional demands of the bishopric, in part because of a concern about the appropriateness of the association with antiquarian work, but perhaps also because that work had fulfilled its function. It would appear that Percy's self-cultivation as a modern minstrel was not maintained in later life. He did, however, hold to his claim on Northumberland descent, which was accepted by James Boswell in his *Life of Johnson*.[55] But by then, of course, the former Thomas Piercy had become Lord Thomas Dromore: surely the highest social and cultural achievement his story of origins could bring him.

Percy, wrote Frederick Furnivall in 1867, "opened to us the road into the Early English home where we have spent so many pleasant hours" (*BPFM*, 1:xx). In this role, the *Reliques* has been less well explored than it has as a key document in romanticism. The publication of the contents of the folio manuscript by Furnivall and Hales is no doubt part of the reason for this. It became possible to see that Percy had been no textual editor, in the terms of the mid–nineteenth century. His manuscript, so attractively presented in the portrait of Percy painted by Joshua Reynolds, is in fact every bit the "parcel of old rags and tatters" Ritson said it to be.[56] The genuine Middle English of the folio was at least a century and a half away from its origins when written down, and even more distanced when it was printed in the *Reliques*. But Furnivall was right to point to the book as a key document for the study of Early, or Middle, English. The *Reliques* created a consciousness of Middle English—even though it still awaited that classification—where there had been almost none. It was a direct influence on Walter Scott and his activities for Middle English and on Joseph Ritson, albeit negatively. Frederic Madden, one of the first scholars to see the manuscript after Percy, was also crucially influenced by his work, so that the *Reliques* lived in the consciousnesses of three generations of medievalists.

The essays on minstrels and metrical romances forcefully shaped thinking on Middle English studies. For a disciplinary field as yet theoretically free-floating and extramural—potentially in the public sphere—this had a number of direct political and institutional consequences. The intrication, in Percy's life, of his literary editing with his personal career and self-fashioning meant that the poetry as he presented it had to be positioned in certain politically and historically explicit ways. The rapid alterations made to the shape of the book, and therefore the presentation of the manuscript, when Countess Percy became the dedicatee represented a moral and political reordering. But Percy had already shaped his material in specific political directions; the association with the Percys that came about in 1764 was largely a consequence, not a cause, of this. The offering of the poems as a hereditary right to the countess made explicit the vision of the relations of literature to class, and between literature and the aristocracy, that Percy had already developed, principally in his theory of minstrels. If, then, with the dedication to the countess and the subsequent reordering of the work and of Percy himself, the principal intervention in the field of Middle English literature of the time vanished into a set of private and closely circumscribed political relations, this is only what had been implicit in the work from the outset.

The successful deployment by Percy of Middle English texts as part of an aesthetic work on the self came at the cost of the political co-opting of the literature by aristocratic interests. The public-sphere existence that Middle English could theoretically have had in the eighteenth century was illusory. Percy developed a romantic, conservative Middle English designed to cement the relations between the ruling class and a certain type of aesthetic persona created by a literary-scholarly work on the self. This had various ramifications: at the level of genre, for example, romance came to dominate Middle English studies for several decades, because romance tended to display aristocracy to advantage and offer positive visions of patronage.

From this political imagining of the Middle Ages, in which the scholar's delight in a Middle Ages of pageant, pomp, and chivalry was matched by his pleasure in strict hierarchical order and feudal government, a persistent scholarly formation arose. It was such men as Walter Scott and Frederic Madden who inherited the legacy of Percy, and it was in their hands and in the hands of men like them that Middle English went into the first half of the nineteenth century as a kind of feudal practice itself: it was pursued by men of humble origins, who deployed Middle English texts (usually romances) as elements of a self-fashioning that involved a negotiation between an aristocratic patron and the supplicant antiquarian on the basis of a shared vision of the past conjured up in the texts.

Middle English, more than a century before its entry into academic institutions, was thus at the outset rapidly and effectively contained as a potential political force, as a discipline-to-be in theory without institutional political alignment or bias. The question remains whether the "barbarous productions of unpolished ages" could have been made popular on any other political terms. What possibilities existed for Middle English in the public sphere in the later eighteenth century? Could there have been a political and critical alternative in the study of medieval literature? What answer there may be surely lies in the career of the most politically radical medievalist of his time.

CHAPTER 2

Turning the World Upside Down
The Unmaking of Joseph Ritson

1803

Early in September 1803 I frequently heard a great Swearing and Noise in his Chambers, and on meeting his Laundress on the Stairs I asked her ye Cause of Disturbance I had heard—She answered, that she believed her *Master was out of his Mind*, for his Conduct in every respect proved him so—and that she was greatly afraid that in his Delirium he would do himself or her an injury.[1]

By 1802, the year he produced his major Middle English edition, *Ancient Engleish Metrical Romanceës*, Joseph Ritson was at the limits of endurance of his self-imposed ascesis. He had been physically ill for years, and probably mentally unstable for some time as well. He suffered from memory loss and hinted at fears of mental illness, of which there may have been a history in his family.[2] He had few friends left and had lost most of his money in financial speculation. Later the following year, a rapid decline began.

Ritson's chambers were in Gray's Inn. On the evening of September 10, he was seen by other occupants in his rooms, surrounded by books and papers, some of which he was throwing on the fire. He was carrying a candle in his hand, and already some of the loose papers were burning. He would let no one in. The steward was sent for, a key procured, and the steward, two porters, and Robert Smith, the author of this account, entered and confronted Ritson:

He appeared much confused on seeing us, and asked how we came in?—We told him by means of the Laundress's Key—He then asked what we wanted? Mr Quin told him we came in Consequence of the great Blaze that appeared in his Chambers—believing them to be on Fire! He answered that his Fire had gone out, and that he was lighting it to make Horse-reddish Tea—

Mr Quin then represented to him the great Danger of making his Fire with loose papers, particularly as there was so many scattered about the Room, some of which had actually taken Fire. (*JR*, 1:288)

Ritson's response was to drive the unwelcome visitors from his chambers with a drawn dagger in hand. Smith succeeded in pacifying the hapless antiquarian on this occasion, but in the days following, Ritson remained unpredictable. He smashed all his windows; at other times he would appear to be at work, telling Smith that he was "writing a Pamphlet proving Jesus Christ an Impostor" (*JR*, 1:289). Ritson was soon removed to an asylum, where he died on 23 September 1803. A story that reached the ears of Francis Douce suggested that on his deathbed, Ritson, an atheist, "with tears in his eyes made his confessions," but Douce, no doubt correctly, believed this "to be a pious lie."[3] In his will, written, as if in a presentiment of the end, just three days before the final madness began, Ritson had asked that his body "be interred...with the least possible ceremony, attendance, or expence, without the presence of a clergyman, and my coffin being previously, carefully and effectually filled with quick lime" (1:291). Ritson, who had neither sought nor received personal advancement from his work in his life, now seemed to want to efface and obliterate all traces of himself in death.

In this resolution, Ritson was thwarted by his old adversary, Thomas Percy, who was equally determined to preserve his memory. It was the bishop who was responsible for procuring Robert Smith's account of Ritson's end, which he solicited through a friend who happened to be a Bencher of Gray's Inn.[4] Percy spread the story of Ritson's last madness among his correspondents at all opportunities, unrelentingly keeping up his campaign against the antiquary in death as in life. Eventually he ensured the publication of Smith's account, first attempting to place it in Henry Weber's *Metrical Romances* (1810) and then securing its publication in Robert Cromek's *Select Scotish Songs*, in the year before his own death in 1811 (*JR*, 1:307–10). Here its inclusion was justified by its presentation as a cautionary tale about "the near alliance between genius and insanity."[5]

The painful and deeply personal story of Ritson's death appears to be everything that should not be contained within scholarship but confined instead to the realm of the private. Yet Thomas Percy not only viewed it as a public property, but ensured that the story would be perpetuated within a *scholarly* frame. Its placement in the world of scholarship, rather than simply its circulation as gossip, seems to have been his ultimate motive in procuring it. The attack on Ritson's private life became for Percy, by then one of the grand old men of literary antiquarianism, the ultimate response to everything Ritson had done in his public life as an editor and scholar in the field of ballads and romances. The vituperative exchanges between Ritson and Percy (originating mainly from Ritson) were both scholarly and personal, in a realm of antiquarianism in which self and scholarship were difficult to separate. An attack on Percy's minstrel theory was an attack on Percy himself. Percy's revenge was equally personal, implying as it did that no viable scholarship could have come from a man so clearly unbalanced.[6]

So Percy, whose own personal mythology of origins began with a document plucked from the flames, circulated another mythic tale, of the demonic Ritson's end with his documents in flames around him. Percy, Cromek, and others who gossiped about him give a strong sense that Ritson had to pay, with his tortured death, for his excesses in life. It is as if his excessive brand of scholarship were not natural, but could only be accounted for as the product of his "unnatural" inclinations: his repudiation of God, his revolutionary politics, his strict vegetarianism, his rumored sexual excess. All that the story of Ritson's end lacks is the Faustian bargain. Perhaps that, too, is buried here: Ritson was his own Mephistopheles; he had struck a destructive bargain with himself. Certainly many of his contemporaries thought him to be the devilish figure of late-eighteenth-century antiquarianism, and some of his own utterances suggest that he deliberately took on this role.

Ritson was born in Stockton, Durham, in 1752. His nineteenth-century biographers tended to exaggerate the gentility of his origins by claiming that his family had originally been landed gentry.[7] But Ritson himself seems to have been unconcerned about what were in fact humble origins; he was the son of a corn grower, from a line of Westmoreland farmers. Ritson's father had moved to Stockton and married a servant in the household of the corn merchant for whom he worked (*JR*, 1:9–10). Ritson seems to have received a solid schooling, and he later displayed his literary interests by publishing poetry. But there was little question of his going to university; around the age of seventeen, he was indentured to a Stockton solicitor and later worked for a barrister (1:41). Bertrand Bronson points out that the bulk of this work was in conveyancing, which, given the importance to it of old title deeds, was probably "peculiarly favorable . . . to the development and fostering of an antiquarian taste" (1:43).

Ritson moved from Stockton to London some time in 1775, where he was employed with a conveyancing firm in Gray's Inn (*JR*, 1:50). He apparently began practicing on his own as a conveyancer in 1780, at which time he also moved into the inn (1:55–56). Deciding to become a barrister, Ritson was admitted to Gray's Inn in 1784 and called to the bar in 1789 (1:123). Various pieces of evidence—not least his obvious lack of means—suggest that Ritson was not very active in pursuing work, tending rather to "let clients come to him" in his chambers (1:141). A post acquired early in 1784, that of bailiff of the Savoy, provided a regular but unspectacular income (1:122–23). Throughout this period, Ritson's main pursuit must have been his self-education in early literature, through which he "made himself one of the best informed men of his time in fields where accurate knowledge was then peculiarly difficult of attainment" (1:56). As would many a scholar after him, Ritson achieved this by a daily tramp to the British Museum.

Ritson also visited Scotland, where he examined, among other things, the Auchinleck manuscript in the Advocates' Library in Edinburgh, in which he discovered the romance of *Sir Tristrem*. He left Britain once, for a tour to revolutionary Paris in 1791 (1:145). In 1801, an unlikely meeting of minds took place when Ritson stayed with Walter Scott in his cottage at Lasswade, where they certainly discussed many antiquarian topics, and Ritson probably passed on his opinions concerning *Sir Tristrem*, which Scott was about to edit (1:250).

In many important respects, Ritson's passage to antiquarianism followed a classic pattern: born in provincial England into a socioeconomically underprivileged family, he benefited from his family's ability to send him to school; a dabbler in literature, he focused his interest through examination of old documents; he entered the law, but only practiced enough to subsist. In the study of early literature he was self-taught, through long periods spent in a great manuscript repository, and he also benefited from access to the libraries of antiquarian friends (1:69). His progress was similar to Percy's, with the difference that Percy, having gone to university, went into that other great employer of antiquarians, the church. Like his rival—and with considerably more justification— Ritson connected himself with the Northumberland of the medieval Percys, whose deeds he admired, and although he was sometimes critical of the land of his birth, he often invoked his connection with Durham and the Borders.[8]

The typicality of the pattern of Ritson's career in scholarship needs to be emphasized because of the fact that he was viewed in his time as outstandingly untypical. His politics and personal eccentricities usually ensured that he was characterized by contemporaries as everything a scholar should *not* be. When one critic said, "He seems to be Deistical, Popish & Jacobitical" after the publication of the notorious *Observations* on Thomas Warton's *History of English Poetry*, he told only half the story.[9] Ritson became an atheist and an aggressive vegetarian, and in the 1790s the Jacobite became a Jacobin. After his journey to Paris, he began addressing friends in his letters as "Citizen" and using the revolutionary calendar. He became part of the revolutionary circle in London and was an associate of the radicals William Godwin, John Thelwall, and Thomas Holcroft. Some of his letters show that he lived in expectation of a coming revolution in Britain, although he could not envisage its precise impact. He was later to become particularly critical of Godwin, but was still an associate of the radicals when several of them were arrested in May 1794. Ritson seems to have been genuinely fearful that he, too, would be put on trial, and Bronson argues that he would have suffered if the outcome of the trial had been a guilty verdict (*JR*, 1:160).

Modern critics, though more sympathetic to Ritson, have tended to confirm his freakishness by suggesting that he was too far ahead of his time to be appreciated in it: Bronson saw him as an editor "approximately sixty years ahead of his time," while for Arthur Johnston it was a century.[10] This is the reverse of what many of his contemporaries argued of Ritson; they thought he was *backward* in his insistence on fidelity to ancient manuscripts. This position is even less valid than that of Bronson and Johnston. Foucault argues that "[i]n any given culture and at any given moment, there is always only one *episteme* that defines the conditions of possibility of all knowledge, whether expressed in a theory or silently invested in a practice."[11] Within the episteme of late-eighteenth-century literary antiquarianism, Ritson conformed completely to the patterns of his time. He did not, and could not, break the bounds of possible knowledges in the last quarter of the eighteenth century. What later scholars have done, noting Ritson's disagreements with his age and his apparent anticipations of scholarly method after comparative philology, is to suggest that Ritson foreshadowed what comparative philology would later make axiomatic. In this view, Ritson took the first few steps on the road to objectivism, away from the path of subjective, fraudulent treatment of early texts, in anticipation of comparative philology's aim to develop an objective approach to editorial and critical methodology.

In fact almost the opposite was the case. Far from anticipating the scholarship and editing made possible by comparative philology, Ritson's principles of editing were precisely an attempt to work in the *absence* of the governing paradigm philology would later provide. He was not taking steps toward scientifically illumined method, but groping in the dark of its absence. Certainly, Ritson's methods appeared to be set against the temper of the times, as when he was criticized for his very fidelity to his manuscript sources, his sacrifice of taste to antiquarian rigor. But to be a failure, to be set against the dominant scholarly expectations—to be, in effect, unmade—this is to be within and governed by the conditions of the episteme.

My first concern here is to expand the account of the state of learning on Middle English literature in the 1770s and 1780s given in the previous chapter by considering Thomas Warton's *History of English Poetry.* Ritson's challenges to this "orthodoxy" can then be reexamined to suggest not that they were aberrantly out of their time, but serious, albeit not widely held, counterpositions within the total sphere of Middle English literature; his *continuity* with his era can be newly stressed. Ritson's politics, and the expression of his politics in his work, can then be considered and, finally, his contribution to the debate about how Middle English texts should be edited. Ritson was unquestionably a radical in many ways; but his own and others' characterization of him as the demonic figure of his time does not, in fact, give a true indication of his place in Middle English.

Barbarism and Civility

In 1775, when Ritson came to London, there was no discipline of Middle English; only retrospection can supply that. There were, however, several key publications central to the literary antiquarian view of "ancient" English. Thomas Tyrwhitt, often labeled "the founder of modern traditions of Chaucer editing," produced his edition of *The Canterbury Tales* in that year, and Ritson became a great admirer of this scholar.[12] The third edition of the *Reliques* also appeared in 1775, and the first volume of Thomas Warton's *History of English Poetry* had been published the year before. None of these works defined itself by reference to a notion of "Middle English" or even of the "later Middle Ages." The study of Chaucer, as I argue in a later chapter, was a defined field in its own right, not so much the study of a great medieval poet as of a great English poet who happened to live in the Middle Ages. The character of the *Reliques* we have already seen. Warton's book was intended, according to its full title, to trace literary history "from the Close of the Eleventh to the Commencement of the Eighteenth Century," and only became a work of medieval studies by default, when Warton failed to complete it.

Warton shared with Percy and many of their contemporaries the assumption that he worked in an enlightened period looking back on an age of barbarism. Believing he was writing "[i]n an age advanced to the highest degree of refinement," Warton suggested that it was natural to be curious about "the transitions from barbarism to civility." He and his readership looked

> back on the savage condition of our ancestors with the triumph of superiority; we are pleased to mark the steps by which we have been raised from rudeness to elegance: and our reflections on this subject are accompanied with a conscious pride, arising in great measure from a tacit comparison of the infinite disproportion between the feeble efforts of remote ages, and our present improvements in knowledge.[13]

Under such a governing view, it became at least as important to these scholars to determine the point at which the process of refinement from barbarism began as it was to periodize the Middle Ages as a middle between antiquity and modernity. The important point for Warton and Percy—who rarely use the term "Middle Ages"—was not the beginning of the Renaissance, but the time or times *within* the Middle Ages when the first glimmerings of refinement could be discerned. So Warton entirely dismissed Anglo-Saxon literature from his considerations, as having "no connection" with his subject, which began with "that era, when our national character began to dawn" (*HEP*, 1:vi).

Although it represents the principal contribution to the study of Middle English to come from within a university in the eighteenth century, *The History of English Poetry* is to modern eyes the least academic piece of writing in the field. As a lifetime fellow and tutor at Trinity College, Oxford, Warton did not have to work hard or deal with the burden of having to sell his texts, and "[i]t was very natural," one biographer suggests, "that Warton should be in a certain sense indolent."[14] Percy's revisions of his essays, particularly the essay on minstrels, and the debate that was carried on in journals and learned societies over issues raised by the *Reliques* were far more scholarly in purpose than the *History*. Warton's work is in many ways the most personal of literary histories: it rambles and digresses, it keeps to no coherent plan, at all times reflecting the whim of its author. Warton frequently gives the impression, when he explains that he will not cover one or another area, that he is inventing an excuse to ignore something he does not want to do. His exclusion of Anglo-Saxon, for example, however justified, was really the result of the fact that he was not proficient enough in the language to read the literature (which he thought consisted principally of "religious rhapsodies" [*HEP*, 1:vi]). He states more than once that he does not intend to discuss Scots poetry, but then covers Dunbar in detail because he is the best poet since Chaucer and Lydgate.

Given its digressive structure and the fact that its errors were legion, it is not surprising that the *History* was bitterly complained about by succeeding scholars. Yet no one seemed disposed to replace the work; instead, a revision was completed once a generation or so in the nineteenth century — by Richard Price in 1824, Richard Taylor in 1840, and William Carew Hazlitt in 1871 — so that it eventually became a bloated compendium encrusted with all the quarrelsome learning of a century of antiquarian dispute and fact-grubbing. The fact is that however inaccurately he transcribed, however dilatory his writing, Warton had culled a vast amount of material from manuscripts few had seen, to create the single greatest resource for Middle English poetry in existence. At the same time, he had augmented existing scholarly ideas about medieval literature and added some influential theories of his own, to advance a powerful account of the early development of poetry and the English language.

It was often speculated that Warton did not complete his original design because of the vitriolic criticisms of the first three volumes by Joseph Ritson.[15] More recent critics take a subtler view: Joseph Donatelli, for example, feels that Warton found it increasingly difficult to shape the "disparate materials" of the fifteenth and sixteenth centuries into the kind of narrative he had constructed around the earlier literature.[16] This is borne out by the way in which Warton's narrative of progress falters when he goes beyond Chaucer. But *The History of English Poetry* was in any case unfinishable. It is a largely paradoxical work, always in danger of running up against its own contradictions, and these paradoxes at the heart of Warton's scholarship made the work irresolvable. The mission to demonstrate the stages of increasing literary and cultural refinement made Warton's account a narrative of progress, showing how poetry, and the English language, had progressed ineluctably from their former barbarity to their current refinement. This meant that much of the poetry studied was, in the then typical fashion, deemed more or less barbarous. But Warton, as a romantic genuinely captivated by the romantic element in poetry, also wanted to valorize the poetry he was studying for itself, as itself.

These two aims always conflict in the *History*. On the one hand, the medieval text stands on its own as valuable; on the other, it can never quite be what it is supposed to be, because, by definition, it is incomplete, on the road to progress but not yet arrived. The point of arrival is the age of refinement in which Warton lives, so that literary history, in Warton's sense, has stopped. Warton, understandably, seems to have found it easier to write about a narrative of progress than to deal with a telos in which history had simply perfected itself and come to an end. The *History* was a narrative of progress for which the end could not be written.

A second, related problem in the *History* is that Warton values romance precisely for its fanciful and exotic nature. The postmedieval trend toward science, reason, and the classics had "produced that bane of invention, IMITATION" (*HEP*, 2:463). Realism, in other words, for Warton is banal, and the romantic refusal of realism is the true stuff of poetry. Yet, like other eighteenth-century critics, Warton tended to value medieval poetry for its historicist possibilities and its realism. Like Percy and Hurd, he had absorbed the idea that what was useful about ancient texts was "the pictures of antient manners presented by these early writers, [which] strongly interest the imagination: especially as having the same uncommon merit with the pictures of manners in Homer, that of being founded in truth and reality, and actually painted from the life" (1:42). The romantic text's value is, paradoxically, precisely in its realism, its imitation.

These paradoxes arise because of Warton's obvious affection for much medieval poetry, combined with his inability, ultimately, to treat that poetry as a product of its historical context rather than the regrettably barbarous material it must always be when measured against the standards of eighteenth-century taste. The *History* is always oscillating between these twin positions, which are clearly a version of the long-standing antiquarian/man of taste dilemma. Romance goes a long way to resolving the dilemma. For Warton the problem was that medieval historical writing (in chronicles) was tasteless and bad; earlier antiquarians, he wrote, no doubt with Thomas Hearne and his edition of Robert of Gloucester's *Chronicle* (1724) in mind, wasted their time on these "obscure fragments of uninstructive morality or uninteresting history" (1:209). The medieval romances were much to be preferred, because they were historical pictures and also appealed to the man of taste and genius.

Like many another, however, Warton found that medieval poetry would usually have been better if it were something other than what it was. Some of the "nervous, terse, and polished lines" of Lyndesay's *Monarchie*, for example, "need only to be reduced to modern and English orthography, to please a reader accustomed solely to relish the tone of our present versification" (2:308). In other words, if the poem were a modern English one, there would be nothing wrong with it; however good Warton finds this medieval poem to be, it is really better as something else. Warton, here, has the typical self-appointed role of antiquary as mediator: the antiquary does the hard work for the man of taste, and this could be seen as the principal function of the *History* as a whole.

Warton began *The History of English Poetry* with one of his favorite topics, in a dissertation titled "Of the Origin of Romantic Fiction in Europe." Ideas about romance were still fluid in this period, when English writers, according to Johnston, "theorized from grossly inadequate knowledge," while the French tended to read the primary texts more closely.[17] A consequence was that much thought in the work of English scholars relied heavily on the work of Sainte-Palaye, Fauchet, and Chapelain,[18] and as we have seen, Richard Hurd was quite candid about his own debt. Warton's account of romance shows distinct traces of the positions of both Hurd and Percy. His view of minstrels, mentioned early in the dissertation, is very familiar: they were the descendants, albeit diminished in role, of the bards, who had been greatly respected figures.[19] But Warton demurred from Hurd's thesis about the origin of chivalry as an expression of feudal society; this placed chivalry, and romance, too late. Elements of chivalry can be found, Warton suggests, in the early Gothic tribes, although it is difficult to see "the seeds of elegance amongst men, distinguished only for their ignorance and their inhumanity," and the "superior pomp" of feudalism overwhelmed "[t]he rude origin of this heroic gallantry" (1:i4r-i4v).

The critical agent in the development of western romance was the Crusades, and the contact they afforded with the fictions of the East. Warton was a staunch orientalist in this respect. Romance represented a turn to the exotic, and the exotic, in Warton's view, was derived from the East: "Amid the gloom of superstition, in an age of the grossest ignorance and credulity, a taste for the wonders of oriental fiction was introduced by the Arabians into Europe." Warton speculates that the "Gothic scalds" may previously have drawn on oriental fiction, without suggesting precisely how (1:i4v). The minstrels adopted the forms of fiction brought by contact with the East, which were then amplified in the work of Pseudo-Turpin and Geoffrey of Monmouth, to form "the ground-work of that species of fabulous narrative called romance" (1:i4v). It was this mode that had its eventual outcome in the work of Spenser.

After a further dissertation, "On the Introduction of Learning into England," the *History* proper begins, with the issue of language. Progress in language, from what Warton calls "Norman Saxon," forms a frame for the work as a whole, because in the continuist narrative, linguistic improvement and literary history cannot be separated. Lacking any philologically informed view of linguistic change, Warton saw it as entwined with the development of literature: a barbarous language was refined by those who used it best, and these were the best poets. English began to be formed out of Norman Saxon, for example, when translations from French minstrel literature into English in the twelfth century introduced new linguistic forms, "circumstances [which] enriched our tongue, and extended the circle of our poetry" (1:115). Poets are, in effect, linguistic "fixers." They do not even have to be very good, as in the case of Robert Mannyng, who, although "uncouth and unpleasing... and chiefly employed in turning the theology of his age into rhyme, contributed to form a style, to teach expression, and to polish his native tongue" (1:77).

The period of greatest improvement of this kind was in the fourteenth and fifteenth centuries, when even a writer as "feeble" as Hoccleve "contributed to propagate and establish those improvements in our language which were now beginning to take place" (2:38). But it was Chaucer, in a common eighteenth-century view, who took the paramount role in this respect. Like Tyrwhitt, Warton thought that Chaucer should not be blamed for, as some would have it, corrupting English with his Gallicisms. Chaucer must only have been reflecting a general prevalence of French in the English court; in any case, he, along with Gower and Hoccleve, "much improved the vernacular style by the use of this exotic phraseology. It was thus that our primitive diction was enlarged and enriched. The English language owes its copiousness, elegance, and harmony, to these innovations" (2:50).

Like other writers, Warton here assumes that one man can influence the course of a language or a culture and that a great poet is someone who shapes the language rather than is shaped by it. Warton finds precedent for this form of influence in Petrarch, who was thought to have revived the taste for Roman history in his time in the French court (2:114). The poet's cultural autonomy allowed Warton to present Chaucer in a way that would remain widely prevalent in the nineteenth century: he is at once a man of his time *and* removed from it. An acute observer of his cultural context, Chaucer is also the great universalizer, someone whose "knowledge of the world... enabled him to give such an accurate picture of antient manners, as no cotemporary nation has transmitted to posterity," and the writer who surprises us, "in so gross and ignorant an age," with his "talents for satire, and for observation on life," because these are "qualities which usually exert themselves at more civilised periods" (1:435).

Chaucerian eminence presents a problem: fifteenth-century literature. Progress can only be seen as interrupted after Chaucer, when there was a partial relapse "into barbarism" (2:51). If Chaucer was like a "genial day in an English spring," when a "brilliant sun enlivens the face of nature with an unusual lustre," then after him "winter returns with redoubled horrors" (2:51). Warton praises Lydgate—a writer toward whom he is kinder than most of his contemporaries—but is in general scathing about the fifteenth century. It was not until the end of that century that "the bonds of barbarism" were broken (2:408), and not until after the reign of Elizabeth—with Protestantism decisively established—that "men attained that state of general improvement, and those situations with respect to literature and life, in which they have ever since persevered" (2:462).

Warton wrote about the Middle Ages and medieval poetry because of an obvious aesthetic attachment to the literature. But like any man of taste in his time, he thought the Middle Ages to be an appalling time of bigotry and popish oppression. The close of the period, at the end of the fifteenth century, was the point at which a "mighty deliverance" was achieved, "in which the mouldering Gothic fabrics of false religion and false philosophy fell together" (2:408). For Warton, this period was the beginning of the establishment of a modernity that was not fully achieved, after the fresh outbreak of popery under Mary, until the seventeenth century. Modernity brings with it refinement—of language, literature, and manners. The two terms, modernity and refinement, are almost synonymous. At the same time, though, and despite the evident benefits, modernity has a cost:

> Setting aside the consideration of the more solid advantages, which are obvious, and are not the distinct object of our contemplation at present, the lover of true poetry will ask, what have we gained by this revolution? It may be answered, much good sense, good taste, and good criticism. But, in the mean time, we have lost a set of manners, and a system of machinery, more suitable to the purposes of poetry, than those which have been adopted in their place. We have parted with extravagancies that are above propriety, with incredibilities that are more acceptable than truth, and with fictions that are more valuable than reality. (2:463)

It is as if true taste and good criticism are always already lapsarian; the condition of their being is the prior passing of a flawed, but more innocent and authentic, era. The paradox of chivalry and its attendant literary form, romance, is that they are the agents of the coming of modernity, because they improve the literature and thereby refine the language, but medieval romance can never truly achieve refinement; it can never, by itself, leap from barbarism. Warton's continuist narrative commits him to a view of the Middle Ages as a time of lost, flawed innocence, on the one hand, and, on the other, modernity as a time of the greatest refinement, which has, however, lost something vital it can never recover.

Turning the World Upside Down

Your blunders are beyond computation, "out of all cess;" and I have neither the leisure nor the patience to detect you in every one. But your ignorance is so amazing and unaccountable, in many of them, that I cannot choose but bestow more attention upon them than I otherwise would do. For instance, how could you contrive to misinterpret, and corrupt the above simple phrase *"hedde ferly,"* as you have done? The lowest person in Trinity college, the porter, nay your old bed-maker, had you asked them the question, would have immediately informed you its meaning was purely this: *The christian man had* ferly (i.e. *wonder*), what it might mean.[20]

As this published address to Warton suggests, Ritson's way into the antiquarian world was entirely adversarial. In the space of a year, he attacked, often in the most intemperate terms, four of the dominant literary figures of the time. To enter the field of Shakespeare studies, he published a critique of the Shakespearian work of George Steevens and Samuel Johnson. In ballad editing, he attacked Thomas Percy.[21] And to impress himself on the study of early English, Ritson wrote perhaps the most violent of all his critiques, an attack on Warton that even he referred to as a "scurrilous libel." Ritson's intent was clear: "I will turn the world upside down," he declared to a friend.[22]

The *Observations on the Three First Volumes of the History of English Poetry* (1782) would alone have been sufficient for Ritson to have been branded as the wild man of late-eighteenth-century letters. There was little public respect to be gained by taking "the genial Thomas Warton" (*JR*, 1:72) to the pillory, a man who had few enemies and many supporters. The *Observations* is a work of astonishing insolence, even by the standards of the time, and Ritson's kindest supporters have found it difficult to excuse. The title, somewhat cheekily, recalls Warton's own earlier work, *Observations on the Faerie Queene of Spenser* (1754), and the work begins with an insultingly presumptuous prefatory note that points out that the volume has been printed in the same size as Warton's *History*, so that it can be bound in with it to form "a very useful APPENDIX."[23] The book is written in the form of a letter to Warton, and the constant personal address to the unfortunate poet gives Ritson's criticisms extra piquancy. Ritson's method has no great subtlety; he simply went through the *History* chapter by chapter, correcting errors and disputing conclusions. The whole is embellished with comments on Warton's ignorance, foolishness, and incompetence, many of them entirely unnecessary to the project of correcting his mistakes.

Most of the criticisms focus either on misinterpretations of medieval words by Warton or on bibliographical inaccuracies that result, in Ritson's probably accurate opinion, from Warton's lack of familiarity with the texts with which he is dealing. Some of his remarks, though, are simply ad hominem attacks on "a thorough-bred Oxonian tory-rory High-churchman."[24] Nevertheless, Ritson many times exposes Warton in bad translations and interpretations. His savage comments quoted at the beginning of this section, for example, were occasioned by Warton's gloss of the lines he rendered as "The cristen mon hedde farly / What hit mihte mene." Warton decided "hedde" must mean "heeded" in the sense of "was attentive to" (*HEP*, 2:231). After a paragraph of pure scorn for this error, Ritson offered the correct interpretation.

Some of the criticisms are simply petty, as when Ritson scornfully noted ordinary misprints in Warton's work. Some are completely wrong, as when he stated that the stanzaic *Morte Arthure* was based on the corresponding passages in Caxton's *Morte D'Arthur*. Concluding his extraordinary work, Ritson wrote that he had "completed my design of exposing to the public eye a tolerable specimen of the numerous errors, falsities, and plagiarisms" Warton had perpetrated, and hoped that the historian would be "sorry" and "ashamed." He professed not to care whether his arguments would have any effect on Warton. A history of a country's language and literature, Ritson said, was "the most interesting and important subject that can be conceived," besides "civil history," and Warton was "the least qualifyed" to undertake such a work. His ignorance was such that he was "certain, at last, of encountering detection and disgrace."[25]

So the most controversial antiquarian of his time introduced himself to the scholarly world. The ensuing battle shook the *Gentleman's Magazine* for months. Much later, in a largely forgiving memoir, Robert Surtees still thought the comments on Warton "indefensible," and neither could Joseph Haslewood defend a work that he thought was "given...in the language of a despot, rather than with the urbanity of a liberal critic," and "evidenced an unprovoked and most indefensible irascibility of temper." Only Harris Nicolas, thirty years after Ritson's death, saw that despite the "occasionally rude style of his language" and "the needless personal taunts," Ritson's motives were not personal but in the interests of scholarly accuracy.[26] Even Bronson misses this point, seeing Ritson as jeopardizing the secure future he could have had "by a step which is, after all allowances have been made, inexcusable" (*JR*, 1:72).

Ritson rapidly confirmed his reputation with his attack on Percy, begun soon after the appearance of the *Observations* in *A Select Collection of English Songs* (1783) and later continued in *Ancient Songs* (1792). At the heart of their *querelle* is the old dilemma, the conflict between the requirements of taste and antiquarian scholarliness. Ritson began, in 1783, by acknowledging the *Reliques* to be "beautiful, elegant, and ingenious," but complained that "they who look into it to be acquainted with the state of ancient poetry, will be miserably disappointed or fatally misled." He went on to imply that Percy had used his high rank to place himself above charges of "Forgery and imposition."[27] He then turned, in "A Historical Essay on the Origin and Progress of National Song," to Percy's notion of the minstrels. Ritson acknowledged the abundant evidence collected by Percy of the respectability of French minstrels in the Middle Ages, but would not allow that this meant *English* minstrels enjoyed the same status. There were wandering performers, he added, who made a living "singing and playing to the illiterate vulgar," but the sources did not suggest "that they were received into the castles of the nobility, sung at their tables, and were rewarded like the French minstrels."[28]

Ritson would later expand his critique of Percy's "forgeries" by casting doubt on the existence of the folio manuscript itself. The extent to which he did so, however, has been greatly exaggerated.[29] Ritson's two principal concerns with Percy's work were always editorial standards and the status of the minstrels. In 1792, he included in *Ancient Songs* his essay "Observations on the Ancient English Minstrels"—a title that must have chilled Percy. Ritson snidely implied that there was no manuscript, without actually stating that this was what he believed. He again attacked Percy's editorial methods and the concept of the minstrel. The argument was essentially the same as in 1783, though with greater illustration from early sources. The minstrels, far from being exalted figures, were in fact neither particularly protected by the aristocracy nor known for performing works they had composed themselves; they were simply musicians, usually living in a degraded state. The statute of Queen Elizabeth's time, declaring that minstrels be "punished as rogues, vagabonds, and sturdy beggars," which Percy had cited as evidence of a late decline in status, to Ritson simply indicated that "As to dignity; it is pretty clear they never had any to lose."[30]

Ritson then proceeded to quote Percy's own comments on the damaged state of many of the poems in the *Reliques* drawn from the folio, and made it clear that he thought manuscript corruption an excuse for the editor's preference of "his ingenuity to his fidelity, without the least intimation to the reader."[31] Ritson, quite correctly, argued that Percy was as much author as editor of some of the poems. He never identified the homology between the minstrels and Percy himself; although he implicitly exposed the importance of the minstrel theory to the socially mobile editor, he nowhere linked Percy's fortunes to the association with the Northumberlands. But he did, explicitly, perceive how Percy had rewritten medieval literature in terms of contemporary taste.

The transformation of Ritson, in popular memory, into the Faustian figure of antiquarianism suggests that he achieved his aim of "turning the world upside down," though it did him little good. But there is a great difference between participating in an epistemic shift, a revolution in knowledge, and simply upsetting the people who espouse an accepted knowledge. To do the former usually involves the latter, but that does not mean that every time the establishment is rocked, a fundamental shift takes place. The reassessment of Ritson that has been going on since his death has tended to rehabilitate him as a man ahead of his time, but this is far from accurate.

Ritson did not have a new paradigm to offer. He had the gospel of accuracy, of pure antiquarianism unreconciled to the needs of the man of taste. Even this aim, as the next section shows, was substantially adapted later in his career. He was the demonic figure of antiquarianism, but not because he was going forward into something new. He was in fact simply offering to do better what was already being done; the entire rationale for *A Select Collection of English Songs*, for example, was to do what Percy should have done in the first place in the *Reliques*.[32] The world is not turned upside down at all. No paradigm is broken, no radical solutions are proposed to problems of editing, no radical visions of the Middle Ages are offered.

Ritson's Middle English Texts: Politics and Editing

As A. S. G. Edwards notes, editors of Middle English after the 1760s did not learn directly from techniques of editing used with classical studies, and so struggled toward a method that owed more to a tradition of modernizing improvement than to techniques of emendation based on textual criticism.[33] In fact Middle English editing has never, according to Tim William Machan, been particularly explicit about textual criticism. As Machan argues, textual criticism was founded on Renaissance humanism, which in turn was based on the idea "that works of the Middle Ages were inherently and variously inferior to those of the Antique or the Renaissance."[34] Consequently an editor of a Middle English text (apart from the works of Chaucer) was faced with a set of editorial principles formulated on the assumption that medieval texts were not worthy of having those principles applied to them.

The tradition of improvement of medieval texts went back through numerous rewritings, in the sixteenth to the eighteenth centuries, of the work of Chaucer, Lydgate, and Hoccleve.[35] Percy was, as we have seen, an editor of the improving kind. This was only in part covert; like other editors of the later eighteenth century, he had a rough system of textual criticism. Percy placed single quotation marks—inconsistently and sometimes misleadingly—around words he had altered. Albert B. Friedman suggests that the *Reliques* "was a victim of its own success," winning a "respect...for popular poetry [which] led eventually to higher standards in ballad-editing, against which the *Reliques* itself came to be measured and found seriously deficient."[36] So Ritson represented part of the logical process of the institution of editorial methodology that the tradition of improvement engendered, a process that Percy himself helped to initiate.

Ritson's method can be summarized as a call for authenticity—authenticity of source and authentic representation of that source—and it was a logical separation of two elements that had hitherto been commingled: the representation of medieval poetry on the one hand and medieval-inspired composition on the other. "The Rime of the Ancient Mariner" would occupy a fundamentally different place in literary circulation from John Pinkerton's "Hardyknute" forgery and Chatterton's Rowley poems. Walter Scott's invented ending to *Sir Tristrem*, written in pastiche Middle English, would be carefully distinguished from the genuine section of the poem. Ritson's method, rather than anticipating the principles of an as yet nonexistent comparative philology, was a development from the standards brought by the *Reliques* and the ballad revival. He did not ultimately provide a viable solution, nor was he able to adhere to his principles consistently. But in rejecting the improvement school, he offered solutions to the problems thrown up since the 1760s. Ritson, far from being a new philologist *avant la lettre*, dealt with the problems at hand, to become, logically, the preeminent scholar of his time.

For all his many challenges to the learning in the *Reliques* and *The History of English Poetry*, Ritson did nothing to challenge the essentially generic partitioning of what he, too, called ancient English. Of his two most medieval works, one was author-focused and was undertaken principally because the work of the author, Laurence Minot, had not been edited before. The second, *Ancient Engleish Metrical Romanceës*, was, as its title indicates, generically based. Ritson's other collections were all based on a single structural concern, either generic, as in *Ancient Songs* and *Pieces of Ancient Popular Poetry* (1791), or regional, as in the various Northumberland garlands, *The Yorkshire Garland* (1788), *Scotish Song* (1794), and *A Select Collection of English Songs*. One well-known exception was the anthology of Robin Hood verse.

Many of these anthologies contained some medieval material, but while Ritson showed a greater ability than most to date his manuscripts, and thereby reinforce a sense of the medieval in his work, there was no more emphasis on a notion of the medieval, let alone Middle English, as an organizing node than in the work of Warton or Percy. The concept of the end of the Middle Ages and the beginning of modernity barely operates in Ritson's work, as his subtitles often suggest: *Ancient Songs*, for example, avowedly covered material "From the Time of King Henry the Third, to the Revolution," thereby suggesting that everything falling in that period was "ancient." The Robin Hood anthology was "A Collection of all the Ancient Poems, Songs, and Ballads, Now Extant...," which did not distinguish its medieval material from later broadside ballads. *Bibliographia Poetica* (1802) spanned the divide as a "A Catalogue of Engleish Poets, of the Twelfth, Thirteenth, Fourteenth, Fifteenth, and Sixteenth Centurys, with a short account of their works." When Ritson took a theme or genre, in other words, his aim was compendiousness, not periodizing into medieval and modern.

Ritson did have genuine methodological and scholarly differences from his peers, but as there were few institutionally sanctioned ideas about ancient literature, this is not so surprising; Ritson's extreme variances from his contemporaries obscure the fact that all the antiquarian scholars had quite different approaches from one another. What set Ritson's work apart was that, through his own studies, he had already acquired most of the knowledge available in the works of Warton and Percy. Warton's *History* was therefore useless to him, because he did not need "a pleasant history to stimulate his interest in medieval literature," but "an accurate reference book" (*JR*, 1:319), and Warton's work was certainly not that. As a learned antiquarian, Ritson did not require to be shielded from the assaults on his taste that early literature might make, so it was for him a difficulty that most of the available writing was predicated on the reconciliation of the man of taste and the antiquarian. Whatever the personal quirks that led to his famously abrasive style, that style must still be seen as a *scholarly* response to a dilemma of scholarship.

Despite these marked methodological variances from the practices of his peers, Ritson did not produce, nor did he attempt to produce, a radically new vision of Middle English literature. Although he devoted much energy to the removal, from the original production of Middle English literature, of the privileged minstrel, in most respects he shared in the vision of the Middle Ages seen by Percy, Hurd, and Warton.[37] Ritson's main concern with his rivals was their failures of accuracy, and in this respect he wanted to do *better* what they were already doing; his methodology was an extension of the principal ideas of Middle English in the period from the 1760s to the 1780s, not a radical turning away from them. Even his view of minstrels was not so radically opposed to that of Percy, as Walter Scott recognized as early as 1824 when he recorded his surprise on finding that Ritson and Percy "have differed so very little as, in essential facts, they appear to have done.... In reality, their systems do not essentially differ."[38]

What Ritson objected to was principally methodological, not conceptual. He abhorred inaccuracy and constantly berated "forgery and imposture," because they distorted a Middle Ages that he treated as an objective historical presence. He proposed, by way of renovation, a pure historicism, a true representation of the Middle Ages and its literature. The man of taste was, inevitably, diminished in importance if not entirely cut out of considerations in this process; Ritson believed that the real man of taste would, like himself, want to appreciate the medieval material for what it was, as it was. This ambition was not, clearly, what contemporary men of taste demanded, as Ritson's lack of worldly success indicates; critical responses to Ritson's work decried his very accuracy — if this was how medieval poets wrote, many critics obviously thought, then medieval poetry was not worth having.

Ritson's *critical* methodology was completely in accord with that of his contemporaries. For Ritson, too, medieval poetry presented pictures of life and manners and was useful for historicist purposes. Consequently, the more objectively the poetry itself was represented, the more accurately it could be read as a historicist document. This was at the heart of Ritson's approach to medieval poetry and informed his editorial methodology. It follows that aesthetically and, more crucially, politically, Ritson did not fundamentally differ from his contemporaries either. The political radicalism for which he was so well known was not often translated into an aesthetic or critical stance; indeed, Ritson appears to have maintained an entirely typical separation between aesthetics and politics where medieval literature was concerned. The same was true of William Godwin in his *Life of Geoffrey Chaucer*, a work that later attracted opprobrium not because of its author's radicalism, but because of his inaccuracy and flights of fancy. As a set of ideas about the Middle Ages, the *Life* was easily assimilable into the conservative vision of social harmony under feudalism, and Godwin completely espoused the traditional value of old literature as a picture of life and manners.[39]

Like his sometime friend Godwin, Ritson did not deploy his revolutionary beliefs in a coherent and systematic fashion as elements of literary analysis. Radical sentiments do find their way, from time to time, into Ritson's prefatory essays, but only when a historicist detail is seized upon as an opportunity for political expatiation, not as elements of aesthetic judgment. *Robin Hood*, unsurprisingly, is the most overtly politically motivated of Ritson's works. Ritson enthusiastically approved of its eponymous hero and what he saw as his proletarian sympathies. Robin Hood was "a man who, in a barbarous age, and under a complicated tyranny, displayed a spirit of freedom and independence, which has endeared him to the common people, whose cause he maintained, (for all opposition to tyranny is the cause of the people,)..."[40] Even with this politically congenial material, however, Ritson produced only a "vaguely radical reading of Robin Hood," as Stephen Knight comments, partly because he accepted the sixteenth-century tradition that saw the outlaw as a displaced aristocrat.[41]

Ritson was capable of extended political judgment on the medieval people he discussed. His own early Jacobite leanings made him always sensitive to issues of kingship, and he dealt harshly with Edward III's claim to the crown of France in his dissertation "On the Scotish Wars of King Edward III," saying that no claim was "more frivolous and worse supported."[42] Ritson was in general contemptuous of the first three Edwards. Yet neither this nor his profound anticlericalism need be explained as the manifestation of a consistent political attitude, rather than the typical eighteenth-century dislike of the church of Rome (compounded in Ritson's case by atheism) and the barbarous doings of medieval kings. Ritson's own prejudices about modern nations also affected his attitude to medieval history. He was generally anti-Scottish, though capable of suspending his dislike when, as he often did, he deplored the actions of the English even more than those of the Scots. A confirmed Francophile, his dissertation "On the Title of King Edward III. to the Crown of France" is markedly sympathetic with the French and condemnatory of Edward's policy.

Ritson would not, of course, have been very sensible to have stuffed revolutionary sentiments in his works in the 1790s, particularly after the treason trial of 1794. As a known supporter of the Revolution, he feared, probably rightly, accusations of sedition. It is in *Robin Hood* that Ritson's most explicit statements appear, where outrightly revolutionary sentiments could be cloaked in historical garb. His lament for the rise of gunpowder over the longbow, which had given "the people . . . the very little liberty they had . . . which their tyrants were constantly endeavouring to wrest from them," gave him a way of talking about the revolutionary freedom of the people (he mentions Tyler and Cade in the same sentence) at a historical remove.[43] The Robin Hood ballads allowed Ritson a kind of historical allegory of proletarian revolution.

Aesthetically, Ritson was also typical in that he did not see much beauty in medieval material. He was a sophisticated reader, admiring, according to Bronson, "poetry of the neoclassical school": "This was to remain his attitude throughout life: English poetry before 1600 was largely exempted from considerations of taste, because of its absorbing historical interest; then came Shakespeare, who was subject to no sort of criticism; and all subsequent poetry was to be judged by the canons of Dryden and Pope" (*JR*, 1:21). Like Percy and his peers, he often saw medieval texts as the barbarous productions of a barbarous era. In the impressive *Bibliographia Poetica* he published in 1802, he wrote of *Piers Plowman* as "a very curious and masterly production" and referred to the "singular merit" of Minot's poems. But the usual targets are also there, particularly in the Wartonian winter that was the fifteenth century: Lydgate gets a longer entry even than Chaucer and Langland, but only so that Ritson can expatiate on "this voluminous, prosaick, and driveling monk," a "stupid and disgusting author, who disgraces the name and patronage of his master Chaucer."[44]

The difference, with Ritson, was that he believed the historicist impulse to outweigh any considerations of taste. Because of this emphasis, Ritson saw clearly that the improvement of poetry rewrote it into a modern context and reduced its potential as a picture of ancient life, rendering it pointless. Just as he linked the historical misprisions of earlier editors, particularly Percy, to bad and unrepresentative editing, so he yoked his own superior historical vision to a more reliable editorial methodology. "If the main interest of the reader was in ancient manners and customs," as Johnston suggests in relation to Ritson, "it was essential that texts be authentic."[45] The two issues could not, ultimately, be separated. Ritson redefined editing in terms of accuracy and fidelity to manuscripts, as Edwards notes, looking back beyond Percy to Hearne and John Fortescue Aland, who "share a randomness of editorial method" but used "considerable care and restraint in the execution of that method."[46] He may also have had the example of Samuel Pegge's *The Forme of Cury* (1780) before him, a type facsimile of a medieval kitchen handbook, which Edwards believes to be the first such edition of a Middle English text (45).

Ritson did not develop editorial methodology much further than Fortescue Aland and Hearne. His main methodological principle, fidelity to the manuscript, had obvious advantages in an era in which editing of the "improving" kind was only imperfectly distinguished from outright fraud. But it also had a number of drawbacks, not least in its sheer utopianism (how far exactly does the editor go before he can call himself accurate? At what point does he deem his edition unreadable?). It makes emendation, where the text seems to require it, difficult, and it does not explain how the editor deals with a text of which multiple manuscript copies exist. The problems created for this kind of editor by the perceived subjectivity of emendation and the troubling question of the point at which emendation becomes infidelity, or even improvement, are evident throughout Ritson's work. Ultimately, "fidelity" is not really a positive proposition so much as a reaction to a perceived infidelity to sources on the part of other editors. Ritson produced accurate texts by the standards of the day, in part because unlike most antiquarians he did his own transcribing.[47] Yet despite an at times fanatical devotion to fidelity, many of his texts were in fact further from the manuscript than a modern edition would be, and his principles of emendation are rarely clear.

Ritson's early announcements of the credo of fidelity were usually formulated in explicit reaction to the perceived distortions of the *Reliques,* as in *A Select Collection of English Songs* and *Pieces of Ancient Popular Poetry,* in both of which he criticized the lack of fidelity (despite the undeniable elegance) of the *Reliques* and proposed to present his poems with more "elegance, fidelity and correctness" than was usually seen in such publications. He printed the poems himself "with no other intentional license than was occasioned by the disuse of contractions, and a regular systematical punctuation, or became necessary by the errors of the original, which are generally, if not uniformly, noticed in the margin, the emendation being at the same time distinguished in the text."[48] But while such apparently clear statements of principle abound in Ritson's writings, the deployment of this method varies from text to text and is not always regular even within the one text. It is not always possible to see exactly what Ritson's view of the function of emendation was or a clear line of development in his editions, although broadly speaking there is a liberalizing in his stance in the later works.

Ritson's *Ancient Songs* reflects the methodology outlined in *A Select Collection* and *Pieces of Ancient Popular Poetry* and puts it to work on medieval material. It provides an example of the logical lengths to which fidelity could be taken. Ritson edited it as a type facsimile, printing a list of abbreviations at the front of the book and giving the poems with contractions, thorns, yoghs, (in some early poems) the Saxon form of the letter *t*, and diacritics intact. The edition illustrates the extreme of the objective historicist position, which sought to clear away all possible mediations between the present and the past. Its editor offered it not to scholars but to the public, given the "favorable attention" shown by the public "to works illustrating the history, the poetry, the language, the manners, or the amusements of their ancestors."[49] Once again, Ritson was attempting to redefine the tradition shaped by the *Reliques:* in these songs, the reader, he warned, "must not expect to find...the romantic wildness of a late elegant publication. But, in whatever light they may exhibit the lyric powers of our ancient Bards, they will at least have the recommendation of evident and indisputable authenticity: the sources from which they have been derived will be faithfully referred to, and are, in general, public and accessible."[50] The approach found little favor; the *Critical Review*, despite approving in general of the work, disliked the style of printing, which was thought "pedantic."[51]

With these three works, Ritson appears to have worked toward a logical editorial practice, consistent with his methodological clarion calls, to embody his ideals of accuracy as far as was practically possible. Yet he never again produced a type facsimile. While maintaining the emphasis on fidelity, Ritson shifted his ground in works of the later 1790s to accommodate the possibility of emendation. Presumably he had discovered that fidelity, in the case of some texts, results in unreadability. It is difficult to say, because he provides no reason for a shift that appears to take him steadily *away* from his ideal of editing. The consequence is that the two works that consist entirely of medieval texts—both late productions—show a freedom that is not consistent with the earlier purist position. Each is an *editio princeps*, of the poems of Laurence Minot and of the several works in *Ancient Engleish Metrical Romanceës*.

The poems of Minot appeared in 1795 under the title *Poems on Interesting Events in the Reign of King Edward III... By Laurence Minot.* They were edited, Ritson announced in familiar style, "with scrupulous fidelity," which nevertheless allowed him to discard what he called the character *y* (i.e., the late form of thorn), while using *z* in its function as yogh. The poems were printed "from the only manuscript copy of them known to exist, of which even the evident corruptions, though unnoticed in the text or margin, are not corrected without being elsewhere pointed out to the reader, in order that he may decide for himself upon the necessity or propriety of the correction."[52] The result is a handsomely printed octavo edition in which the poems are laid out unadorned by line numbers or notes on the page. Notice of emendation is thrown to the end of the text, in a list of "Original Readings, corrected in the Impression." These are generally conservative and uncontroversial and are not indicated in the text itself. In addition to these, Ritson has in three places supplied extra words, in square brackets, where there appeared to him to be omissions in the text.

The late work *Ancient Engleish Metrical Romanceës* returned to Ritson's typical form of a genre-based anthology, but has much in common with *Poems on Interesting Events.* It shows some evidence of the mental stress that killed Ritson in the following year—he writes of "the malignant and calumnious personalitys" of the critics, "a base and prostitute gang of lurking assassins, who stab in the dark, and whose poisoned daggers he has allready experience'd"—but it is generally a very sound work, strikingly accurate and useful.[53] It contains, in three octavo volumes, a dozen romances, including *Ywain and Gawain, Launfal, Lybeaus Desconus, King Horn,* and *Sir Orfeo.* Ritson edited most of them by going to the manuscripts himself (two poems, *Squyr of Lowe Degre* and *Knight of Courtesy,* were taken from black-letter editions). He adopted a style of printing much the same as that of the Minot edition, giving each poem on unadorned pages entirely in modern type (although he included line numbers in the margins, perhaps because of the greater length of the poems compared with Minot's). The first volume was prefaced with a rambling "Dissertation on Romance and Minstrelsy," and more than 130 pages of notes appear in volume 3.

The most striking thing about both these editions is their evident accessibility and commitment to attractive readability. They are both, in this respect, far distant from the type facsimile of *Ancient Songs* and clearly accommodate the contemporary reader of taste. The shift in editorial procedures, which are much the same in both works, does not make complete sense when compared with modern conceptions of emendation, but it does make sense when considered as a reconciliation of antiquarian rigor with readerly taste.

In *Ancient Engleish Metrical Romanceës,* Ritson began with a ritual denunciation of Percy, accusing him of printing "scarcely one single poem, song or ballad, fairly or honestly." Nevertheless, he went on to make a significant concession on the question of editing:

> To correct the obvious errours of an illiterate transcribeër, to supply irremediable defects, and to make sense of nonsense, are certainly essential dutys of an editour of ancient poetry; provideëd he act with integrity and publicity; but secretly to suppress the original text, and insert his own fabrications for the sake of provideing more refine'd entertainment for readers of taste and genius, is no proof of either judgement, candour, or integrity. (1:cix)

Had Percy signaled his emendations properly, "He would have acted fairly and honorablely, and giveën every sort of reader complete satisfaction. Authenticity would have been uniteëd with improvement, and all would have gone wel" (1:cxlii). Some important concessions are made here. Notably, the new position, which is a long way from the editorial ideology of the type facsimile, is based on the production of another figure in medieval literary production who has been, in his own way, as influential as the minstrel. This is the "illiterate transcribeër," the bad scribe, in other words. There is no point, Ritson appears to have realized, in editing from a manuscript accurately if what is in the manuscript is already in some sense wrong, if the text is barbarous to a second degree because of the activities of the minstrel's evil twin, the bad scribe.

The "illiterate transcribeër" in effect allows Ritson to begin considering the needs not just of "the austereëst antiquary," but the man of taste and genius as well (1:cxlii). Here and in *Poems on Interesting Events* there are strong suggestions of a concession to the modern readership. In both editions, the poems are significantly modernized, more so, in fact, than they would be in modern editions, with the rendering of thorns as "th" and the addition of plentiful modern punctuation. It was late in life that this far less austere Ritson distanced himself from the severity of a Hearne, recalling a satirical couplet written on this antiquarian: "Pox on't, quoth Time, to Thomas Hearne, / Whatever I forget you learn."[54]

Both the poems of Minot and the romances are conservatively emended, but in a fashion that is not always consistent in its aims or achievement. As Edwards suggests in a discussion of *Ancient Engleish Metrical Romanceës*, Ritson's "sense of the relationship between the activity of emendation and its indication is not always very clear"; the same could be said of the Minot edition.[55] As in Minot, Ritson provided a list at the end of *Metrical Romanceës* of the original readings that in the text he had corrected, without indication, and he also surrounded some readings in the text with square brackets, without putting them in his list. The two practices, as Edwards rightly observes, are not obviously connected.

Nevertheless, a coherent pattern is observable in both works, although it is not completely consistent or properly explained. In *Poems on Inter-*

And for to amende p^t we mís do,
In cleí or p^t we clynge and cleue ;
And mak vs euene w^t frend and fo,   55
And ín good tyme to take vr leue.

Nou hauep good daí, gode men alle,
Hauep good daí, ʒonge and olde,
Hauep good day, boþe grete and smalle,
And graūt m^{c}cí a poufend folde.   60
Ʒif euer J míʒte, ful fayn J wolde,
Don ouʒt p^t weore vnto ʒou leue.
Críst kepe ow out of cares colde,
For nou ís tyme to take mý leue.

Figure 2. Two pages from Joseph Ritson's editions. Left: The lyrics of *Ancient Songs* (1792) were presented in type facsimile. The minstrel is presumably a French one, as it was in this work that Ritson attacked Percy's notion of a special class of English bards. Right: The opening page of *Ancient Engleish Metrical Romanceës* (1802) is a strong contrast in style. By permission of the Rare Book and Special Collections Library, University of Sydney.

METRICAL ROMANCEËS.

YWAINE AND GAWIN.

ALMYGHTI god that made mankyn,
He fchilde his fervandes out of fyn,
And mayntene tham, with might and mayne,
That herkens Ywayne and Gawayne:
Thai war knightes of the tabyl rownde,
Tharfore liftens a lytel ftownde.
Arthur, the kyng of Yyngland,
That wan al Wales with his hand,
And al Scotland, als fayes the buke,
And mani mo, if men will luke,   10
Of al knightes he bare the pryfe,
In werld was non fo war ne wife;
Trew he was in alkyn thing,
Als it byfel to fwilk a kyng.

esting Events, Ritson seems to have emended in three distinct categories that to a modern editor would constitute only one. There are five silent emendations of manuscript word division: Ritson prints "de lice" for MS "delice" and "tharein" for MS "thare in," for example, without any indication that he has done so. Second, he has included three square-bracketed additions, each time to mark an interpolation of his own where he thought there must be a gap in the text. Third, and this is the only category actually explained, there is a list of twenty-three original readings that he emended given at the end of the text. There is no signaling of these emendations in the text itself, however, so that the reader can only know they are there by going to the list and then backtracking through the text. And as the square brackets of the second category are nowhere explained, the 1795 reader could only ascertain that they indicated interpolations by going to the actual manuscript.

The practice in *Metrical Romanceës* is exactly the same. Square brackets are put around interpolations, while other emendations are listed at the end. Anomalies remain; a few emendations are not noted by either technique, suggesting that Ritson either misread the manuscript or silently emended. Three italicized letters at line 1976 of *Ywain and Gawain* are completely mysterious unless the reader looks at the manuscript and discovers that these letters are partially obscured by a dark spot. But nowhere does Ritson explain that this is what italicizing indicates, nor does he italicize at any of the many other parts of this poem obscured by discoloration.

What appears to be happening here is that Ritson is providing a not quite consistent technique to cope with two constraints. In contrast to his earlier use of the type facsimile, Ritson's later editions all exhibit the apparent desire to give the text in a modern and unmediated fashion, to bring the text on the page as far from its manuscript appearance and toward a modern printed appearance as possible. But at the same time he had to practice what he so vehemently preached, "fairly and honorablely" editing with fidelity, noting all deviation from the manuscript. He seems to view it as sufficient, therefore, to limit the intrusive presence of emendations by noting them *only* in one place: either in the list at the end or with square brackets in the text, but never both. He could, of course, have eschewed the square brackets and included these emendations in his final list as well, but actually putting words into the text that were not in the manuscript perhaps struck him as a step on the road to the wholesale invention of stanzas he so deplored in Percy and Pinkerton.

To give Ritson his place in the editing and study of Middle English should be to re-place him firmly in the late eighteenth century, as the editor who responded to the problems that period posed to editing with a set of workable principles. His principles were not consistent and, in the course of evolving throughout his career, did not result in a reliable methodology. For all the vehemence of his attacks on what he thought bad editing, there are signs, in his evasion of a coherently explained methodology, that he was not himself always comfortable with emendation. In these respects, Ritson was the most important, the defining figure, for Middle English in the last fifteen years of the eighteenth century. If Ritson was to the scholars of his time a demonic figure, then to the later nineteenth century his failure in life had a different import. The fable the nineteenth and twentieth centuries tell is that of misunderstood genius, of the man whose personal quirks prevent his forward-thinking from being recognized. Both narratives project a ready-made self on Joseph Ritson, and it is the selfhood of Ritson that needs to be reassessed.

A Scholar Unmade

Ritson's near-total failure to make a favorable impact on scholarship in his lifetime cannot be fully explained by his commitment, in his works, to the antiquarian over the man of taste. In some of his most important works, Ritson had made significant concessions to the reader of taste. In any case, works such as Minot's poems and even *Ywain and Gawain* from the romance collection could not reasonably be criticized by readers of taste in the way that the undigested ballads had been. No competent reader could have bracketed Minot's easy verse, no matter how barbarous it was perceived to be, with the unedited ballads. And with *Ancient Engleish Metrical Romanceës*, Ritson had in fact hit upon what was to be the most fashionable medieval genre of the new century's first decade. The problem was not, or not only, in the nature of the material. Neither were his works significantly disfigured for the era's reader by his inimical political opinions. In fact, the work that allowed Ritson the widest expression of his political views, *Robin Hood*, would become by far his most popular production. It was the man, the self, of Joseph Ritson that his contemporaries rejected, and as long as that self was sufficiently notorious to have existence beyond the works, the works were treated as an extension of that self and accordingly rejected.

Ritson's considerable projections of self in his most argumentative material must be balanced against his apparent carelessness of personal advancement. Ritson did not seek patronage, never dedicated his works, and did not place his name on any of his texts other than *Ancient Engleish Metrical Romanceës*. He sought, by contrast, to advance his work according to a much more idealistic model, into both scholarly and popular forms of circulation. He offered *Pieces of Ancient Popular Poetry* "to the patronage of the liberal and the candid, of those whom the artificial refinements of modern taste have not rendered totally insensible to the humble effusions of unpolished nature, and the simplicity of old times; a description of readers, it is to be hoped, sufficiently numerous to justify a wish that it may never fall into the hands of any other."[56] This phrase could have stood as the dedication for all of Ritson's works, but his hopes for an enlightened general public were not, of course, fulfilled.

This self-effacement from his texts was furthered in Ritson's editorial principles, which even in their later form largely removed the improving editorial self from the work. The problem with this practice was not that it was ahead of its time, but that it left no way in which to promulgate the material. Ritson found no mechanism to make his scholarship acceptable or desirable. At the same time, in the absence of the artistic fashioning of the self, Ritson's outward presentation was constructed by his enemies. His dying wish was for complete self-effacement but, ironically, his enemies kept him alive.

In 1806, the *Edinburgh Review* published an anonymous review of Ritson's *Ancient Engleish Metrical Romanceës* and a work called *Specimens of Early English Metrical Romances,* by George Ellis, a retired diplomat and sometime poet. The latter work, a series of amusingly ironic plot summaries of romances, had become a popular guide to the genre after its publication in 1805, while Ritson's book was already neglected. The reviewer does not approve of much in Ritson's scholarship; he is critical of the introduction, although he does not outline his criticisms, forbearing because of Ritson's claim in the dedication that it was written in bad health and spirits. The reviewer feels that Ritson's attack on Percy's editing is "urged with far too much grossness."[57] But he approves of the work in many respects. *Ancient Engleish Metrical Romanceës* was "the first comprehensive and general work" on the topic (390), "the romances are judiciously selected, and we have already praised the well-known accuracy of the editor" (392). Rather shrewdly, the reviewer goes on to suggest "that Mr Ritson was, both by talent and disposition, better qualified to assail the opinions of others, than to deduce from the facts which he produces a separate theory of his own" (393). "Ritson's talents," he feels, "were better adapted to research than to deduction, to attack than to defence, to criticism than to composition" (395).

Ellis's book is singled out for almost unalloyed praise. Although it does not present actual editions of the romances, it is valuable in that it might lead people, having read it, to go to the romances themselves. Ellis "has brought the minstrels of old into the *boudoirs* and drawing-rooms ... so that the age of chivalry, instead of being at an end for ever, may perhaps be on the point of revival" (396). The reviewer goes on to praise the merits of the romances generally: "They hold out to us, like Shakespeare's players, the abstract and brief chronicles of the time, and demand the serious consideration of every historian. Even in a literary point of view, their merit is not contemptible" (411). Despite the "indifferent fate" of

Ritson's romance edition, it would be worthwhile, he concludes, to see a new edition; a university, perhaps Cambridge, should consider the project.

There is much here that is discerning and at times prophetic: chivalry was indeed about to live again in the boudoirs of the bourgeoisie. The whole review reflects a familiar dichotomy of scholarship: the opposition between Ritson and Ellis is that between antiquarianism and taste, raw text and mediation, barbarism and elegance. Undoubtedly no one person was in a better position to comment on the state of the study of Middle English romance at this time, and no one person would do more to shape its immediate directions than this anonymous reviewer: he was Walter Scott.

CHAPTER 3

The Last Minstrel
Walter Scott and the Decade of Romance

1804

In Walter Scott's 1820 novel, *The Monastery*, the foppish Euphuistic courtier, Sir Piercie Shafton, makes some familiar claims on a medieval lineage: " 'I...am by birth nearly bound to the Piercie of Northumberland whose fame is so widely blown though all parts of the world, where English worth hath been known.' "[1] The legitimacy of this claim is suspect, however:

> I know something of this Piercie Shafton. The legitimacy of his mother's descent from the Piercie family, the point on which he is most jealous, hath been called in question. If harebrained courage, and an outrageous spirit of gallantry, can make good his pretensions to the high lineage he claims, these qualities have never been denied him. (223)

The question of Sir Piercie's legitimacy is not much more than a sidelight in this novel, which is chiefly concerned with the fortunes of the families of Glendinning and Avenel, but at the end, issues of birth and lineage, blood and legitimacy, suddenly come into the foreground at the moment when the novel's domestically focused plot intersects with its surrounding historical context. Halbert Glendinning, who has fallen in with troops under Lord Murray, wants to marry Mary Avenel; Morton, of the Douglas family, objects, thinking Halbert to be too lowborn. " 'This is but idle talking,' " Murray (who is himself illegitimate) responds:

> [I]n times like these, we must look to men and not to pedigrees.... Times of action make princes into peasants, and boors into barons. All families have sprung from one mean man; and it is well if they have never degenerated from his virtue who raised them first from obscurity. (472)

Morton is unimpressed. " 'My Lord of Murray will please to except the house of Douglas,' said Morton, haughtily; 'men have seen it in the tree, but never in the sapling—have seen it in the stream, but never in the fountain' " (472).

In the same chapter, Piercie Shafton's true origins are revealed: his mother's father was a tailor, and " 'she was wedded by wild Shafton of Wilverton, who, men say, was akin to the Piercie on the wrong side of the blanket' " (478). Piercie then announces his engagement to Mysie Happer, the miller's daughter whom he has been improbably courting. Murray reflects that it was unlikely the marriage would have been made public, had not Shafton's mean origins been revealed. Piercie responds:

"When I am once more mine own man, I will find a new road to dignity."
"*Shape* one, I presume," said the Earl of Morton. (481)

What can Morton mean? Cast out of the great Northumberland family by his revealed illegitimacy, prepared to reveal his intent to marry Mysie Happer, Piercie Shafton has nothing left to him but to shape his own dignity. Given Morton's belief in the organic naturalness, and imperviousness to lower ranks, of the aristocracy, then it must follow that Piercie has no other alternative than to take his destiny into his own hands.

Walter Scott himself, in his various accounts of his life, displays a similar equivocation, an unwillingness to link the place a man occupies in society with what he can shape for himself. In the fragmentary memoir begun in 1808 and the introductions and notes to the collected editions of his works, Scott often presents the view that a man is born into his station and occupies himself as he may. He is particularly careful to dissociate literary activity from social station, repeatedly stating that his character was settled *before* he became a writer: "my habits of thinking and acting as well as my rank in society were fixed long before I had attained or even pretended to any poetical reputation and...it produced when acquired no remarkable change upon either."[2] Certainly, Scott continues, "success in literature" has given him access to "the first circles in Britain. But there is a certain intuitive knowledge of the world to which most well educated Scotchmen are early trained that prevents them from being much dazzled by this species of elevation."[3]

Elsewhere, Scott wrote that he was comparatively indifferent to literary success or failure, because he did not feel "the passion for literary fame" as strongly as some. He had not become an author, he wrote, until he was thirty, "and at that period men's hopes, desires, and wishes have usually acquired something of a decisive character, and are not eagerly and easily diverted into a new channel."[4] Literature could not affect his standing, which was fixed long before: "My birth was neither distinguished nor sordid. According to the prejudices of my country, it was esteemed *gentle,* as I was connected though remotely with ancient families both by my father's and mother's side."[5]

Like Morton's tree without a sapling and stream without a spring, Scott's social standing is a strangely static matter. Owing nothing to external shaping and certainly not to literary activity, Scott views his station in society as asocial and natural. It follows from this that the aesthetic life, the life of the poet, editor, and novelist, is *solely* aesthetic, incapable of penetrating into the realm either of the self or the social; it is something the gentleman pursues without its having any effect on his essential self. In the "General Preface to the Waverley Novels," published in 1829 after the "secret" of his authorship had been officially revealed, Scott is equivocal about authorship and presents throughout a studied indifference to the aesthetic life. The preface begins in the third person in a way that underlines the separation between the person of the writer and the inner self. In order to write about his "compositions," Scott says, "the author... feels that he has the delicate task of speaking more of himself and his personal concerns, than may perhaps be either graceful or prudent." Having begun in the third person, he concedes the artificiality this might bring to the narrative, and in what is "perhaps an indifferent sign of a disposition to keep his word...he proceeds in the second paragraph to make use of the first [person]."[6]

The split signaled here between the authorial-aesthetic and another, more real, self seems reluctantly reconciled. It was, of course, a split deeply ingrained in Scott's career. Notoriously, he had for many years kept his aesthetic persona quite separate from his self as Walter Scott, bart., by first creating "the Author of Waverley" and then consistently denying that he and that person were one and the same. The occasion for the Magnum Opus edition, as Scott called it, was the "revelation" that Scott was the author of *Waverley*, which had come in the wake of his financial collapse of 1826. But before then, it was one of the worst-kept secrets of the literary world: "The mystery about the author of *Waverley*," as John Sutherland observes, "is nothing compared to the mystery of why the author of *Waverley* persisted in the ruse."[7]

The anonymity of the publication of *Waverley*, Scott says, was in the first instance explicable by the author's caution toward this new venture, but this, he concedes, hardly explains his continued anonymity in succeeding editions: "I can render little better reason for choosing to remain anonymous, than by saying with Shylock, that such was my humour," Scott relates, and adds that he hardly needed more literary fame. "[M]y place in society [was] fixed, — my life had attained its middle course. My condition in society was higher perhaps than I deserved, certainly as high as I wished, and there was scarce any degree of literary success which could have greatly altered or improved my personal condition."[8] According to the official mythology, Scott was socially and personally "fixed" in this way long before; J. G. Lockhart remarked of Scott that as early as 1801 his character "was completely formed and settled."[9]

Despite these ritual denials of the influence of the aesthetic persona on the social, Scott's is a famous and well-documented case of literary self-fashioning. Scott's birth was, technically, "gentle," his family an old and respectable one. Scott magnified this respectability, however, by focusing not on his recent antecedents but on the more remote past, a past of heroic exploits by Border chiefs. He liked to think of himself as having sprung, as Sutherland puts it, from "earlier, greater generations of Scotts," overlooking the more recent past in which his father was a moderately successful lawyer, whose own father had been a sheep-farmer (*LWS*, 3).

Scott was born in Edinburgh's Old Town, into surrounds unanimously described by Scott's biographers as filthy and squalid.[10] Scott spent little time there as a child, and it was not long before his father was prosperous enough to move the family to the New Town. Nevertheless, it was Scott's own efforts in adulthood that set him on his path to Abbotsford, where he liked to style himself the "Laird," and to general regard as the most celebrated Scotsman of his time. It was neither his modest career as an advocate nor his equally modest inheritances that allowed Scott to acquire the land on which he built his dream castle and to buy up all the land around it. Neither did his baronetcy, his enormous popularity, and preeminence in Scottish letters arise from workaday pursuits. It was, of course, his art, whether the publicly acknowledged narrative poems of his earlier career or the novels of later years, that shaped Scott's persona and worldly success. And the Scott persona was at all points imbricated with this art; the gulf between the two that Scott liked to pose was, like so much else in his life, an elaborate front.

My concern here is not Scott's role as a medievalizer in his poems and novels or the impact of his work on a medievalizing of social life in the nineteenth century, which have been well written about by Alice Chandler and Mark Girouard. Scott and his work, as these writers have convincingly shown, were pivotal in the development of the nineteenth-century promotion of a modern chivalry as an ideology legitimating the practices of, initially, the aristocracy and, later, the newly emergent middle class.[11] Scott's specific importance for Middle English lies in one of his earlier works, the edition of the Middle English romance *Sir Tristrem*, found in the Auchinleck manuscript. This work does not usually take up much space in critical discussions of Scott, perhaps because, despite its obvious links with his other activities, it is so unrelentingly scholarly that it is difficult to place alongside the oeuvre of the great entertainer. Conversely, the edition is not often used by medievalists because of the outdated extravagances in its scholarship.

But *Sir Tristrem*, according to one view, can be considered a foundation text in the study of Middle English. Edgar Johnson, conceding the errors of Scott's scholarship, stated that the edition placed Scott "high among the pioneers who called this entire body of romance material to the attention of the world." For Arthur Johnston, it "stands as the first great edition of a medieval romance," one that "pointed the way to the scholars who produced the Early English Text Society editions later in the century."[12]

Sir Tristrem was genuinely a departure. Scott was innovative in privileging a single poem, rather than printing an anthology. In this respect, *Sir Tristrem* can be seen as anticipating the scholarly volumes of the EETS. But Johnston, despite noting the "wild conjectures" (187) of Scott's scholarship, does not make enough of the fact that Scott's *Sir Tristrem* has its important links with the formation that produced the *Reliques* and Warton's *History*. Scott's scholarship belonged as securely to conservative romanticism as Percy's, and his editing of the Middle Ages was, as much as the *Reliques*, a tool for self-shaping and part of a process of social advancement.

The editing of *Sir Tristrem* belongs to a formative time in Scott's literary career, the early years of the nineteenth century. His German translations and early poems were behind him, and his true literary popularity was to begin with the works that appeared from 1802, in which he exploited the ballad form. The first two volumes of *Minstrelsy of the Scottish Border* appeared in 1802 and a third in 1803, and at the same time Scott was writing what would become *The Lay of the Last Minstrel*, the first of his long poems. *Sir Tristrem* appeared in 1804, though Scott had largely completed it by the end of 1802 and chose to delay its publication (*LWS*, 92). These three projects arose from very similar impulses and were originally conceived as belonging together in the one book. *Sir Tristrem*, the least popular and least regarded of the three, has to be seen not just as scholarship but as part of the complex narrative of self-fictionalizing and self-creation, the consolidation of aristocratic connections and the invention of a poet, that Scott developed in the works of these early years.

The *Minstrelsy* was the decisive work of Scott's early career. It was, as Jane Millgate has argued, "both the starting point for a lifetime of self-allusion and a model for the many variations Scott was subsequently to devise, as annotator, editor, and self-commentator."[13] It is also the work in which Scott began to shape, amplify, and put to work a sense of self motivated by genealogical connections with the Border regions and the Middle Ages. With rather more historical claim on his genealogy but with the same aim of being "protected and caressed" in view, Scott deployed many of Thomas Percy's tactics. The *Reliques*, as Scott himself acknowledged, had had a great impact on him from the age of thirteen.[14] The very title Scott adopted is an obvious homage to Percy, accepting as it does the centerpiece of Percy's scholarship. To Millgate, the *Minstrelsy* was "the direct product of the shock of recognition" Scott experienced when he read Percy (6).

Like Percy, Scott sought and found an aristocratic patron, the earl of Dalkeith, later the duke of Buccleuch, who had already helped Scott gain a sinecure as sheriff of Selkirkshire and who was to become an important patron.[15] The earl, furthermore, was the head of the Buccleuch family, to which Scott was related, and the embodiment, as Millgate notes, of the Border tradition: "Scott was claiming his heritage, seeking to be true to his past and his place—in personal, familial, and historical terms" (6). This "truth," though, does need to be regarded as of a specific kind; it was one that wrote out of that personal history the lawyer father, the sheep-farmer grandfather, and modest origins.

When *The Lay of the Last Minstrel* outgrew its place as one of the modern versions of ballads in the *Minstrelsy,* Scott developed it, too, as part of this complex of myths of origins. *The Lay* is a modern Border ballad, as Scott explains, and was "intended to illustrate the customs and manners which anciently prevailed on the Borders of England and Scotland."[16] The book was dedicated to the earl of Dalkeith. The poem, as Sutherland puts it, "principally asks to be read as an obsessional exercise in name narcissism, a fantasia on what it is to be a 'Scott'" (*LWS,* 102). The *Lay* plays incessantly with the Scott family history, from which most of its major characters are drawn; it "is less a poem," Sutherland dryly observes, "than a totem pole in verse" (103).

The main narrative of the poem is enclosed by a frame-tale in which the minstrel of the title, who has survived the revolution and is now, in 1690, the last of his breed, seeks the patronage of Anne, duchess of Buccleuch.

> The last of all the Bards was he,
> Who sung of Border chivalry;
> For, well-a-day! their date was fled,
> His tuneful brethren all were dead;
> And he, neglected and oppressed,
> Wished to be with them, and at rest.
> No more, on prancing palfrey borne,
> He carolled, light as lark at morn;
> No longer, courted and caressed,
> High placed in hall, a welcome guest,
> He poured, to lord and lady gay,
> The unpremeditated lay.[17]

The role of minstrel here is easily recognizable as an embodiment of Percy's vision, even if this minstrel is not a medieval one and lives in a diminished time as "A wandering harper, scorned and poor," begging from door to door, tuning "to please a peasant's ear, / The harp, a King had loved to hear" (4). The opening of the *Lay* is a poetic enactment of Percy's theory and history of the minstrels, which is further supported by later visions of minstrels in action within the narrative of the *Lay* itself. The Last Minstrel, despite his lowly appearance, is shown as entering fully into the bardic role of his medieval counterpart.

When the duchess of Buccleuch and Monmouth, more out of sympathy than confidence in his powers, it would appear, invites the Minstrel into her castle of Newark and asks him to sing, he seems barely able to tune his harp. But then a magical transformation takes place: "when he caught the measure wild, / The old man raised his face, and smiled; / And lightened up his fading eye, / With all a poet's extacy!" (8). The magical, druidical function of the bard is glimpsed here. Besides the link to Percy's minstrels, there is a connection with Scott himself, who often wrote of the ease with which his poetry flowed.[18]

The framing minstrel-patron relationship within the poem, furthermore, obviously complements a relationship Scott himself desired between himself and the wife of his patron, Harriet, countess of Dalkeith and later duchess of Buccleuch. Writing in 1830, Scott claimed that he had written the *Lay* in response to the wishes of the countess,[19] heightening the parallel with the minstrel of the poem, who composes for an earlier member of the Buccleuch family. In reality, it seems, Scott had in fact begun the poem before the countess made her request, so that the 1830 preface represents a retrospective intensifying of the minstrel-patron relationship.[20] At the end of the poem, the minstrel is indeed rewarded with patronage: "close beneath proud Newark's tower, / Arose the Minstrel's lonely bower" (193), in a motif that Sutherland regards as "a fairly broad hint" on the part of Scott, who was in fact seeking a home at the time and "had his eye on a property at Broadmeadows, 'close beneath proud Newark's tower'" (*LWS*, 104, 103).

The edition of *Sir Tristrem* grew out of, and symbolically capped, this narrative of minstrelsy and aristocratic protection, and in this respect, it was for Scott another text through which he developed his genealogically based revision of himself.

The First Minstrel

The romance of *Sir Tristrem* was discovered by Joseph Ritson in 1792 in the Auchinleck manuscript, which had been donated to the Advocates' Library by James Boswell's father in 1744. Ritson identified the poem as the work of Thomas the Rhymer of Erceldoune, the quasi-legendary figure known in his role as supposed author of prophecies and as hero of a poem and ballads in which he becomes a consort of the queen of the fairies. John Pinkerton had already speculated that the lost Tristram poem mentioned in a passage in Robert Mannyng's *Chronicle*, and ascribed to a Thomas there, could be in the Auchinleck manuscript, and Ritson assumed that this was what he had discovered. It is perhaps surprising, given Ritson's habitual skepticism and the thinness of the internal evidence, that he so confidently accepted the authorship of Thomas, but once made, the connection proved tenacious.

To Scott, who had the Auchinleck manuscript in his possession for long periods, the Rhymer's authorship was certain and meant in turn that the poem was Scottish rather than English. No one, not even Scott, was in any doubt that the manuscript was English and contained English poems. But the association with Edinburgh in its modern history and the promotion of its importance by Scott gave the manuscript a special place in Scottish medievalism. It became, for a time, almost an honorary Scottish manuscript, as the reclamation of *Sir Tristrem* for Scotland and the prominence of Auchinleck poems in other productions of this decade would suggest.

The passage in Mannyng referring to a romance about Tristram written in "quaint Inglis" is ambiguous; his words can be read as referring to a romance composed *either* by "Thomas of Erceldoune" or an even more shadowy "Thomas Kendal":

> I see in song, in sedgeyng tale
> Of Erceldoun & of Kendale,
> Non þam says as þai þam wroght,
> & in þer sayng it semes noght;
> þat may þou here in sir Tristrem;
> ouer gestes it has þe steem,
> Ouer alle that is or was,
> If meñ it sayd as made Thomas,
> But I here it no mañ so say,
> þat of some copple som is away.[21]

As this is the only surviving mention of a Kendal, it was the slightly more solid "Thomas Lermont the rimer of Ercildon," as Pinkerton had referred to him, who was usually said to be the author of the now-discovered Tristram romance.[22] This Thomas was known from the prophecies attributed to him and some scant biographical details, which Pinkerton had discussed in 1786, at which time he also speculated that the romance might be found in the Auchinleck manuscript.[23] When Ritson discovered the Auchinleck Tristram romance, he was helped in his identification by evidence in the first line of *Sir Tristrem*, which associates the romance with Thomas of Erceldoune. Because of souvenir-hunting, the line is damaged, but a catchword at the end of the previous gathering supplies the placename: "I was a[t erþeldoune] / wiþ tomas spak I þare."[24] This, of course, appears to indicate that this Thomas was not—or not directly—the author of the romance, though Ritson apparently thought that Thomas might have referred to himself in the third person.[25]

Scott was directly influenced by Ritson. The improbable meeting of the two ideologically opposed antiquarians occurred in August 1801 in Scott's house at Lasswade.[26] It seems likely that both *Sir Tristrem* and the ballads of the *Minstrelsy* were discussed.[27] Scott became firmly convinced of the authorship of Thomas and the Scottishness of the poem, and set about convincing others, particularly George Ellis, a friend who was often consulted by letter during the process of editing *Sir Tristrem*. There is, Millgate writes, "an element of the obsessive and the simply stubborn in Scott's determination to win over the English scholar to his own view of the poem's origins and status" (*WS*, 11–12). It is tempting to conclude that Scott had to convince himself, under the guise of persuading others; certainly the letters show him, in his determination to have Thomas as author of a Scottish poem, making up his mind about other texts before he has even seen them and theorizing ahead of the evidence. When Ellis, for example, told Scott of the Thomas who is named in the Anglo-Norman version of *King Horn*, Scott wrote back in early 1804 to say, "Far from being daunted with the position of the enemy, I am resolved to carry it at the point of the bayonet, and, like an able general, to attack where it would be difficult to defend." He continued:

Without metaphor or parable, I am determined not only that my Tomas *shall* be the author of "Tristrem," but that he shall be the author of Hornchild [i.e., *King Horn*] also. I must, however, read over the romance, before I can make my arrangements. Holding, with Ritson, that the copy in *his* collection is translated from the French, I do not see why we should not suppose that the French had been originally a version from our Thomas. The date does not greatly frighten me, as I have extended Thomas of Ercildoune's life to the three-score and ten years of the Psalmist, and consequently removed back the date of "Sir Tristrem" to 1250.[28]

Unmistakable here is what Millgate calls the "missionary zeal" with which Scott set about his work on *Sir Tristrem*. "If the gospel was to be preached," she argues, "it was essential that the genuineness of the text, its authentically Scottish origins, be demonstrated."[29]

By late 1802, *Sir Tristrem* had outgrown the *Minstrelsy*, but the anthology was used to announce the career of Thomas the Rhymer, early Scottish poet. The second volume of the *Minstrelsy* included, in three parts, balladic material about Thomas, in which the hand of Scott is progressively more intrusive. The first part consists of a conflation of an oral and a manuscript version of the tale of "True" Thomas's dalliance with the queen of the fairies; in the second, Scott pulled together "the printed prophecies vulgarly ascribed to the Rhymer."[30] The third section was Scott's own composition, a ballad imitation in which he fantasizes the occasion for the performance of *Sir Tristrem*. Thomas-as-minstrel is depicted entertaining his guests at a feast in Erceldoune with Arthurian tales, specifically one about Tristram. The guests fall silent when Thomas begins to play, "And harpers for envy pale. . . . In numbers high, the witch-ing tale / The prophet pour'd along; / No after bard might e'er avail / Those numbers to prolong."[31] At the end of his performance, Thomas is summoned, just as his legend maintained, back to Fairyland by a magical hart and hind.

So Thomas, even before the publication of *Sir Tristrem*, was now an even more glamorized version of the Percyan minstrel figure. He was not simply a minstrel, but his own laird—Scott made much of the fact that Thomas was not just "The Rhymer," but "of" Erceldoune. As laird, poet, seer, near wizard in fact, Thomas represents the apotheosis in the study of Middle English of Percy's poet-priest.

In the editorial material Scott appended to these poetic fragments, all the basic claims that would be elaborated in the 1804 edition were already in place. Thomas's biography is outlined (2:244–50), his association with prophecy discussed (2:257–77), and, finally, his authorship of *Sir Tristrem* is asserted (2:283–85). This is a masterly argumentative slide, supported by poetic fragments that mix manipulated authenticity with outright (if acknowledged) fabrication. Thomas the Rhymer was well known in legend as a prophet, but only to Robert Mannyng, and that very equivocally, as a *poet*. In the *Minstrelsy*, Scott prepared the way for the more thoroughgoing discussion of 1804 with a mixture of argument and eloquent balladic illustration. Readers coming to *Sir Tristrem* in 1804 must have found it difficult to remember that there was no solid basis for Thomas's *poetic* reputation whatsoever.

When the edition appeared, it was headed by an unequivocal title page: *Sir Tristrem; a Metrical Romance of the Thirteenth Century; by Thomas of Ercildoune, called The Rhymer*. The claims implied here were explicitly repeated in the first line of the introduction, which amplifies the arguments for all the major points suggested in the *Minstrelsy* and then builds on these assumptions to range far beyond the poem itself to create a sweeping argument about medieval Scottish culture. Scott begins with an account of the life of "the earliest Scottish poet" (*ST,* v). Thomas dwelt in the village of Erceldoune, modern Earlstoun, in a tower that is still visible. On the basis of evidence in rolls and charters, Scott concluded that he must have been born in the 1220s. Assuming that Thomas composed the poem in "the flower of his age," *Sir Tristrem* can be placed some time soon after 1250 (ix). Scott then presents various mentions of Thomas and his prophecies in the chronicles of Barbour and Wyntoun, in the *Scalachronicon*, and in Harry's *Wallace*, anecdotes from which "We may collect . . . that he was, in his own time, a distinguished personage." Furthermore, because of evidence that he was acquainted with the earl of March, "some degree of rank and birth" can be argued for Thomas (xv).

Scott then dealt with the tradition of prophecies and the Rhymer's dalliance with the queen of the fairies before turning to Tristrem himself. Tristrem's tale was not invented by Thomas, but derived ultimately from "authentic history" transmitted via "Welch authorities" (xxii). Through a learned discussion of Celtic sources, Marie de France, and Chretien de Troyes, Scott arrives at the conclusion that the Tristram story appeared to have been known in France around thirty years before the composition of Thomas's poem. Did Thomas, then, "translate his poem from some of those which were current in the Romance language?" Or did he take it direct from "British" (i.e., Celtic) sources, the same sources from which the French minstrels derived it (xxxiv)? For Scott, of course, there could be no question: Thomas was the original composer, not a translator. Noting the association of the Border region with Arthurian story, Scott concluded that the Arthurian legend, derived from original Celtic sources, had still been current in the region in the mid–thirteenth century. Thomas's home at Erceldoune is "on the borders of the ancient British kingdom of Strathclwyd," which suggests that Thomas "collected the materials" of *Tristrem* there: "The story, although it had already penetrated into France, must have been preserved in a more pure and authentic state by a people, who, perhaps, had hardly ceased to speak the language of the hero" (xxxix). Thomas did *not* translate, but composed the poem himself, and he had direct access to the original Celtic material, "with which the Anglo-Norman romancers were unacquainted" (xlv–xlvi).

Here, the Celtic bards, the original priestly poet-historians of Percy's formulation, are brought to life. Notably, not only is Thomas placed in nearly unmediated contact with them, but the bards are put in contact with a real Tristram, the hero whose language they probably spoke. One last mediating step was required, however; Scott argued that the poem as it has survived was not actually written down by Thomas, but transcribed by a second person, a southern scribe who spoke with Thomas. This, ingeniously, allows for the existence of the supposed mid-thirteenth-century Scottish poem (disturbingly short of Scottish forms) in the English manuscript of the 1330s (lxxxii–lxxxiii). It allows the poem to be everything that, on the surface, it is not. Thomas of Erceldoune, early Scottish poet, baptized by John Pinkerton, sponsored by Joseph Ritson, is thus confirmed by Walter Scott.

Scott also had to deal with the French version, now attributed to "Thomas of Britain," of the Tristram story, which he knew from the manuscript fragments owned by Francis Douce. Scott turned the reference to "Thomas" in this version to account, despite Douce's (correct) view that his manuscripts dated from before the thirteenth century. Scott simply argued that the reference must be to Thomas of Erceldoune, so that this French version was *derived* from the Scottish bard's work. "As the one [work]," Scott argued somewhat circularly, "therefore, is affirmed to be the work of Thomas, and the other refers to a Thomas who composed such a work, the connection betwixt them is completely proved" (xlv). Orthodox opinion about the English romances—held by Warton, Tyrwhitt, and Ritson—was that they had all been translated from French.

Scott was now able to put quite a different argument: "if Thomas of Erceldoune did not translate from the French, but composed an original poem, founded upon Celtic tradition, it will follow, that the first classical English romance was written in part of what is now called Scotland" (xlvi–xlvii). English minstrels, he adds, did not begin translating romances until 1300, and they were not composing their own until a century after that (lv).

Thomas of Erceldoune was therefore established as the originator of vernacular romance in Britain. But he was not alone. Building on his argument, Scott then constructed a school of poets working around Thomas. He took such known names as "Kendal" and "Hutcheon of the Awle Royal" and suggested that there were "probably many other poets, whose names and works have now perished," all of whom "flourished in the court of Scotland" (lv). Next, Scott provided this school of poets with a corpus of poems. Existing Scottish poems, such as *Gawan and Gologras* and *Eger and Grime*, were attached to the school; northern English poems such as *Galoran of Galloway* (i.e., *Awntyrs of Arthur*) were dragged across the border to join them. *King Horn*, too, seemed to Scott not only likely "to be of border origin" (because of its northern setting) but "may have been the composition of Thomas of Erceldoune himself" (lvii), a statement made on the basis of the mention of a Thomas in the Anglo-Norman version of the poem. As a final extravagance, Scott suggested that the "romance of *Wade*, twice alluded to by Chaucer, but now lost, was probably a border composition" (lxi), and added it to the vibrant literary culture of thirteenth-century Scotland.

The minstrels of this impressive school were the "natural depositaries of the treasures of Celtic tradition" (lxv). They were working well in advance of their fellows south of the border, as Scott proposed:

> While the English minstrels had hardly ventured on the drudgery of translating the French romances, or, if they did so, were only listened to by the lowest of the people, our northern poets were writing original *gests* "for pride and nobleye," in a high stile and complicated stanza, which the southern harpers marred in repeating, and which their plebeian audience were unable to comprehend. In one word, the early romances of England were written in French, those of Scotland were written in English. (lxv)

"English," here, means lowland Scots. Scott had agonized over the vexed question of the origin of this dialect, which some said was not directly related to English, but resulted from the parallel linguistic development of a dialect introduced by a Germanic tribe. Pinkerton had argued this in 1786, pressing the Picts into service as a Germanic or Gothic tribe that had brought its language, in a tribal migration, from Europe to Scotland, just as the Angles and Saxons had brought theirs to England. Although defeated in 843 by Celts, the Picts kept their language, which eventually displaced Gaelic.[32] Over the centuries, this language became "less Gothic, and more near to the language now termed Scotish," just as Frankish had developed into French over centuries and Saxon, in the space of three hundred years, had become "the English of Chaucer."[33] Far from being a debased and barbaric version of English, as the common view had it, lowland Scots was to be viewed as a "Doric dialect" of English.[34] It was a Germanic language — Pinkerton despised Celts — having its own provenance and dignity.

Scott was never entirely convinced by this argument, which always troubled him — "These vile picts still disturb my slumbers," he wrote to Ellis in 1801.[35] In *Sir Tristrem*, Scott does not refer to Pinkerton, but accepts that the "vile Picts" were a separate Gothic tribe with their own parallel Saxon tongue (*ST*, xlix). Partly for this reason, there "was a tract of country including all the south of Scotland, into which the French or Romance language was never forcibly introduced" (l). So the school of Thomas produced an "English" literature, which, however, was uncontaminated by French. "Teutonic" was the "principal component" of this language, which "was never banished from court" in Scotland or "confined to the use of the vulgar," as had happened in England (lii).

After some more argument about language, Scott rounded off his case, concluding: "By this system we may also account for the superiority of the early Scottish over the early English poets, excepting always the unrivalled Chaucer. And, finally, to this we may ascribe the flow of romantic and poetical tradition, which has distinguished the borders of Scotland almost down to the present day" (lxviii). The nationalist appeal and motivation of the overall argument are unmistakable. At a stroke, Scott has reversed the usual judgment that sees the French as the originators of most romances; he has discovered a preeminent poet, and a thriving school of poets around him, at work in the Scottish court at an early date; he has put these poets directly in touch with Celtic tradition. Finally, he helps his reader to see that the English language received its greatest boost out of the barbarism of Saxon not from English writers, but from one Scottish poet and the school that worked with him.

Many Scots men of letters in the late eighteenth century and early nineteenth wanted to purge the Scots dialect of its distinctive forms, to bring it closer to the English language. As Robert Crawford argues, this "was not an anti-Scottish gesture, but a pro-British one"; if "Britain" were to become a genuine cultural and political entity and Scots were to share in it, they needed to speak in the language of power: "Language, the most important of bonds, must not be allowed to hinder Scotland's intercourse with expanding economic and intellectual markets in the freshly defined British state."[36] Scott's argument simply sidestepped this concern. Drawing on earlier arguments about the separate development of the lowland dialect, Scott deployed a Middle English poem as an authentication and legitimation of Scottish national origins.

Border Disputes

Sir Tristrem was not destined to become a famous publication in the manner of the *Minstrelsy* or the *Lay*. Scott's publisher Archibald Constable was wary of *Tristrem*, and it appeared in an edition of only 150 copies (*LWS*, 92, 93). This may have been in part, as Sutherland suggests, because of "the scandalously sexual nature" of the poem (93). John Leyden, Scott's helper who had done much of the work of transcribing, had stopped when he reached the word "queynte," and the duke of Roxburghe declined to be the dedicatee.[37] The edition was, nevertheless, a success and was followed by three further editions in the following fifteen years before it was canonized as part of the *Poetical Works*.

The successive editions were in part forced by modifications to the theory built up around Thomas the Rhymer. Like Percy with the *Reliques*, Scott had to concede some points in order to reinforce others. The antiquity of Thomas's poem, in particular, rested on a house-of-cards of an argument. In 1807, a student named Henry Weber contacted Scott with information about the Middle High German *Tristan* of Gottfried von Strassburg, which Scott conceded to Ellis was "a sort of knockdown blow to all my system about the Rhymer" and the Scottish origins of Tristram tales.[38] But Scott resolutely adhered to other contentions, never giving up the idea that the poem was a very early Scottish romance and that Thomas of Erceldoune was the earliest Scottish poet.

It is worth noting that despite vigorous attacks from English scholars on Scott's arguments, the "Scottish" *Sir Tristrem* and its poet have had a remarkable afterlife, continuing almost to the present day. In his 1824 revision of Warton's *History of English Poetry*, Richard Price argued for the French origin of the story in the Douce fragments, which were therefore composed by a Thomas who predated Thomas of Erceldoune. He also cast doubt on whether the Tristram tale mentioned by Mannyng was the Auchinleck version at all, and said that *Sir Tristrem* was not even Scottish.[39] The dialect authority Richard Garnett contributed a similar debunking in the 1840 revision of the *History*, attacking in particular the claims for Scottishness, while Thomas Wright added that Thomas of Erceldoune was "a legendary character, and I will as soon believe the poem to be written by him, as I would that it was written by the king of the fairies."[40]

Scott, however, never withdrew from his central views, other than to admit the priority of some Continental versions of the Tristram story. J. G. Lockhart, printing *Sir Tristrem* in Scott's *Poetical Works*, conceded that Thomas the Rhymer could no longer be viewed as the originator of

Tristram romances, but insisted on Thomas of Erceldoune as author and on the poem's Scottishness.[41] *Sir Tristrem* was edited for the Scottish Text Society in 1886, and excerpts from it appear as late as 1966, as the first poem in the *Oxford Book of Scottish Verse*, where only a bracketed question mark against Thomas's name alludes to any dispute over the attribution.[42]

Thomas and Walter

Scott's *Sir Tristrem* by Thomas of Erceldoune began life as a Border ballad. The *Minstrelsy, Lay,* and romance were all interconnected, and, as Millgate argues, "It is also important to keep in mind that [Scott] believed all three works to have had their roots in the Borders" (*WS*, 11). Appropriately, then, what *Sir Tristrem* turned out to be was the story of an audacious border raid, an inverse cultural-colonial maneuver through which the primacy of Scottish intellectual life in the Middle Ages was established over that of England. So successful was it, in its limited way, that no one since has been quite sure where the border really is. *Sir Tristrem*, in this sense, was not simply an event in scholarship or publishing, but a tool in a kind of cultural politics. Scott was aided in his border raid by the fact that the absence of a well-defined linguistic or cultural entity called Middle English allowed bold appropriations of the culture to be made. To claim the *Sir Tristrem* of 1804, then, as the first great edition of a medieval romance is to miss the point that in 1804 it was not an English romance at all. The formation within which it emerged produced it as a Scottish text.

This Scottishness can be further explained as not simply a product of Scott's patriotism—as a cultural politics—but as an element in a practice of the self also seen in the *Minstrelsy* and *Lay*. Like Percy, writing himself into the medieval Border world from the English side via the Northumberlands, Scott wrote himself into the world of Thomas of Erceldoune, which was of course the world of his ancestors. Scott was a modern minstrel, inspired by the example of Thomas Percy, who enjoyed a privileged relationship with the aristocratic patrons whose sense of history he cherished and honored. At the same time he is no mere outsider to that history, but genealogically implicit in it. In the *Lay*, he portrayed the mutually sustaining relationship of the minstrel and the aristocratic patron, in a way that mirrored relationships he was himself cultivating and later writing into his accounts of his life and art. In the *Minstrelsy*, he furthered a Percy-like vision of medieval ballads and their creators, and he demonstrated his own minstrel powers, with somewhat more candor than the bishop, in his modern ballad imitations. And there he depicted the greatest of his minstrels, Thomas the Rhymer of Erceldoune, in action.

In *Sir Tristrem*, he cemented the minstrel's reputation, and then literally wrote himself into the complex he had described. For in the Auchinleck manuscript, the poem of *Sir Tristrem* is unfinished. Early in the process of editing, Scott decided to complete the poem himself. Like the ballad imitations of the *Minstrelsy*, this would be an acknowledged modern version.[43] The poem appeared with fifteen concluding stanzas in a pastiche of the poem's meter, form, and language, telling of the deaths of Tristrem and Isolde. In his invented ballad "Thomas the Rhymer" in the *Minstrelsy*, Scott had described this part of the tale of Tristram, as told by Thomas. Now he took it a further step, writing *as* Thomas:

> Ac Tristrem hath tene,
>   His wounde gan him wring,
> To hostel he hath gene,
>   On bedde gan him flinge
> . . . .
>
> On Tristremes bere,
>   Doun con sche lye;
> Rise ogayn did sche nere,
>   But thare con sche dye
>   For woe:—
> Swiche lovers als thei
> Never schal be moe.
>   (*ST*, 193, 200)

The introduction to *Sir Tristrem* proves the primacy of the Scottish poet, Thomas of Erceldoune, but the concluding fifteen stanzas of the poem then replace this poet with Scott himself. Scott (who, "at an early age, called himself 'the Rymour'")[44] *becomes* Thomas, by completing what Thomas had begun, in a kind of foreshadowing and an early announcement of the position Scott himself would later take as premier bard of Scotland in his day, a position for which he staked a claim the year after *Sir Tristrem* with the publication of the *Lay*. The *Lay*'s internal representation of the minstrel-patron relationship and its productive genealogizing of minstrel and aristocrat are anticipated by the more dramatic concretizing of the medieval and modern minstrels' relations in *Sir Tristrem*. Here, then, there is a productive meeting of self-shaping with cultural politics. What Scott invents in the *Tristrem* edition is not simply an acceptable version of a proud Scotland, but the kind of Scotland he, as a literary nationalist, would like to live in. The relative openness of early history in an era in which the study of the empirical documents was in a state of flux allowed flexible appropriations. Just as Pinkerton rewrote early Scottish history to bring in Gothicized Picts and marginalize the Celts, just as Percy reinvented the Northumberlands, Scott fashioned the homeland that suited him. In Scott's scholarship, the self builds its context, and that context fashions the self.

"Indolent and Cursory Readers"

The efflorescence of Middle English romance in this period continued when George Ellis, Scott's pen-friend, produced his *Specimens of Early English Metrical Romances* in the year following the publication of *Sir Tristrem*. John Ganim, noting that the promoters of romance in the period "adopted strongly conservative and hierarchical political views," suggests that romance at this time "almost certainly appealed to an anti-republican bias."[45] Ritson, of course, can scarcely be included among the conservatives, but Ganim rightly points out that "his version of romance is consistent with the idealizing patterns of late-eighteenth-century antiquarianism" (153). In these texts, "the Middle Ages was presented as a critique of modernity, a critique of industrialization, urbanization, and democratization. The social world imagined in this scheme idealized both aristocracy and folk. The aristocracy was imagined almost entirely in terms of chivalry" (152).

At the same time as they accorded with these broad political currents, however, editions of the Middle English romances were also much more private documents, as technologies of the self. A romance issued initially in a print run of 150 copies cannot really be thought of as an important political technology, however indubitably it expresses or mirrors the conservative views of the individual who produced it. Like most romance editions of the period, *Sir Tristrem* presents a time of an idealized political hierarchy and, in the figure of Thomas, the cultural and political nobleman Scott himself wanted to be. The arguments it makes, in this respect, have less to do with the state of Napoleonic Europe than with the personal placement of Scott in a Scotland enthusiastic about its place in Great Britain.

There was still a separation between the kind of modern medievalizing in *The Lay of the Last Minstrel* or the *Border Minstrelsy* and the real medieval studies in *Sir Tristrem*. Real medieval literature remained intractably barbarous, as far as the majority of readers was concerned. Ellis's *Specimens* was precisely designed to address the problem of the gulf between the two kinds of medievalism.

Ellis was a retired diplomat, sometime poet, and cofounder of *The Anti-Jacobin*—which alone would have recommended him to the Scottish poet—when Scott made his acquaintance, initially through letters, in 1801. The pair had a mutual friend in Richard Heber, the member of Parliament for Oxford who was an antiquarian and famous book collector. Ellis's *Specimens of the Early English Poets* (1790) was designed to represent "all the most beautiful small poems which had been published in this country during the sixteenth and seventeenth centuries" and began with poets of the reign of Henry VIII.[46] In 1801, Ellis published a revised version of this work, designed to complement Warton's *History* and offering a "Historical Sketch of the Rise and Progress of the English Poetry and Language." This new edition encompassed medieval verse and foreshadowed Ellis's most medievalist work, *Specimens of Early English Metrical Romances* (1805), a work that shows the influence of his detailed correspondence with Scott.

Invoking "Mr. Warton's very learned and entertaining, though desultory work," Ellis announced that he had no intention of trying to "supersede" it in his revised version of *Specimens of the Early English Poets*.[47] This announcement appears to place Ellis's work in a precisely defined scholarly lineage. It is also characterized by the mixture of respect for Warton and the feeling that more needed to be done, which was typical of thinking about the *History of English Poetry* throughout the nineteenth century. But Ellis quickly makes it clear that he does not conceive of his book as existing in a domain of pure scholarship for the scholarly. His work does not "interfere" with the collections of Percy, Pinkerton, Ritson, and others (1:ix). In the *Specimens*, the needs of the general reader are in view.

Ellis's specimens began with Laȝamon, and included Robert of Gloucester, Robert Mannyng, Adam Davie, Langland, Gower, John Barbour, Chaucer, Andrew Wyntoun, Lydgate, Juliana Berners, and the Scottish Chaucerians. His approach, like Warton's, was to discourse eloquently about the poetry with liberal illustrations from the poets. The result is elegant rather than comprehensive, though surprisingly detailed, balancing an undeniable scholarliness with the need for a gentlemanly distance to be maintained. Speaking about the difficulties of the language of medieval poems, Ellis announces that he has adopted modern spelling, "for the convenience of indolent and cursory readers" (1:10). Elsewhere, he sets up a dichotomy between the "the historical antiquary" and "[t]he more indolent reader" (1:260). Despite his quite considerable scholarly knowledge, Ellis is concerned to wear it lightly, and to be seen to wear it lightly, in a work that constantly has the interest of the indolent and cursory reader in view. Ellis is obviously a historical antiquary, yet, as a retired gentleman-scholar, he gives the impression that he is at heart an indolent reader, whose needs he projects onto his own text.

Like Warton, Ellis gives an overview of the development of the language, as represented in the work of various authors. Although Robert of Gloucester is the first of his listed authors, Ellis's discussion begins with Anglo-Saxon times. He considers the pre-Conquest language and times in brief, and then prints *The Battle of Brunanburh*, with accompanying translations, one literal, one a poetic paraphrase. Like many early writers, Ellis could not fully comprehend the workings of the Anglo-Saxon alliterative versification and followed Tyrwhitt in concluding that "it must still remain a doubt, whether the Anglo-Saxon verses were strictly metrical, or whether they were only distinguished from prose by some species of rythm" (1:12). He rejected the notion that the Conquest had the decisive role in the change of the language (1:38–39) and concluded that the loss of the Saxon terminations was the principal cause of the gradation that took place (1:6). In the time of Laȝamon, Ellis surmised, the Saxons and Normans were beginning to unite and speak one language (1:76).

Ellis evidently felt no great need to be compendious. "After quitting Layamon," he continued, "we shall waste little time on the compositions of his immediate successors" (1:81). Noting in passing the *Ormulum* and *Saint Marharete,* works on which later scholars would place so much importance as examples of Semi-Saxon, Ellis made the rather whimsical decision to print instead *The Land of Cokaygne* in full. He then proceeded to the period of main interest, discussing and excerpting Robert of Gloucester (whom he thinks dull) and Robert Mannyng ("industrious" and "elegant" for the time [1:123]) and discussing minstrels. In the fourteenth century, he picks out Richard Rolle ("very popular and learned, though inelegant" [1:146]), Laurence Minot, and Langland, to whom he accords particular praise:

> [I]t must be confessed, that this writer has taken every advantage of a plan so comprehensive and convenient [ie the dream-vision scheme], and has dramatized his subject with great ingenuity. His work may be considered as a long moral and religious discourse, and as such, is full of good sense and piety; but it is farther rendered interesting, by a succession of incidents, enlivened sometimes by strong satire, and sometimes by the keenest ridicule on the vices of all orders of men, and particularly of the religious. It is ornamented also by many specimens of descriptive poetry, in which the genius of the author appears to great advantage. (1:148)

Despite not understanding Langland's alliterative meter any more than he understood the Anglo-Saxon, Ellis was able to make this judgment and at the same time identify (without of course naming it) the phenomenon of the alliterative revival. Warton had thought Langland's alliterative poetry must "disgust the reader" (*HEP,* 1:267), but Ellis simply concluded that alliteration, to an ear used to it, was probably as euphonious as rhyme is to modern ears, and he referred the reader to Percy's essay on the subject. Langland's work presented "an entertaining and useful commentary on the general histories of the fourteenth century" because of "its almost innumerable pictures of contemporary manners" and "connection with the particular feelings and opinions of the time" (*SP,* 1:166).

John Gower's reputation was generally poor in this period, and Ellis argued that the poet was not likely ever to be popular, because "few modern readers" will want to read works of the length of *Confessio Amantis* in "obsolete English" (1:178). Nevertheless, parts of this poem, he suggests, are worth reprinting, and he gives the tale of Florent entire. Chaucer is treated in typically adulatory tones, particularly where *The Canterbury Tales* are concerned. Although the *Tales* are fragmentary and therefore imperfect, the work "contains more information respecting the manners and customs of the fourteenth century, than could be gleaned from the whole mass of contemporary writers, English or Foreign." The *Canterbury Tales* "abounds" with "poetical beauties," ensuring its author "the first rank among the English poets, anterior to Shakspeare" (1:212). Stating that there was little point in copious quotation from Chaucer, given the availability of his work, Ellis offered various extracts, principally of passages tending to illustrate Chaucer himself: the Host's description of Chaucer in the General Prologue; Chaucer's self-referential descriptions in the *Parliament of Fowls* and *Legend of Good Women*, as well as the opening of the *Book of the Duchess* and a very brief part of *Troilus and Criseyde*. In the remainder of the essay, Ellis devotes attention to Barbour, Wyntoun, Lydgate, Hoccleve, James I, and others.

The result was a major contribution to scholarship on Middle English. There was, of course, an element of the bluffer's guide to Ellis's work—this is, after all, what is implied by the title he used and reused, "specimens." Ellis never promised completeness of coverage, and he presents only what he thinks the indolent reader needs to know of historical antiquarianism. Inevitably, this produced a very personalized and somewhat detached stance, as exampled in his preferring the sprightly *Land of Cokaygne* to the tortuous, but philologically useful, *Ormulum*. Ellis's succeeding work, *Specimens of the Metrical Romances*, developed this detachment into an art form.

This work is even more devoted to indolence and cursoriness than its predecessor, putting ever more distance between the nineteenth-century readership and the medieval romance. It was divided into six categories: Arthurian romances, "Anglo-Saxon romances" (*Guy of Warwick* and *Bevis of Hampton*), Anglo-Norman romance (*Richard Coer de Lyon*), Charlemagne romances, romances of oriental origin (*Seven Sages of Rome*), and miscellaneous romances, which include *Florice and Blauncheflour, Sir Isumbras, Eglamour of Artois*, and *Amis and Amiloun*.

Ellis did not edit these romances, but retold them in his own words, done into a slightly archaized language, laced with original quotations, modernized, and with obsolete words glossed. He prefixed a detailed essay on romance, which occupied about half of the first volume. With these three volumes and without reading a single romance, readers could acquaint themselves intimately with the contents of some twenty medieval romances—about a third of all that were known in the period—without encountering any barbarous language and in addition being told exactly what to think about them.

Retelling the tale of Bevis of Hampton, for example, Ellis begins by noting the marriage of Bevis's father, late in life, to a younger woman:

"Our author remarks that such a choice was very imprudent; and as his remarks are not always equally just, we take great pleasure in recording this instance of his sagacity."[48] In the course of the narrative, Bevis fights with a boar, which "was distinguished from other boars by a contemptuous disregard for beech-mast and acorns, and by an unnatural predilection for human flesh" (2:107). Bevis blows his horn, but "[t]he boar, whether from sleepiness, or from a natural indifference to such music, took no notice of the defiance" (2:108). Another key episode is described thus:

> Bevis on his return found Josyan perfectly familiarised with the lions, whom however she could not forgive for eating her chamberlain: she therefore proposed to hold one of them by the neck whilst her lover attacked the other: but he insisted on fighting the two together; and such was the comfort which he derived from the presence of his mistress, and from the conviction of her perfect chastity, that he cut off both their heads at one stroke. The lovers now dined, and, after duly bewailing the loss of the faithful Boniface, mounted on Arundel and pursued their journey. (2:136)

By developing this ironic rhetorical mode to retell the romances, Ellis managed to reconcile what most scholars had seen as the two irretrievably diverse elements of romance. While valuable for their pictures of manners and customs, romances traditionally troubled scholars with their lack of moral seriousness and their unrealistic use of fancy and fantasy. Even the most sympathetic scholars of Middle English found it hard to forgive romance authors for this reckless mélange; most felt the need to explain away the unrealisms. The popular theory of the Eastern origin of most of the marvels that had found their way into English romance was one such explanation, allowing the view that decent pictures of English life and manners had been infected by something oriental and essentially foreign.

Ellis simply did away with the need for explanations by retelling the stories in an attractive way and highlighting with irony the parts that any enlightened reader would find ridiculous. The fundamental contradiction for most writers on medieval literature, and particularly romance, was that its value lay in its reflections of society, but the very mode of medieval writing seemed to flout reflective realism by incorporating nonsensical fantasy. No scholar admitted to enjoying the whimsical aspect of romances; as Johnston suggests, the reading of romances had always been disapproved of in some quarters, "whether on literary or moral grounds."[49] Ellis mocked the unrealisms of romance, but at the same time rendered them newly enjoyable, as irony. Readers could read Ellis's retellings not with furtively guilty enjoyment, but in the safe knowledge that they were participating in the correctly knowing and mocking nineteenth-century attitude.

Medieval literature in the Ellis version is then doubly distanced. Just as Percy and Scott had exoticized their texts, Ellis renders them strange and (literally) inaccessible. Readers have no direct access to the texts, despite being given copious details about the manuscripts from which they were drawn, and then have an ironic stance forced on them. *Specimens of Early English Poets* had operated by transcending the gap between medieval and modern, but the later text puts the division back in place through irony. The reader cannot help but feel located in the present of 1805, a more objective, sober, historically realist time. The reader laughs, with Ellis, at the foolish and amusing inability of medieval writers to conform to the high standards of historical objectivity set in the late eighteenth and the nineteenth centuries. The failure of the romances is their falling between two stools; failing to be, on the one hand, historically accurate and useful or, on the other, fiction of a convincingly realist order. Scholars could not develop a literary discourse that would explain the romances as literary objects, but they kept reading them and editing them. Like modern academics who find reasons to watch soap operas or *Star Trek*, Ellis, Scott (and for that matter, Percy and Samuel Johnson) could not elevate the romances to the status of art, but for all the mockery and irony, neither could they talk themselves out of reading them.

This distance, of course, also means that it is difficult for Ellis to make it sound as if he takes this literature seriously. Irony is endemic in the *Metrical Romances*. But as a tendency, it is no more than an explicit version of an attitude that is never far from the writing of even those most favorably disposed to medieval literature. This attitude is quite simply the belief that the literature lacks much intrinsic merit. The insistence with which the importance of the literature, as representing the manners and customs of our ancestors, is stated and restated barely masks the fact that literary merit is scarcely ever detected. Scholars could happily confess to being captivated by ballads or romances—as Scott did, recalling his first reading of the *Reliques*—but they were usually at a loss to explain this in terms of literary merit.

On the contrary, most scholars were more or less candid about what they felt were the shortcomings of the literature to which they devoted themselves. Scott, for example, despite his great investment in *Sir Tristrem*, was nearly put off from his balladic conclusion because "the villainous cramp stanza of our Thomas almost scares me."[50] He goes on to refer contemptuously to stock minstrel phraseology, such as "Bidene" and "Of yore," as the "legitimate crutches which prop the hobbling stanza of the Minstrels" and which he could use for his imitation, "but if it is expected that any thing like the graces of modern poetry can be introduced into such a sketch I fear it might be as well required that a modern dancing Master should open his Ball dressd cap-a-pie in Sir Tristrems armour."[51]

In nearly a hundred pages of introduction to the poem, Scott spent scarcely a word on poetry as such, and when he did, he acknowledged the romance was "close, nervous, and concise even to obscurity" and said that most romances were characterized by "a tedious circumlocutory style" (*ST*, lxxxiv). Here, again, he was aided by his theory that Thomas had related his poem to another minstrel, because that second minstrel could be, and was, blamed for what the poem had become.

Currying no favor, seeking no preferment, Ellis wrote with more independence than most. Where he thought poetic merit was present, he said so, but he did not hold back from critique of what he thought absurd or inelegant; to the contrary, he made a style out of it. He also took a notably independent line on some articles of faith. Like most writers, Ellis absorbed a Percyan vision of minstrelsy, restating the view that the minstrels were composers and reciters, patronized by "wealthy nobles," whose practices ultimately derived from those of the northern skalds.[52] In the eleventh to thirteenth centuries, Ellis thought, the minstrels were "a privileged class" (1:128). So much is very familiar. But Ellis is referring to those who composed in French, and finds it far less likely that minstrels whose language was English could have had an analogous position before the mid–fifteenth century, when "our language had been successively improved by the writings of Gower, Chaucer, and Lydgate" (1:131). He has seen, here, a flaw in the Percy theory, that English was not likely to have been the language of those protected and caressed by aristocrats who, for the most part, spoke French.

Similarly, although Ellis clearly approves of chivalry, he made it clear in the *Metrical Romances* that he was strikingly at odds with his contemporaries in viewing the feudal system as an evil. Like Hurd, Ellis saw romances as having developed from the requirements of a new, hierarchically organized aristocratic class. But unlike other writers, Ellis did not simply conflate feudalism and chivalry. "[T]hat scene of confusion called the feudal system" contributed to the rise of a hereditary nobility, a circumstance crucial to the genre of romance, but it also led to localized government and magistracy focused on aristocrats, which was a "monstrous system."[53]

This antifeudalism is unusual, particularly from the anti-Jacobin. Unlike Percy or Scott, Ellis had no need to write himself into medieval literature, so his writing has an initial appearance of objectivity that theirs lacks. It is the objectivity of the conservative gentleman, a man who can afford not to become personally engaged in the literature he is discussing because, ultimately, that literature is rather flawed and therefore to be engaged in not too deeply, but indolently and cursorily. Ellis's engagement in literary antiquarianism was not his life's work, and he did not return to it after *Metrical Romances*. By taking excerpts from medieval literature, by couching it in his own reasoned prose, and particularly by rendering it intelligible in normalized English, Ellis performed the opposite of the self-historicizing of Percy and Scott. He decontextualized and dehistoricized the literature. It is true that what ostensibly made it valuable was the extent to which it offered pictures of medieval manners and customs, but Ellis could only do this by transcending the cultural and historical gap between his readers and the Middle Ages and rendering the literature in an intelligible, *un*historicized version, for easy consumption by the armchair litterateur.

"A Drudging German"

The editor of the last important text of the decade of romance was a man almost as unfortunate as Joseph Ritson, who had produced the first. Henry Weber was Scott's amanuensis and later himself an editor of the literary material Scott began pouring through the Ballantynes' printing and publishing business, of which he was part owner. Weber edited texts associated with the 1513 battle of Flodden Field in 1807, obviously as a spin-off project from Scott's *Marmion,* and later produced editions of the plays of Beaumont and Fletcher and John Ford. Weber's contribution to Middle English was his *Metrical Romances of the Thirteenth, Fourteenth, and Fifteenth Centuries* of 1810. Unlike Ellis's *Specimens,* this was a genuine edition, in scope reminiscent of Ritson's *Metrical Romanceës* and in approach more in the school of Scott and Ellis.

In the last years of the decade, before the first hints of financial disaster had appeared, Scott was still envisaging vast literary publishing programs. He entrusted to Weber a projected edition of metrical romances in 1808 and set about trying to raise support through subscription.[54] Weber originally envisaged a comprehensive publication of all the romances, one that would aid the production, he hoped, of a dictionary of medieval English.[55] It was an ill-fated project from the outset: subscriptions were not forthcoming, and Scott, who had originally planned to add some notes to the publication himself, refused to put his name on the title page. Weber then could not find a London publisher, so Archibald Constable had to take it on.[56] In its reduced form, the work contained *Kyng Alisaunder, Sir Cleges, Lay le Freine, Richard Coer de Lyon, The Lyfe of Ipomydon, Amis and Amiloun, The Seven Sages of Rome, Octavian, Sir Amadas,* and *The Huntyng of the Hare,* in three volumes, together with, in the now standard fashion, a learned introduction, notes, and a glossary.

The volumes were attractively presented octavos, with the text ornamented by line numbers alone, on generous pages. Notes and Weber's record of his corrections from the manuscripts and variant readings were thrown to the end of each volume. The longer romances were divided into chapters, with italicized plot summaries standing as headnotes. Editorially, Weber proved to be no more accurate than his peers—nearly

20 percent of the lines show some variance from the manuscript versions, according to Kurt Gamerschlag (213)—though this is not particularly remarkable for the time. To produce his texts, Weber sometimes had to conflate manuscripts, always preferring the older manuscript as the base text. *Kyng Alisaunder,* for example, was constructed from the Bodleian and Lincoln's Inn manuscripts, to produce an "edition...as perfect as the two existing MSS. could make it."[57] *Amis and Amiloun* was printed from the Auchinleck manuscript on the grounds that it was the most "ancient," with its "defects" repaired from a manuscript owned by Francis Douce (1:lii–iii). *The Seven Sages* was printed from the copy in the Auchinleck manuscript, with missing sections supplied from MS Cotton Galba E.ix; even though the latter was "perfect," it was, Weber thought, a century later than the Auchinleck version (1:lv).

Several references to Ritson, in tones as respectful as those used for Scott, Ellis, and Douce, suggest that Ritson's strictures were having some filtered-down effect. Principles of presentation of manuscript originals were clearly spelled out:

> In preparing these romances for the public, it was the wish of the editor, without in the least disturbing a single letter of the old text, to render their perusal as accessible to general readers as possible. For this reason, the longer ones were subdivided...regular punctuation was introduced, capital letters were used to distinguish names of persons and places, the abbreviations were reduced to the peculiar standard of orthography, employed in each particular romance, and the Saxon letters for th, gh, and y, discarded. In all these points excepting the first, the accurate Ritson has given an example to the editor. (1:lxiv)

Weber's introduction is without either the strained ideological arguments of Scott or the elegant ironies of Ellis. It is a scholarly piece of work, marked by a depth of reading, particularly in Continental sources, that few others, with the probable exception of Douce, could have offered. In addition, while Weber does not wholeheartedly commit himself to a case for the literary merit of his poems, there is a strain of unashamed appreciation for the poetry in his writing, rarely glimpsed in the work of other scholars of the time.

As later writers would do, Weber claimed for the romances a solid but secondary status in the canon: "With all their imperfections," they are nevertheless comparable to "the prolix and wire-drawn moralities and second-hand narrations of Gower, Occleve, and Lydgate," despite the generally higher reputation of these poets (1:ix). Inevitably, the romances are deemed to throw "great light upon the manners, customs, and vernacular language of their age," which might otherwise be forgotten (1:x). Explaining his principles of selection, given the abandonment of the original comprehensive plan, Weber gives as his principal criterion "intrinsic merit," which he leaves, at first, unexplained (1:xi). He turns instead to the idea of the romantic, traveling back over the territory covered by Ellis, Scott, and Warton, to deal, with rather less embarrassment than any of these writers demonstrates, with the marvels that abound in this form of poetry. Weber points out that marvels are found not solely in romance, but also in epic poetry, before making the Wartonian conclusion that the marvelous creatures of romance ultimately derive from Asia (1:xii).

Weber then turns to the interesting point that while the *origin* of romance has been debated at length, few have considered the causes of the *decline* of romance, which he attributes to the "diffusion of science" in the time of the Reformation, the appearance of classical learning after the dissolution of the monasteries, and, "above all," the printing press (1:xiii). At this point in history, "[t]he nobles began to read, instead of listening to the recitation of strolling minstrels" (1:xiii). With the appearance of a "middle rank" (1:xiii) in society and the introduction of system at all levels, "it began to be the fashion to ask after instruction also," rather than simply amusement (1:xiv). (So romance, in Weber's view, dissolves back into the historical function from which, so Percy had maintained, it had originally derived.) This shift, however, did not come easily. "The higher ranks would still leave the new systematical writers, for the works of mere imagination," while "the lower classes" kept listening to romances, in their reduced form as ballads (1:xiv). Romance would only collapse, finally, when it was reduced to "the vehicle of allegory" (1:xv), as in Spenser, to await its contemporary revival.

Weber restated the orthodoxy—no mention of *Sir Tristrem* is made at this point—that English romances were late translations from French (1:xvi). He declines to discuss whether the translations were improvements or otherwise on their originals, but regrets "that the choice of subjects for translation was not always the most judicious" (1:xvii), before noting that there is evidence that some of "the most romantic productions" might have been lost, "while the dull wire-drawn history of Guy of Warwick, and the mystic lucubrations of such poets as Hampole and Occleve were carefully preserved" (1:xvii). Here Weber is inclining toward that classic posture of supporting medieval literature but wishing that it were something other than what it is. Concluding, he claims the "most valuable" of the romances to be *Kyng Alisaunder, Ywain and Gawain,* and *Sir Tristrem.*

> But most of them have something attractive; and few, even of those which remain unpublished, are entirely worthless. In some of them the general cloud of dulness is now and then dissipated by a few brilliant lines.... Others, though their poetry and versification are gen-

erally very mean, are rendered attractive by the romantic wildness of the tale, such as Sir Launfal, Le Beaus Desconus, Ipomidon, and Amis and Amiloun. All of them demand the attention of those who would form a true judgment of the manners, amusement, and modes of thinking which obtained in the darker ages, and of that, perhaps most wonderful of all human institutions, the chivalrous and feudal system. (1:xviii–xix)

Here, then, in familiar form are all the accepted wisdoms about the romances and their value, enlivened by what in context are claims for poetic merit verging on radical boldness. The literature is, regrettably, inferior, but is useful for its depiction of customs and manners. Nevertheless, in detecting "romantic wildness," if he cannot explain exactly how it manifests itself, Weber sees the link between this kind of literature and the poetry of Scott and, perhaps, Coleridge. In his comments on individual poems, he takes his literary appreciation even further. The introductory material to *Kyng Alisaunder* is enormously well researched and scholarly, but this is balanced by some genuine literary appreciation of a romance that boasts "a greater share of good poetry" than most others in English (1:xxxiii). "The lines are less burdened with expletives, and exhibit far better versification" than other poems; they "frequently possess an energy which we little expect"; "the short descriptions of nature...are frequently very delicate and beautiful," while the animation of the battle scenes and processions "would not disgrace the pages of Chaucer" (1:xxxiii). When Weber then goes on to quote two sections of the poem in order to commend their virtues, his work has taken a direction that few others were prepared to consider. In fact, he uses a method more typically associated with twentieth-century close-reading techniques, when he lauds and then quotes the poetry, in order to let it resonate on the page.

The edition was a failure. Scott and Weber had thought there would be a market for it, but Ellis was probably the more correct when he suggested "that the Tristrem had gone through two editions, simply owing to the celebrity of its editor's name; and that, of a hundred that had purchased the book, ninety-nine had read only the preface and notes, but not one syllable of True Thomas's 'quaint Inglis.'"[58] And Scott's introduction, though it did not compete with Weber's for scholarly learning, had a sustaining narrative, that of *Tristrem*'s and Thomas's Scottishness. Weber had no such appeal, and neither was his collection the best chosen to demonstrate the intrinsic poetic merit he claimed existed in the poems. The lengthy *Kyng Alisaunder* opened the collection and can scarcely have found many devoted readers, let alone many who could see, with Weber, where it was as good as Chaucer. By avoiding material already published in Ellis's *Metrical Romances* and Ritson's *Metrical Romanceës*, Weber left himself with an eclectic and generically rather confusing selection. Even given all of these factors, the book could have succeeded as a collector's item, but in this regard it was probably let down by the absence of Scott's imprimatur.

The claim for the importance of this edition, then, must be made with several qualifications. It raised the possibility of literary and poetic merit; it viewed the early form of the language not as a barbarous encumbrance but as of interest in itself and of use to future lexicographers. But on the small pond of medieval literary study at the beginning of the nineteenth century, it left hardly a ripple as it sank to the bottom.

Neither the case of Ellis nor that of Weber presents the dramatic relations of patronage seen in Scott's *Sir Tristrem*. Both scholars, nevertheless, worked within a field of possibilities for literary publication and criticism set up by Walter Scott. Ellis was a mentor-turned-student of Scott's, an adviser on the *Tristrem* edition who became the advised on the *Specimens of Metrical Romances*. Weber was a protégé of Scott's from the beginning of his antiquarian career in England, whose publications were all overseen by the novelist. More specifically, all three were inspired by the contents of a single manuscript, the Auchinleck. Scott, of course, had had this in his possession for months at a time and took *Sir Tristrem* from it. Ellis, through Scott's good offices, was able to use the Auchinleck manuscript as the structural heart of his work, basing on it, in whole or in part, his retellings of *Arthour and Merlin, Roland and Vernagu, Otuel a Knight, The Seven Sages, Floris and Blancheflour, Lay le Freine,* and *Sir Degaré,* of his twenty romances.[59] For Weber, too, it was important. He printed *Lai le Freine, Amis and Amiloun,* and *The Seven Sages* from it, and referred to it constantly.

No other single manuscript of medieval English commanded so much attention as this one in the first decade of the nineteenth century. As the generation of literary antiquarians immediately before had been fixated on the Percy Folio, so this generation was devoted to the Auchinleck manuscript. In constantly stressing the "ancientness" and "perfection" of the versions of romances in this manuscript, Scott, Ellis, and Weber were at once confirming the investment of scholars in a key originary text and consecrating an ur-text that would withstand the rigorous skepticism of any Ritsonian. Although it was Scott who most overtly linked his quest for social mobility and his literary self-shaping to this text, all three scholars were connected in their quests for the literary respectability of the material they championed.

George Ellis, plainly, did not *need* to link his fortunes to his literary work. He was not a young scholar on the make, but a retired diplomat who had sufficient leisure and money to indulge his antiquarian hobby. Correspondingly, there is not a shred of editorial rigor, but a great deal of elegant whimsy, in the *Specimens of Early English Metrical Romances*. It is noteworthy that neither this work nor the specimens of early poets has any form of dedication.

The peculiar case of Henry Weber is rather different. Weber was born Heinrich Weber into the Moravian Community in Saint Petersburg in 1783, to a German father and an English mother. He grew up in England and was sent to Germany for his secondary education. In 1803–4, Weber was back in Britain, studying medicine at Edinburgh, but in 1806 was studying in Jena. With the defeat of the Prussian army at the battle of Jena and Auerstedt by the Napoleonic forces, the university was closed, and Weber returned to Edinburgh, where he met Scott in 1807. Gamerschlag believes that they met after Weber wrote to Scott to outline Gottfried von Strassburg's *Tristan* to him. Weber had no money and little employment; Scott hired him and soon came to rely on him for editorial, transcribing, and filing work.[60]

Gamerschlag suggests that Weber's ambition was to support himself through medicine, which would enable him to follow his true love, literature. But Weber never completed his studies and acquired instead a prodigious knowledge of languages and medieval romance. This fitted him for the editing of such works as the *Metrical Romances*, but left him perpetually poor. Like other scholars, Weber dedicated his collection to a rich aristocrat. Elizabeth, marchioness of Stafford and countess of Sutherland would have appeared a wise choice of patron: the marchioness's husband, George Granville Leveson Gower, second marquis of Stafford, was a trustee of the British Museum and had become, after his retirement from politics, a patron of the arts, possibly under the influence of his wife. Although he inclined toward the visual arts, he also had literary interests and was a founding member of the Roxburghe Club in 1812.[61] But Weber does not appear to have developed this association or derived particular benefit from it. In almost every other way, Weber's *Metrical Romances* plays not on invented connections to aristocracy, but on scholarship. The true patron is no aristocrat, but Scott himself. It was Scott's name that Weber wanted on the book, and Scott's refusal probably cost it its slender chances of success.[62]

Weber was a Jacobin, but he supported, unsurprisingly, the English cause in France. Again, though, John Ganim's broader point holds; Weber's edition was thoroughly caught up in the formation of romantic scholarship that had produced Scott and Ellis, and was inserted within the characteristic relations of patronage of that formation. Like Scott, Percy, Hurd, and others, Weber was unashamed in his admiration of chivalry and feudalism. But Weber's is also a scholarly work with hints of an aesthetic appreciation. In this respect, he was a product of a tradition to which Scott had no access: a German schooling and university training. Weber had studied classics, history, and geography, as well as English, French,

Hebrew, and Greek.[63] He also taught himself an astonishing array of classical, medieval, and modern languages.

To someone who had grown up speaking German and English and later learned medieval German and English languages, the reading of Middle English romances must have been a relatively simple matter. With his wide linguistic learning, Weber in effect had the bases for comparative philology and had been schooled in the same educational apparatus that would within a few years produce that discipline. It is unsurprising that he shows signs of being able to write appreciatively of the romances using a belletristic vocabulary, without perceiving barbarity. What Weber entirely lacked was a readership, in the absence of which he needed patronage: not the protection and caressing of aristocrats, but a genuinely scholarly community. Weber was denied this. He was to suffer a strangely Ritsonian fate.

At Christmas 1813, Scott had invited Weber, as he often did, to dine in his house. Before dinner, as both were sitting in the library, Scott observed Weber looking at him with a fixed stare. Scott asked what was wrong, and Weber replied: " 'Mr Scott . . . you have long insulted me, and I can bear it no longer. I have brought a pair of pistols with me, and must insist on your taking one of them instantly.' "[64] Scott fobbed Weber off; the unfortunate amanuensis was later restrained and suffered a breakdown. He recovered, relapsed, and, in October 1816, was committed to a lunatic asylum with a dementia supposedly brought on by too much study of texts.[65] The hagiographic Lockhart, for whom Weber was "a mere drudging *German,*" tells us that Scott paid the hospital bills, and Weber died in the hospital fifteen months later.[66]

The etiology of Weber's madness can only be guessed at. Too much reading of Middle English texts seems a romantic cause, perhaps rather less plausible than the years of near starvation, penury, and displacement Weber endured during the troubled time of the beginning of the century. Strikingly, though, the failure of patronage and the failure of scholarship to take the editor where he wanted to go seem to have played a part, as the drama enacted in the presence of his mentor, Scott, suggests. Shortly before the event concerning the pistols, Weber had been on a walking tour in the Highlands. Scott had provided letters of introduction, and it appears that at Dunrobin Castle (the Sutherland seat of the dedicatee of *Metrical Romances*), Weber and his party got drunk and out of hand. Scott, annoyed, then monitored Weber's drinking on his return. This, combined with exhaustion and a fever contracted on the tour, "probably" "worked together to produce the unlikely clash" with the pistols.[67]

Middle English, by the end of the first decade of the nineteenth century, was still implicated in relations of patronage and questions of genealogy, and was fueled by romantic notions about feudalism, chivalry, and an ordered past. The result was a field curiously distanced and alienated from itself: it was neither "Middle" nor "English"; it was focused on Edinburgh, not London. First formed amid Thomas Percy's ambitions, briefly academicized by Thomas Warton, and further exploited as an object of middle-class cultural politics and practices of the self in the early nineteenth century, by 1810 the study of Middle English was seemingly locked into a relationship between upwardly mobile middle-class freelance intellectuals and an aristocracy keen to secure its difference to precisely this middle class through appeals to tradition and genealogy. The next transformation for Middle English formalized and institutionalized this relationship.

CHAPTER 4

Turtle Soup and Texts
From the Roxburghe Club to
the Camden Society

1812

It was said of the battle that "such deeds of valour [were] performed...
as had never been previously beheld; and of which 'the like' will probably never be seen again. The shouts of the victors, and the groans of
the vanquished stunned and appalled you as you entered." The same eye-
witness wrote: "How many champions, once clad 'in complete steel' for
that contest, now sigh, as they gaze upon their suspended armour—their
'haubert, helm, and twisted mail,' their gloves of steel, and battle axe
of slaughter—sigh, to think upon the dearly-won spoils of that memorable day!" The most famous engagement was between an earl and a
marquis, and at their clash, "All eyes were turned—all breathing well
nigh stopped...every sword was put home within its scabbard—and not
a piece of steel was seen to move or to glitter save that which each of
these champions brandished in his valorous hand. See, see!—they parry,
they lunge, they hit: yet their strength is undiminished, and no thought
of yielding is entertained by either."[1]

The marquis triumphed over the earl in this passage of arms. But the
chivalric struggle did not take place on a blood-soaked field in Europe.
The scene was a dining room in Saint James's Square, London, and its
more heroic dimensions existed only in the florid metaphor of Thomas
Frognall Dibdin, librarian to George John, second Earl Spencer. The battle was the auction of the library of the duke of Roxburghe, and the aristocratic dueling was over a rare book, the Valdarfer Boccaccio of 1471.
Spencer and the marquis of Blandford were the main bidders at the sale
of this book on 17 June 1812, and they contested until the astonishing
price of £2,260 was successfully offered by Blandford. The two noblemen
had driven up the price unprecedentedly; nobody had paid a four-figure
sum for a book before, and the fame of both book and sale were assured.
Skirmishing on other days was equally impressive; one agent bid so lavishly and effectively that it was rumored he was buying for Napoleon
himself. Bibliomania—the phenomenon described by Dibdin in 1809—
had reached its height.

Dibdin was an attendant to Spencer when he witnessed the "battle"
that he was later to recast in chivalric terms. At his instigation, eighteen

bibliophiles met for dinner at a tavern on the evening of the sale, in celebration of the day. They included Earl Spencer (in the chair), George Granville Leveson Gower (the Earl Gower who was the husband of Henry Weber's dedicatee), Sir Mark Masterman Sykes, the MP for York, and Sir Samuel Egerton Brydges, MP for Maidstone. Gentlemen included George Isted, who had inherited books from his great-grandfather, Thomas Percy, and the Oxford MP Richard Heber, who at his death in 1833 left eight houses full of books that took three years to sell. In the course of dinner, it was decided that the occasion would be ritually observed on the same day each year. The Roxburghe Club was formed.

The eighteen became founder members, and they soon enlisted six others, including William Cavendish, duke of Devonshire (it was for him, not Napoleon, that the mystery bidder had been working at the Roxburghe sale). The following year, membership was extended to thirty-one, and thereafter, gentlemen, such as Walter Scott in 1823, took up the increasingly sought-after vacancies after election, while quasi-dynastic principles were apparently observed for aristocrats, such as Viscount Althorp, Spencer's son and heir. The club preserved this social division within its ranks; its members always included a handful of the notable aristocrats of the day, one of whom was always president, while the roles of vice-president and treasurer were usually filled by gentleman members. "These who in some measure fed on the crumbs that fell from the master's table," it was later written, "were in a position rather too closely resembling the professionals in a hunt or cricket club."[2] Whatever its internal social divides, the club was united in an imperiously exclusive stance toward the outside world, for which it became notorious. When it began producing books, it jealously kept them from nonmembers, a practice that attracted widespread resentment.

It was soon resolved that the club should have a bibliophilic purpose and that each member should "furnish the Society with a REPRINT of some rare old tract, or composition—chiefly of poetry."[3] But it was two years before Surrey's *Certaine Bokes of Virgiles Aenaeis, turned into English Meter* was presented to the club as its first fruit, an accurate indicator that for many members it was the annual dinner that was the real business of membership. Some of them never produced their editions, while at one dinner, fifteen Roxburghers ate fifty pounds of turtle and two haunches of venison at a cost of £85. On the bill, servants' dinners are marked down at seven shillings and the waiters received one pound: "The final items," the club's historian drily observed, "appear to have been the sole economy."[4]

When Spencer died in 1834, he was succeeded in the chair by Edward Herbert, Lord Clive, later Earl Powis, and in 1835, written regulations were introduced. The membership was extended to forty, and each member was required to contribute a book. A subscription of five guineas was introduced for the first time, and the revenue was to be spent on "printing some inedited Manuscript, or in reprinting some Book of acknowledged rarity and value."[5] The rules also stated that no more than one hundred copies of each book should be printed, two to be made available to each member, the spare copy to be presented by him to a friend or to a public institution. Under this mechanism, some Roxburghe editions did enter the wider world, but one hundred was a maximum rarely reached, and in general the aim was to keep the books out of the hands of the public and even out of libraries.

Celebrating bibliomania, the club seems to have tried to preserve a sense of the rareness of the works being edited and reprinted by reproducing them only in rare editions. Nevertheless, in this way, a major mechanism for the production of early literature was set up. The subscription mechanism would become in the nineteenth century the resolution of the dilemma that had retarded publication of medieval literature in the eighteenth, the conflict between the requirements of the man of taste and the scholar. To be popular, and therefore to make money, required tailoring texts in the manner of Percy; to be scholarly, like Ritson, was to be despised and bankrupted. The subscription mechanism attempted to guarantee the more scholarly product for which editorial advances had created a demand, by bringing together in advance a community of people who would willingly pay for production. The need to create something salable was, in theory, circumvented.

The mechanism represented in the Roxburghe Club, though, cemented the somewhat feudal relations between aristocrats and aspiring litterateurs exploited by Percy. The social divide within the club sometimes recreated the relationship of supplicant artist to great lord. Dibdin himself was the most conspicuous example. Few men of the time could have based their careers more solidly on books and the patronage they could attract than he. Dibdin at first combined the two most typical career choices of antiquarians, studying law but then entering the church, before he became a bibliographer, bringing himself to the notice of Earl Spencer with an introduction to editions of classical literature that he published in 1802. Spencer became his patron, helping him along in his career in the church and making him the librarian at his seat of Althorp, which the earl built up to be one of the great private collections. Dibdin published many books on books and is credited with fueling the trend for book collecting, which he celebrated in his 1809 work, *Bibliomania*. His talents, however, were suspect, his books "amusing...but full of verbiage and follies, and abounding with error."[6]

At the end of a decade of romance publication, it was natural that someone like Dibdin should turn the business of book collecting into a species of romance. Romance had so far permeated relations between the scholar and the hoped-for aristocratic patron that it became a rhetoric in which all kinds of dealings could be described. Bibliomania is a romantic pursuit; the rich and powerful aristocrats of the day become chivalrous questing knights, and the books on which they expend vast sums become spoils won in battle. And the humble bibliophile becomes the romancer himself.

The Clubs and Their Editions

Writing in 1928, the Roxburghe Club's historian noted that half of the members had been public-school educated, and of those, half went to Eton. "Seventy-three have been peers and seventy-six members of Parliament: four-and-twenty have been clergymen and the same number have been called to the Bar: about twenty have been professors, fifteen librarians of public institutions, twenty soldiers, and twenty men of business: three have been famous writers and about fifty have written books: three have been Prime Minister."[7] The club was an establishment bastion, its early members representing the new British ruling-class elite that had been forming in the decades since the 1780s.[8] In this respect, it was hardly likely to alter the conservative cast of the editing of medieval English. Spencer, its founding president, had been first lord of the Admiralty under Pitt until 1801, a period that saw the Battle of the Nile. Other members in 1812 were less directly involved in the Napoleonic conflicts, but in this social grouping at this time, the republican sympathies of a Ritson would have been unimaginable.

At first the club had little to do with Middle English; the romance publications of the previous ten years may well have satisfied taste for a time, if not glutted the market, and there was little call for other genres. In addition, the Roxburghe — appropriately enough for a club commemorating the sale of an incunable — began with the purpose of reprinting books rather than editing manuscripts, and in its first five years most of its productions were of sixteenth-century literature. Middle English made its appearance when Sir Mark Masterman Sykes presented, as the club's sixteenth production, Lydgate's *The Churl and the Bird* in 1818. Later, Earl Gower presented a volume of John Gower's verse in French and Latin, Thomas Ponton edited the stanzaic *Morte Arthur* (1819), E.V. Utterson edited *Chevalere Assigne* (1820), and Sykes presented another Lydgate poem. The most significant Middle English production of the club's early years came about when, in the mid-1820s, output had begun to fall away and it was obvious that some members would never fulfill their editorial duty. A new mechanism was instituted, allowing an outsider to edit a text, the expense of which was to be borne by a member.[9] The first text to appear in this fashion was Frederic Madden's edition of *Havelok the Dane,* presented to the club by Earl Spencer, its editor remunerated by £100. Under this scheme, Middle English became a regular, though still never dominant, feature of club production: Madden produced *William of Palerne* in 1832 and Joseph Stevenson *The Owl and the Nightingale* in 1838. Much later, in the 1860s, Frederick Furnivall would begin his own career in Middle English by editing for the club.

Nevertheless, in its first few decades the club did not operate with or promote a coherent notion of Middle English. Even the learned Madden was no more precise about *Havelok* than to call it an "ancient" romance. The club's principles were never any clearer than the regulations of 1835 made them, so it remained resolutely dilettantish in its approach. No one was laying down any particular procedures or standards; many of the scholars were as much interested in turtle soup as texts, so publishing decisions reflected personal whim and editorial standards were wildly variable.

In 1823, the new member of the club, Walter Scott, began his own equivalent club in Edinburgh. The Bannatyne Club began on very similar lines to the Roxburghe, with regulations stipulating a membership of thirty-one, an annual subscription, and a brief to publish material relating to Scottish antiquities. Its founder members reflected a more middle-class basis than that of the Roxburghe, and included men in the world of trade, such as Scott's publishing and printing associates, James Ballantyne and Archibald Constable, and David Laing, the Edinburgh bookseller and antiquarian who served as the club's secretary throughout its life. Gradually, new members were admitted until the total reached one hundred in 1829.[10] Like its predecessor, the Bannatyne Club published eclectically: collections of letters, old historical works, parliamentary proceedings, the histories of noble houses, and accounts of trials formed much of its early output. There was relatively little literature: Henryson was published early, then an Alexander romance, and later, *Sir Gawain and the Green Knight* and other Gawain romances and ballads. But Middle English was rare among its publications.

Obviously influenced by the Bannatyne Club and its founder, the Maitland Club was established in Glasgow in 1828. A subscription society, it began with fifty members, later increased to one hundred, with the earl of Glasgow as its president but a largely gentlemanly membership. In 1829, Scott, J. G. Lockhart, and the literary historian David Irving became members. The club's aim was "the printing and publication of Works illustrative of the History, Literature, and Antiquities of Scotland."[11] In the by now typical model, members received copies of all productions free, but some copies were also reserved for libraries at the discretion of the committee. It was also resolved that any particularly important production could be printed in excess copies and offered for sale to the public, though "on a paper differing in size or quality from the Members' copies" (7). A very similar club, the Abbotsford, was founded in Edinburgh in 1833, the year after Scott's death, its object being "the printing of Miscellaneous Pieces, illustrative of History, Literature, and Antiquities."[12] Its founder and secretary was William Barclay David Donald Turnbull, a young Edinburgh lawyer who did much antiquarian work with his club and the Maitland Club, which he joined at the same time as starting the Abbotsford; later, David Laing was its leading light.

Like the clubs on which they were modeled, the Abbotsford and Maitland produced an eclectic variety of antiquarian publications. Both, however, devoted considerable space to Middle English literature, partly because it was clearly an interest of Turnbull's. He edited *Bevis of Hampton* for the Maitland Club in 1838; and for his own club, *Roland and Vernagu* and *Otuel a Knight* (1836), *Arthour and Merlin* (1838), and *Guy of Warwick* (1840). These publications simply perpetuated the earlier obsession with romance, and all were taken from that honorary Scottish volume, the Auchinleck manuscript; only because of its presence there, presumably, could the English *Bevis* appear with the Scottish-focused Maitland Club. (The brief of the Abbotsford Club was broader; its interest was in the antiquities of the countries about which Scott wrote.)

The Roxburghe Club continued publishing throughout the nineteenth century; the Bannatyne Club closed in 1861, the Abbotsford effectively ceased in 1844, and the Maitland closed in 1859. Between 1812 and the late 1830s, these clubs were responsible for almost the entirety of Middle English production. The Roxburghe was alone in the field until 1823, and even when a publication came from elsewhere, it was typically done by someone who was a member of the club. Despite their variations, the character of their publications was similar, editorially and critically. There were significant overlappings in personnel, and in general, a coherent character for Middle English was constructed in the period.

There were, however, two important publications in Middle English of this period that did not belong to this formation (they were the more easily separated from it by the lack of any broad unifying term). In 1813, the Lancashire vicar and topographer Thomas Dunham Whitaker published a C-text of *Piers Plowman* in his *Visio Willī de Petro Plouhman*, the first new edition of this work since Robert Crowley's two and a half centuries before. Whitaker's main concern, as far as the period was concerned, was to establish Langland as the first satirist, and as the Father of English Poetry in preference to Chaucer. Whitaker conceived of his poet much as others had imagined Chaucer:

[T]he author of these Visions was an observer and a reflector of no common powers. I can conceive him (like his own visionary William) to have been sometimes occupied in contemplative wanderings on the Malvern Hills, and dozing away a summer's noon among the bushes, while his waking thoughts were distorted into all the misshapen forms created by a dreaming fancy. Sometimes I can descry him taking his staff, and roaming far and wide in search of manners and characters; mingling with men of every accessible rank, and storing his memory with hints for future use. I next pursue him to his study, sedate and thoughtful, yet wildly inventive, digesting the first rude drafts of his Visions.[13]

Langland is here the observant social realist, going among all ranks and taking his impressions back to the study, a conception of poetic activity also common in Chaucer studies (as will be discussed in chapter 7). Charlotte Brewer, who has traced the fortunes of Langland studies from the sixteenth century to the present day, suggests that the passage is also reminiscent of the early Wordsworth, with its description of a poet wandering widely in nature and recollecting his impressions in tranquility.[14] In this respect Langland, in Whitaker's hands, is a kind of protomodern poet, just as Chaucer had been to Renaissance scholars and would be later in the nineteenth century. Whitaker thought that despite the corruption of Langland's times, some kind of national awakening could be perceived in this period: "While, however, the national *morals* had been gradually declining, the state of national *intelligence* had suddenly risen to that point of elevation, at which satire will always be attempted as an instrument of correction, and seldom without effect. It is never the growth of an age wholly barbarous."[15] The implication here is that Langland is part of a cultural resurgence, but then, in his turn, he helps to further that resurgence, just as Chaucer was often credited with having renovated a barbarous English language.

Whitaker could not classify his work within a period that could comprehend the romances and Chaucer in one coherent field, as neither "Middle English" nor a usable synonym was available as a term. Instead, Whitaker framed the text in a way that placed it in a lineage of antiquarian literary scholarship very familiar to its potential readership. Percy is recognized because of his essay on Langland's verse, which had appeared with the *Reliques*. The learned footnotes refer many times to George Hickes's *Thesaurus*. The volume is dedicated to Richard Heber, who lent two of the three manuscripts used by Whitaker for the edition, in the typical antiquarian mode of friendly exchange. The book did not *look* like something from this lineage, however; Whitaker dealt with the demands of this text by printing it in a sumptuous black letter, with proper nouns and the Latin passages printed in red. Along the bottom of each page he included a Modern English paraphrase in roman type. Brewer says that the book was not a great success, probably owing to the presentation, which "rendered it inaccessible to the casual reader."[16] Also, it was simply not what was being read at the time as Middle English literature, and it is doubtful whether a clearer edition in roman type would have been any more successful. Whitaker did the right things with his author by creating him as a poetic eminence, but the time of this text was yet to come.

In the year following this publication Whitaker brought out a much simpler book, an edition of *Pierce the Ploughman's Crede*, reprinting it from an edition of 1553 without notes or glossary. Thereafter, he returned to his more characteristic pursuits of writing local histories and planting trees.

The nonclub publication destined to have a far greater impact appeared a few years later; predictably, it was another contribution to romance. Malory's *Morte Darthur* was better known than most Middle English texts when Robert Southey reedited it in 1817, having remained among the tiny corpus of Middle English prose to be read beyond the sixteenth century, after several black-letter reprintings. The last new edition had been William Stansby's black-letter printing of 1634. Suddenly, however, it was back in vogue, with the appearance of two new reprints in 1816, followed by Southey's edition. Both 1816 texts could be seen as following on from the vogue for romance, but neither resulted from a strong antiquarian impulse. Each appears to be a bookseller's initiative, aimed at securing as wide a distribution as possible; both were based on Stansby's edition, but both used normalized and modernized orthography. Southey's edition was of a different order, more obviously antiquarian by origin, being based on Caxton and preserving Caxton's fifteenth-century English. This was a lavish two-volume folio, whereas the 1816 editions were duodecimos.[17]

In 1817, as it happened, Southey's republican play written two decades before, *Wat Tyler*, also appeared. But this was a pirate edition that caused the now conservative poet much embarrassment; there was nothing in his presentation of Malory's Arthurian cycle that differed from the conservative vision of romance and the Middle Ages seen in other scholarship of this time. Southey admires chivalry in his introduction to Malory, and even takes some trouble to demonstrate that despite literary hyperbole, "The prowess of the knights of Romance ... is not much exaggerated."[18] But Southey has little to say about Malory's work itself; the bulk of his thirty-two-page preface is concerned with his author's sources, most of which he found morally wanting. Although an author, Southey stated, is to some extent bound by the materials he inherits, it was nevertheless "the fault of the author that so many of the leading incidents should shock, not merely our ordinary morals, which are conventional and belong to our age, but those feelings which belong to human nature in all ages" (1:xv).

Like Whitaker, Southey benefited from loans of manuscripts from Heber's massive collection in compiling his introduction, and the Caxton text was lent by Earl Spencer. But it was the Stansby version, in the cheaper 1816 reprints, that made possible the great nineteenth-century revival of this work.

Whitaker's *Piers* had the potential to open up a rather different medieval England from that popularly imagined, but it had little immediate impact. Southey's Malory accorded with the norms established by romance editing. Within the clubs themselves, a number of shared characteristics are evident. They continued the all-male character of Middle English, if not antiquarian publishing generally. They combined, to greater or lesser degrees, the aristocracy with middle-class antiquarians. A great number of the antiquarians practiced the law; rather fewer were in the church. The book trade appeared for the first time as a milieu in which antiquarians were produced. A few of the clubs' middle-class members, especially in the early part of the century, relied on the antiquarian work they were able to procure, but the usual pattern was for members to be in employment. The clubs were almost entirely nonacademic organizations. Their publications were relatively lavishly produced, usually in quarto on good paper, and they were not generally made available to the public. In their period of dominance, the focus of antiquarian activity in this field shifted, once again, from London to Scotland. Just as important are some of the things the clubs did not do: committees did not assess the offered publications for suitability or desirability; they never set down anything in their rules about editing or scholarship. Editors, in these matters, had a free hand, and for precedent they tended to look back to Scott, Ellis, and Percy. Ritson's scholarship, if not his editing, was often respected.

These aspects, combined, in practice meant that there was nothing to challenge Middle English as it had emerged in antiquarian work from Percy to Scott. Introducing *Guy of Warwick* in 1840, Turnbull wrote:

Mr Ellis considers it as no less certainly one of the dullest and most tedious [of early fictions]. Our ancestors, doubtless, thought otherwise, and M. De la Rue held a very opposite opinion. I fully concur with Mr Ellis.

But, heavy and protracted though it be, in a philological point of view, and as illustrative of ancient manners, this Romance possesses considerable interest.[19]

Condensed here are all the accepted ideas about medieval literature: the editor has selected a romance; treading the line between taste and scholarship, he is as equivocal as editors always had been about the literary value of the material; the modern aesthetic judgment of the work, not the possible medieval judgment, is superior; pictures of life and manners are the justification for publishing it, alongside philological value. It is easy to be left wondering why someone like Turnbull bothered with the text at all, which, despite its realist value, he finds dull, tedious, heavy, and protracted.

Because of the natural uniformity of their publications, the clubs tended to homogenize even further the style of editions, and consequently the available Middle English literature was constructed according to quite narrowly conceived criteria. Abbotsford and Maitland Club editions, dominated by Turnbull and Laing, were often almost indistinguishable, and overall, all four clubs shared a basic format for presentation.

Roxburghe Club editions were, at the outset, almost negligible in scholarly terms. The precedent set by the inaugural volume was often adhered to. William Bolland's reprint of Surrey simply claimed that the text was "faithfully printed from the original edition in the library of Dulwich College," and apart from a dedication to the club members and the standard list of members, it contained no other prefatory material. The text was printed in black letter, without apparatus of any kind. In later editions, editors often included a paragraph or two on the manuscript or print from which the text had been taken. The text would then be presented, without notes, line numbers, or any other form of scholarly apparatus. Printing in black letter was the norm, with manuscript contractions retained. These early productions can barely be considered editions at all; they were really no more than attractively printed diplomatic transcripts.

Deeper scholarship was an option, if the editor wished; the solicitor James Heywood Markland's edition of two Chester Mysteries has a lengthy and erudite introduction showing a real depth of knowledge. The text is printed accessibly in roman type, and variant readings from other manuscripts are recorded at the foot of the page.[20] No trend was set by this work of scholarship, however; a Middle English work that appeared the following year, the edition by the Lincoln's Inn barrister Thomas Ponton of the stanzaic *Morte Arthure*, followed the more dilettante format, presenting the text in black letter, "faithfully printed from the original manuscript in the British Museum, with all its abbreviations, obsolete words and spelling, and literal and grammatical errors."[21]

In keeping with the Roxburghe Club's concern with printed books rather than manuscripts, its editions were often illustrated with facsimiles of early woodcuts. The Abbotsford and Maitland clubs also typically employed black letter and illustrated their works more lavishly than the Roxburghe. The resultant frontispieces and mock illuminated capitals, however, were often more neo-Gothic than medieval. Charles Kirkpatrick Sharpe was a frequent illustrator of these editions. In Turnbull's *Arthour and Merlin*, Sharpe's frontispiece is a line drawing of questionable relevance to the Middle English text. In it, a woman lies asleep on an opulent bed, the upper half of her body exposed, while two horned demon figures leer over her. On a stool at the bedside, there is a large book, bound with clasps. Where the Roxburghe Club did attempt some fidelity to a fifteenth-century model for its books, the Scottish clubs recreated their texts more in terms of what the nineteenth century thought was "medieval."

Abbotsford and Maitland editions did, however, attempt to provide more scholarly frameworks for their texts. The result was less coherent than the Roxburghe's unambitious reprints. Turnbull tended to write introductions of some substance, though no great learning. He was neither a great editor nor a skilled reader of manuscripts, and his editions tend to reflect the opposite ambitions to be scholarly on the one hand and to produce an attractive nineteenth-century book on the other. Turnbull's *Arthour and Merlin* opened with several lines of black letter and a very elaborate illuminated capital involving entwined dragons, leaves, and human faces. This largely ornamental purpose is then replaced by a more scholarly look, as the rest of the romance is printed in roman type. Editorial principles are somewhat random: long *s* and *v* for consonantal *u* are retained, but *th* replaces thorn. Rather than emending, Turnbull signals what he perceives to be a textual problem by printing "sic MS." in a footnote, thereby avoiding proposing any solution. There are no textual notes and no glossary.

Turnbull's other editions follow this general pattern. By printing diplomatically and using the notation "sic MS." to absolve himself of the need to emend, Turnbull turned out editions quickly, and they were then illustrated according to a standard format. It is doubtful whether he could have done more, given his lack of skill with manuscripts. His editions frequently show such basic confusions as *u* for *n* and *v* for *u*. Just as he did not commit himself to extensive editing, Turnbull limited his role as a scholar by indicating that it simply was not necessary to make more than a few genteel remarks on the material being edited. Turnbull opened *Arthour and Merlin* with what he called "Exordial Observations," a coy and somewhat pompous way of avoiding the more scholarly sounding "Introduction." Editing *Bevis of Hampton,* he everywhere set aside scholarly questions as not worth pursuing. So on the question of the actual existence of Bevis, "in order to save much expense of time and final discomfiture, it may be as prudent to waive the general question of pedigree."[22] Like Warton, Turnbull thought the romance was of French origin, but "the point is, on the whole, of comparative indifference" (xvi). The bibliography on the romance is "extensive," but the reader is referred to other sources, in order to avoid "dry detail" (xvii). And finally, criticism too is evaded: "An analysis of the romance were absolutely a work of supererogation, as the volume, it is hoped, is not destined to blockheads; and, should it unfortunately lapse into the hands of such, no summary or exegesis could possibly 'lighten their darkness' " (xvii).

Not everything in this period was produced by the clubs, but when a medieval edition appeared outside of a club, it was usually edited by someone associated with a club. David Laing was able to produce his own material because he was a bookseller and could sell it himself; Edward Vernon Utterson, literary antiquary and a barrister of Lincoln's Inn, eventually set up his own press. They offer contrasting cases in the world of literary antiquarianism of the time. Laing was the son of an Edinburgh bookseller, apprenticed to his father at fourteen, although he did do some study at Edinburgh University. It was when he became a partner in his father's business in 1821 that he devoted himself to scholarship in early Scottish literature. In 1827 he became a fellow of the Society of Antiquaries of Scotland and was later able to give up the bookselling business.[23] Utterson was educated at Eton and Trinity Hall, Cambridge, and entered Lincoln's Inn in 1794. He was later a fellow of the Society of Antiquaries, and after 1835 he lived in the Isle of Wight, where his Beldornie Press produced early literature in small print runs.[24]

Despite his interest in Scottish antiquities, Laing did publish a relatively large amount of Middle English, partly because of the continuing confusion over what exactly was Scottish and what was English in the Middle Ages. Laing published his first book, *Select Remains of the Ancient Popular Poetry of Scotland* in 1822, suggesting that these poetic remnants "are valuable, no less in enabling us to trace the history and progress of our language, than in assisting us to illustrate ancient manners and amusements, of which they often contain the liveliest representations."[25] This odd and ill-produced book is really two quite distinct things; the second part contains ballads, undoubtedly Scottish, many of which are drawn from the Bannatyne manuscript (after which the club had been named). The first part contains several works that, at least by implication, are supposedly Scottish but are mostly in fact Middle English. These include *The Taill of Rauf Coilyear, The Awntyrs of Arthur, Sir Orfeo, Thomas of Ersyldoune*, and *The Pistel of Swete Susan*. A little scholarly hedging was needed to retain some of these poems for Scotland, though Laing was assisted by the still prevalent, and very helpful, assumption that a poem existing only in an English dialect and an English manuscript might nevertheless be, in a truer, original version, from somewhere else.

Hence, *Sir Orfeo*, printed by Ritson from the Harley version, is taken by Laing from the Auchinleck manuscript, guarantee enough, in the right hands, of Scottishness. Laing notes Robert Henryson's version of the story and prints several extracts from it. Nowhere does he actually *say* that *Sir Orfeo* is a Scottish poem, but nowhere does he say it is not. Because of its Scottish affiliations, via Henryson and the Auchinleck manuscript, it finds its way into this collection. Likewise, *Thomas of Ersyldoune*, printed from the manuscript in the Cathedral Library, Cambridge, is Scottish—or would be, if it existed in a truer version. It is *"impossible"* to imagine, Laing says, that it *"could have been written by any other than* Thomas *himself, however much it may have suffered by subsequent interpolation"* (102). John Jamieson, the Scottish lexicographer, Laing notes, claimed a Scottish origin, despite the absence of a Scottish copy of the poem. Furthermore, Huntly Bank, where Thomas meets the fairy queen in the poem, is not only in Scotland, but is still popularly known as the Rhymer's Glen and is in fact to be found in Abbotsford, Scott's estate (Lockhart later said that the glen is the background to Landseer's 1833 portrait of Scott).[26] What greater authority could be imagined for the Scottishness of the poem than the fact that the Wizard of the North had literally bought into it? On these various grounds, another Scottish poem, albeit one existing only in an English version, was constructed.

Laing made no such pretensions in his edition of *Sir Degaré*, produced for the Abbotsford Club in 1849. Although not formally wound up until 1866, the club was moribund from 1844, and it was left to Laing to dispose of its remaining assets with a last few editions, of which this was one.[27] Laing printed from the Auchinleck version, and the edition included several facsimiles of the woodcuts and pages in Wynkyn de Worde's edition. There are no notes and no glossary, and the overall effect is similar to Turnbull's Abbotsford editions. The editing, like Turnbull's, is erratic. It is unclear why Laing uses a special character for yogh in his text and preserves long *s*, while silently altering thorns to *th*. There are random modernizings in his text — "did" for MS "dede" in line 5, for example — and basic mistakes such as "was" for MS "nas." Laing produced these editions and another of *Early Metrical Tales* (1826) without putting his name on the title page.

In 1817, E. V. Utterson published *Select Pieces of Early Popular Poetry.* He indicated his editorship only with "E.V.U." on the imprint page, and the two volumes were published not by himself but by reputable London booksellers. The work had a dual intent: first, to print some of the romances hitherto only known in Ellis's summarized versions, on the grounds that readers would now want to see them as they really were. "The untutored Polynesian," Utterson wrote by way of explanatory metaphor, "is much more an object of interest and curiosity, with no other clothing than his war-mat and feathered helmet, than if fully equipped in the costume of European society."[28] The second volume contained humorous poems, and Utterson claimed that it had been the recommendation of "that accurate and intelligent antiquary Ritson" that such a volume be printed (1:xvii). Most of the poems were taken from early printed editions, and Utterson relied principally on the Garrick collection of early prints in the British Museum for the romances he printed in the first of his two volumes.

In his fluent introduction, replete with learning inherited from Percy, Warton, Ellis, and also Ritson, Utterson opened by noting the interest in literary antiquities of the past thirty years and the attendant publications. These circumstances, he continued, meant that it was hardly necessary to apologize to the public for requesting "its patronage in favour of the little work now submitted to its acceptance." Recent scholars "have thrown much light on various particulars relating to our manners and history during the middle ages" (1:v). There is more to be done:

[I]f in the occasional republication of portions of our early literature few additional illustrations of received opinions are now to be discovered, yet the revival affords corroboration of former conjectures, which is thus strengthened into conviction; it affords materials for the philologist wherewith to analyse the structure of our language, or suggests to the poet interesting images of ancient manners, which, chosen by taste, and remodelled by genius, tend to enliven the narrative, and increase its interest. (1:vi)

Utterson then went on to explain and justify interest in the rude work of minstrels, as having a pleasing simplicity in the view of "the present enlightened state of society" (1:vii). Minstrel work was the principal form of enjoyment of the upper classes in the Middle Ages. "Simplicity," Utterson argued, is the great virtue of the minstrel romances, "accompanied, it is believed, by great accuracy of representation in those parts of the narrative which referred to the dress and habits of the personages introduced" (1:ix). The humorous poems of the second volume were less easily justified on these grounds; indeed, there was the problem of a "phraseology" which might be thought sometimes to "swerv[e] from the language of decency" (1:xvii). But here readers are asked to remember the contrast between the refinement of the present era and the less delicate language of the Middle Ages.

The lengthy and fluent, if very standard, introduction and a moderately scholarly presentation of the texts make this a far more detailed and competent piece of scholarship than anything published by the Roxburghe Club before Markland's *Chester Mysteries*. Although, in keeping with the Roxburghe format, Utterson used black-letter editions as the source rather than manuscripts, retaining printers' contractions, he did provide line numbers and occasional footnotes. Utterson did not emend, but in footnotes he often suggested solutions to obscure readings. At the end of volume 2, there is a thirteen-page glossary.

In his edition of *Chevalere Assigne* presented to the Roxburghe Club three years later, Utterson reverted to the standard club format. A three-page introduction and a small glossary of about forty words comprise its only scholarly apparatus. The edition is printed in black letter, complete with abbreviations as they appear in the manuscript. Comparison with the manuscript (BL MS Cotton Caligula A.ii) shows that Utterson's treatment of the scribal forms is eccentric: *y* and thorn are represented by one character in his edition, though the scribal forms are easily distinguishable; Utterson also retains yoghs, but not long *s*. Some macrons are preserved, other words that have a macron in the manuscript are silently expanded, and yet others have macrons where there was not one in the manuscript. Some contractions are accurately represented by superscripted abbreviations, such as "þᵗ" for *þæt*, but other instances of such superscription are interpolated. Altogether, this is not so much a consistent attempt to represent manuscript forms as a randomly archaized rendering, in 1820, of a poem in manuscript as its editor imagined it might have been printed by de Worde or William Copland. The editor here is playing not the minstrel but the sixteenth-century printer.

In 1839, Utterson published his *Kyng Roberd of Cysylle*. This was released, anonymously, in a print run of thirty copies, which he then seems to have given away to friends. It is a small and elegant volume of only twenty-seven pages. After a minimal introduction, the text is given in roman type, with no medieval characters and without apparatus, notes, or glossary.

The editions of this period evidently encapsulate some variations: Markland's *Chester Mysteries* is scholarly in a way that looks ahead to the format of scholarship later in the century; Utterson's *Robert of Sicily* is no more than a bijou; Laing's *Select Remains* has the ideological purpose of furthering early Scottish literature. Laing and Utterson came from social backgrounds that differ in important ways. Their trajectories are opposed: one relied on bookselling for an income that enabled antiquarianism, the other followed antiquarianism and set up his own press. Book production was for one, trade, which he wanted to escape; for the other, the mark of gentlemanly dilettantism, which he embraced.

Despite such local variations, the character of these enterprises is broadly very coherent. The clubs enabled the circumvention of the taste/antiquarianism dilemma, but at the expense of the circumvention of scholarship. Although some club books were reviewed by scholarly journals, this was usually only when they had been edited by an outsider, as Madden was when he did *Havelok* for the Roxburghe. Club insiders needed never to fear much scrutiny from the outside world of letters. In effect, it was open to the individual to be as much or as little the scholar as he wished. A zero degree of scholarship was often achieved in those Roxburghe editions where the greatest labor expended probably occurred at the printing shop when the type was set up. The overall output in Middle English increased, but it was directed at a far narrower readership than ever before. Scholarship stagnated; reference to Percy, Warton, Ellis, and Ritson was de rigueur, but exploration beyond the widely available books of these writers was relatively rare. As far as Middle English was concerned, certain assumptions were now an orthodoxy. The literature was rude and simple, but the first could be excused and the second was a virtue; its principal use was an illustration of manners and customs, and secondarily it was philologically interesting; the best of it was of minstrel composition; and it was composed mostly for the upper classes, for whom it formed the principal diversion.

Despite the persistence of these assumptions, which cemented the conservative assumptions of earlier scholarship, this literature was not generally being used in the overt promotion of self by the clubmen. Medieval literature was still assumed to be a product of patronage, but the men editing it were not usually men on the make seeking to reproduce this patronage in their own lives. Harrison Steeves, noting the "social gulf" between the upper and lower echelons in the Roxburghe Club, did suggest that some of the humbler members "actually lived largely by the commissions of their wealthier associates,"[29] but there is in fact little basis for this. Although it is true of Dibdin and Joseph Haslewood, of the first thirty-one members of the Roxburghe almost all were in some form of reliable employment and many combined this with inherited property. The clubs' "feudalism" lay not so much in their internal workings as in the imperious relation they had to the rest of the world, from which they withheld their precious texts.

Why, then, given the lack of interest in public sale, did such men bother to edit at all? Clubs other than the Roxburghe did not even offer the attraction of annual revels. There was no money in it; many editors apparently cared so little about advancement that they did not put their names on what they did. But club membership had more subtle effects on selfhood than bald grasping after patronage. Middle English was just one kind of literature that, in an era of bibliophilia, was being projected in subtle ways through the mechanisms of the clubs and private printing as a demonstration of self.

Middle English and the Mastery of Time

Although an editor of club books could, as Utterson did in *Select Pieces of Early Poetry*, display the findings of quite substantial research, it was equally open to him to avoid anything he did not want to do. Turnbull's comment, that an analysis of *Bevis* was not required as the volume would not fall into the hands of blockheads, perhaps had a simple practical use: he might not have wanted to do the work or been capable of much extended analysis. But the comment is also a telling one, full of implications about the readership and the scholarly community in which these texts were circulating at the time.

Through this comment and in the general attitude evident in his editions, Turnbull gives some idea of who he thinks his readers are. We are of course able to know exactly who his readers were because of the club mechanism, but Turnbull allows a sense of what *kind* of people he thinks they are. He constructs a sense of community; he is addressing men who are essentially like himself. He implies that he *could* do an analysis of the romance, but there is no need to because the men he wants to read it, the people he knows are its only readership, will read it just as he reads it. They are men like himself, sharing his assumptions, and nobody needs to be told what he already knows. Conversely, anyone who *cannot* read the volume as Turnbull and his intended readership would read it is by definition a "blockhead" and not worthy of the literature. Anyone who needs the scholarship spelled out to them is not worthy of access to it. The clubs are, of course, communities in an obvious sense, but through attitudes such as this a slightly more subtle notion of community is created, community based on exclusion and absence, clubs being, after all, as much exclusive as they are inclusive. That which is not discussed is that which cements the group; those who have to discuss it do not belong to the group. Whether they were earls or apothecaries' sons, clubmen were united at a level that cut across their undoubted social divisions. They all belonged to an aristocracy of learning, a "cultural nobility."[30]

What had happened to Middle English was that it had reached a quite logical destination given a trajectory that had always constructed it as a form of mediation between supplicant scholars and the upper classes. The *Reliques* had, in effect, been an offering to the Northumberlands; Ritson had offered his productions to an imagined inquiring public. Club editors offered their productions to one another: "To the members of the Roxburghe Club this reprint of The Hors The Shepe and The Ghoos is dedicated and presented by their obedient servant M. M. Sykes," as one typical dedication runs. The circle was closed; a community was constructed, one that placed the less wealthy scholar alongside his likely aristocratic audience. Like any efficient matchmaking agency, the clubs ensured the mutual satisfaction of all concerned. The poorer scholars were assured of funds for their editing labors; the wealthier scholars were provided with a like-minded community.

In theory, this meant that the former constraints on Middle English were loosened. These editors did not have to alter their texts in ways that would please potential aristocratic patrons, and in practice, they did not do so. They did not edit their texts into ideologically acceptable artifacts (with the exception of Laing in his reclamation of English poems for Scotland). Neither did they have to concern themselves with the problems and questions of editorial methodology, which had been such an issue since 1765. By constructing for themselves a readership and effectively cutting off any other possible readership, the clubs ensured that little criticism would be forthcoming, thereby removing pressure from editorial practices.

In practice, all that this meant was that Middle English was perpetuated in its conservative, prince-pleasing role. The theoretical freedom was available only to people who would not use it. Everyone in the clubs was united in support of a vision of the Middle Ages inherited from Scott and Percy. Textual criticism was barely possible, when clubmen simply edited in a way that ensured the retention of an antique look. It did not much matter that every peculiarity of the manuscript or early print was reproduced, so long as there were enough macrons and contractions in the edited result for it to look authentically medieval.

Scholarship, in these conditions, now had little value as an agent of self-shaping. The scholar had accepted, in effect, a certain attitude toward self-presentation by being a member of the club in the first place, so that the projection of self lay not so much in the *work* done on the self through the literature as in the attitude expressed by having produced the literature at all. Before Madden's editions for the clubs, the literature was uniformly produced according to one or two basic formats; it was effectively unedited, often unreadable, and, we can assume, largely unread. (Even within the small circle of club members, it is hard to imagine too many of these enthusiastic diners making their way through the texts. When one complete set of Bannatyne editions went under the hammer in 1828, the books "were all in an uncut state."]³¹ It was not scholarship but *belonging* that mattered in the clubs. Antiquarian literature was an excuse for belonging to a club.

For these men, their ability to print early literature was part of what Pierre Bourdieu calls "the aesthetic disposition."³² This involves "the accumulation of a cultural capital . . . which can only be acquired by means of a sort of withdrawal from economic necessity."³³ The club editors were principally men who were rich enough not to experience economic necessity. Editing early literature was not, for them, a mechanism of social and economic aspiration, but part of that casual attitude to the world of scholarship, the deployment of "unintentional learning," as Bourdieu calls it, which characterizes the life of leisure deriving from the possession of abundant economic and cultural capital (28). Unintentional learning is a form of competence acquired by someone who already has a grounding in "legitimate culture" (28); it is the extension of officially sanctioned and institutionally acquired knowledge in a casual way outside institutional frameworks. The clubmen were mostly well educated, but they did not live by directly deploying those educations, in the way that academics do. Their deployment of learning was in demonstration of an aesthetic disposition. Bourdieu writes:

> The aesthetic disposition, a generalized capacity to neutralize ordinary urgencies and to bracket off practical ends, a durable inclination and aptitude for practice without a practical function, can only be constituted within an experience of the world freed from urgency and through the practice of activities which are an end in themselves, such as scholastic exercises or the contemplation of works of art. (54)

Thomas Percy had used his educational capital to free himself from urgency; after the *Reliques*, his works could be seen as tasteful ends in themselves. Ritson knew urgency and was killed by it, precisely because his works were not ends in themselves, but always involved the practical function of making money and bringing worldly success. Scott, after *Sir Tristrem*, elevated the aesthetic disposition into a way of life. The clubs were formal mechanisms for the demonstration of the aesthetic disposition. It is true that they hid within their ranks some men, such as Dibdin, Haslewood, and perhaps the younger Madden, who were not well off and could not "bracket off practical ends," but for the most part, they provided a visible means by which men of economic independence could perform that "destruction of riches"—the squandering of money—through which "Economic power... asserts itself" (55).

Many club members, particularly the aristocrats, were or had been prominent in the ruling-class elite that Linda Colley describes as having established itself in this period. By the end of the eighteenth century, there had been a sharp rise in public school and university attendance by aristocrats, and shared education helped consolidate the class.[34] It is not surprising that the learned pursuit of bibliomania was for many in the ruling class what they did when they were not pursuing their legal or parliamentary careers or managing their aristocratic estates. For some, their fine personal libraries formed their principal interests outside their work. Most of the first thirty-one Roxburghers had their own libraries. Spencer's, of course, was famous, and other aristocrats, such as the duke of Devonshire, had considerable personal collections. But so too did the middle-class gentlemen: Sir Joseph Littledale is said to have taken "little interest in outside matters except in the library he collected."[35] Sir Mark Sykes was another with an impressive library; on his death, his brother Sir Tatton Sykes (described by the *DNB* as a "patron of the turf")[36] inherited it along with the baronetcy. Later, running into financial trouble, he had to choose between selling his famous pack of hounds or the library. "While he made the decision his 'anxious old huntsman stood outside the library door. A gentleman could forgo his books, but not his hounds, and the library was sold in 1832 for over ten thousand pounds.' "[37] As we have seen, Utterson had his own press, and so too did Sir Samuel Egerton Brydges. Some gentlemen hunted, some had libraries or produced books; both are forms of conspicuous consumption.

Unlike hounds, though, books potentially demonstrate another aspect of the aristocrats of culture: their mastery of time. Bourdieu proposes:

[T]o possess things from the past, i.e., accumulated, crystallized history, aristocratic names and titles, châteaux or 'stately homes,' paintings and collections, vintage wines and antique furniture, is to master time, through all those things whose common feature is that they can only be acquired in the course of time, by means of time, against time, that is, by inheritance or through dispositions which, like the taste for old things, are likewise only acquired with time and applied by those who can take their time.[38]

Their libraries demonstrated the clubmen's mastery of time; their club books, too, were manifestations of their ability to take the time to deploy their cultural capital.

These remarks, of course, pertain not just to Middle English but to antiquarian production of early texts in general. The clubs promoted even vaguer ideas of chronology and of what was medieval than the scholars of the eighteenth century had done. There was no sense of "Middle English" as a coherency in the work of the Roxburghe Club, while the Scottish clubs often confused the issue even further by claiming English texts as Scottish. It is unlikely that anyone before Frederic Madden was recognizing, in the multitude of club productions, the Middle English texts as belonging together. As late as the end of the 1820s, the only coherency that was recognized in this respect was that of the genre of medieval romance.

Amateurism and dilettantism were thus enshrined in work on Middle English, and no sense of a discipline was possible. Change would come with a reappropriation of antiquarianism by middle-class scholars in a way obviously suggested by the model of the clubs, but arising from the general sense that scholarship ought to be a less exclusive affair.

Clubs versus Societies

On the thirty-third anniversary of the Roxburghe Club's first meeting, an aggrieved Frederic Madden was drafting a letter to its president, Earl Powis. Madden had a problem. He wanted permission to redo his edition of *Havelok the Dane* for the Camden Society. The London-based subscription society wanted the text, but Madden had already been refused permission to reuse his earlier edition. The response of the Camden Society was simply to ask someone else to edit the text, over which, of course, the Roxburghe Club had no control. The man chosen was the prolific journeyman antiquarian Thomas Wright. No choice could have angered Madden more. Wright was not remotely the editor Madden was; his work was usually carried out rapidly and without Madden's attention to accuracy. Wright, furthermore, was a close friend of James Halliwell's, whom Madden had despised at least since he helped expose Halliwell as the thief of some manuscripts from Trinity College, Cambridge.

Madden had to be tactful to Powis. The draft of his letter carefully points out that the publications of the early clubs benefited the few and the rich, while the newer societies, such as the Camden and the Surtees Society, were making early literature available in a popular form. It was not surprising, he wrote, that the societies wanted to reedit material once circulated in the clubs, for club books "can scarcely be said ever to have been <u>published</u>."[39] Madden urged his case by telling Powis that his work for the society was not remunerated, and that by doing it he would "confer a benefit on our early literature." And, he wrote—approaching what was no doubt the real point—he would be spared "the mortification of seeing my own work tortured...by the critical fangs of a supplanter" (fol. 65r). But this he seems to have thought unsuitable for the earl's eyes, and he crossed it out.

When Madden wrote in 1845, the near monopoly of the clubs on literary antiquities was ended. The Surtees Society had begun in 1834 with the object of printing antiquities relating to the northern counties, and when the Camden Society began four years later, it had to reprint its first book after the initial run of five hundred was oversubscribed.[40] It was not surprising, in this era of increasing interest in historical antiquities for their own sake, that the clubs' exclusive dealing should be disapproved of. What is much more surprising is to find that this attitude had existed since the clubs' beginnings. There had in fact always been those who intensely disliked the way the clubs went about their business, either because of their restrictive practices or because of the opposite belief that what was produced was fundamentally worthless. Because of their exclusive print runs, "instead of diffusing knowledge, they [the Roxburghers] selfishly cut off the springs which should feed it; and, instead of promoting the interests of Literature, they materially injure them," wrote one complainant to the *Gentleman's Magazine* as early as 1813. The contrasting view was put by a writer in the Scottish press who complained that "a Bannatynian is a sort of literary scavenger, whose duty it is to save from oblivion all kinds of rubbish."[41]

Why should anyone have cared what a few dozen rich men did in their spare time? What did it matter if a handful of MPs and lawyers held an annual dinner at which they gave each other poorly edited reprints produced at their own expense? Obviously there was at least a latent belief at the time that literary and historical material were in the public domain and formed part of a shared heritage. It is typical of English medieval studies in this period that people never complained about their lack of access to their heritage until they felt they were being denied it by someone else — the elite Roxburghers or later the Germans and Danes. Bibliomania, essentially the pursuit of dilettantes, gradually gave way to a more scholarly and protoprofessional antiquarianism. But bibliomania clearly should be seen as having impelled the more scholarly pursuit.

The new societies greatly extended the franchise of learning. In the first enthusiasm after its establishment, the Camden Society had twelve hundred members, each paying an annual subscription of one pound. John Gough Nichols, in 1862, characterized the society's interests as political treatises, general chronicles and histories, ecclesiastical history, historical documents, rolls of expenses and inventories, personal memoirs and diaries, letters, travels and topography, genealogy and heraldry, poetry and old literature, and philology.[42] A sense of disciplinarity emerges here, and it is not surprising that the work of societies such as this eventually became absorbed into more official and academic institutions, when these began to take over scholarly work in the 1880s and 1890s. Philippa Levine proposes that the foundation in 1886 of the journal *English Historical Review* "marked the academic arrival of the professional historian."[43] In 1897, the Camden Society was merged with the Royal Historical Society and no longer produced anything under its own name.

What the societies did *not* do was to provide a decisive break in the nature of textual editing of Middle English or provide a paradigm shift in criticism. The methodologically uncertain editing of the clubs can be seen as late as the middle of the century, as Laing's and Turnbull's editions suggest. An early Camden Society production, Thomas Wright's edition of *Richard the Redeless*, is no more advanced than their work. Although it boasted the by then standard scholarly trappings of preface, glossary, and notes, Wright's conclusions and arguments are anything but closely and convincingly argued. His lack of research is reflected in the diffident tone of his writing. In the brief preface of less than four pages, Wright suggests that the manuscript *"seems* to be of the beginning of the 15th century"; the poem *"seems* to have been intended as a continuation" to *Piers Plowman*; "The scribe . . . *seems* to have been a partizan of the opposite party [to Richard's enemies]"; and "It has been thought advisable to add a slight popular glossary."[44] Both notes and glossary are similarly uncommitted and ill-researched: "*A leyne uppon other*, I suppose means *one laid upon another*" (54). Where Wright is unsure of a gloss, he leaves a question mark in brackets after the word. The reader who used Wright's glossary to interpret the words about the partridge, which "heipeth his heires, and hetith hem after," would find the following glosses: for *heipeth*, "crowdeth (?)"; for *heires*, "eggs (?)"; and for *hetith*, "warmeth (?)" (61). This is hardly indicative of much linguistic research. The editor is uncertain of the meaning of the verbs and nouns in the line, and so of the line's meaning, but it has neither provoked him to find out what it means nor stopped him from editing the poem.

Wright's scholarly shortcomings were well known in his own time. They arose directly from the fact that he was not a man of means and relied on volume of output, not accuracy. His father had been a bookseller and printer; he himself went to Cambridge only because a neighbor saw his talents for literary work and funded his education. Settling in London, Wright made a living from rapidly produced antiquarian works, such as a history of Essex written on scant firsthand acquaintance with that county. He produced texts of all kinds, some of them for wealthy patrons, and only in later life benefited from a civil list pension.[45] Cruelly, and somewhat loftily, Richard Garnett referred to Wright's "want of scholarship and acumen" in an article of 1847–48, saying that he would "never be more than a third or fourth rate personage, bearing about the same relationship to a scientific philologist and antiquarian that a law-stationer does to a barrister, or a country druggist to a physician."[46] Garnett was very much of the Madden camp. To Madden's circle, both Wright and Halliwell were fair game because of their implication in the Trinity theft. Garnett's article, which also attacks Halliwell, makes it clear that there was an accepted lineage of work in early English that still, in the late 1840s, accepted tasteful work in the tradition of Percy, Warton, and Tyrwhitt. Men such as these "were something more than mere mechanical transcribers of ancient poetry. They had enlightened views of the true functions of an editor in this department of literature, and we overlook their occasional inaccuracies and errors in consideration of the learning, the elegance, and good taste of their illustrations, and the originality of their remarks" (317).

What is striking here is that this is not an unscholarly commitment to taste on the part of Garnett, a man of massive linguistic learning. Garnett, who began with a career in the church and later became assistant keeper of printed books in the British Museum, was among the very first scholars in Britain to understand the importance of comparative philology. In England, however, comparative philology reinvented rather than rejected the work of the tasteful eighteenth-century scholars: being a philologist did not mean you stopped being a gentleman. Garnett's attack on such "[h]alf-learned smatterers" (323) as Halliwell and Wright concluded with praise for (his friend) Madden's edition of Laȝamon's *Brut*, leaving no doubt about who was in the correct lineage and who was not.

Madden, too, had benefited from comparative philological learning by this time. Even his first Middle English edition in 1828, *Havelok the Dane*, is of a different order of learning from its fellow editions in the Roxburghe Club. The pages of this book, with their line numbers, manuscript readings at the foot of the page where Madden had emended the text, and notation of the manuscript folio numbers must have seemed extraordinarily cluttered to club members used to black-letter texts adorned with the occasional facsimile woodcut, while the lengthy and learned introduction must have caused much spluttering of turtle soup. *Havelok* is an indication that there was something happening, even before comparative philology had taken hold, in Middle English. Something quite different from the Roxburghe Club's bijou editions was possible, even if only in a small, learned circle.

The Roxburghe, Bannatyne, Abbotsford, and Maitland clubs were all in full swing after 1833. The arrival of the new philology in England, Hans Aarsleff proposes, occurred in 1830, with the appearance of N. F. S. Grundtvig's prospectus for the publication of Anglo-Saxon texts and of Benjamin Thorpe's translation of Rasmus Rask's Anglo-Saxon grammar.[47] As these publications suggest, it was Anglo-Saxon studies rather than Middle English that would feel its full effects, but comparative philological learning begins to become evident in some Middle English editions from the late 1830s. It is in such Camden Society texts as John Robson's *Three Early English Metrical Romances* (1842), the reviled Halliwell's *Thornton Romances* (1844), and James Morton's *Ancrene Riwle* (1852) that a scholarly mode can be seen that would later be continued in the Early English Text Society and in twentieth-century Middle English. In

Halliwell's discussion of the decline of the system of contractions in fifteenth-century manuscripts and Morton's learned analysis of the grammatical forms of the *Ancrene Riwle,* what is being displayed is a form of educational capital gained through learning: not riches, nor mastery of time, nor dilettantish good taste.

As the clubs were first rivaled, and later outstripped, by the Camden Society, the center of gravity of the study of Middle English again shifted. Three of the four clubs were in Scotland, and two of those in Edinburgh; all were in some way tied to the aristocracy, even though the aristocrats did little or no editing themselves. The Camden Society relocated medieval studies firmly back in London, where, apart from the work going on in Germany, it would remain until it became a subject for export from the late 1860s. The subject passed completely into the hands of men of the middle class, including its lower echelons, who were making their way via their educations rather than inherited property. For some, such as Wright, this allowed the making of a living—if a precarious one— from antiquarian work itself, presaging the conditions in which professionalism could emerge.

Wright was more a roaming hired gun than a true professional; there was no real institutional structure within which he could work, and he could not escape the need for the patronage of the wealthy. Frederic Madden cannot be said, either, to have been the first professional in Middle English, because although his editorial work was closely tied to his curating of the British Museum's manuscripts, he was not actually employed to be a scholar of Middle English. His laborious transcription of the two manuscripts of the *Brut* went on for many years in the evening hours after his day's work. Madden undoubtedly had the learning and the attitude to be a professional, but conditions were still not quite right for him to be able to take on such a role.

Because of comparative philology, English scholars were belatedly realizing that if they did not take charge of Old English, the Germans and Danes would. It was an accident that Thorpe saw Grundtvig's prospectus for a Danish initiative in the editing of Anglo-Saxon texts at the printers and was able to preempt Grundtvig. The hasty organization by the Society of Antiquaries of an English program for publication saw the reclamation of Anglo-Saxon. Anglo-Saxon studies therefore took on national importance in the nineteenth century, just as it had done in the sixteenth century.[48]

No one had such concerns for Middle English. Later, the fear that Continental Europeans would do more and better work on Middle English than would English scholars was used as a spur to reluctant editors and readers, but Middle English, unlike Anglo-Saxon in the 1830s, did not have a dormant institutional apparatus at Oxford and Cambridge that could be jolted into wakefulness. By mid-century, Middle English had not much more than the Camden Society and London's Philological Society, founded in 1842, to give it life. The Philological Society always combined the academic with the dilettante, and allowed the coexistence of a range of different competencies. Madden, the great scholar of Middle English in the middle third of the century, is an example of an increasingly uneasy alliance between the discipline's two facets as a privatized technology of the self and its emergent national importance.

PART II

⁜

Nationalism and
the Selling of Middle English

✧

"The Deadly Poison of Democracy"

Frederic Madden, Scholar-Knight

1839

These three stories of chivalrous violence arose from a period of a few months in England in 1839.

In that year "a rather ominous matter," as Thomas Carlyle understatedly called it, seemed to threaten social order.[1] In July, this "matter"—the condition of the working class in England—violently manifested itself in a clash between protesters and police in Birmingham. The *Gentleman's Magazine*, that guardian of correct taste and genteel behavior, recorded "[t]he daring and outrageous manner in which those deluded men calling themselves Chartists, have for some time past conducted themselves at *Birmingham*, in breach of the peace and in defiance of the law," and related that sixty London policemen had been sent to Birmingham by rail on 4 July to quell the threat.[2] There, in an area known as the Bull Ring, they confronted two thousand Chartists:

> On the police desiring the mob to disperse, they refused, and a dreadful conflict ensued. In the affray, many of the Chartists suffered severely. Nor did the police escape considerable injury. One of them was stabbed in the abdomen by a dagger, and another was wounded badly under the ribs, apparently by a similar weapon. In about three quarters of an hour after the conflict began, some troops of cavalry arrived, and on their appearance the Bull-ring was instantly abandoned by the rioters. (192)

Late in the following month, around one hundred thousand people converged on a castle in Ayrshire. Many of them traveled on the new railway line to Liverpool, which had proved so convenient to the London police a few weeks earlier, before transferring to one of two recently commissioned iron steamboats to Ardrossan and completing the journey with a further rail trip.[3] The modernity of their travel contrasted with its purpose, for these people were traveling to a medieval tournament at Eglinton Castle. There would be a procession with a Queen of Beauty at its head, a jester, a feast with dancing afterward (for select guests), and, as the main business of the day, jousting by fully armed knights on horseback and later a melee. Enough of the visitors also expected the torrential rain that all but destroyed the event on its first day for "the feudal appearance of the display," as the *Gentleman's Magazine* put it, to be "sadly marred by thousands of umbrellas."[4] Although rescheduled to a later, drier day, when it went ahead with some success, the tournament entered popular memory as a rained-out disaster, one of its abiding images, thanks to the caricaturists of the day, being of mounted knights protecting their armor with umbrellas.[5]

The satire was largely politically motivated. The ridiculing of the event indicated not a predisposition against romance as such, but a satire of a particular appropriation of it. The Eglinton Tournament was the creation of young Tories. Lord Eglinton, who owned the castle and largely created the event, was strongly influenced by Disraeli and the Young Englanders, and one of the clear impulses for the staging of the event was the indignation of young Tory nobles at the handling of Victoria's coronation by a straitened Whig government the year before, when some of the more costly traditions of coronation had been abandoned.[6] The tournament was in part inspired by a desire to show the shabbily unchivalrous Whigs how ceremony was done, and admission was open only to political sympathizers. Tickets were free but made available to applicants on the basis of declared political affiliation. Existing letters of application show that this was well understood by the public; one applicant presented his political credentials to the tournament organizers by telling them that he and his wife, armed respectively with a sword and a candlestick, "nearly killed a Radical at the rising in 1819 and on that occasion it was the public opinion that my wife ought to have had a pension."[7]

About seven weeks after the tournament, another knight traveled north on an important quest. Battling by turns wild men of the forest, giants, serpents, and wolves, this knight journeyed to his rendezvous at the Green Chapel in October 1839 — at least as far as modern readers were concerned — when Sir Frederic Madden, keeper of the manuscripts in the British Museum, published the first edition of *Sir Gawain and the Green Knight* in his anthology of Arthurian romances and ballads, *Syr Gawayne: A Collection of Ancient Romance-Poems*, published by the Bannatyne Club.[8] In this volume, the club's coterie of one hundred aristocratic and upper-middle-class men could read for the first time about the appearance in Arthur's court of a threatening and monstrous Green Knight, about Sir Gawain's subsequent quest to the Green Chapel as representative of Arthurian chivalry in fulfillment of his bargain with the Green Knight, and his successful endurance of the challenge he met there.

Like the London policemen and the Tory knights, Sir Gawain discovered that leaving the capital and going north on chivalric business can be a dangerous occupation. Each of these narratives involves some form of perceived threat to traditional values, as they are represented in metropolitan culture, and in each case, the threat is dealt with by armed, officialized violence, either in its literal form or acted out in a ritualized version. So the police are sent north to suppress the working-class insurgency; a band of knights goes north to celebrate romantic conservative traditionalism, and a solitary knight goes north (Madden thought his destination to be in Cumberland) from the capital, the center of civilized, chivalrous values, to meet the monstrous force that has threatened its reputation.

Each text, to a greater or lesser degree, invites a reading as romance, and the success or failure of the central enterprise in each depends to a large extent on how like a romance it is perceived to be. The knights at Eglinton thought they were reenacting romance, particularly as they understood it from Scott's *Ivanhoe*; Arthur's court vindicates Gawain, seeing his quest as properly completed and fulfilling the ameliorative function characteristic of romance; in the *Gentleman's Magazine* account of the Bull Ring riot, the police fulfill the role of romance knights, keeping the peace disturbed by the "deluded" and by implication monstrous Chartists. In each case, the questing knights overcome initial difficulties to prevail in their chivalric mission.

The more like a romance the narrative shape of the story is, the more a represented traditional authority—the Arthurian court, the police and the forces of order they represent—is vindicated. Possible counterreadings of each text, and consequently of the authority depicted in them, tend to come with a generic reevaluation. The Eglinton Tournament's detractors, to extract political satire from the event, rewrote it as farce. Sir Gawain, shamed by what he perceives to be his failure, is less confident of the successful completion of his quest than are the courtiers, and so is far less certain that he has fulfilled the generic requirements of romance, a doubt that creates one of the poem's interpretative cruxes.[9] What the *Gentleman's Magazine* does not say in its characterization of the "daring and outrageous" Chartists is that the Bull Ring riots were provoked by police attacks on what had hitherto been peaceful demonstrations.[10]

The apparently coincidental set of resonances, echoes, and near allegories between such texts results from a broader, more determinate structure within which this collocation of events was no coincidence at all. As we have seen, the genre of romance dominated in the study of Middle English texts well into the nineteenth century. Even when other texts gradually became available, medieval romance and its representation of chivalry continued to provide a model, as Mark Girouard has shown, for social behavior; chivalry was a code of behavior for gentlemen, and romance was its handbook.[11] Men from the middle class who wanted to distance themselves from their own involvement in trade or, like Scott, translate themselves into pseudoaristocrats, tended to associate themselves with romance. Aristocrats who wanted to dignify their often recent titles with the overtones of tradition and aristocratic triumphalism that medieval literature could bring often associated themselves with romance and gave patronage to those who edited it for them.

The dominance of the genre of romance in the study of Middle English led, as John Ganim puts it, to the Middle Ages themselves being envisioned as a romance; it is a genre that, "defined as escapist and utopian, is emplaced as the stereotypical genre of the Middle Ages."[12] Although it did not close down the possibilities for radical appropriations of medievalism, the adoption of the Middle Ages as romance left a conservative legacy for Middle English in the early nineteenth century. The Middle Ages offered a softened, humanized hierarchical system, one in which everyone—unlike the Chartists—knew his place.[13] Feudalism was a more "natural" version of the class system; for Carlyle, because it preceded the cash nexus, medieval feudalism ensured a more symbiotic relationship between upper and lower classes, in which aristocrats were not just "governors" but "guides of the Lower Classes."[14]

Frederic Madden was the most learned Middle English scholar up to his time, and he helped put the discipline on its modern footing through such editions as *Syr Gawayne*. But he remained in many ways part of the conservative formation of medieval studies from which, as was seen in the previous chapter, his work first emerged. He was an implacable opponent of anything hinting of radicalism and was naturally opposed to Chartism. In May 1839, his friend the bibliophile Sir Thomas Phillipps wrote to him to warn him to get "the most precious" manuscripts of the British Museum together to be carried off in the event of a Chartist attack on the Museum.[15] A belief in the likelihood of such attack in 1839 could hardly have directly influenced Madden in an edition he had by then been working on for several years, but it is nevertheless striking that fears of violent attack on the center of culture by a monstrous force that does not know its place are found both in the romance and in the editor's immediate political context. The point is not that Madden made a choice in the direction of a conservative political allegory, but that, having been one of the first to realize exactly what the contents of MS Cotton Nero A.x were, he chose to edit not *Pearl, Patience,* or *Cleanness,* but *Sir Gawain and the Green Knight.* It was *Sir Gawain and the Green Knight* that spoke most directly to such an editor as Madden and to his probable readers, and it was most likely to be attractive to the club through which he published it. In its public role, the romance was implicitly opposed to political events inimical to the conservative elite.

In a more private role, it was also the text most likely to assist Madden's personal advancement. In 1837, while he was preparing *Syr Gawayne,* Madden was appointed to a rather curious group known as the Gentlemen of the Privy Chamber. Madden's main role, in the year following his appointment, was to assist in the production of a memorial that the Gentlemen proposed to present to the new queen, claiming what they believed to be their ancient privileges. Their leader was a man named

Lucius Hooke Robinson, who at one meeting described the function of the group as follows:

> Although meeting together for the friendly discussion of Private Rights, and disclaiming every particle of Political motives, yet our Gentlemen could not be blind to the wickedness or turpitude of those, who would destroy every venerable Institution, or who, by open or treacherous means, would infuse the deadly poison of Democracy into the minds of a generous and unsuspecting People.[16]

In his membership of such a group as this and in his general political disposition, Madden was simply another in the line of antiquarian scholars who had come from the margins of the lower middle class and whose antiquarianism was allied with one or the other end of the political spectrum: usually conservative, as in the cases of Percy, Scott, and Thomas Warton, sometimes Jacobin, as with Ritson and Weber. The tendency of the conservative scholars to want to keep the lower classes in their place is juxtaposed with their own considerable ambitions for social mobility, which is often justified as a *return* to an (imagined) prior social elevation: hence Percy's appeal to an invented genealogy and Scott's favoring of his medieval ancestors. In Middle English editing up to the middle of the nineteenth century—not surprisingly—such social ambitions were far better served by virulent political conservatism than by Jacobinism.

Madden's romance anthology was distributed in a print run of 128 copies among like-minded gentlemen, many of whom, no doubt, did not read it. Its impact, therefore, cannot be exaggerated, nor can it be compared to a famous event attended by one hundred thousand people or a broadly supported movement of social protest. To look at it economically, the Eglinton Tournament, according to contemporary estimates, cost about £40,000.[17] The damage done in the Bull Ring rioting was estimated by the *Gentleman's Magazine* at £30,000 to £40,000. The entire costs of *Syr Gawayne*, including a bonus of £50 paid by the Bannatyne Club to Madden, were around £440.[18] But a small edition of a romance—in a disciplinary field that was gradually growing in influence—can be regarded as one of what Foucault describes as "infinitesimal mechanisms," which can be seen as having its place at the base of an ascending model that takes in much broader forms of power.[19]

Madden: Trajectory and Patronage

Madden's work provides what appears to be such a clear break with the scholarship of Percy, Warton, and Scott that a broad consensus has arisen that proposes him as having set the discipline of Middle English on its modern footing. Hans Aarsleff suggests that the study of Middle English "would have been very different without Madden's model editions and without a clear view of the historical development of the language."[20] Robert and Gretchen Ackerman state that Madden "may fairly be said to have set the canons of what we regard today as responsible editorial scholarship." The *Gawain* edition has been especially privileged, Robert Ackerman suggesting that it "stood in strong contrast to" and "left far behind" the productions of Madden's predecessors, while for A. S. G. Edwards, Madden offers what appears to be the "first wholly systematic formulation in Middle English editing" in *Syr Gawayne*, which has "the components of a genuine critical edition."[21] In this way, Madden is constructed as harbinger of modernity in Middle English studies. Yet his life, career trajectory, and use of Middle English texts reveal many backward links to an earlier scholarship.

Like Scott's, Frederic Madden's origins were humble and only on the fringes of gentility. Like both Scott and Percy, he turned away from the dominant profession of his family to pursue literary-antiquarian studies. Like Percy, he attended Oxford University, though only briefly, and he was unable, for lack of money, to complete his studies. Like both, Madden looked back beyond the reality of his immediate family to what he believed were more genteel origins. He was born in 1801 into a Portsmouth family whose principal occupation was in the military, but he showed no inclination toward this profession, turning instead to antiquarianism (*FM*, 3–4). By his late teens Madden, the youngest of four sons, was languishing in Portsmouth, without employment or prospects, his father refusing him the money that would have been needed for university (7). In his chosen field of antiquarianism, Madden had published some minor essays, but without money, he required patronage to progress beyond modest hack writing. In 1824, following the lead of a friend, Madden contacted Henry Petrie, keeper of the records in the Tower of London, seeking work as a transcriber of manuscripts for the Commission of Historical Record. After an "audition" in which Madden read a twelfth-century manuscript to Petrie's satisfaction, his application was successful (8). Madden had broken into the world of metropolitan antiquarianism, albeit in a very precarious fashion, and his lifelong engagement with manuscripts had begun. He worked for the commission for four years, laying the foundations of his great expertise as a paleographer. He also met at this time, through Petrie, many of the scholars who would become his friends: men such as Philip Bliss and Bulkeley Bandinel, the Oxford librarians; Francis Douce; and Francis Palgrave.

Madden's escape from laborious piecework into reliable employment came as a result of Middle English romance and aristocratic patronage. In August 1825, Madden discovered the early Middle English romance of *Havelok the Dane* in the Bodleian Library, a text known but thought to have been lost.[22] What followed resulted entirely from the typical antiquarian form of circulation in which a text cemented relations between scholars. Madden was only in a position to discover the romance in the first place because of the friendship with Bliss, which gave him access to the manuscript. The following year, he was credited with the discovery in J. J. Conybeare's *Illustrations of Anglo-Saxon Poetry*.[23] Madden was later encouraged to edit the work by Palgrave,[24] and then early in 1827 he offered to edit *Havelok* for Earl Spencer as a publication for the Roxburghe Club, of which Spencer was president.

It is likely that Madden had had some contact with Spencer before this, but the *Havelok* edition, which Spencer quickly accepted, secured the relationship. It was an astute choice of patron: Spencer was not only one of the foremost antiquarian aristocrats, but also, most important, a trustee of the British Museum. Madden's edition appeared in 1828 to widespread approval. It brought him many scholarly connections: Christian Molbech, librarian at the Royal Library in Copenhagen, enthusiastically reviewed the publication and remained an occasional correspondent of Madden's; N. F. S. Grundtvig, introduced by Molbech, became another correspondent and met Madden when he visited London. Another important connection was established when Sir Walter Scott wrote in praise of the edition to Spencer.

Late in the year of the publication of *Havelok*, Joseph Planta, principal librarian at the British Museum, died. Within hours of his death, Madden wrote to Spencer to notify him that he would be applying for the vacancy that would be created.[25] The following day, he wrote again to undermine the claims of another candidate, "Mr T. W. Horne . . . whom your Lordship will recollect better by his compilations of an Introduction to Bibliography, and an Introduction to the Scriptures, than by any knowledge of MSS. or even the capability of reading one."[26] Spencer replied cautiously on the following day, saying that he had written to the archbishop of Canterbury "to remind him of my former mention of you, and to state my wishes for your eventual success on this occasion." He warned, however, that there were many applications, "and as I have no other claim than the desire he knows I have for the interests of the British Museum, I am not very sanguine of success."[27]

Despite this diplomatic tone, Spencer appears to have had Madden's interests at heart. Planta's death brought about a move up the ladder for everyone: Henry Ellis succeeded to the principal librarianship, Josiah Forshall became keeper of the manuscripts, and Madden was brought in as assistant keeper to Forshall. He owed his success not so much to his undoubted suitability for the job—which, as earlier unsuccessful applications had shown, guaranteed nothing—but to the goodwill of friends like Bliss, who secured testimonials for him, and the favor of the man he would later call his "illustrious patron," Spencer,[28] which in turn owed much to the edition of *Havelok the Dane*.

Like many of his predecessors in the study of Middle English, then, Frederic Madden was a man who linked his personal fortunes to his antiquarian studies, using Middle English literature as a medium between himself and the aristocrats and antiquarians who could help him in his ambitions. He gave his own inflection to this; he was not, like Percy and Scott, a poet, able to put himself forward as a modern embodiment of the minstrel. Instead, he became the first scholar to approach something like professional status within the study of Middle English. Madden was not an academic and never completed a degree, but his career represented the partial institutionalizing of Middle English in that he attached his role as editor to a role as official custodian of literature, as keeper of the manuscripts, the position he succeeded to in 1837 when Forshall retired, in the British Museum.

The combination of these two roles was not, however, a requirement of the keeper's job. Madden acted like a leisured gentleman and man of letters — which is how he wanted to be perceived — by putting before the public his editions of medieval texts, but somewhat ironically, his editing work actually filled much of his leisure. Although Madden's career represents the bridge for Middle English out of amateurism and into professional scholarship, out of the aristocratic clubs and into official institutions, he was never able fully to professionalize himself as an editor, and remained for most of his publications dependent on one or another form of patronage. In this, as in much else, Madden's work was a contradiction, a contradiction that arose from a devotion, on the one hand, to ideals of pure scholarship that were new in medievalist-antiquarian study and, on the other, to a limiting program of literary endeavor linked to political conservatism and allied to the immediate past of medievalist antiquarianism as a means of self-shaping that circumscribed the achievement of his editions.

Editions, Politics, and Self

Madden's first major work was *Havelok*, said by the Ackermans to mark "the true beginning of FM's scholarly career" (*FM*, 11). It is a landmark edition in many ways, both in Madden's career and in the study of Middle English. The circumstances of its production helped someone who was no more than a promising young scholar to the patronage that secured his position in the museum and to a material basis for his later eminence. It was the first Roxburghe Club edition prepared by an outsider, and as such was simply in a different realm of scholarship from the club's previous productions. What it understandably lacked in philological rigor it made up for in paleographic expertise, as Walter Skeat, when he edited the text years later, would acknowledge.[29]

Havelok was printed in a run of eighty copies, which was large for the Roxburghe Club, and brought Madden one hundred pounds as editor. The title page gives the full title of *The Ancient English Romance of Havelok the Dane; Accompanied by the French Text: With an Introduction, Notes, and a Glossary*, with "Havelok the Dane" and "Roxburghe Club" highlighted in red black-letter type. Next follows, as was typical, the roll of the thirty-one club members, with Spencer set above it and the remainder in strict social hierarchy: two dukes, two earls, two viscounts; then the Honourable and Reverend G. Neville Grenville, then the baronets, including Walter Scott, and one knight, followed by the gentlemen and clergy in alphabetical order. Madden's fifty-three-page introduction follows, before the text is announced by a single page emblazoned with "Havelok" in large black-letter type. There is no dedication, but instead a paragraph of acknowledgments at the end of the introduction.

The text that follows would have been, to those who could read the signs, an announcement of editorial rigor. Madden's text of *Havelok* is printed (with a generosity that would make modern publishers jealous) on one hundred quarto pages, with line numbers and with basic textual notes thrown to the foot of each page. Manuscript folio numbers are noted, and manuscript paragraphs are noted with initial letters in large type. The text is in roman type, with modern punctuation supplied and contractions silently expanded, as in a modern edition. The letter *u* is printed for *v*, and vice versa, as in the manuscript. Following the text are two French versions of the Havelok story, one of eleven hundred lines from a manuscript in the Herald's College; the other, Gaimar's version from a British Museum manuscript, collated with two manuscripts from Durham and Lincoln. Madden thought this version to be an abridgment of the other French text. There then follow the textual notes, copiously for the English version, very briefly for the French.

Despite this general scholarliness, it is perhaps the glossary that is the great achievement of this edition. A typical entry indicates the astonishing thoroughness (for 1828) with which Madden went about this work:

AGEN, *prep.* SAX. [*on-gean*] Against, 1792. *Ageyn*, 493. 569. 2024. &c. *Ageynes*, 2153. 2270 &c. *Ayen*, 489. 1210. 2799. *Yen*, 2271. *Ageyn*, Toward, 451. 1696. 1947. Upon, on, 1809. 1828. *Ageyn him go*, 934. Opposite, by his side, so as to bear an equal weight. *Ageyn hire*, 1106. At her approach. *Ageyn the lith*, 2141. Opposed to the light, on which the light shines. V. R[obert of] Gl[oucester] R[obert de] B[runne] Chauc. Wynt. [Gawin] Doug[las' *Aeneid*]. Gl[ossary] Lynds.[30]

It has to be remembered that this was published by a club that countenanced the minimal scholarship of something like E. V. Utterson's *Chevalere Assigne* and its forty-word glossary, and that, as late as 1844, James Orchard Halliwell simply declined to do a glossary to his Camden Society edition of the Thornton romances on the grounds that many of the words appeared in other editions.[31] Even more tellingly, Madden was operating without the dictionaries a modern editor has. This glossary is not simply notable for impressive scholarship; Madden edited the romance as if he expected people to read it, and he gave them all the aid they needed to read it.

The introduction offered a discussion of *Havelok* under three heads: "The Historical and Traditional evidence on which the Story is founded," "Remarks on the originality and style of the English poem, compared with the French text, and on the period of its composition," and an "Account of the Mss." (*H,* iv). It reveals a typical thoroughness on Madden's part. Madden was a functional and plain, though very readable, writer. In all his editions, he devoted most of the space to demonstrating the literary genealogies of the text or texts at hand, drawing on his always very expansive reading. There is little literary criticism as such. Essentially, Madden follows the format that was established when Percy revised the essay on minstrels, by quoting copiously from sources, analogues, and other textual evidence and commenting on the quotations.

By far the bulk of the *Havelok* introduction is taken up with the first heading, where abundant antiquarian learning is on display. Madden began by adducing the standard raisons d'être of the study of ancient poetry: the romance's "value... as an accurate picture of the manners and customs of former times" and the fact that it "illustrate[s] the history and progress of our early poetry" (iii). To this he added a formulation not new, but newly privileged in this edition, the "Glossographical" value of the text. The glossary, Madden explained (in echo of Henry Weber), was intended as "an additional contribution towards that great desideratum A DICTIONARY OF THE OLD ENGLISH LANGUAGE" (lv). Madden privileges here a motive for the study of early texts that was to become more prominent later in the century. The literary text is treated as valuable because it is a linguistic archive. In this regard literary value is of no account at all. As literature, the text has a value entirely self-reflexive in that it illustrates the "history and progress" of poetry simply by being itself. Under the other head, the value of the text is, as ever, dependent on the degree to which it can be represented as documentary realism. Arguing this out, Madden relies on a familiar dichotomy:

> The demarcations of Fiction and History, now so rigorously observed, were at that early period unknown or neglected. The rhyming Chronicler, and the monkish Historian who wrote in prose the events of ancient times, received with the same degree of credence every circumstance handed down to them by document or tradition, and not possessing the means or the judgement to discern between truth and falsehood, admitted into the sober page of History legends founded on the wildest efforts of imagination. Hence it is, to use the language of Percy, that the historical narratives of the North so naturally assume the form of a regular Romance. (xliv)

In a whole range of romance texts, Madden considered, "real historical personages and events" could be traced, "mingled with a mass of fable and invention" (xliv). This was the way in which *Havelok* could be read, as being based on "transactions which we cannot wholly reject as fabulous" (xlv). Making a rather subtle distinction in conclusion, Madden suggested that "whether we regard the tale at present as a web of mingled truth and fiction, or as a pure creation of fancy, we must admit that for ages it was chronicled and read, and in the immediate province to which it so particularly refers, was considered quite as much intitled to belief, as any other portion of our National Annals" (xlv). This is, in effect, a point about the text's likely reception that goes beyond simple dichotomous considerations of truth and fiction.

The second heading is only briefly addressed, and its promise of literary discourse on "style" and "originality" is not, predictably, fulfilled in the terms in which it might now be understood. By "originality" Madden means not authorial innovation in language, but the question of whether all English romances before the time of Chaucer were, as Tyrwhitt, Ritson, Warton, Ellis, and Scott maintained, actually translations from earlier French romances (xlv–xlvi). Madden argued that *King Horn* could be considered entirely an English work, and that furthermore there must have been many native English writers writing in French. The French *Havelok*, he felt, "might also have been composed by a native of Britain" (xlvii).

Briefly commenting on literary style, before turning to his descriptions of the manuscripts, Madden proposed that *Havelok* was not written by someone "conversant with the Court," as poetry in English "was abandoned to the peasants" while nobles listened to lays, romances, and fabliaux (l). The poem's "greatest singularity and value," Madden suggested, might be "that it presents the only instance exstant of a Romance written for the 'comonalty,' [*sic*] exhibiting faithfully, in the vernacular dialect, the language, habits, and manners of the period" (l). "[M]ore amusing" than *Tristrem* or *King Horn*, "the Romance will bear comparison with any other composition of that age, and is, in many respects, superior to every specimen we possess prior to the time of Langland and Chaucer" (l).

Madden quoted the following lines as an example of the poet's "real poetical feeling":

The heu is swilk in here ler,
So the rose in roser,
Hwan it is fayr sprad ut newe
Ageyn the sunne, brith and lewe.

He compared them with the following lines from *The Complaint of the Black Knight* (then thought to be by Chaucer):

123

And that the flowers of mani divers hue
   Upon her stalkes *gonne for to spread*
   And for to splaye out here leves in brede
   Again the sun, gold-burned in his sphere,
   That downe to hem cast his beames clear.[32]

Madden makes no more of this comparison, and a few remarks on rhyme
and pronunciation conclude this section. As Weber had done, Madden
simply lets the resemblances resonate on the page, the positive judgment
on the author of *Havelok* flowing, of course, from the prior and uncontested (if in this case illusory) authority of Chaucer; literary value simply consists in nearness to the language of Chaucer. This method is the
limit of literary criticism anywhere in Madden's work. Although he seems
quite comfortable passing this literary judgment and arguing for the poet's
literary achievement, these remarks constitute only a few lines in an introduction of more than fifty pages in which observations on manuscripts
and sources obviously came more easily to him.

   The critical reaction to the *Havelok* edition was, for a Roxburghe book,
relatively rich. T. G. Repp, while criticizing the Roxburghe and Bannatyne
clubs, commended Madden for the care he had taken with the edition,
but regretted that he had not said enough on language (the "glossographic"
aspect of the text). This was because Repp could not allow literary value
to the romances: "It is not on account of their taste, their poetry, their
metrical, or any other beauty, that the old English or Norman romances
are particularly interesting to the scholar." Vernacular medieval literature, with the exception of Chaucer, is a poor man's classics: "Only he
who cannot read Homer, or Ariosto, or Chaucer, or Spencer, or the mas-
terpieces in the ancient northern literature, will bother himself with the
pedant's investigation, seeking for beauties where there are none or few."[33]
Others were more favourably disposed on this question. The writer in
the *Oxford Literary Gazette* almost repeated Madden's words in writing
of the poem's "value, not only in a glossographical point of view, or as
an accurate picture of the manners and customs of former times, but also
as serving in a singular manner to illustrate the history and progress of
our early poetry." This reviewer called the poem a "rustic Odyssey," ce-
menting the relation of vernacular English literature to the classics rather
more favorably than had Repp.[34]

   Like Repp, but for very different reasons, S. W. Singer argued that Madden had not done enough on language. Singer was no comparative philologist; his critique was delivered, in gentlemanly fashion, in a privately
printed pamphlet that maintained the pretense of being a letter written
to Francis Douce. Its criticisms of the glossary to *Havelok* are often laugh-
ably wide of the mark, and Madden had little trouble disposing of them
in a "letter" addressed to Petrie, in reality his own privately printed pamphlet, fifty-seven copies of which he distributed among friends.[35]

A more significant response came in 1833, in an article in the Cambridge publication, *The Philological Museum*. The author noted that Madden was to edit the *Brut* of Laʒamon for the Society of Antiquaries, and regretted "that some Saxon scholar" could not be found to do it. Madden, the writer continued, was "a laborious and praiseworthy enquirer into the middle period of our language" but no Anglo-Saxon expert, as several lexical errors made in the notes to *Havelok* showed.[36] The article in which this critique appeared was uncompromisingly titled "On English Praeterites," and it was signed I. M. K. This was John Mitchell Kemble, the formidable philologist and Anglo-Saxonist. Madden, according to the Ackermans, took more notice of these brief remarks than of Singer's whole document, and went on "to improve his knowledge of English philology" as a result (*FM*, 12). The contrast between Singer's obliquely genteel approach and Kemble's no- nonsense philological critique, buried as it was among Germanic verb paradigms, could hardly be more stark.

Perhaps the most personally gratifying remarks on *Havelok* for Madden were those of Scott, addressed not to Madden but in a letter (a genuine one) to Spencer himself. He "speaks of it in a way so flattering to myself," Madden wrote to Philip Bliss, "that I scarcely can repeat his words, but among his other praises he writes that 'few Antiquarian works have been so accurately & so rationally edited,' & is very warm in his approbation of the Glossary."[37] Such an endorsement, made direct to the president of the Roxburghe Club and Museum Trustee, was as useful as any correction of a philological point. Madden was quick to propose to Scott, later in the same year, that the Bannatyne Club take on *Syr Gawayne*. But that much-delayed project was not to be Madden's next edition. The years 1830–32 were particularly busy for Madden. He was now established in the museum and, on the basis of *Havelok* and his journal articles, had become a scholar and editor of note; he appears also to have thrown himself into work after the death of his first wife early in 1830.

This was also the period of a sudden national interest in Anglo-Saxon texts and the beginning, Aarsleff suggests, of the new philology in England. In 1830, the Danish Anglo-Saxonist Grundtvig published his prospectus for the publication of Anglo-Saxon texts. When English scholars realized that a foreigner was preparing to purloin their literary heritage (in which, hitherto, they had shown little interest), they acted rapidly in response. A committee of the Society of Antiquaries began commissioning rival publications, effectively hijacking Grundtvig's program, and the Dane retired from the field.[38] Madden was commissioned at this time to edit the two texts of Laʒamon's *Brut*—still considered principally a "Saxon" work—a task that would occupy him for the next sixteen years. In the meantime, he also accepted the commission for editing the romance of *William and the Werwolf* (now known under the title Skeat gave it, *William of Palerne*). This was another Roxburghe edition, this time under the patronage of John Campbell, earl of Cawdor; it appeared in 1832 and offers a marked contrast to *Havelok*.

In the standard format, the book opens with an ornate title page, which is followed by a dedication from Cawdor to the president and members of the Roxburghe Club; the list of club members follows, before Madden's introduction. This introduction consists of seventeen pages of literary history, which first deals with the reception of the romance since its first public notice in 1781 and then turns to the story itself, the unique manuscript, analogues, and possible sources. After the length and thoroughness of the *Havelok* introduction, this introduction appears a little functional, everything in it somewhat reduced. The outlines are very recognizable: a framework of literary history derived from wide reading, illustrated by many footnotes, with the typical appeals to linguistic and literary value. As in *Havelok*, Madden interrupts the flow of historical learning only momentarily to suggest that of the writer's "ability as a poet we ought on the whole to form a favorable judgment," despite the constraints of the meter on his poetry. Madden quotes some verses "which would seem to mark the author capable of better things" — as ever, the text would have been good literature if only it had been something else.[39]

At somewhat greater length, Madden argues for the value of this text as "the earliest specimen of unrimed alliterative metre yet discovered" (xiv). Because of this romance, Madden continued, it was now possible to "trace the English language step by step from the year 1300, since the writings of Robert of Gloucester, Robert of Brunne, Robert Davies, William of Shoreham, Robert Rolle, and Laurence Minot, lead us up to the precise period when our poem was composed, and which forms the connecting link with Langland and the subsequent writers" (xiv–xv).

The glossary, too, is sufficient, without approaching the thoroughness of *Havelok*. Parts of speech are given, but not etymologies; one-word glosses are common. But the fundamental differences between *William* and *Havelok* are found elsewhere in this edition, and may help to explain Madden's apparent retreat from the standards set in 1828. In the first place, Earl Cawdor foisted on him a very unscholarly device, in two letters addressed to Cawdor himself, titled "On Werewolves." The enchanted werewolf of the *William* story presents, of course, the old problem for the reader of romance: the stubborn unwillingness of the medieval writer to stay with documentary realism. The letters were written by Algernon Herbert, a minor antiquary whose *DNB* entry records him as "the author of some remarkable works replete with abstruse learning," which were, "however, discursive, and his arguments...inconclusive."[40] Herbert did not try to explain away the werewolf, but delved into the recurrence of this creature in various literary texts and in folklore. It is hard to imagine Madden's being very pleased with the presence of this arcane learning in his text, particularly as, at forty-five pages and in a larger typeface than Madden's introduction, the letters are clearly privileged over the scholarly work.

Even worse, from Madden's point of view, must have been Herbert's conclusion that "werewolf" was likely to mean not "man-wolf" but "war-wolf."[41] Madden had clearly told Cawdor at some point during the editing that he disagreed with this etymology as provided in the first letter. This only had the effect of provoking the second letter, in which Herbert affirmed that he had given Madden's objection further consideration, "and, after several times doubting, have satisfied myself that it was not an incorrect opinion" (25). Madden had the last word: in the glossary, completed after the writing of the letters, he offered a mini-essay on the word "werewolf" in refutation of the contentions of A. H.

Most striking of all in this odd edition is the text itself, a starkly rigorous presentation of the manuscript in type facsimile rather than roman type. The text is unemended and all manuscript contractions are faithfully reprinted, with only a key at the beginning for guidance. There are no line numbers, though manuscript folio numbers are provided; there are no explanatory notes, and seven pages of textual notes provide readings where there are obvious errors in the text. Despite its obvious attempt to imitate a manuscript, the immediate effect of this edition is to resemble a black-letter print, which renders the exercise doubly anachronistic. It must have been a challenge to most of its readership of thirty-one.

William and the Werwolf represents an odd confluence of several different scholarly-antiquarian impulses, at the most crucial period of the century in the study of medieval literature. By printing in "saxon" rather than roman type, Madden was going against what would become the dominant trend of the new philologists, who introduced the practice of using roman type and whose work Madden himself would soon defend in public. But in producing the text in the way he did, Madden was giving the highest expression of the utopics of editing he advanced again and again in his published work throughout his career. Accurate representation of the manuscript is a fanatical theme of Madden's, and he constantly criticises his predecessors for not having transcribed accurately. Yet this produces a contradiction, for Madden also believed that the point of producing medieval literature was to make it available not only to such a coterie as the Roxburghe Club, but also to the general public. This was a kind of duty owed by the gentleman to the public. The rigorous edition of *William*, with its contractions and Saxon characters, hardly accorded with this aim.

William and the Werwolf was also contradictory in combining the latest scholarship of a no-nonsense prophilologist with the impressionistic Horne Tookery of Algernon Herbert. Bizarrely, a book about a werewolf exhibits throughout an inability on the part of the two people who compiled it to agree on what the very word means. In *Havelok*, Madden only had to deal with such difficulties in the form of critique from outsiders; in *William*, he had to put up with it in the work itself. For these reasons, which probably derived from a more active interference by the work's patron than Spencer had exercised, it seems likely that Madden devoted less industry to *William*, and this is reflected in the final product. Born from the conflicting impulses of aristocratic patronage, club publishing, scholarly editing, and antiquarian speculation, *William* is something of a werewolf itself, doomed, as part scholarly work, part coffee-table book, to be a hybrid creature.[42]

Although Madden brought to these works new standards of accuracy in transcribing, he had little to say about editing or textual criticism in them. Through the 1830s, he labored on what was to become his best-known work, the anthology of ballads and romances that would contain *Sir Gawain and the Green Knight*, and in this work, he elevated his concern with accuracy into a credo. "The poems here taken from original manuscripts," he wrote, "are printed with a scrupulous regard to accuracy, and the abbreviations left as written, but, for the convenience of the reader, a list of these is annexed, and the words are written at length in the Glossary and Notes."[43] All the texts in *Syr Gawayne* are, in fact, more austerely representative of their manuscript origins than modern standards would demand. Although roman type was used rather than black letter, the use of scribal forms potentially made reading a text in this collection a denser form of historical work than the easier modern edition, as the reader shuttled between the list of medieval contractions and the text itself. Furthermore, the actual appearance on the page is an attempt to represent that in the manuscript. In *Sir Gawain*, the metrical feature of the bob and wheel at the end of each stanza is printed as it appears in the manuscript (with the bob set to the right and separated from the main text by a double vertical line), rather than clearly delineated as in modern editions. Emendations are sparing, and all manuscript readings are thrown to notes at the foot of the page. The text is, then, a type facsimile, as A. S. G. Edwards notes, "the ultimate solution before the age of photography" to the problem of presenting the text exactly as it is in the manuscript.[44]

In his statement on editing, Madden provides a rationale for editing in Middle English, as Edwards noted, and furthermore he contrasts what he is doing with his significant predecessors. As a theoretical position, though, there is nothing new here. Accurate representation of manuscript originals had been an *issue* in Middle English editing from the moment Ritson first criticized Warton and Percy, if not before; the mere fact that someone had now appeared who could, more or less, represent the manuscripts accurately (in the way we now view accuracy) does not mean that a point of origin can be found in which a radical break with the

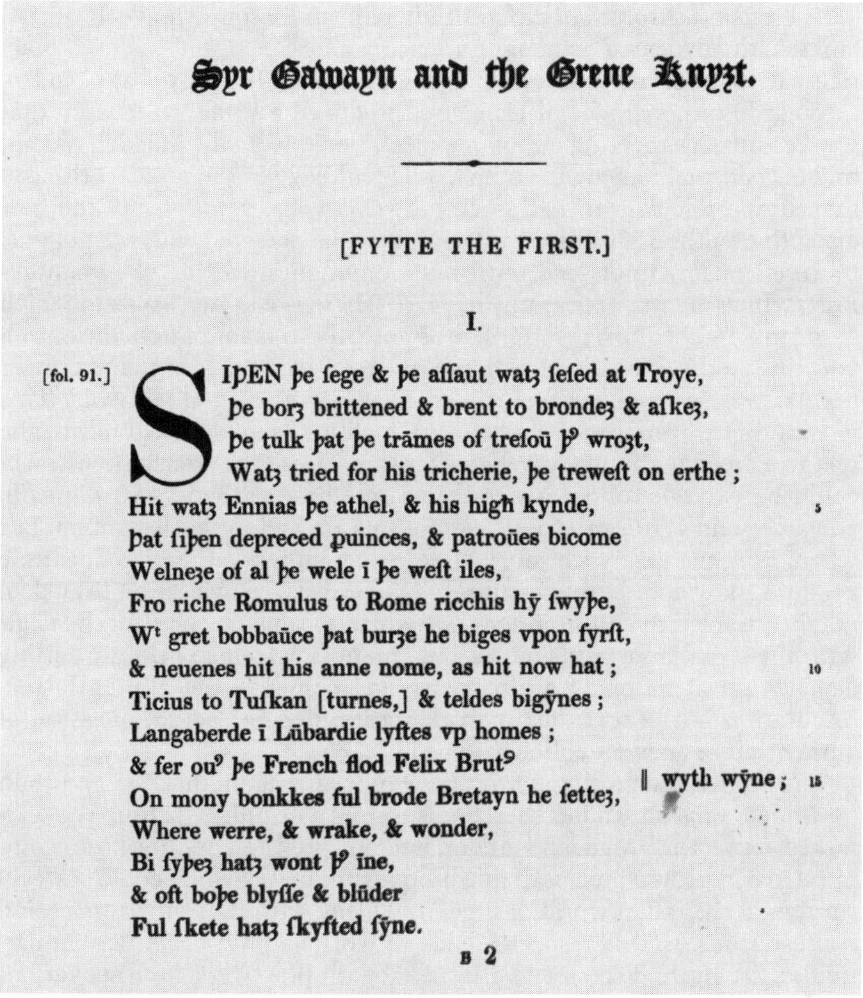

𝕾𝔂𝔯 𝔊𝔞𝔴𝔞𝔶𝔫 𝔞𝔫𝔡 𝔱𝔥𝔢 𝔊𝔯𝔢𝔫𝔢 𝕶𝔫𝔶𝔷𝔱.

[FYTTE THE FIRST.]

I.

[fol. 91.]

S IÞEN þe fege & þe affaut watȝ fefed at Troye,
þe borȝ brittened & brent to brondeȝ & afkeȝ,
þe tulk þat þe trãmes of trefoũ ſ⁹ wroȝt,
Watȝ tried for his tricherie, þe treweft on erthe ;
Hit watȝ Ennias þe athel, & his higñ kynde,   5
Þat fiþen depreced puinces, & patroũes bicome
Welneȝe of al þe wele ĩ þe weft iles,
Fro riche Romulus to Rome ricchis hỹ fwyþe,
Wᵗ gret bobbaũce þat burȝe he biges vpon fyrft,
& neuenes hit his anne nome, as hit now hat ;   10
Ticius to Tufkan [turnes,] & teldes bigỹnes ;
Langaberde ĩ Lũbardie lyftes vp homes ;
& fer oũ⁹ þe French flod Felix Brut⁹
On mony bonkkes ful brode Bretayn he fetteȝ,   ‖ wyth wỹne ;   15
Where werre, & wrake, & wonder,
Bi fyþeȝ hatȝ wont ſ⁹ ĩne,
& oft boþe blyffe & blũder
Ful fkete hatȝ fkyfted fỹne.

B 2

Figure 3. A founding moment in Middle English studies? The opening page of *Sir Gawayn and the Grene Knyȝt* in Sir Frederic Madden's famous edition, *Syr Gawayne: A Collection of Ancient Romance-Poems* (1839). By permission of the State Library of Victoria.

past had taken place. Madden's method is obviously *defined* by that of his predecessors, in that he does what he thinks they should have been doing all along: "The truth is, that editors of our old poetry have, with few exceptions, paid too little attention to the system of writing used by the early scribes, and the consequence is, that but a small portion of all that has been published will bear collation with the originals. I say this *advisedly*, having myself compared most of the poems edited by Ritson, Pinkerton, Weber, Percy, Ellis, Hartshorne, and others [i.e., with the manuscripts]. It is time this were remedied" (*SG*, xlv).

There is no *theoretical* difference here from Ritson, who with similar fanaticism advocated accuracy in editing and contrasted his own practice with that of his predecessors. The difference is solely that Madden, through his paleographical expertise, produced a level of accuracy that we recognize as meeting our own expectations. Notably, Madden did not find his editorial remedy in comparative philology or the textual criticism that grew up within it. Although he was a vocal supporter of the new discipline in the 1830s, little trace of it can be detected in *Syr Gawayne.* Its true impact is not seen until his monumental edition of Laȝamon's *Brut,* which did not appear until 1847.[45] There is a strong sense in which Madden's 1839 editorial statement is actually in favor of *non*editing, advocating a pure or nearly pure homology between manuscript and printed text (as was seen, in a different way, in *William and the Werwolf*). This is a kind of editorial utopianism, in which Madden wants to *return* the text to a preeditorial purity. What is far from clear is how such utopianism could be extended more generally as an editorial theory. *Sir Gawain, Havelok,* and *William of Palerne* are unique and authorless texts. But when, as is the case with most Middle English texts, there are multiple versions, how could utopian editing choose between variants? (Madden, notably, tended to edit unique texts; when he took on the *Brut,* he dealt with the two manuscripts by printing them side by side.) Utopic editing depends on a notion of authenticity and demands the authentic representation of the text, but it works best when the actual question of authenticity is never explicitly raised.

The modern enshrining of *Syr Gawayne* and its methods as an origin for Middle English studies therefore suggests a nostalgia, behind the warranted respect for Madden's undoubted editorial talents, for an uncomplicated accuracy, a prelapsarian editorial simplicity, which could scarcely survive in the fallen world of modern editing with its controversies and contestations. In this respect Madden's work and *Syr Gawayne,* in particular, are quite disconnected from modern practice. The discovery of an origin dehistoricizes that origin precisely at the moment it is nominated, for it is then that the historical origin becomes, in effect, the furthest point to which modernity can be stretched back in time. To say that *Syr Gawayne* is the origin of Middle English studies is simply to say that it is modern, that it did then what we do now. But this kind of origin relies heavily on a perception of identity that excludes difference. When Madden and *Syr Gawayne* become the moment of the inception of modern Middle English editing, an identification occurs because modern scholars are happy to adopt the familiar aspects of Madden for themselves: his accuracy, his utopic desire to represent the original, unadulterated manuscript. Correspondingly, they have to ignore other aspects of Madden's work in which identity with modern practice is not so readily observable. Scholars have focused on Madden's edited *texts,* but far too little on the material that surrounds them, where many ideas can be found that are very much at odds with modern scholarship.

There is in fact more in Madden's scholarship that forms a *link* with that of his predecessors than a break from it. Viewed in relation to the overall scholarship in *Syr Gawayne,* the editorial credo is a very small and arguably insignificant part, almost the last thing Madden wrote in an introduction that runs to more than forty-five pages. In that introduction and in other scholarly material, there is a great deal that sits very uneasily with a notion of Madden as forerunner of contemporary Middle English studies. In the first place, it is worth noting that *Syr Gawayne* does not equal *Sir Gawain;* unlike every other edition Madden produced, this work was designed from the outset as an anthology, not as an edition of a single text. Anthologies claim a different kind of authority for their editors from that which derives from a single-text edition; the editor of *Syr Gawayne* set himself up as an expert, not in Middle English literature specifically, but in everything relating to "that celebrated knight," Sir Gawayne. *Syr Gawayne* is Madden's claim on a whole genre, and in this respect it looks back to Percy's *Reliques of Ancient English Poetry,* Pinkerton's *Ancient Scotish Poems,* Scott's *Minstrelsy of the Scottish Border,* and Ritson's *Ancient Engleish Metrical Romanceës.*

More tellingly, there is the simple fact that as far as Madden was concerned, *Sir Gawain and the Green Knight* and the other poems in the collection were not Middle English. This term, although available in the work of Jacob Grimm, was still not part of the conceptual apparatus of English scholars in the 1830s, and it appears nowhere in *Syr Gawayne.* The subtitle of the anthology, "A Collection of *Ancient* Romance-Poems," is interesting in this respect. Although Madden dated *Sir Gawain* quite accurately, the imprecise "ancient" is reminiscent, again, of the titles of Percy's, Pinkerton's, and Ritson's collections. Modern scholars tend not to refer to perhaps the single most remarkable thing about *Syr Gawayne,* which is that far from claiming them for the nascent study of Middle English, Madden announced many of the poems to be Scottish, including *Sir Gawain and the Green Knight* itself. On the basis of the North-West Midlands dialect in which it is written, Madden stated that MS Cotton Nero A.x is one of "the oldest manuscripts containing *genuine* Scotish poetry" (*SG,* 303). He did not quite suggest that the manuscript was Scottish, but proposed that the poems in it had originally been composed in Scotland, then transmitted to and written down in the south: "There is sufficient internal evidence of their being *Northern,* although the manuscript containing them appears to have been written by a scribe of the midland counties, which will account for the introduction of forms differing from those used by writers beyond the Tweed" (301). This is precisely the argument made by Scott for *Sir Tristrem* and by Laing for other poems. As they did, Madden produces an ur-poem that is nowhere to be seen, but which has precisely describable characteristics, though only from observation of a text that is not that poem.[46]

Havelok had launched Madden's career; *Syr Gawayne* capped it and celebrated it. When he had gained the assistant keeper's position, with the help of Spencer and the *Havelok* edition, Madden set about consolidating his social position. Once more with the help of Spencer, and many others, Madden sought a knighthood and became a Knight of the Hanoverian Guelphic Order in 1833 (*FM*, 16). He later set about obtaining a grant of arms (and dropped the *k* from the end of his Christian name). The Frederick Madden, Esq., who had edited *Havelok* became the Sir Frederic Madden who edited *Syr Gawayne*, which he worked at intermittently throughout this period of consolidation. The resultant work can be seen as a celebration of the position, both scholarly and social, for which Madden had worked so hard during the decade since he had discovered *Sir Gawain and the Green Knight*. *Syr Gawayne* is a work that focuses more than any other he edited on chivalry and deeds of knighthood. The structural core of the anthology is the figure of Gawain, and the introduction is principally an explication not of the anthologized poems themselves, about which Madden says very little, but of Gawain and his character. Madden writes as if at some level he believed in the reality of his central figure, whom he describes as if he were a real person, a single unified figure whose life can be traced "from his birth to his burial-place" (xxvi).

To maintain this idea, Madden continued to read medieval texts as documentary realism, valuable for the way they revealed "details of the manners and customs of our ancestors which were otherwise unobtainable," as Arthur Johnston has put it.[47] Madden found *Sir Gawain and the Green Knight*, with its detailed descriptive passages, congenial material for such a mimetic reading. The Christmas revels at Hautdesert, for example, are an indication "that the feasting and jollities of that season were kept up in the fourteenth century in Scotland in a manner not to be excelled by English pageantry" (310). Gawain's northward journey— so often the locus of discussions of realism in the poem—is traced carefully, and a suggested location is given for the Green Chapel (320–21). Items of dress also provoke comment: the headdress of Bertilak's lady is seen as an accurate detail of "the female coiffure in the reigns of Richard the Second and Henry the Fourth" (324).

Such readings are, of course, circular. The stanzas in which the arming of Gawain is described, for example, are "valuable for the minute description they contain of the mode of completely arming a knight at the close of the fourteenth century" (314). Madden goes on to explain the procedure of arming, meticulously describing the process just as it is seen in *Sir Gawain* and providing in brackets the poem's technical words for the different pieces of armor. Although Madden refers the reader to a contemporary text on armor, the note exemplifies the circular reasoning of the reading for realism: the arming scene in *Sir Gawain* shows us how a knight was armed, and we can tell it is right because we know how knights were armed from reading the scene in *Sir Gawain*.

Reading from such a perspective, logically there can only be one Gawain, and that Gawain must therefore have a consistent character. Variance in that character, in texts, is therefore the result of authorial interference. Madden's task is to guide us through "the history, character, and exploits assigned to our Hero Syr Gawayne" (xi), restoring the true characteristics of the "real" Gawain. Madden's treatment of Gawain as character is where his practices of editing can be linked to his practices of the self. In making his offering, Madden completely reinvented the figure of Gawain for his era, rehabilitating the figure known to most English readers in the 1830s from the rather tarnished version given by Malory. Madden went to less well-known French sources in which Gawain was represented in a more courtly role. While it was certainly permissible to Madden that Gawain should "have been famed more for his various intrigues than his constancy" and be known for "his influence with the fair sex" (xxxiii)—Madden had taken his turn at trying to be a Regency-style rake—he objected to those texts that presented Gawain almost as a villain. He dismissed those writers who "calumniate" Gawain (xxviii), particularly Malory, in whose work Gawain's character is "traduced, and his history misrepresented" (xxix). Madden focused instead on the French romances in which Gawain's "character for valor and courtesy re-appears in its original lustre" (xxx).[48]

Gawain, in short, is a gentleman. The *Gawayne* anthology was a canon of Gawain stories, together with an authorized biography, correcting impressions of the knight's villainy and offering him to other gentlemen as an English hero, the major Arthurian figure, Madden proposes, before he was superseded by Lancelot and Tristram in later texts (cf. xxvii). Madden's characteristic formula for Gawain is "our hero," which might suggest a nationalist strain in Madden's writing through a reclamation of the knight so well known to *French* romance in the newly discovered British romance. But nationalism is not a strong theme in Madden's scholarship. Madden was of course explicitly addressing a much narrower community in the one hundred gentlemen and aristocrats whom he knew to be his direct readership, the latter-day chivalrous men to whom he offered his narratives of medieval chivalry and deeds of knighthood, and to whom Gawain was being offered as "our" hero.

Just as Gawain was a gentleman, so too was Madden a knight. He was literally so, of course, but there is also a metaphorical dimension in which Madden is the questing hero in pursuit of the truth about Gawain's character. Like Gawain, Madden had to venture into exotic territory in order to restore the knight's reputation, just as Gawain had to restore that of the Arthurian court. There is, then, more than mere contiguity in the fact that Sir Gawain, like conservative gentlemen in the late 1830s, knew what to do with monstrous threats that came from the north. It was only in the romance text, rather than the religious poetry of Cotton Nero A.x, that Madden could find a narrative for his times and his class. In a very localized and specific form of work on the self by a relatively obscure scholar, there is nevertheless a capillary point of a power that was ultimately contested at a level that comprehended the political and social conduct of a nation.[49]

Madden was undoubtedly the outstanding figure in Middle English in this period, and like many such figures, he embodied contradictions. His practices as an editor look forward to the coming professionalism, but also back to romanticizing dilettantism. If we must have origins for modern Middle English studies, then we have to accept that while we take much from Madden, the lineage of our current practices goes back to the often mediocre scholarship of such men as Thomas Wright, James Orchard Halliwell, John Robson, and James Morton. Their Camden Society editions — Halliwell's Thornton romances, Morton's *Ancrene Riwle* (which should be exempted from the charge of mediocrity), Robson's metrical romances, Wright's *Richard the Redeless* and *Political Songs* — produced in the period 1838–52, represent the kind of scholarship that would be taken up by the EETS.[50] These editors had their faults, but the format for scholarship they pioneered is the one that persists today. "Bad" scholarship is not excluded from originary status by its "badness." The difference between these scholars and Madden is that they were not romanticizing a past in order to fashion their present.

1848

In London in November 1847, Marx and Engels addressed a meeting of the Fraternal Democrats, who were allied with the Chartists. Speaking after Marx, Engels said that he was "of the opinion that the first decisive blow from which the victory of democracy, the liberation of all European countries will ensue, will be delivered by the English Chartists."[51] Early the following year, as revolutions broke out across Europe and Britain awaited the revolt Engels predicted, Queen Victoria was sent to the Isle of Wight and the duke of Wellington was put in charge of the forces that would protect London from insurgency. Thousands of men were sworn in as "special constables," an ad hoc force with ill-defined duties that would suppress the coming revolution. Frederic Madden, though forty-seven years old and of sedentary lifestyle, was quick to join up. His experiences that year, predictably, hardened his hatred of democracy.

By this time, Madden's career had completely stalled. His monumental edition of Laȝamon's *Brut*, one of the great editions of the nineteenth century, had at last appeared. Another monument, the edition of Wycliffe's writings begun in collaboration with Forshall, would appear in

1850. But both of these were essentially projects of the early 1830s that had dragged into the next decade. The antiquarian ardor Madden expresses in his diary and letters of the 1830s is gone by the late 1840s, and he would henceforth edit principally for money. He was also stuck in the keeper's position, passed over for promotion to the principal librarianship when Henry Ellis retired, which worsened his famously sour relationship with the man who did succeed, Antonio Panizzi. Madden's letters of the 1850s and '60s often exhibit bitterness directed at the museum and the work of the younger, emerging scholars. By 1848, Madden's career had taken him across an epistemic shift in scholarship. Far from pointing the way to the postphilological era and the EETS, Madden was clearly left behind by the scholarship that emerged from the new philological ascendancy of the 1840s. It is not a question of Madden's having rejected the new theoretical approach, for he was an early sympathizer, but he did lack the ability to remake himself as the new sort of scholar. The fact that Madden's *Havelok, William and the Werwolf,* and *Sir Gawain* were soon reedited by the EETS could be seen as signaling the respect of the new generation for his work. But equally well, as I will argue in the following chapter, they exhibit a concern to capitalize on Madden's excellent texts by completely replacing everything he said about them in his introductions and notes. There is a sense then in which Madden's editions were rendered, or perceived as, obsolete within a few decades.

The problem was a broad one, no less than the beginning of the disappearance of a way of life. For Madden, the editing of medieval literature was simply the duty a literate gentleman owed to society: were he richer, he once wrote, he would spend the money in occasionally "printing some relic of the olden times, which every man who can afford it, and is a lover of our early literature is bound, in my opinion, to do."[52] The contradiction here is that Madden writes as if he were a man of leisure who could afford—like the richer book club members—to cultivate a dilettantish pose. In practice, this was far from the truth. Madden *acted* like a man of letters, but was of course a salaried officer of the museum, dependent on his pay. His entire reputation rested on work that was performed *not* as part of his official duties, but that filled the very leisure time that made him a gentleman. The paradox was that to project the image of a scholar, he scarcely had time to be a gentleman. To promote relics of olden times, what was really needed was professionalism, a professionalism that would break up the closed circle of club production.

The coming of comparative philology brought with it a professionalization of Anglo-Saxon studies that flowed into the study of medieval literature generally. This professionalization came at the cost of a curtailment of the function of the literary gentleman-antiquarian. Aarsleff writes that the study of Middle English effectively began in the 1830s but, given that most scholars still thought of the period simply as "old English" and given the continuity with a study that had been going on since the

1760s, it would be better to say that *conditions* for that study were entrenched at this time. Very soon, academicization would begin, when the London colleges began teaching English. What was happening was that the antiquarian study of literature was being taken out of the hands of aristocrats and those bourgeois who wanted patronage from them and was being given to the middle class without any need for aristocratic patronage to be attached. The careful controls of the clubs on output would be removed, and most of the clubs themselves would wither away. Aristocrats, in any case, would have problems of their own in the course of the nineteenth century that would divert their attention from dilettante literary study. Many of the great libraries shifted, by the end of the century, from noble estates to more public institutions, as did Spencer's in 1892.

Other forces, well documented by Chris Baldick, Ian Hunter, and others, were at work that would require literary study to be pressed into service as an increasingly broad-based program aimed at the middle class. University College London—then called London University—had opened its doors in 1826, King's College in 1829. Philology and historicism would be developed by the literature professors at these institutions as the way to approach medieval literature, and as the function of literary teaching grew through the middle years of the century, what developed was a form of mass education focused on the middle class. Through literary schooling, as Hunter has convincingly argued, what had formerly been "the aesthetico-ethical practice of a minority caste" now "acquired a new deployment and function as an arm of the emergent governmental educational apparatus."[53] The exemplary figure who emerged under these conditions, the critic, and his "capacities and standing" "were the product of a quite different minority caste practice from which the man of letters emerged as an exemplar for his own class" (133). The era in which a single authoritative literary figure could join a minority caste by ethical self-shaping through literature was giving way to a time in which the broader spread of this technique would proceed in alliance with a "governmental technology" (133). Madden, who had not completed his university degree and was in no way an educator, was left as perhaps the last practitioner of the antiquarian technology of self-shaping.

The study of Middle English would now become associated with, if not yet wholly integrated into, the coalescence of techniques and disciplines that would emerge later in the century as the business of English departments. Yet Middle English, apart from the ever-useful Chaucer, was still not a popular or well-understood field. The closed circulation of the antiquarian period was in part responsible for this, but even when clubs did try to publicize their material, they were usually disappointed. The Bannatyne Club, for example, printed overruns of some of its editions for public sale, but this practice failed to receive support.[54] Apart from the general lack of understanding of medieval literature and language and the stigma of barbarism, what had been produced was too narrowly directed at specific class interests to be of broad appeal. By 1848, romance was still overwhelmingly the preferred Middle English literature outside Chaucer, and romance had been highly tailored to minority class interests. Middle English, to be more generally bourgeoisified, needed a new appeal; even when that transformation was successfully accomplished, its promotion would require a devotion to the cause of early literature nothing short of fanatical.

The man — and at the time, it was still inevitable that it would be a man — who fitted these requirements was also a special constable in 1848. But the young Frederick James Furnivall, unlike Frederic Madden, would be moved not to disgust but sympathy by his experiences in the year of revolution. His sympathies would directly inform his approach to medieval literature. Middle English was about to become democratic, liberal, bourgeois, patriotic, and even, in time, Middle and English.

CHAPTER 6

"Go-a-head-itiveness"
Frederick Furnivall and Early English

1867

At six in the evening on 23 July 1866, Sir Frederic Madden and his son Arnold walked into Great Russell Street from the British Museum and, heading west, went down Oxford Street before crossing via side streets to Piccadilly to avoid the crowds. They then arrived at Hyde Park, where thousands of protesters were gathering to agitate for voting reform. Madden had soon seen enough, and later congratulated himself on having left before the "rioting" (as he called it) began, in which part of the park railings were torn down. His response was typically blunt: "Instead of Police, I wish a body of troops had fired point blank into the scoundrels! <u>Reform</u> indeed."[1] But the mood was with the protesters, and the second Reform Bill was passed a little more than a year later, in August 1867. Madden had by then retired from the museum and moved to the smart new suburb of Bayswater. Three days after the passing of the bill he was out walking his dog near his home and had a brickbat thrown at him from some houses under construction. Madden complained to a policeman, who told him nothing could be done unless plainclothesmen were employed to keep an eye on such "cowardly ruffians." "This," Madden fulminated, "is one of the effects of <u>raising the lower classes</u>, and <u>giving them Holidays</u>."[2]

So the old fear of the mob remained in Madden's mind. He was in many ways an embittered man, who had seen many of his hopes, both personal and professional, disappointed. In thirty years, he had failed to progress beyond the position of keeper of the manuscripts. He and his bitter rival, Antonio Panizzi, retired around the same time, but Panizzi received more liberal terms than Madden. Age and a considerable degree of respect for the gray eminence of the study of Middle English had not softened any of his views. Madden would remain an influence on Middle English after his retirement. W. Carew Hazlitt consulted him, to good effect, for his revised edition of Warton's *History*, which appeared in 1871, and Walter Skeat was another who benefited from his advice and help. But the era of Madden's style of Middle English study was long over. Romance was no longer the genre of dominance. Medieval literature was no longer in the hands of conservative aristocrats and those who would benefit from serving them. Worse, from Madden's point of view, was the fact that the very elements within society from which the study of Middle English had insulated him had now seized control of the discipline. Those same people who wanted to give the lower classes holidays also wanted to give them books, literature, even romance. The heritage so painstakingly reconstructed by the antiquarians as a marker of hierarchical difference between the classes was now being reshaped by the liberals to reconcile precisely these class differences.

The year 1867 saw the publication of Hazlitt's *Hand-Book to the Popular, Poetical, and Dramatic Literature of Great Britain* and Richard Morris's Middle English textbook, *Specimens of Early English*. Henry Bradshaw became the librarian at Cambridge University Library and wrote "The Skeleton of Chaucer's Canterbury Tales," in which he first outlined his theories on Chaucer's rhymes and pronunciation.[3] Frederick J. Furnivall began the Extra Series of the Early English Text Society, for which Skeat reedited *William and the Werwolf* (1867) and *Havelok the Dane* (1868). But the most symbolic of the events in the transformation of Middle English was the complete edition, which appeared in 1867–68, of Percy's Folio manuscript.

For a century, the manuscript that still served as a founding document of modern Middle English studies had remained distant, grail-like, glimpsed by one or two fortunate questers who came close to it but were prevented from grasping it. Madden had seen it and transcribed some poems from it, but was prevented by Percy's descendants from editing it. Cash delivered the grail to Furnivall and John W. Hales. Percy's descendants, who had tended the manuscript for so long, allowed Furnivall to borrow it for six months and copy it for £150. Furnivall had not driven a very hard bargain, presumably unaware that the folio had been offered for sale to the British Museum two years before for £300, when Madden, perhaps rating revenge higher than national heritage, offered only a hundred guineas for the manuscript he had not been allowed to copy more than thirty years before.[4]

In his pamphlet calling for subscribers to the proposed edition, Furnivall noted that the contents of the *Reliques* had been "household words" for a hundred years, wherever English literature had been studied. The *Reliques* had inspired Southey, Coleridge, Burns, and Scott, and had "been the delight of untold thousands of boys and men. Yet not one in ten thousand of all these readers has ever known how much or how little of the different poems was really ancient, how much was sham antique of Percy's own." Distinguishing the expectations of Percy's day from his own, Furnivall continued,

> Now "in a polished age like the present," as Percy has described his own time, a judicious antiquary (unlike Ritson) might possibly be pleased with such treatment of manuscripts as the Bishop's was; but

in an age which (like our Victorian) has, thank Heaven, lost that kind of polish, a judicious antiquary would get judiciously furious at such tampering with a text, and demand imperatively the very words of the manuscript. After their production he might listen to any retouchings and additions of editors clever or foolish, but not before. He cares first for the earliest known authority (however late it may be), and its sentiment, not for the "interesting and affecting" alterations made in "a polished age."[5]

When the edition appeared, Furnivall suggested that Percy had regarded the manuscript "as a young woman from the country with unkempt locks, whom he had to fit for fashionable society." In due course, "his young woman was accepted by Polite Society, taken to the bosom of a Countess, and rewarded her chaperon with a mitre. No one objected to the change in the damsel's appearance save one cantankerous attorney."[6] Furnivall hoped that "we are all now on Ritson's side": "To tell the truth, and tell the whole truth, of a text or MS. is an editor's first duty. That done, let any amount of cooking or editing follow; its extent will be known, and no harm done" (1:xx).

Bishop Percy's Folio Manuscript was only one of many projects being managed by Furnivall in the 1860s. He had founded the Early English Text Society in 1864, the Extra Series in 1867, and the Chaucer and Ballad Societies in 1868. Although the folio edition, by comparison, was just one relatively minor achievement, Furnivall showed an acute sense of the importance of Percy's place and achievement within the literary-historical evolution of Middle English studies and later English literature. Retrospective recognition of Ritson should not obscure that achievement, Furnivall argued: "[Percy] led the van of the army that Wordsworth afterwards commanded and which has won us back to nature and truth. He opened to us the road into the Early English home where we have spent so many pleasant hours" (1:xx).

Paying respect to Percy, locating him as founding father, Furnivall also took pains to *distinguish* what Early English had become, in 1867, from what it had been a century before. Furnivall's comments here are as near as he comes to a credo on editing.[7] He rejects Percy's way of producing "sham antique," but also tempers Ritson's utopics of representation with a pragmatic commitment to emendation, which is acceptable so long as it is done openly. The rival forms of scholarship of a hundred years are here put in their historical place, and there is no need, Furnivall implies, to reopen such antiquarian debates as the Ritson-Percy conflict. Modern, mid-Victorian scholarship has moved on; it acknowledges the importance of its predecessors, but it is operating in an age in which "polish"—editorial tampering—must not be allowed to obscure the text. Modern scholarship, in other words, is objective; it seeks to preserve the exact record of history in the "earliest authority" and render it up to the gaze of a modern era, which must not shape that record in its own image.

Furnivall's position shows a utopianism of its own. He wants to have his text and cook it; the edited text must be at once the "very words of the manuscript" and subjected to "any amount of cooking or editing." Nevertheless, though Furnivall, notoriously, was not a particularly accurate editor, he at least applied this potentially contradictory practice consistently, bringing a new regularity and uniformity to the presentation of Middle English texts. Although EETS texts were often rushed and consequently poor, in editorial theory they had benefited from the scholarly controversies of the 1830s and 1840s. By the 1860s, one edited Middle English text looked much like another, and by the end of the decade, there were ever more to choose from. But who would want to read them, and why?

Middle English, Humanism, and Patriotism

Frederick Furnivall, born in 1825, was a child during the philological controversy of the 1830s. He emerged as a force in London letters from the Philological Society, of which he was cosecretary from 1853 and sole secretary from 1862 almost till his death in 1910. He was early exposed to Germanic philology as a student, from 1841 at University College, where he was taught Greek by Henry Malden, who in turn had learned from Friedrich Rosen.[8] He also took German, chemistry, and mathematics. He went to Trinity Hall, Cambridge, a generation after men who would later influence him strongly: John Mitchell Kemble, Frederick Denison Maurice, Richard Chenevix Trench, and Alfred Tennyson. On returning to London, like many an antiquarian before him Furnivall turned to the law, studying at Lincoln's Inn from 1846 and being called to the bar at Gray's Inn in 1849 (*FJF*, 14). By this time, however, there was little doubt about where Furnivall's real interests and inclinations lay; on settling in London in 1847, he joined the five-year-old Philological Society.

Furnivall, then, was of a generation that missed the controversy of the 1830s and received the new philology as an orthodoxy. The young turks of the controversy were to Furnivall's generation the established scholars: Joseph Bosworth, Richard Garnett, Trench, Benjamin Thorpe, Kemble. Furnivall's close associates, as William Benzie points out, were of the younger generation of scholars: Henry Benjamin Wheatley, a reeditor of the *Reliques*, Richard Morris, Walter Skeat, Alexander Ellis, Henry Sweet, and Gilbert Murray (79). All of these men came to prominence in the 1860s and 1870s.

Furnivall was born into a comfortably middle-class family. His father was a doctor of medicine, a rather stern Tory and evangelical. Furnivall inherited his father's political assumptions, and as a student was very devout. But the influence of the socialist John Malcolm Ludlow, whom he met in the late 1840s, began a process of political and social reeducation and the gradual shedding of earlier beliefs. It is also clear that the context of the medievalizing, reforming, and often turbulent 1830s and 1840s had its effect on Furnivall. Far from insulating himself, Madden-style, from social strife, Furnivall recreated himself in response to the main concerns of the times.[9] Like many another, he became rapidly more liberal as a young man, passing through muscular Christianity (the muscularity survived) to Christian Socialism and, eventually, agnosticism. He also became less and less interested in science and more exclusively concerned with literature.

The mature Furnivall is usually portrayed as one of the great Victorian eccentrics. Remembered as much for his young ladies' sculling club as for his furious row with Swinburne over Shakespeare criticism, and said to be the model for Kenneth Grahame's Rat in *The Wind in the Willows*, he is to one historian "a man of turbulent character, part clown, part scholar, a charlatan of fanatical integrity.... Teetotal, non-smoking, vegetarian, over-exercised, he was also an agnostic and an anti-sabbatarian, who married a lady's-maid and compounded the offence by leaving her."[10] Yet Furnivall was not really at odds with his era, despite his ability to abrade the sensibilities of all with whom he came in contact, friend and foe alike. Behind such trademark extravagances as the pink ribbon tie, there was a great deal about Furnivall quite typical of the liberal, reform-oriented middle-class gentleman of the second half of the century. What made him remarkable was that he got more done than anyone else, and did so by expense of his own conspicuously boundless energy. "Your 'go-a-head-itiveness' puzzles me sometimes," the urbane Skeat wrote to him in 1866, "but it's an element of success."[11] The way Furnivall got things done did arouse perplexity among such calmer men as Skeat, but it was also typical, a classic exemplification of Victorian entrepreneurialism. As John Gross rightly points out, if Furnivall's "energies had taken another turn [he] might have covered a continent with railways."[12]

But Furnivall's energies were diverted into literature. In his teens, he took the well-trodden path of Arthurian romance to early English, influenced by Tennyson's new poem, "Morte d'Arthur," in 1842. The German scholar Alois Brandl, who had "it on Furnivall's authority," claimed it was this poem that "first kindled in him the flame of his enthusiasm for the older literature." John Munro, editor of the commemorative *Frederick James Furnivall: A Volume of Personal Record*, recorded the same experience in more colorful terms, noting that Tennyson's poem "turned his attention to that distant past wherefrom faint but audible voices called to him, sometimes in the very accents of his own warm-hearted humanism and his own comprehensive democracy; and he grew more and more convinced that these forefathers' voices should be made audible and significant to modern men."[13]

Munro's statement has benefited from a great deal of hindsight; Furnivall's democracy was not yet "comprehensive" in 1842, and it was many years before he sought in earnest to make those distant voices audible. But Munro neatly captures the nature of Furnivall's later enterprise and, indeed, the whole tenor of philology after midcentury. Late in life, commended by a colleague for his services to English philology, Furnivall responded, "I never cared a bit for philology; my chief aim has been throughout to illustrate the social condition of the English people in the past" (*VPR*, 43). The important trend that brought English philology into the mainstream of later nineteenth-century thought, seen here and in Munro's summary, is its tendency to move outward from words to the people who used them. It was one of the peculiarities of the Philological Society that—the battles of the 1830s being won—it "did not create a forum for the new philology in England. On the contrary...the most striking fact about the Society's work during the first twenty years is the virtual absence of non-English, Germanic philology."[14] The search for verb paradigms and sound changes—linguistic *traces* of the past—was soon supplemented in English work by a broader concern with the source of those traces: real people.

In the form in which Furnivall read it in 1842, before *Idylls of the King,* Tennyson's "Morte d'Arthur" was framed by a prologue entitled "The Epic," which represents the "Morte" itself as an example of modern minstrel performance. The minstrel is represented as Tennyson's friend, "the poet Everard Hall."[15] "The Epic" opens "At Francis Allen's on the Christmas-eve," where the host, "The parson Holmes," Everard Hall, and the Tennysonian narrator discuss "How all the old honour had from Christmas gone" (2:1). It is mentioned that Hall has composed a twelve-book Arthurian epic, but destroyed it by throwing it on the fire. At the urging of his friends, he recites the "Morte d'Arthur," obviously as a fragmentary verbal performance from the lost, greater whole. Despite the trappings of classical epic, the poem more obviously invokes the romantic mythology of the destroyed whole, tantalizingly represented in the transcription of a fragmentary oral performance, like "Kubla Khan" or the Ossian poems. The "Morte," without the *Idylls,* is a relique.

Although the original "Morte" is as much an elegy as the later version, the theme of death and absence is strongly counterpointed by a theme of renewal opposed to death, circularity rather than finality, return rather than absence. The poem laments Bedivere's realization that "the true old times are dead / When every morning brought a noble chance" (2:14), but just as quickly celebrates the possibility of renewal: "The old order changeth," Arthur responds; "yielding place to new, / And God fulfils himself in many ways, / Lest one good custom should corrupt the world"

(2:15). Bedivere watches Arthur disappear on the barge to Avilion, "Revolving many memories," and at this point Hall falls silent (2:16).

The narrator goes to bed and dreams that he sails "with Arthur under looming shores," until, between waking and sleeping near dawn,

> To me, methought, who waited with a crowd,
> There came a bark that, blowing forward, bore
> King Arthur, like a modern gentleman
> Of stateliest port; and all the people cried,
> "Arthur is come again: he cannot die."
> Then those that stood upon the hills behind
> Repeated—"Come again, and thrice as fair;"
> And, further inland, voices echoed—"Come
> With all good things, and war shall be no more."
> At this a hundred bells began to peal,
> That with the sound I woke, and heard indeed
> The clear church-bells ring in the Christmas morn.
> (2:17–18)

In this framework, dropped from the poem when it was incorporated into the broader plan of the *Idylls*, Arthur becomes both the type of his nineteenth-century chivalrous counterpart, the modern gentleman, and a type of Christ. The *rex futurus* is Arthur but also Christ, and Christliness, if not Christianity, is by implication closely associated with chivalry in the poem. Christmas, lamented at the outset as an empty form, finds its content in a Christianity revived by its fusion with modern gentlemanliness and the imagined Arthurian-chivalric past.[16]

This vision presents the smiling face of Germanic philology. Furnivall, claiming inspiration from this poem and caring not a bit for philology, drew heavily on the pervasive Victorian belief encapsulated in Tennyson's poem: the idea that hope for a class-divided, industrialized, and sporadically rebellious society lay in some form of medievalizing of that society. Furnivall, like so many others, would lose his faith in the Christianizing aspect of the formula in the late 1850s, but this, in Benzie's view, actually increased his faith in his medievalist activities: "Furnivall felt very acutely this disruption to the faith of his childhood and youth, and the buoyant fervor and piety with which he had lived the evangelical life was now redirected with fresh, optimistic, and compensatory energy to more secular ends: the celebration and reclamation of the golden ages of England peopled with noble, heroic ancestors" (*FJF,* 22).

Philology, too, took on this mission. The work of Rask and Grimm led in England not only to R. G. Latham's often reprinted textbook on grammar, but also to a much more humanist version of itself in which not medieval words but medieval people were the chief interest. It was in this spirit that Furnivall rejected pure philology in favor of the social condition of people, and in this he was preceded by perhaps the greatest popular philologist, Richard Chenevix Trench.

When Trench moved to London to become dean of Westminster, he also joined the Philological Society in 1857. In the society, he rediscovered some of the friends he had known in Cambridge when he was a member of the elite society, the Apostles.[17] A noted scholar of Scripture, Trench was professor of divinity in King's College, London; his second interest was in language. For him, as Hans Aarsleff puts it, "theology and exegesis were bound up with philology since both served the cause of Christian instruction in the tradition of the English Church and gave promise of an ultimate reunion of divided Christianity" (231). In the mid-1840s, Trench delivered a series of lectures on language at the Diocesan Training School in Winchester, published in 1851 as *On the Study of Words*. A later series of lectures was published as *English Past and Present* in 1855, and these books, in Aarsleff's view, "did far more than any previous publication to make language study popular" (234–35). Both were issued in numerous editions.

No great philologist, Trench had the gift of "clear and interesting exposition" (231). He was interested not in the origin of language, "not in etymological metaphysics, not in conjectural history, but in history" and "the spiritual and moral life of the speakers of English" (238). Language, Trench argued, "contains so faithful a record of the good and of the evil which in time past have been working in the minds of men, we shall not err if we regard it as a kind of moral barometer, which indicates and permanently marks the rise or fall of a nation's life. To study a people's language will be to study *them*."[18] This kind of philology was deeply appealing to Furnivall, who in the later 1850s was turning away from religion and toward historical-philological study. Trench adopted a metaphor of the times to describe language as "fossil poetry." Just as in fossils, "curious and beautiful shapes of vegetable or animal life, the graceful fern or the finely vertebrated lizard" might be preserved, "so in words are beautiful thoughts and images, the imagination and the feeling of past ages, of men long since in their graves, of men whose very names have perished... preserved and made safe for ever" (4–5).

This kind of thinking by Furnivall and Trench came eventually to an inevitable result, one of the profoundly important projects of philological thought of the nineteenth century: the *New English Dictionary*, later to be published as the *Oxford English Dictionary*. Whether the credit for the initiation of this massive project should go to Furnivall or Trench is not an important issue here.[19] The idea of the *Dictionary* was an inevitable product of its time, which found its most able promoters in these two men. The impulse was not simply linguistic, but expressed in the linguistic field the 1850s' rhetoric of empire and expansionism. If language were an index of a culture—if a nation could be mapped in its language—then the *Dictionary* was a lexical cartography of the empire of the English language. Furnivall, as Roman Dyboski shrewdly pointed out in his memoir, did not lack the "modern Englishman's Imperial patriotism," and "an ideal still nearer and dearer to his heart than the material extension and consolidation of the British Empire was that even more ample and splendid intellectual empire of England, for which new provinces are conquered by every lecture on English literature and every lesson of the English language given in any part of the world" (*VPR*, 41).

English nationalism is not much in evidence in the study of Middle English before the 1850s, because there was little to be gained from claiming such evidently barbarous material as the national heritage. As we have seen, as late as 1839 Madden was happy to imagine an exotic, Scottish *Sir Gawain*. Philology allowed the scholar to see regular processes of linguistic change connecting modern words to medieval, where earlier generations had seen only hopeless barbarisms. Victorian imperialism provided the occasion for the development of nationalism as the key element in the study of early English. Patriotism did not account for all of Furnivall's interest in these texts, but it was, in effect, his sales pitch.

However neatly Furnivall's expansionist project for English analogizes Victorian imperialism, his nationalism was not jingoist or xenophobic, but a logical expression of the increasingly liberal stance he had taken through the 1850s. Furnivall's loss of religion as a ground for socialism corresponded with a decade of Victorian foreign expansion and landmarks in the history of science that undermined fundamentalist views of the Bible. Seamlessly, the subject positioning of loyal liberal patriotism offered to an enlightened man in a great empire took over in Furnivall's self-presentation from his earlier justification of good works on religious grounds. When Furnivall cofounded, with F. D. Maurice, J. M. Ludlow, and others, the London Working Men's College in 1854, he was a committed Christian Socialist, principally teaching English grammar (*FJF*, 51). Munro claims that by the end of the decade, which saw the publication of *Origin of Species* in 1859, Furnivall's shift away from religious belief had begun, and in 1869, when Thomas Huxley coined the word, "he could term himself an 'agnostic.'"[20]

Literature, and particularly Middle English literature, was there to fill the gap. In 1858, Furnivall was lecturing on *Piers Plowman*—"because of its sketch of working men in the fourteenth century"—and on Ruskin, Tennyson, and Chaucer (*FJF*, 52). Munro believed that Furnivall's reading of the ecclesiastical satire *The Land of Cokaygne*, which he edited in 1862, contributed to his attitudes to the church. Furnivall had thrown himself into medievalist editing at this time, bringing to it his typical blend of overachievement and carelessness of detail. Munro records Furnivall's "earliest editorial labour" (*VPR*, xlvi) as being an edition of Henry Lovelich's *Merlin* (under the title *Seynt Graal*), which appeared with the Roxburghe Club in 1861–63, but Furnivall must in fact have been working all at once on that large project, Robert Mannyng's *Handlyng Synne*

(Roxburghe, 1862), and *Early English Poems and Lives of Saints*, which also appeared in 1862 as part of the Philological Society's *Transactions* for that year.

As editor of the *Transactions*, Furnivall had found himself short of material for the volume recording the activities of 1858. His solution was to fill the space with early English texts, a decision no doubt inspired by his labors for the Roxburghe Club. In the typical antiquarian fashion, Furnivall looked for help to an eminent authority. "Can you tell me," he wrote to Madden early in 1859, "of any early English M.S. (in London), before 1300 if possible which would take up from 100 to 150 octavo pages[?]" Madden proposed that Furnivall consider the saints' lives in MS Harl 2277, the first part of Robert of Gloucester's *Chronicle*, and *Handlyng Synne*.[21] Furnivall used the saints' lives in the *Transactions* volume and borrowed a manuscript of *Handlyng Synne* for use in his edition.[22] He repeated his procedure of providing Middle English texts in the *Transactions* for 1860–61.

These activities led to the decisive event for the study of Middle English of the second half of the century: the founding of the Early English Text Society, first of Furnivall's many subscription publishing societies. Munro notes that the Roxburghe Club was not democratic enough for Furnivall, who wanted "greater output" than it could offer (*VPR*, xlvi). The Philological Society would not provide it, deciding, with the backing of members who did not believe the society's work was to be exclusively in the field of English, that the expense of printing editions in the *Transactions* "was draining the society's financial resources" (*FJF*, 119). There was another pressing factor: the *Dictionary*, which the Philological Society had resolved to embark on in 1858, was to be based on etymological principles. Someone had to provide the otherwise inaccessible material on which those etymologies would be based.[23]

So in 1864 Furnivall simply founded his own society. Although originally tied to the *Dictionary*, the Early English Text Society rapidly expanded into a nationalist project of its own, with the simple motivation of publishing all of early English literature, as a matter of duty and moral benefit to the nation. The intent, as originally expressed, was "to print all that is most valuable of the yet unprinted MSS. in English, and also to re-edit and reprint all that is most valuable in printed English books which, from their scarcity or price, are not within the reach of the student of moderate means."[24] There was also a special purpose, reflecting Furnivall's early reading, to publish Arthurian material in the first few years. No criterion of value was ever articulated, as there did not need to be while Furnivall maintained the simple aim of printing all there was to print. He called for volunteers and, asking them to approach texts as colonial pioneers might approach an untamed land, required them to dedicate not only their own lives to editing early English, but their sons' as well:

[T]he men they [the EETS committee] want are "the resolute members" referred to in the last Report; men who do not think the right
way to get through their work is to be afraid of it or let their stom-
achs turn at it; but men who know they have a work to do, and mean
to do it; men who can look 270 MSS and books in the face, and say
quietly, "Well, at 9 a-year, we shall clear you off in 30 years;" who
can look at £60,000 worth of work, and say, "At £1000 a-year, you're
to be cut down in 60 years; and if I can manage 30 of them, my boy
can settle the other 30."[25]

The spur to these resolute men should be simply duty; the effect of their
labor, moral and national. In his report for 1871 Furnivall noted that the
society's output had decreased because of "the absorbing interest" of
the Franco-Prussian war, before using "the love of Fatherland" shown by
both sides in this conflict to remind readers of

the memorable words of Professor Seeley... "Classical studies may
make a man intellectual, but the study of the native literature has
a moral effect as well. *It is the true ground and foundation of patriotism*...I call that man uncivilized who is not connected with
the past through the state in which he lives, and sympathy with
the great men who have lived in it." The Committee again declare
that they can take no lower ground for the Society's work than
this. Not dilettante Antiquarianism, but duty to England, is the
motive of the Society's workers; and they do not hesitate to call on
all men interested in Literature who can feel that motive, to come
forward and help them in their work.[26]

In his 1873 report, Furnivall stressed duty once more, again with a terri-
torial metaphor, and wrote:

It is not fitting that the ruling tongue of the world should longer
allow its history to be unknown, by leaving the documents of that
history unprinted; it is not right that men who bathe in the full
stream of English Literature should longer rest content with not
exploring, and making plain to all, the sources of the great river
they enjoy. The study of the past is the best training for right judgment and action in the future; and on an Englishman, no past has
such a claim for regard as that of his own fair land.[27]

The EETS unquestionably transformed Middle English studies, making
more texts more readily available than ever before. Although the print
runs do not look so much greater than those of the clubs, the society's
flexible subscription mechanism meant that texts that proved popular

were often reprinted, according to demand; in addition, while the clubs had a measured pace of annual production, Furnivall would turn out as many texts in a year as the subscription base would allow. And in university and public libraries, a single copy might gain a readership bigger than that of an entire antiquarian club. In the first year of the society, 145 subscribers sent in £152, and 481 pages of material were printed. In 1865 this had increased to 260 subscribers, £384, 950 pages, and by 1870, 580 subscribers (actually a decrease from the previous two years) paid £796 for 971 pages. By this time, the Extra Series had been created to handle reprints and early printed books, and in 1870 it had 240 subscribers paying £504 for 664 pages.[28] Furnivall would never admit to being content with these figures, and always suggested that more texts could be handled. In 1871 he claimed to have enough material and editors to use up £1000 a year in both Original and Extra Series, more than twice what the two series combined were averaging.[29]

There was nothing to compare with this output. The Camden Society had achieved print runs of 1,200, but only by being far more selective in what it printed; the Roxburghe Club was still producing texts in the 1860s and may even have benefited from the interest created by the EETS, but it continued its restrictive practices. A subscriber base hovering around 300 to 600 members is obviously still small measured against the perceptions of a whole society, which might buy thousands of copies of Tennyson's *Idylls*. But it should be remembered that many of these subscribers were teachers in schools and universities, and many more were members of such learned societies as the Philological Society, so that the opportunities for the publicizing of Middle English literature were now greater than at any time before. Certainly, many of the texts were obscure and unattractive to all but the specialist, but at the same time many great texts were becoming readily available for the first time: *Sir Gawain and the Green Knight, Pearl, Cleanness*, and *Patience* in 1864, the alliterative *Morte Arthure* in 1865, and *Piers Plowman* from 1867.

Like any mail-order system of purchasing, the society had its limitations. Furnivall found that not all readers were thoroughly delighted by the product they received. Some, unsurprisingly, simply found the material too difficult to read. It is hard to imagine many men or women having the skills and patience to work through the alliterative *Morte* or *Sir Gawain*, even with Morris's primer, *Specimens of Early English*, to one side. Many must have thought that they would be fed a diet of swashbuckling romance, perhaps leavened with Tennysonian morality, a still quite reasonable expectation of medieval literature in the 1860s and indeed encouraged by the society's early Arthurian emphasis. This problem may have contributed to the decline in subscribers after the initial steady rise of 1864–68. Furnivall's response to subscriber complaints was to offer "duty" as simply transcending any other motive for reading:

They [the Committee] want to lift the motive for joining or continuing in the Society, from "I care for this class of Texts; I don't care
for that," into one of duty to our Country and her Literature, so that
those who don't care for Anglo-Saxon may yet be glad that those
who do shall get a couple of Texts yearly, while those who don't care
for late Texts may be pleased at less learned folk than themselves
getting Texts they can read.[30]

This is a scheme of cross-subsidy in which, rather unrealistically, subscribers are expected to pay for and put up with texts in which they have
no interest for the greater good of the reading public and the nation. While
there were, no doubt, many members who were prepared to do just this,
there were few who had large financial resources to spare for Furnivall's
projects. Very few of the subscribers were wealthy, philanthropic men.
The EETS was thoroughly middle class; Furnivall was very conscious of
this, and proud of the success of the middle class at large in becoming
"the mainstay of General Literature and Art." He felt that "Antiquarian
Literature," too, could be captured from the upper class (as represented,
in particular, in the Roxburghe Club) by the middle class.[31] Furnivall
did not woo the aristocracy and so could not benefit from its money. He
would have known that aristocratic bibliomania had subsided; even so,
it is very difficult to imagine Furnivall having the requisite tact to gain
aristocratic patronage.

It had also been suggested to Furnivall that he might attract subscribers
by printing in black letter and making the texts "as nearly facsimiles of
the originals as modern type could make them." Furnivall rejected this
proposal, "however popular it is, or might prove," and employed an interesting metaphor:

On a true literary antiquarian the so-called type facsimile of an old
book produces just the same feeling that the bran-new restoration
of an old cathedral-window does on the real lover of old architecture.
The old, broken, crumbled lines, and irregular curves, give place to
the sharply-cut edges and regular convexities of modern mechanics;
the old tone of time to the glare and glaze of modern surfaces. *C'est
magnifique, mais ce n'est pas la guerre.* The Reproduction may be
handsome, but it is not Antiquity, not what that is, was, or ever
could have been; and its quasi-imitation of the original is but a re-
pellent to the true antiquarian.[32]

What Furnivall rejects here is the conception of old literature as invested
with cultural capital deriving from its display of antiquity, in which value
derives from antiquity itself rather than textuality. Editorially this means
the firm rejection of the notion that the ideal representation of an antique text might lie in a utopian reproduction; an edition should not strive

to be a quasi imitation, but must recognize its own mediatedness — a principle established in the 1830s, reiterated as a tenet of the EETS, and underlying all modern editions.

From Ancient to Early

The volume of EETS productions in both Original and Extra Series makes it difficult to survey the field. For the first time, Middle English was being edited by many people, rather than one dominant figure — though the dominating figure of Furnivall is never far away in any EETS edition. Morris, Skeat, and Wheatley all emerged as editors and scholars in their own right, but many of the EETS editors were cajoled by Furnivall out of a literary obscurity to which they rapidly returned after completing their work. Many, like Morris and Skeat, were clergymen whose training was their Oxford or Cambridge education. As a result of the lack of truly skilled editors and Furnivall's haste to throw texts into print, much of the early EETS work was bad, as Benzie records (*FJF*, 150). Bradshaw was perhaps the most knowledgeable man involved with the EETS, but he was a chronic procrastinator who, despite his many plans, never produced a book. He at least influenced Skeat, originally a mathematician and later an Anglo-Saxon professor, whom he helped learn to read manuscripts.[33] Richard Morris, prolific in the early days of EETS, produced a page of transcript from Nero A.x that was shown to Madden, who thought it so bad he was "thoroughly disgusted" by the kind of editing it implied, and wrote that Morris's work would be "worthless."[34]

The society did not therefore always represent an advance in scholarship on the era of Madden. It did not define a field of "Middle English." That term was emerging at this time, but, as the name given to the society suggests, was far from prevalent. Despite explicit, programmatic statements of *purpose* from its founder, the EETS did not really represent a sustained and coherent body of editorial theory or literary criticism. Furnivall knew what he wanted to do, but did not show an equivalent concern for how it was done. The EETS did, though, represent the regimentation of a body of Middle English literature in scholarly guise for the first time. EETS editions may not have been truly coherent, but they *looked* as if they were. A certain basic format, consonant with the democratic aim of the club, established conventions for editions. Material surrounding the texts drew on what had become standard scholarly conventions in the antiquarian period: the introduction or preface, textual notes at the end of the book, and a glossary. No longer was it open to an editor to avoid the glossary if he did not feel like doing it, as Halliwell had done as late as 1847 with his *Thornton Romances*.

The quality and rigor brought to these parts of the text, however, varied greatly. J. Rawson Lumby's glossary to his edition of *King Horn* with fragments of *Floris and Blauncheflur* (1866) usually gives only a one-word interpretation of each word and a line number, though very occasionally part of speech or case is given and, apparently randomly, an etymology. George Perry's *Morte Arthure* (1865) gives part of speech for all words in the glossary, but no etymologies. Morris's *Early English Alliterative Poems* (1864) often gives several words as possible meanings, no parts of speech, and sometimes etymologies that extend to quotations from other texts, a practice that he might have taken from Madden's expansive glossary to *Syr Gawayne.* Skeat, in his prentice work *Lancelot of the Laik* (1865), gives etymologies for most words.[35]

The prefaces to these works were often far less expansive than those of the earlier antiquarians, a sign that despite the constraints under which they worked, the antiquarians had had considerable license for their scholarly speculations. Lumby's *King Horn* has a fifteen-page preface that begins with descriptions of the manuscript used (Cambridge UL Gg.4.27.2), and a comparison of the beginnings of this text with those of Harley 2253 and Laud 108 in the Bodleian. Two and a half pages are devoted to linguistic matters, in which "peculiarities of dialect and grammar" are explained, and the remainder, more than half of the whole, is given to plot summaries.[36] The first paragraph of this preface exemplifies the laxness of some of the EETS work; it opens with a solecism and closes with the inaccurate information that the Cotton library burned "at the Museum in 1731."[37]

This format for the preface was quite typical, and is also seen in the fourteen-page prefaces of Skeat's *Lancelot* and Perry's *Morte,* though both these writers are more lively than Lumby. Skeat spends his first page demolishing the worth of Joseph Stevenson's Maitland Club edition of the text, to conclude "that the former text can seldom be safely quoted for the purposes of philology," and Perry indulges in a rare moment of aesthetic valuation in referring to "Arthur's beautiful lament over Sir Gawaine, and his touching reflections on his dead knights." "The writer of this romance" he thought "was assuredly not wanting in the feeling of true poetry."[38] In other respects, their remarks are confined to standard questions of dialect, meter, manuscript, grammar, and orthography.

The edited texts themselves are much more uniform. Their principal distinction is two innovations that reflect the dual scholarly and public placement these texts were designed to achieve. Furnivall's stricture against the type facsimile was law for the EETS; from the beginning, all manuscript contractions were expanded, but italics were used to highlight the letters derived from the expansions. Second, explanatory side notes accompanied all texts, glossing the more difficult passages. The uniform expansion of contractions signals a scholarly stance taken on an issue that had always been treated haphazardly in the past, while the explanatory glosses obviously point to an awareness of the needs of an imagined general public.

The accuracy of the texts and the value of emendations also vary widely. It had become increasingly the norm for editors to do their own transcribing, though texts included for comparison might be transcribed by another.[39] This did not, of course, ensure accuracy when the editor was not particularly careful himself. Benzie records that Thomas Wright, editing *The Book of the Knight of La Tour-Landry* (1868), confessed under questioning from Furnivall "that when he found that the first proof sheet tallied with the manuscript he decided that no further check was necessary." And although Furnivall set exacting standards, "his own work was not at all times flawless or meticulous" (*FJF*, 150).

Texts were not, under these circumstances, always accurate, and the apparatus was often thin and frankly speculative. In *Pearl*, for example, Morris only emends the most obvious manuscript errors, noting the manuscript reading in a footnote. Far more often, he leaves the original reading, and adds a conjectural footnote: in line 10, "þurȝ gresse to grounde hit fro me yot," "yot" is glossed "Got (?)." This is standard practice throughout where Morris is uncertain. Skeat, too, is inclined to retain a difficult manuscript reading and record a tentative query at the foot of the page: "So in MS. Should we read 'in to'?" or "After 'day' we should perhaps insert 'he.' " Perry, in the *Morte,* makes few suggestions.

This reluctance to intervene decisively makes the editor look like a far less commanding and authoritative figure than the often magisterial antiquarians of the past. This was inevitable, given the lack of either a Middle English dictionary or an English etymological dictionary. The scholar's best chance to elucidate something he or she did not understand was still through the old antiquarian method of correspondence with learned peers, a leisurely method that worked better when there was not the great pressure of time Furnivall imposed. Furnivall himself was an expert at this form of correspondence, and was one of the first to make extensive use of the plain postcard—which some still looked down on as rather vulgar—hundreds of which, containing various philological queries, survive in his correspondence. As they became more confident in their work, however, some editors simply created their own authoritative discourse out of nothing other than the supreme confidence that they were right. The humble Skeat of *Lancelot of the Laik* can hardly be recognized in the Olympian figure who later edits Langland and Chaucer. Like many scholars at this time, Skeat worked at incredible speed;[40] to produce what he did, he simply would not have had time to make inquiries at the calm antiquarian pace. The assumption of authority was almost a necessity.

The EETS further broke with antiquarian tradition in adopting a mode of text-ordering that relied principally on the intertextual relations of a given text, rather than its presence in a particular manuscript, or its relation to other texts on the basis of a shared character. The old anthologies, based on a manuscript such as the Auchinleck or a character such as Gawain, were gone, and in their place, scholars printed sources and analogues. A "vertical" principle of order was established, as opposed to the "lateral" one seen in the *Reliques* or *Syr Gawayne.* This procedure was a notable feature of Furnivall's Roxburghe *Merlin* and *Handlyng Synne,* both of them compendious volumes in which the English texts were accompanied by various French sources, in places, where the correspondences warranted it, printed side by side with the English for ease of comparison.

EETS editors were not given to great speculation on literary or other matters. This would, in part, have been the result of the time pressure that made it expedient to follow the same basic format, but it also reflects the still uncertain relation of this kind of literature to the modern literature a gentleman read and understood. While Perry thought the *Morte* to be good literature and Morris concurred with Madden's high valuation of the work of the *Gawain*-poet, there is always a note of apology on the editors' part to readers whose basic assumption is probably that literary value cannot possibly be concealed beneath such language. Morris gives a summary of the poems in the hope that this will "give the reader stomach to digest the whole" — hardly a promising metaphor. Although they contain "uncouth" terms, this only reinforces the philological value of poems that, in Madden's opinion, were "*equal to any similar passages in Douglas or Spenser.*"[41]

Philological and literary value, as Morris conceives them, are in an uneasy dichotomy of mutual exclusion. Philological value tends to result from the uncouthness of the language, which renders literary value impossible; literary value arises from the passages that can be compared with more accepted authors and that are therefore not uncouth. In his edition of *Genesis and Exodus,* similarly, Morris urged the reader not to be "disappointed" by the lack of "poetic skill," but to accept that the historical interest and "philological value of the poem, fully compensates him for the absence of great literary merit, which is hardly to be expected in a work of this kind."[42] In striking this note, the editor is apologizing for the very specificity that led him to edit the text at all. This, in turn, creates that contradictory moment in which the editor says that the poem is at its best when it is most like something else. In fairness, this is probably less Morris's own opinion than the result of his attempt to popularize a text whose virtues would not be immediately apparent to a general readership.

As Benzie states, Furnivall and many of his contemporaries were "only mildly interested in questions of evaluation and criticism." Literary value was less important to them than historical fact as it was revealed in a text; for them "literary value *was* the authentic primitive purity of the text" (139). It seems to have been enough that the text existed at all in an accessible version; its value is intrinsic and immanent, and correspondingly does not need to be demonstrated by assertions of literary or historical worth. Merely by being produced, an early English text apparently adds value to English culture. Furnivall often referred to the fact that England had lagged far behind Germany in printing its literary heritage and used this as a spur: the society, he wrote in 1868, was determined "not to rest till Englishmen shall be able to say of their Early Literature, what the Germans can now say with pride of theirs, 'every word of it's printed, and every word of it's glossed.' England must no longer be content to lag behind."[43] But given that the teaching of medieval literature was not widespread and print runs were still relatively small, Furnivall seems to imagine that sheer volume of production is all that is needed to rival the Germans.

The ideological drive of the EETS is also less evident in individual texts. It was Furnivall's repeated stress on the mission to reclaim the national heritage that ensured that overall, whatever the commitments of individual editors to this program, the EETS had an apparently coherent direction. This was greatly reinforced by the title, the Early English Text Society, because this was the first society to bear a name that referred to its actual activities, rather than to an illustrious predecessor or patron. Furnivall's emphasis on what he called "early" textuality, enshrined in the society's name, helped bring about the important transformation from "ancient" to "early." "Early English" was effectively a transitional term before the more precise and philological "Middle English" became generally current. "Ancientness" was disappearing. One of the subtle shifts in the scholarship seen in EETS editions is from a conception of medieval literature as alien, attractively exotic but far removed from modern history and modern aesthetics, to medieval literature as the cradle of modern literature, as continuous, in an unbroken chain, with modernity.

It is significant in this respect that in the first year of the society there was a symbolic handing-on of the scholarly baton from Madden to the EETS scholars. One of the first things Furnivall did when establishing the society was to contact Madden, as he had done when editing the *Transactions* volume. Madden, unsurprisingly, disliked "that jackanapes Furnivall," who represented everything the older man despised.[44] Madden also did not like the society's chances: "I don't think the scheme will succeed, nor do I place much confidence in Mr F. and his friends. However, I shall subscribe to the undertaking, as the <u>motive</u> is good, whatever the result is."[45] Nevertheless, Madden was forthcoming with help and permission to reedit his own key texts, presumably because his long-held desire for the more widespread publishing of medieval literature overcame his dislike of Furnivall. It was fortunate, too, that he came to respect Skeat, a courteous and tactful correspondent.

The change from one era to the next is most obvious in two of the society's productions in its first year, Richard Morris's editions of *Sir Gawain and the Green Knight* and, in a separate volume, *Pearl, Patience,* and *Cleanness*. In editing *Sir Gawain*, Morris received permission to reuse Madden's text and glossary, and he also used Madden's description of the manuscript almost unaltered. In these aspects, the text is effectively a reprint of Madden's great Bannatyne edition. But the two editions of the same unique text could hardly be more different visually, ideologically, and in scholarship. On the page, Morris's text looks quite different from Madden's, with the expansion of contractions, the addition of side-notes, and the bob and wheel indented in the way that they have been in all editions since, where Madden had imitated the look of the manuscript. Even more important differences lie in the framing effects of the edition. Madden had printed the poem in an anthology, a kind of book closely modeled on eighteenth-century antiquarian editing. His structural focus was an Arthurian character, and the poem was called *Syr Gawayn and the Grene Kny3t*, using archaized spellings in emphasis of antiquity; it was ancient, and Scottish, and probably the work of Huchowne of the Awle Ryal. Morris's structural focus was the poem itself; he titled it with the rather less archaic *Sir Gawayne and the Green Knight* and gave it a precise generic subtitle, "An Alliterative Romance-Poem." For him, the poem was early and English. Madden's argument for Scottishness is dismissed, and in the dialectal forms that allowed Madden to make his argument, Morris sees only "great philological worth."[46] The reclamation of the poem for England, furthermore, relies in part on an argument about literary value. If the poems had been transcribed from one dialect to another, as Madden proposed, any original "literary merit" they may have had would have been "destroyed." "But the poems before us are evidently the work of a man of birth and education; the productions of a true poet" (viii). Although Morris privileged the romance by editing it separately, he did redress the generic balance by presenting the other three poems of MS Cotton Nero A.x, under the title *Early English Alliterative Poems, in the West-Midland Dialect of the Fourteenth Century*. This could hardly be more explicit about the concern to replace the manuscript and its poems firmly in England and the late Middle Ages.[47]

Within ten years of the founding of the EETS, the study of Middle English had been radically altered. By the end of 1874, the society had produced fifty-eight titles in the Original Series and twenty-three in the Extra Series. In addition to the texts already discussed, *Hali Meidenhad*, the English treatises of Richard Rolle, *Ayenbite of Inwyt*, the *Gest Historiale of the Destruction of Troy*, Barbour's *Bruce*, and Skeat's editions of the A-, B-, and C-texts of *Piers Plowman* had been produced, in addition to many other less well known Middle English texts and some Anglo-Saxon texts. The Extra Series had reprinted *Havelok*, *Chevalere Assigne*, and *William of Palerne* and had begun Lovelich's *History of the Holy Grail*. The first three parts of Alexander Ellis's work on early English pronunciation had appeared. Skeat and Morris had produced, with the

Clarendon Press, a revised version of Morris's *Specimens of Early English.* The society's workers had, in the space of a few years, provided a literature and the means with which to read, teach, and study it.

In addition, the society was responsible for the promotion of the study of Middle English in schools and universities. Furnivall instituted a system of prizes for the best pupil in exams on English before Chaucer, and in 1866 these were awarded at institutions including Oxford; Trinity College, Dublin; King's College, London; University College, London; and the Universities of Edinburgh and Glasgow. This was achieved through Furnivall's network of scholarly contacts: Joseph Bosworth at Oxford; John Brewer at King's College, London; Henry Morley, professor of English at University College from 1865 (and said to be the first man to make English his full-time profession);[48] John K. Ingram at Trinity College, Dublin; David Masson at Edinburgh; and others in Manchester, Glasgow, Saint Andrew's, and Belfast. The importance of the EETS was not simply its tangible results, but the way in which it allowed Furnivall to set up a community of scholars whose activities could be labeled and made coherent, raised to disciplinary status and disseminated among students. Finally, and not the least important, Furnivall pioneered Middle English as a subject for export, making contacts in, and recruiting several editors from, Germany and gaining subscribers to the EETS in Australia, India, and the United States, where his contacts were James Russell Lowell and Francis Child.

And all the riches of early English were to be had (in theory) by any member of any class, in the knowledge that he or she was performing a duty to the nation, for two pounds and two shillings a year.

Middle English in the Public Sphere?

The Early English Text Society resulted from a confluence of various philological activities that had gone on from 1842, together with liberal reform manifested in a concern with education, in a context of imperialist expansion. The Roxburghe Club would have suggested the subscription method, and the Philological Society, the open, democratic format, with the example of the Camden Society, too, suggesting the possibilities of a more democratic publishing mechanism. The EETS looks recognizably like a continuation of antiquarian tradition since 1765, and there is indeed a lineage from Percy to Madden to Furnivall. The same generic interest in romance, particularly Arthurian romance, is crucial in Furnivall's early work, the same emphasis on early texts as pictures of life and manners.

It is not difficult to see, however, the fundamental social and political transformation of the study of Middle English capped by the formation of the EETS, which serves therefore as the moment of rupture with the prior tradition. Clubs had given way to societies, antiquarians to scholars, aristocrats to the middle class, old philology to new. As Early English assumed a role in which it was aimed at supplementing or replacing classical literature and religion in its new place within liberal education, the narrow direction of the doings of "our ancestors" to the aggrandizement of the editor and his patrons, as had been the practice from Percy to Madden, was opened out with the new recognition that early English texts had become a matter of national importance. While it was still possible to edit for aristocrats in the Roxburghe Club—Furnivall was a relatively prolific contributor—the EETS rapidly achieved near official status as purveyor of medieval literature. Early English was handed to— or forced upon—a general, middle-class readership; it was democratized and reinvented as national heritage. Once wrested from the mechanism of aristocratic patronage, it was no longer principally a minority practice of the self, the tool of isolated antiquarians, but promulgated by apparently selfless scholars as a generalized technology of aesthetic cultivation for the masses.

The changes encompassed in this shift lend themselves to the ascending, continuist model of knowledge, that narrative in which scholarship goes on improving itself by increasing, through the effort of its practitioners, its own objectivity. This is precisely the narrative that Hans Aarsleff and, in a different context, Michel Foucault have warned against. Characterizing what he sees as the second phase of the broad shift from the classical to the modern episteme, Foucault proposes that "knowledge in its positivity changes its nature and its form." It is not a case, he warns, of the critical importance of "the discovery of hitherto unknown objects, such as the grammatical system of Sanskrit." General grammar did not become philology, natural history biology, or the analysis of wealth political economy "because all these modes of knowledge corrected their methods, came closer to their objects, rationalized their concepts, selected better models of formalization—in short, because they freed themselves from their prehistories through a sort of auto-analysis achieved by reason itself." For Foucault, there was a change in knowledge itself at the turn of the century, an "irremediable modification." In the case of philology,

> if Grimm and Bopp attempted to define the laws of vowel gradation or consonant mutation, it is because Discourse as a mode of knowledge had been replaced by Language, which defines objects not hitherto apparent (such as families of languages whose grammatical systems are analogous) and prescribes methods that had not previously been employed (analysis of the rules governing the modifications of consonants and vowels).[49]

As a manifestation of the arrival of new philology in England, the EETS is not the logical, improved successor to the antiquarianism of Percy, but ultimately part of an epistemic shift that, in 1966, Foucault felt we could not fully understand, "probably because we are still caught inside it" (221). This statement contains its own contradiction; the fact that Foucault can say it is a sign of an ability, however partial, to stand outside the episteme that arose in the early nineteenth century. In part because of such work as Foucault's, the statement is less obviously true now; what *is* clear is that it was completely true in the 1860s, when scholars had an unbreachable confidence in their modernity and objective improvement on the approach of their antiquarian predecessors.

The full ramifications of this epistemic shift are not witnessed, in the case of Middle English, until the founding of the EETS in 1864. By the time of the establishment of the Extra Series and the Chaucer Society in 1867–68, the time of the reform that saw the enfranchisement of nearly a million people, Furnivall's mechanisms for the extension of the national heritage franchise to the English people were all in place. Yet at the same time as this rupture broke the hegemony of aristocrats and their values over Middle English—the very point when a genuine public-sphere mechanism appeared to have been implemented, one that could guarantee a copy of every text for anyone who could afford the reasonable sum of a guinea a year—a gap between laypeople and initiates opened up.

The EETS was far ahead of the equivalent developments in education that would make early English literature more readable and understandable—indeed the EETS fueled some of these developments, with its encouragement of textbooks and examinations. What the EETS failed to do was develop the apparent potential for medieval literature to ride on the back of pre-Raphaelitism, Ruskinian Gothicism, and Tennysonian Arthurianism to broad public interest; what it substituted instead was a mechanism tending toward the privatizing and institutionalizing of medieval literature, which would eventually be largely the preserve of those who had acquired skills from an education that was still very much for the few.

This occurred despite Furnivall's stated intentions and the nondisciplinarian, philologically vague, and hence supposedly nonexclusive principles on which the EETS operated. If Furnivall had been a better philologist, the society might have been called the Middle English Text Society or the Medieval Text Society. But his real breadth of philological knowledge was questionable, at best. His own writings show only a general understanding of the field and "Early English," which has taken on a retrospective clarity, for Furnivall simply meant anything from the tenth to the seventeenth century.[50] Alois Brandl recalled that Furnivall "was not a philologist of thorough linguistic training: I should not even care to assert too positively that he could conjugate an Anglo-Saxon verb" (*VPR*, 10).

Yet the democratically fashioned "Early English" that was the result of this philological looseness was not long in redefining itself and finding its place in the academy. The 1867 annual report of the EETS lists

352 subscribers. Around 100 of these lived in London, about 40 in Scotland (principally Edinburgh and Glasgow), 36 in or near Manchester, 24 in Oxford and Cambridge, and about 20 outside Britain, chiefly in the United States. The remaining minority were in other English cities and the countryside. There were a few aristocrats, but subscribers consisted overwhelmingly of private gentlemen who added "Esquire" to their names. The appearance of several rectories and vicarages in the addresses suggests the interest of intellectual clergy, while Robert Rumney esq., of the Ardwick Chemical Works near Manchester, and George Muntz, of the Albion Tube Works in Birmingham, were perhaps educated managers who rallied to Furnivall's call to duty. Relatively few subscribers, as the surprisingly low figure for Oxford and Cambridge suggests, were academics; about 20 libraries subscribed.[51]

By 1879, most subscribers were still British residents, but many more libraries, some overseas, had subscribed. By 1905, however—when the subscription was still a guinea for each of the series—there had been a dramatic change. Of 287 subscribers, more than 230 took both the Original Series and Extra Series. Of the total, almost 200 were institutional subscribers such as colleges and libraries, private and public. Sixty-one of the libraries were in the United States alone. Gone are the country vicars of the 1860s, and many of the individuals are clearly academics, men such as A. S. Napier, former Merton Professor of English Language and Literature; Walter Raleigh, Oxford's foundation literature professor in the previous year; and George Saintsbury, literature professor at Edinburgh. The U.S. addresses suggest an almost purely academic interest.[52]

In one respect, this represents the success of Furnivall's plan. Through international libraries, a vastly increased and global readership could be achieved, at no further cost to the EETS. But of course Furnivall's plan for the reenfranchisement of the population in the national heritage was entirely defeated by this trend. Evidently, as the general lay readers who had subscribed in the 1860s and 1870s died or let their subscriptions lapse, they were simply not replaced by others like them. In fact, the 1905 subscriber list suggests that without the successful dissemination of the society's texts in institutions abroad, particularly in the United States, the discipline's flagship might well have collapsed for lack of local support before Middle English secured itself as part of "Eng Lit" at the old universities. Furnivall still pounded the nationalist drum, but now with a rather doleful beat: "the Society's experience has shown the very small number of those inheritors of the speech of Cynewulf, Chaucer, and Shakspere, who care two guineas a year for the records of that speech. 'Let the dead past bury its dead' is still the cry of Great Britain and her Colonies, and of America, in the matter of language."[53]

Furnivall seemed not to be able to see his great success—he had created a subject for study—perhaps because, in doing so, he had apparently destroyed any chance for a nonacademic, public-sphere community of readers, a society rather than a "Society." Had Furnivall assisted Middle English in its "political suicide"? In the conclusion of this book, I want to consider that question; before doing so, it remains only to look at the critical role of Chaucer studies in the progress of Middle English to institutional and academic status.

CHAPTER 7

"Wise and Gentle Speech"
From the Chaucer Society to the Universities

1900

In his poem *The Regement of Princes*, completed in 1412, Thomas Hoccleve recalled the dead poet he named his dear master. He tells how he commissioned an image of the poet, which appears in an early manuscript of the poem found in the Harleian collection. In this famous picture, Chaucer is seen in old age; he is pointing at a stanza of Hoccleve's, which reads:

Al thogh his lyfe be queynt, the resemblaunce
Of him hath in me so fressh lyflynesse,
That, to putte othir men in remembraunce
Of his persone, I haue heere his lyknesse
Do make, to this ende in sothfastnesse,
That thei that haue of him lest thought & mynde,
By this peynture may ageyn him fynde.[1]

Chaucer's outstretched hand points at the words "lyknesse" and "sothfastnesse," as if to cement Hoccleve's purpose, linking image, word, and person in an unbroken memorializing circle.

Almost five hundred years later, this image was once again the key to remembering Chaucer. It was reproduced in 1900 in photographic facsimile as one of the illustrations to *The Portraits of Geoffrey Chaucer* by M. H. Spielmann, a Chaucer Society copublication produced to commemorate the quincentenary of the poet's death. The image, Spielmann wrote, "is here reproduced from a photograph taken with the latest improvements, so that the relative tones and values may be set forth on the page in a degree of perfection and completeness never before attained."[2] Spielmann and the Chaucer Society here celebrate not just the pivotal place of the poet in the Middle Ages, but also the technologies of modernity that have allowed his image to be reproduced anew. It was a good time for remembering Chaucer. Frederick Furnivall and the many contributors to the Chaucer Society could justifiably say that there was now a respectable subject called Chaucer studies. They could look with satisfaction on the criticism and scholarship devoted to the poet, which con-

Figure 4. The Hoccleve portrait of Chaucer, circa 1415, thought to be the original portrait from which all others derive. From MS Harl 4866, by permission of The British Library.

firmed his important place in university curricula. They knew that, after decades of compromises, a modern scholar had produced the definitive edition of Chaucer's works, completed just three years before.

The Hoccleve portrait was vital to the project of remembering Chaucer in the nineteenth century. It had been attached to Chaucer's work in one form or another throughout the century, so that it was this image more than any other that readers relied upon for their ideas about Chaucer's appearance. And, in turn, the image was used as a guide not just for how Chaucer looked, but for conceptions of his character as well. Increasingly, in fact, nineteenth-century scholars explicitly remembered Chaucer in a way oddly analogous to the way Hoccleve had claimed to remember the poet and had asked his readers to recall him. Nineteenth-century scholars remembered Chaucer in a fashion that had precedent going back to the sixteenth century: as an unparalleled observer of human nature and as the almost single-handed renovator of a barbarous language. This was a tradition, of course, that was underpinned by the *distance* between the later scholar and the medieval poet, whose achievement was thought the more colossal because of the alien and barbarous time in which he lived:

163

Yet when we further recollect that they [Chaucer's "best works"] were written in a remote and semi-barbarous age, that Chaucer had to a certain degree to create a language, or to restore to credit a language which had been sunk into vulgarity and contempt by being considered as a language of slaves, that history and the knowledge of past ages existed only in unconnected fragments, and that his writings, stupendous as we find them, are associated, as to the period of their production, with the first half-assured lispings of civilisation and the muse, the astonishment and awe with which we regard the great father of English poetry must be exceedingly increased.[3]

Here, in his 1803 biography of the poet, William Godwin encapsulates a common view of Chaucer. This allowed scholars to see Chaucer as both of his time (as a great observer of everyday life) and out of it as well (as someone who stands intellectually and linguistically apart from the Middle Ages). In both roles, what impresses Godwin is Chaucer's incipient modernity despite his enormous distance from the modernity in which Godwin writes.

In the later nineteenth century, this attitude would not disappear, but would be accompanied by a way of remembering Chaucer that was paradoxically close to Hoccleve's. Hoccleve was anxious to secure a personal relationship to Chaucer, as David Carlson suggests, because the *Regement* was a major plea for patronage, which could be enhanced by an association between its author and the recently departed poet.[4] In a way that is symbolized by their recurrent use of the Hoccleve portrait, scholars in the later nineteenth century remembered Chaucer much as Hoccleve had asked his readers to remember him in 1412. Rather than emphasizing the great distance between themselves and the poet, they wrote about him almost as if they, too, had known him.

This apparent paradox resulted, in part, from the influence of comparative philology on such men as Furnivall, Walter Skeat, and Henry Bradshaw. Because they understood the processes underlying linguistic change, they did not simply dismiss medieval language as barbarous, and, writing in an era of decline in religion, they were less inclined to the prejudice against the Roman Catholic Church that colors earlier attitudes to the Middle Ages. A better understanding of Chaucerian language and of the time in which he lived lessened the apparent distance.

But there was more at work than a new scholarly objectivity. Nineteenth-century scholars reacted very subjectively to Chaucer as well. Seth Lerer has noted that most of the fifteenth-century poets, like Hoccleve, wrote as if they had been personal friends of Chaucer's: "virtually all Chaucerians throughout the century seek to establish their relationship to Chaucer by appealing to some kind of personal relation to the poet. Either by claiming friendship or imagining a sort of tutorial acquaintance, these writers try to sustain Chaucer's presence in their work."[5] This posture should not be taken at face value, Lerer argues. Nineteenth-century critics did not have this possibility of closeness to Chaucer available to them, yet to an unusual degree, they absorbed the rhetoric of the fifteenth-century writers; they wrote as if in some sense they *did* know Chaucer better than other people did, and they knew him in some kind of personal way. The Hoccleve portrait and the status of Chaucer as *auctor* allowed for this construction to happen, in a way that could not happen with any other Middle English writing.

The scholarship that emerged from this formation was crucial to the last phases of academic acceptance of Middle English studies.

"Our Glorious Old Poet": Chaucer from Thynne to Wright

Unlike almost the entire body of Middle English literature, some of the work of Geoffrey Chaucer had always been accessible since William Caxton's first edition of the *Canterbury Tales* in 1478. The mission of Chaucer editors from Thomas Tyrwhitt onward was consequently very different from that of editors of early English from Hearne to Furnivall. Insofar as they were rescuing Chaucer's text, they were rescuing it not from obscurity but from bad editions. They were promoting the poet with the help of a considerable tradition of acclaim for his importance rather than one of complete indifference on the part of the reading public. Bolstered by rich tradition, Chaucer's work, by the nineteenth century, tended to circulate in quite different social and cultural forms and exchanges from those forced on other Middle English texts. The standard criticism of the antiquarians was that they valued old poetry just because it was old. "Old poets" are usually "only valuable because they are old," as Robert Southey wrote in 1807. Chaucer's poetry was not just old, however, but obviously good, and so stood outside antiquarian forms of value and participated in more generally shared regimes of value; as Southey continued, "[N]othing but his age prevents Chaucer from being universally ranked among the greatest poets of his country."[6] Chaucer was not, like everything else in post-Conquest literature, "Early English"; Chaucer was already literature. "[T]he affecting parts of Chaucer," as Wordsworth wrote in 1801, "are almost always expressed in language pure and universally intelligible even to this day."[7]

This segregation of Chaucer's work from, rather than its inclusion in, early English was typical of attitudes to the poet after Caxton's time. The antiquarians responsible for the retrieval of early English were attracted, in various ways, to the *difference* of the medieval text. Difference might be negatively imagined, as in the linguistic barbarousness of an old ballad, in which case the text is valued for the way in which it is of interest despite its barbarism, or it might be more positively conceived, as when a text is recommended for its philological value: "philological value" resides precisely in the *difference* between the medieval and modern forms of a word.

The retrieval and dissemination of the work of Chaucer, as Southey's remark suggests, were based on precisely the opposite principle. Despite having lived in the linguistically and culturally barbarous fourteenth century, Chaucer was valuable for his *identity* with modernity. After Caxton, Chaucer's editors and commentators again and again commended him for the way in which he transcended his time to write poetry that was as good as modern poetry. Certainly, Chaucer was regrettably medieval in his tendency to write low and unserious tales; he was incurably of the church of Rome (though both problems could be mitigated). But with the perpetuation of the notion that Chaucer had in effect created modern English by his linguistic innovativeness, he was established not simply as premier medieval poet, but as a great poet for any era.[8]

Dedicating his edition of Chaucer's works to Henry VIII in 1532, William Thynne argued for his interest in Chaucer primarily on linguistic grounds. Intellectual and cultural sophistication are indicated in refined language, he proposed, such as that of the Greeks and Romans. Among Englishmen, there have been those who "haue right well and notably endeuoyred and employed them selves / to the beautifyeng and bettryng of thenglysh tonge." In Chaucer's works, Thynne argued, there was a beautifying of the English tongue the more remarkable for having happened in an age in which a general barbarousness, probably ordained by God, had obtained. In Chaucer's works

> is so manyfest comprobacion of his excellent lernyng *in* all kyndes of doctrynes and sciences / suche frutefulnesse in wordes / wel accordynge to the mater and purpose / so swete and plesaunt sentences / suche perfectyon in metre / the composycion so adapted / suche fresshnesse of inuencion / compendyousnesse in narration / suche sensyble and open style / lackyng neither maieste ne mediocrite couenable *in* disposycion / and suche sharpnesse or quicknesse in conclusyon / that it is moche to be marueyled / howe in his tyme / whan doutlesse all good letters were layde a slepe throughout y[e] worlde / as the thynge whiche either by the disposycion & influence of the bodies aboue / or by other ordynaunce of god / semed lyke and was in daunger to haue utterly perysshed / suche an excellent poete in our tonge / shulde as it were (nature repugnyng) spryng and a ryse.[9]

Chaucer's linguistic and poetic eminence remained a truism of criticism after Thynne. George Puttenham declined to look beyond the period of Edward III in his study of poetry because "there is litle or nothing worth commendation to be founde written in this arte" after the

Conquest, which had altered the language and brought "a certain mar-tiall barbarousnes" to English culture.[10] Chaucer and Gower were poets "of the first age" (48), and Chaucer was "the most renowmed of them all" (49). To a 1643 chronicler Chaucer was "the *Homer* of our Nation."[11] John Dart, in the life of Chaucer prefixed to John Urry's edition of 1721, found one of Chaucer's great virtues to be his observation of nature, which set him apart from other medieval poets: "As he had a discerning Eye he discovered Nature in all her appearances, and stript off every disguise with which the *Gothick* Writers had cloathed her: He knew that those Dresses would change as Times altered; but that she her self would al-ways be the same, and that she could never fail to please in her simple attire."[12] Here emerges Chaucer the realist, who, like Shakespeare, is for all time because the reality, or nature, that he observes is unchanging, while the fanciful distortions of other "Gothick" writers bound them to their (barbarous) time. Although Dart did not believe that Chaucer's verse was regular, "His Language, how unintelligible soever it may seem, is more modern than that of any of his Cotemporaries, or of those that fol-lowed him at the distance of Fifty or Sixty years, as *Harding, Skelton,* and others; and in some places it is to this day so smooth, concise and beautiful, that even Mr. *Dryden* would not attempt to alter it."[13]

Chaucer, to Dart, is somehow more modern than the era in which he lived and even, paradoxically, more modern than poets of the century after his death. This construction of Chaucer as both medieval and mod-ern was characteristic after the fifteenth century. As Lee Patterson re-minds us, Chaucer was constructed not principally as a father but as a master by his successors in the fifteenth century. But Dryden's securing of Chaucer as "the father of English poetry" introduces a new conception, linked to the invention of Chaucer's realism. "By returning poetry to the universality of human nature, Chaucer escaped [the Middle Ages]," Patterson writes. "And he was not merely a Renaissance rather than a medieval poet: more to the point, he was the first poet who lived in our own, postmedieval time—the first modern poet and hence the father of English poetry."[14]

Such a notion entailed the absolution or excusing of the poet from his more medieval faults, the "great wants" that, Philip Sidney wrote, were "fit to be forgiven in so reverend antiquity."[15] Writers on Chaucer from the sixteenth to the nineteenth century therefore tried to find ways around such manifest faults as the bad language in the mouths of some of the Canterbury pilgrims. The more adept writer could turn this into a strength, in that it could be seen as another aspect of Chaucerian realism and imitation of nature.[16]

The dual role of the poet as medieval and modern was confirmed at the outset of the nineteenth century in Godwin's substantial (if highly spec-ulative) biography. The worth of a writer, Godwin felt, must be judged by absolute standards, without concession to the situation of the man.

At the same time, though, it is difficult to ignore the poet whose circumstances will be "topics of interesting research."[17] By this dual standard, Godwin wants to evaluate Chaucer in terms of all literary history, but without sacrificing his interest as a poet belonging to a particular context. He could therefore argue that Chaucer's "best works," such as the *Canterbury Tales*, "have an absolute merit, which stands in need of no extrinsic accident to show it to advantage, and no apology to atone for its concomitant defects. They class with whatever is best in the poetry of any country or any age." At the same time, we are astonished by the assurance with which Chaucer wrote, given that he lived "in a remote and semi-barbarous age" (2:582). Likewise, in 1831, Robert Southey, perhaps with Godwin's book in mind, said that Chaucer, with Spenser, Milton, and Shakespeare, was of "the first class" and that he achieved what he did "with a half-formed language: retaining what was popular, and rejecting what was barbarous, he at once refined and enriched it."[18] In this view once again, Chaucer is of his time and transcends it; a medieval poet, he is also the first of the moderns. Through his linguistic innovation, he begins the work of constructing modernity.

Among the consequences of this strong tradition of Chaucerian eminence was the tendency for Early English studies and Chaucer studies to remain quite separate well into the nineteenth century. Chaucer's work did not require the specially created publishing mechanisms that printed other early English works, because it was already a commercial property. As the mission of most antiquarians was the retrieval of unjustly neglected literature, Chaucer did not require their attentions. Before Thomas Wright produced his edition of the *Canterbury Tales* in 1847–51, there was an almost complete separation between work on Chaucer and work on the rest of Middle English. While Percy, Ritson, Scott, Pinkerton, and Madden read Chaucer, they did not write on him or edit his work. Tyrwhitt, on the other hand, edited no Middle English other than Chaucer. Thomas Warton did deal with both, but clearly thought of Chaucer and Gower as marking a boundary between Saxonism and modernity. Wright, by contrast, did extensive editing work in all of Middle English, and his *Canterbury Tales* was published by the Percy Society in its series entitled Early English Poetry, Ballads, and Popular Literature of the Middle Ages.

Before Wright's edition signaled this fusion, however, Tyrwhitt's edition of the *Canterbury Tales* (1774–78) enabled a series of imitations to be produced by enterprising booksellers that for a time ensured that Chaucer would be explicitly in the realm of a cultural property other than Early English. Most Chaucer editions up to the 1860s were plundered from Tyrwhitt and from sixteenth-century prints for works other than the *Canterbury Tales*. The result was that by midcentury there was no scholarly edition of Chaucer. In 1855, F. J. Child wrote to Frederic Madden from Harvard to ask which edition of Chaucer he should use for

scholarly articles he planned to write on the language of Chaucer and
Gower. Madden's habitually sour tone, in his survey of the field, should
not obscure the fact that there was much for the scholar to be pessimistic
about:

> at present I despair of seeing an Edition of Chaucer given by a scholar
> who is sufficiently versed in MSS. to give the text strictly as it is
> <u>written</u>. In regard to the Editions, Tyrwhitt's, as you are aware, is
> very objectionable, and Urry's below contempt. Wright's edition of
> the Canterbury Tales is certainly intitled to more consideration.
> The Harleian MS. 7334 he prints from, is a very fine & fairly writ-
> ten volume, on vellum, but not of so early a date as he supposes—
> I should say, <u>not earlier than 1420</u> and the scribe is apt to fall into
> errors both of <u>commission</u> and <u>omission</u>. It is believed, that Mr W.
> really took Tyrwhitt's text for his groundwork, correcting the orthog-
> raphy by the Harleian MS. but it is only by a long & careful colla-
> tion the fact could be proved. The edition of Chaucer published by
> Pickering, in 1845, is only valuable for the Memoir of Chaucer pre-
> fixed by Sir H. Nicolas.

Madden concluded by recommending to Child that he "procure & follow the new Edition of Chaucer by <u>Rob.t Bell</u>" because he knew "no
better or more worthy Edition of our glorious old Poet."[19]

This state of affairs existed because the very familiarity and popularity of Chaucer as an author had actually hindered scholarly endeavor.
Always quick to criticize the scholarship of the 1770s, the nineteenth-
century antiquarians were not equally quick to try to better it. Despite
the many nineteenth-century complaints about Tyrwhitt's shortcomings
as an editor of Chaucer, edition after edition in the nineteenth century
was deeply indebted to—if not outrightly plagiarized from—his *Canterbury Tales.* Tyrwhitt's understanding of grammar, to the era of comparative philology, looked weak; some of the manuscripts he used were of
little authority; he did not fully understand Chaucer's meter; and his
principles of emendation did not accord with the standards of the nineteenth century. But he did what no one was prepared to do for the next
seventy-five years by going to a significant body of manuscripts of the
Canterbury Tales and doing the work of comparing them.[20] Into the confusion left at the time of Thomas Speght, Tyrwhitt brought an order to
the tales that is the basis of most succeeding schemes, and he knew
enough to drop from the work *The Plowman's Tale* and *Gamelyn.* His
"scholarly responsibility" and "relative deference to the medieval documents themselves" suggest that Tyrwhitt should be considered "the
founder of modern traditions of Chaucer editing."[21]

The immediate consequence of Tyrwhitt's reestablishment of Chaucer's importance was that Chaucer could be promoted not so much as

premier medieval poet but as one of the great English, or British, poets, *despite* his medievalness. To borrow from Lerer's description of Boccaccio's treatment of Petrarch, Chaucer is historicized as a man and dehistoricized as a writer.[22] This is abundantly evident in the collected editions of the British poets for which there was a great vogue in the late eighteenth and nineteenth centuries. In 1773, just before Tyrwhitt's edition, Hugh Blair's collected English poets had begun with Milton. Thereafter, such collections usually placed Chaucer at the beginning of the English or British poetry they claimed to define. Robert Anderson's important work, *A Complete Edition of the Poets of Great Britain*, published in thirteen volumes in London and Edinburgh in 1792–95, opened with the works of Chaucer and unequivocally placed the poet as "certainly the first person in England to whom the appellation of a poet, in its genuine lustre, could be applied."[23] As in most of these series, Anderson simply reused Tyrwhitt's text for the *Canterbury Tales.*[24]

This assumption about Chaucer, and the editorial shortcut, then characterized series after series. In 1822, a series entitled The British Poets: Including Translations filled the first six of its one hundred volumes with the works of Chaucer edited by S. W. Singer.[25] In 1845 the London publisher William Pickering issued *The Poetical Works of Geoffrey Chaucer* in six volumes as part of his series, the Aldine Edition of the British Poets. In 1854–57, Robert Bell, a historian, biographer, and journalist, issued his series, the Annotated Edition of the English Poets, which appeared in monthly volumes at 2s 6d each. *The Poetical Works of Geoffrey Chaucer* in eight volumes formed the first volumes of this series. In 1866, a new Aldine edition appeared, with Chaucer's works edited by Richard Morris.[26]

Each of these series claims to be representing British or English poetry, and each anchors that poetry in the work of Chaucer, who therefore, for all his medievalness, is also, at least implicitly, the harbinger of modernity. This is Chaucer "the post-eighteenth-century Poet," as Ralph Hanna puts it, "whose *Works* sat easily on the same shelf with those of Shakespeare, Keats, and others, in a volume commensurate."[27] None of these editions fulfilled the requirements of scholars. They plundered Tyrwhitt for the *Tales* and early prints for other texts, and they often reprinted Tyrwhitt's introductory essays. Sir Harris Nicolas's memoir of Chaucer, said by Eleanor Hammond to be the first useful biography, appeared in the first Aldine edition of 1845 and was thereafter often reused.[28] The series editions tended not to have such basic markers of scholarliness as line numbers and rarely featured critical comment more recent than Tyrwhitt's. They capitalized, in other words, on the poet's salability as a national literary figure, and did so with a minimum of scholarly or editorial work.

The first sign of a scholarly break with this tradition came with Wright's Percy Society edition of the *Tales*, the first since Tyrwhitt's in which the editor went back to manuscripts.[29] This became the principal edition of the *Tales* for nearly half a century, and it was this that Francis Child went on to use, despite Madden's endorsement of Bell. As Thomas Ross notes, Wright's edition has since gained a certain celebrity because in it Wright appeared to have stumbled on the best-text method of editing by selecting one manuscript as his base text, even though that manuscript, Harley 7334, has since fallen from favor.[30] In fact it is almost certain that Wright's choice of a single manuscript arose from the expediency of a journeyman antiquarian rather than strong editorial theory. Although Wright was undoubtedly knowledgeable, his editions often reflected in their superficiality his need to turn out material rapidly; diligence, in Wright's case, would have been costly. His *Canterbury Tales* is a more painstaking work than some of his editions, such as his *Richard the Redeless* produced for the Camden Society in 1838, but it shows many signs of haste, as, for example, in the fact that it has no glossary. There is also good reason to suspect that Madden was correct to suggest, in his letter to Child, that Wright had barely edited at all, instead using Tyrwhitt's text with the spelling altered in accord with Harley 7334.[31] Wright's text, nevertheless, did place the *Canterbury Tales* unequivocally within the framework of Early English. The fortunes of the two areas of study would not again be disentangled, and the same people would lead scholarship in both Chaucer studies and Middle English more generally from this time on.

Modern Chaucer: Skeat, Furnivall, and Bradshaw

The genealogy of nineteenth-century Chaucer editions to 1866 clearly shows that the poet's work was substantially invested with symbolic capital, in a way that allowed many profitable editions to appear in the general literary marketplace. At the same time, no real advances had been made on the scholarship of Tyrwhitt's 1775–78 edition, and these advances were not to come until after the establishment of the Chaucer Society. Why was it so difficult to surpass Tyrwhitt? The cases of Thomas Wright and Robert Bell suggest the answer. These were professional antiquarians and men of letters, men who worked to a schedule and relied on their work for their income. Wright no doubt saved himself weeks of labor by not including a glossary and by his use of Tyrwhitt's work, which allowed him to go on to the next of the 129 works attributed to him in the British Library's catalog. Bell, issuing the national poetic literature at an octavo volume a month, must have been similarly busy.

It was the subscription societies that were producing the real editorial advances of the day. Men such as Bell could sell the national literature, but they could not ready it for academic acceptance and render it satisfactory to scholars who could with more and more certainty distinguish real Chaucer from imitations. The result is a move that appears contradictory. The popular poet's work was taken away from the businessmen of the Strand and Covent Garden and put in the hands of the philologers. Wright's Percy Society edition of the *Tales* was the first move in this direction, and within a few years, the Chaucer Society would effectively take over the production of Chaucer's work. The cheap octavos would not go away, but notions of "Chaucer" would now be constructed and handed down by a small group of increasingly academic scholars.

It was Frederick Furnivall, of course, who had the most profound influence on the unifying of Chaucer with the rest of Middle English. He, too, did this while maintaining a clear separation of the two fields, in two different societies. It was never the mission of the EETS to print Chaucer; in Furnivall's mind Chaucer apparently belonged somewhere else. Furnivall, as a publisher, had to consider his minute market very closely; he judged, and judged correctly, that it would sustain two separate societies, each charging an annual subscription of two guineas (if the EETS Extra Series is taken into account), and there was apparently little risk that subscribers would feel that Chaucer should have come to them for the two guineas they had already paid for the EETS. It is worth noting that Furnivall later speculated that the market would bear a Lydgate and Occleve Society, and was completely wrong.[32] Only Chaucer could stand alone in this way. Yet the ultimate effect was the linking of Chaucer and Early English. Without sacrificing any of Chaucer's eminence as a poet of modernity—indeed, he enhanced it—Furnivall re-placed Chaucer firmly back in his time. One effect was to enhance the conceptual status of "Middle English."

It is no accident that soon after the establishment of the Chaucer Society, the term "Middle English" in its fuller sense began to come into widespread use. It was Skeat (later to be a professor of Anglo-Saxon who did most of his work in the area of Middle English) who helped establish "Middle English" in its modern sense. And it was in Skeat's work more than anywhere else that Chaucer Studies, a genuine disciplinary area ripe for plucking by the academy, was established and the conditions created for the study of Anglo-Saxon, of Chaucer, and of earlier Middle English to coalesce as Old and Middle English. Skeat gave Middle English coherence; although some popular writers on language would continue to use the more complex ways of compartmentalizing the language, a de facto coherence was given by Skeat, Morris, Bradshaw, and other scholars of their time who began treating the whole post-Conquest period as a linguistically unified entity.

In Chaucer, furthermore, the period found its supreme author-persona. The need for authors, as we have seen, was such a strong characteristic of early scholarship that, in their absence, they were invented or conjured up out of vague references. So, variously, the minstrels, Thomas of Erceldoune, Huchown of the Awle Ryal, and other equally shadowy authors were called into being to suit the needs of editors. Chaucer suffered from none of the disadvantages of these authors. He could justifiably be given a pivotal place in literary history. He was for Skeat the second poet after Shakespeare, or at worst equal with Milton; for Furnivall, "the second greatest poet of our country, the fourth greatest of the world."[33] And Chaucer also fulfilled, and fulfilled better than anyone else except perhaps Langland, that primary function of early English: the illustration of the manners and customs of our ancestors.

Skeat, again, was instrumental in securing Chaucer in this role. In 1894, after nearly three decades of work on fixing, canonizing, and academicizing Chaucer's oeuvre, Skeat's compendious Clarendon Chaucer, as it was known, appeared. This project has a look of utopian definitiveness about it. David Lodge's fictional academic, Morris Zapp, aimed to end Jane Austen studies by producing a body of critical work on the novelist so comprehensive that it would leave nothing to say: Skeat's work looks as if he had a similarly comprehensive ambition. "The present edition," he wrote, "comprises the whole of Chaucer's Works, whether in verse or prose, together with a commentary (contained in the Notes) upon every passage which seems to present any difficulty or to require illustration."[34] The edition also featured a life of the poet, and the seventh volume (published in 1897) printed the poems attributed to Chaucer but deemed spurious.

A utopian and positivist ambition was at the heart of Furnivall's societies: the EETS took on the task of printing all there was of early English, and the Chaucer Society had a similarly all-encompassing mission. The Chaucer Society did not produce the definitive edition itself, but it did do the extensive preliminary work that was necessary for it to come into being. It was the society, through the activities of Furnivall, Bradshaw, and Skeat in particular, that found the best manuscripts; Bradshaw's rhyme-tests helped sort the spurious work from the genuine; the Bradshaw Shift in tale order (which has proved a less durable contribution) seemed to have ordered the *Canterbury Tales* so far as they could be ordered, and the biographical searches initiated by Furnivall had produced most of the biographical material that would ever be known.

A great deal of this work was done by Furnivall himself, who, although not truly an editor of Chaucer, brought many manuscripts into print.[35] He acted as a coordinator for the activities of increasing numbers of scholars in England, the United States (Child), and Germany (Bernhard ten Brink). Furnivall produced several parallel-text editions of the *Canterbury Tales* and others of Chaucer's works, and in his important six-text edition of the *Tales,* despite a typically eccentric commitment to print three manuscripts from public institutions and three in private hands, he brought the famous Ellesmere and Hengwrt manuscripts into prominence. He provided a forum for the scholarship of the dilatory Bradshaw, which might not otherwise have appeared, and also encouraged Skeat, who acknowledged in the Clarendon Chaucer a great debt to Furnivall (*CC*, 4:vii).

Furnivall was closely involved in the process of organizing the Clarendon Chaucer, a much delayed and troubled project. This edition had been commissioned as early as 1864, under the general editorship of John Earle, the professor of Anglo-Saxon at Oxford, with the assistance of Bradshaw and William Aldis Wright, the librarian at Trinity College, Cambridge. As it happened, the publisher Alexander Macmillan had previously proposed to Bradshaw that he edit a small edition for the Globe series, but Macmillan courteously deferred this project when the larger one (known as the Library edition) was commissioned.[36] However, the edition did not progress in Earle's hands, and he resigned in 1870 with nothing achieved. The position was then offered to Aldis Wright, who declined it, and Skeat, who proposed Bradshaw instead.[37] Bartholomew Price, the secretary of the Clarendon Press, offered the job to Bradshaw in November 1870.[38]

Bradshaw's response illustrates his typical blend of wild enthusiasm and paralyzing laziness. He consulted Skeat and Aldis Wright, drew up a comprehensive proposal specifying exactly which poems would appear in which volumes, and drafted a four-page reply, all by the afternoon of his receipt of Price's letter.[39] Price, having put the proposal before the delegates of the press, was able to tell Bradshaw they had accepted his proposal by the end of the month.[40] But within days, Bradshaw was writing to Alexander Macmillan, with very cold feet, now worrying that the Clarendon edition would take him too long and involve too much work, even with the help of Aldis Wright and Skeat. In addition, he said he felt half committed to the smaller Globe edition for Macmillan. In December 1870, Bradshaw wrote to Price to back away from the Clarendon Chaucer.[41] Then, strangely, he wrote to Furnivall to say he would edit Chaucer's minor poems for the Chaucer Society, which Furnivall had been pressing him to do for some years.[42]

The project then languished. Furnivall himself offered to edit the Library Chaucer for Oxford in 1874, but his stock was never high at Oxford and the proposal was quickly rejected by the delegates.[43] Next, in 1879, Macmillan's Globe project was revived, now to be under the joint editorship of Bradshaw and Furnivall. This was potentially the ideal combination of "go-a-head-itiveness" and editorial care; soon, however, Furnivall, Bradshaw, and Macmillan, at whose suggestion is not clear, were considering producing a Library edition themselves, with the Globe edition to appear later. "The thing really seems to be taking shape," Bradshaw wrote of the latter project to Furnivall in August 1879, but these proved to be famous last words.[44] Macmillan's Globe and Library editions never materialized, and neither did Bradshaw's Minor Poems.

While these projects went nowhere in the 1870s, yet another popular, accessible edition appeared. This was Walter Skeat's *Poetical Works of*

Geoffrey Chaucer, published in 1878, another hybrid text that was essentially a revamping of Robert Bell's edition, prefixed with an essay by Skeat and using for the *Canterbury Tales* Wright's text. It featured notes from Speght, Tyrwhitt, Wright, and Skeat himself. Yet again, the easy option had been taken, and Chaucer remained without an authoritative edition. Despite the fact that at least two scholars—Furnivall and Skeat—were prepared to do the work required to produce either the Clarendon Press's proposed Library edition or Macmillan's more modest Globe edition, it was obviously in the comparatively easy reedition of Bell by Skeat that the profits lay for both editor and publisher, the more so as the market was not crowded by a monumental edition. Neither the Library nor the Globe edition was expected to make money quickly. Macmillan told Furnivall that the Globe edition would not make money for twelve to fifteen years, while a Library edition would make money, but would involve a greater initial outlay.[45]

At some point in the later 1880s or early 1890s—exactly when is not quite clear—Skeat was commissioned to produce what became the Clarendon Chaucer.[46] The monumental work at last appeared in 1894, some thirty years after it was first proposed. It could scarcely have appeared much earlier, however, given the major groundwork done by Chaucer Society publications, particularly in the 1870s. The Clarendon Chaucer reflects many influences: the combined thinking of Bradshaw, Aldis Wright, Furnivall, and Skeat himself; Skeat's "trial run" in his revision of Bell; the activities of the Chaucer Society over a quarter of a century; and the financial commitment of the Clarendon Press. The result marked "the beginning of a new epoch in Chaucer scholarship," according to A. S. G. Edwards, "the beginning of its Modern Age." Edwards states that while much of Skeat's work may be outmoded, his texts were the basis for most "subsequent editorial work."[47] Skeat brought Chaucer to modernity.

Moral Chaucer

Despite their many differences, one feature is shared by most of the nineteenth-century editions, up to and including the Clarendon Chaucer. This is a frontispiece or a cover showing the Hoccleve portrait of Chaucer. It is by far the most prevalent image of the poet in nineteenth-century editions. It also, therefore, informed opinions on what kind of person Chaucer was, and it was explicitly referred to by editors in this role. Bell, although he did not print the picture in his annotated edition, described it, and suggested that the "mixture of gravity and sweetness in Occleve's portrait conveys the perfect image of a character not less remarkable for its rare combination of power and sympathy, than for the variety of accomplishments by which it was graced."[48] If Chaucer satisfied the need of a generation of scholars for an author-persona, the

(714)

Tho' Chaucer is dead, I've had his likeness put here who've forgotten him may find him again.

¶ Al-þogh his lyfe be queynt, þe resemblaunce[1]   4992
Of him haþ in me so fressh lyflynesse,
þat, to putte othir men in remembraunce
Of his persone, I haue heere his lyknesse
Do makë, to þis ende in sothfastnesse,   4996
þat þei þat haue of him lest[2] þought & mynde,
By þis peynture may ageyn him fynde.   4998

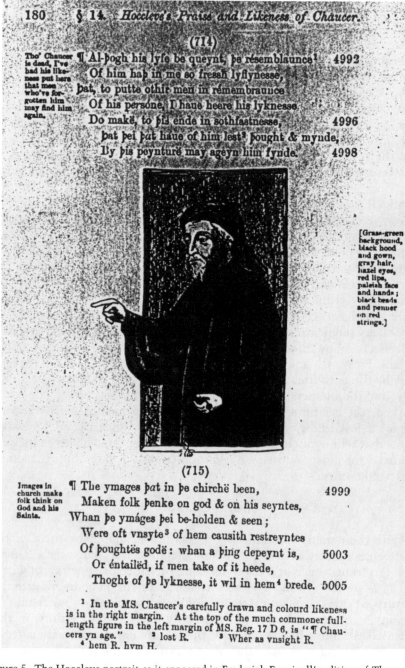

[Grass-green background, black hood and gown, gray hair, hazel eyes, red lips, paleish face and hands; black beads and penner on red strings.]

(715)

Images in church make folk think on God and his Saints.

¶ The ymages þat in þe chirchë been,   4999
Maken folk þenke on god & on his seyntes,
Whan þe ymáges þei be-holden & seen;
Were oft vnsyte[3] of hem causith restreyntes
Of þoughtës godë: whan a þing depeynt is,   5003
Or éntailëd, if men take of it heede,
Thoght of þe lyknesse, it wil in hem[4] brede.   5005

[1] In the MS. Chaucer's carefully drawn and coloured likeness is in the right margin. At the top of the much commoner full-length figure in the left margin of MS. Reg. 17 D 6, is "¶ Chaucers yn age."   [2] lost R.   [3] Wher as vnsight R.
[4] hem R. hym H.

Figure 5. The Hoccleve portrait as it appeared in Frederick Furnivall's edition of *The Regement of Princes*, published by the EETS in 1897. The image appeared in this form in most Chaucer Society publications.

Hoccleve portrait gave them their idea not only of what such a persona should look like, but of what his character was as well. Skeat's Clarendon Chaucer reproduces the celebrated portrait in a facsimile of the manuscript page, as the frontispiece of volume 1. Elsewhere, however, the image had always appeared in more or less stylized and reduced form, no doubt because as it stands in the manuscript, the picture does not fit conveniently on an octavo page. Consequently, in most versions, the image consisted only of the portrait of Chaucer, usually set in the framing rectangle, but entirely detached from Hoccleve's lines. In the portrait represented this way Chaucer simply points into blank space, to the viewer's left. In this fashion, the portrait appeared, sometimes in more than one place, in almost everything produced by the Chaucer Society, of which it was the de facto emblem. Only in Skeat's revision of the Bell Chaucer was the poet reattached to the context of Hoccleve's poem, though in a way that makes Hoccleve's lines entirely subservient to the purpose of representing Chaucer. It is Chaucer's name, not Hoccleve's, that appears above the stanza, which is placed *beneath* the portrait so that Chaucer still points into blank space.

Here, what used to be a text of Hoccleve's is now purely about Chaucer. The decontextualizing of Chaucer in this way breaks the memorializing circle of text, poet, and image. Chaucer now looks very much as if he is standing at a window, and his pointing hand no longer refers to Hoccleve's act of memory in a self-confirming circle, but extends beyond the frame into the nineteenth-century page. As a decontextualized pointer— a guide—Chaucer here overlaps his own medieval space and the space of the nineteenth-century reader, for whom Chaucer is pointing the way.

While the Hoccleve portrait was used and reused, with Chaucer progressively detached from his fifteenth-century context, the Ellesmere representation of Chaucer as pilgrim, which Furnivall reproduced in color in his six-text edition, was less popular. This image has become far better known in the twentieth century, in part perhaps because it fits well with our view of Chaucer as an ironist whose irony extended to his own self-representation. Nineteenth-century scholars were rarely comfortable with Chaucer as a humorous writer, particularly when that humor was of the low kind. They needed their Chaucer to be a much more serious individual, and the Hoccleve portrait offered just this man. It represents visually what Furnivall, Skeat, and Bradshaw did textually with their author. Editors, as did Bell, saw in the Hoccleve Chaucer rather than Ellesmere's slightly absurd pilgrim the kind of man they wanted, and needed, Chaucer to be. However regrettable Chaucer's tendency to spoil a *Knight's Tale* with a *Miller's Tale* or *Reeve's Tale,* whatever his lack of seriousness, Chaucer could always be retrieved as the man of "gravity and sweetness" so clearly portrayed in the Harleian manuscript.

Chaucer's "bad" work was explicable in ways that recovered a truer Chaucer. Skeat, for example, despite his belief that apparent autobiograph-

Figure 6. The Hoccleve portrait as used in Walter Skeat's revision of Robert Bell's *Poetical Works of Geoffrey Chaucer* in 1878. Hoccleve and his act of memory are here forgotten.

ical allusions in the work were unreliable, proposed in the Clarendon Chaucer that the death of Chaucer's wife, probably in 1387, was responsible for the "coarseness" of some of the tales: the Miller's, Reeve's, Shipman's, and Merchant's tales and the Wife of Bath's prologue "can hardly be defended. All these may confidently be dated after the year 1387" (*CC*, 1:liii). (Skeat does not go on to explain whether he thinks it was the poet's grief or the loss of a softening feminine influence that brought about this change.) Chaucer, in the Hoccleve portrait, was Chaucer with this coarseness under control, a wise and serious individual. Chaucer, like other writers of early English, was an illustrator of manners and customs, but he was also more than this. He was an exemplar: moral Chaucer.

This construction of Chaucer was most explicitly developed by Furnivall. Whatever else it was, the Chaucer Society was part fan club, and, as with everything he did, Furnivall worked on Chaucer with a sense of furious mission. Although as ever it was not quite clear *how* the publishing of Chaucer was to achieve national moral amelioration, Furnivall wrote as if Chaucer, the man and his literature, could be the center of a program of moral renewal. In a pamphlet of 1871, Furnivall began what appears to be a standard work of biographical criticism. Establishing a chronology of the canon and a life of the poet, Furnivall detected "a late spring for Chaucer's poetical powers, then a steady advance to the full summer of his genius, followed by a slow autumn of decay, and ended by the chill of death."[49] Gleaning evidence from *The Complaint unto Pity* and the *Book of the Duchess*, Furnivall concluded that Chaucer had suffered from an early, unrequited love affair that "began when he was 21 [and] kept him miserable for eight years" (35). He then proceeds to a lengthy comparison of the *Parliament of Fowls* with the *Teseida*.

To this point, Furnivall seems wholly within the expectations of nineteenth-century criticism. Suddenly, however, Furnivall puts an end to this mode:

> Here for the present I must break off, as I haven't time to study further the rest of the poems just now, and have been for six weeks, and am still, away from almost all my books and literary friends, among bluebells, honeysuckles, laburnums, cuckoos, and nightingales; Chaucer's daisies under my feet, his heavenly harmony of birds about me, and his bright old England all around. (91)

If readers had thought about it at all, they would probably have assumed that Furnivall was writing from his legal chambers in Lincoln's Inn or from the British Museum, to which he made a daily visit when in town and where conditions for antiquarian scholarly work could hardly be more favorable. But by announcing that he is instead in his country retreat at Egham, outside London, Furnivall creates an odd but eloquent moment. Writing *about* Chaucer, in the way late-nineteenth-century London allowed a scholar to do, is suddenly replaced by something much more primitive and immediate: being absorbed into Chaucer's England. It is at this point of unmediated contact with the English countryside Chaucer knew that Furnivall turns to the man himself via the Hoccleve portrait (which appears in the stylized engraved form of the Chaucer Society as the frontispiece to this work):

> The face is wise and tender, full of a sweet and kindly sadness at first sight, but with much bonhommie [*sic*] in it on a further look, and with deepset, farlooking, grey eyes. Not the face of a very old man, a totterer, but of one with work in him yet, looking kindly, though seriously, out on the world before him.... One feels one would like to go to such a man when one was in trouble, and hear his wise and gentle speech. (93)

Chaucer, here, is scarcely more distant from the perceptions of his admiring follower than he was from Hoccleve's memory. It is almost as if he could follow the direction in which he points and step from the frame as moral exemplar and spiritual counselor to us moderns.

This trope of personal contact with the poet does have its comical reverse side. Furnivall expresses his displeasure with Chaucer's bad writing in personal and admonitory terms. The poet should have been "ashamed of himself for this most lame and impotent" conclusion to the *Book of the Duchess*; "he ought to have been caned for it" (42). Chaucer's life records threw up some unpleasant surprises for Furnivall, such as the apparent involvement of the poet in the abduction of Cecily Chaumpaigne, which he thought "looks bad, but was probably not criminal."[50] He found it much more difficult to deal with a possibility raised by Henry Bradshaw when he wrote to Furnivall in 1873 with an ingenious suggestion concerning a possible connection between *Troilus and Criseyde* and John of Gaunt and his mistress Katharine Swynford. Bradshaw's point was only about dating *Troilus*, but Furnivall, overinterpreting, assumed that Bradshaw was saying *Troilus* was written with an immoral aim. His response is almost hysterical: "If the Troilus was really written to justify John of Gaunt's concubinage, the fact is the worst blow to Chaucer's character that has yet been given." He quickly mounted an argument against the suggestion, on the grounds that *Troilus* would not have been a consolation poem for John of Gaunt because it was a tale of *thwarted* love. Furnivall promised to check the relevant dates, "And I've full confidence that either they'll dispel your supposition, or that otherwise we can repel it. It'd be an awful blow if you're right. I should like to kick Chaucer if he wrote Troilus for such a purpose. He can't have done it."[51]

Bradshaw had made no such suggestion, but Furnivall's wild extrapolation from Bradshaw's letter expresses a horror of patronage gone morally wrong, the poet pandering to his master's lecherous desires with a justificatory poem. The kind of poet who would do something like this was not, apparently, one whose wise and gentle speech was likely to be consolation when one was in trouble.

Few scholars wrote in Furnivall's overtly emotional fashion, and this peculiarly strong sense of a personal relationship with the poet is not quite recreated in Walter Skeat's writings about Chaucer. Skeat shows no evident desire to kick or cane the poet; nevertheless, his approach explicitly proposes that he is able to look to Chaucer over the heads of such hapless intermediaries as the scribes, in order to commune with the poet himself. Implicitly, Skeat too wants to speak to, or does actually speak with, Chaucer. He once wrote that the language of the fourteenth century "has long been as familiar to me (as far as such a result is possible) as the language of the present day."[52] Skeat, thirty years after humbling himself before *Lancelot of the Laik,* here all but claims to be a native speaker of Chaucer's language, and his editorial approach to Chaucer is arguably justified on this basis.

An editor, of course, is supposed to know better than others what his text is trying to say, but as A. S. G. Edwards convincingly demonstrates, Skeat's attitude was apparently that he knew better than the manuscripts and perhaps better than Chaucer himself. Referring, in memorable phrase, to Skeat's "emendatorial impetuosity," Edwards suggests that Skeat's own account of his use of the manuscripts does not tell the whole story. Editing the *Canterbury Tales,* Skeat used Ellesmere as his base text, but is not consistent in his recording of variants adopted from other manuscripts, and he does not properly describe his practices of emendation, which are more extensive than he admits.[53] "Skeat's gifts as an editor," Edwards concludes, "did not include the patient sifting of manuscript evidence. He possessed a clear conviction of his capacity to get to the heart of the matter without any sense of the necessity of communicating to his reader the bases on which decisions had been arrived at."[54]

Some readers, at least, were aware of this facet of Skeat's editing as early as 1908, when Hammond wrote that in his editing of the *Tales* "Skeat has not devoted to the MSS such examination as Morell or Tyrwhitt made, and . . . his editorial procedure, a century and more after Tyrwhitt, is guided by the erroneous supposition that the true Chaucerian readings may be picked out intuitively."[55] Through such procedures, Skeat produced a Chaucer rendered smoother, more regular, than any before. Skeat was responsible for smoothing out manuscript orthography, if necessary inventing a form not in the manuscript, and a further result of this "is the appearance of a Chaucer who generally wrote verses of great regularity."[56] Skeat, in short, produced a Chaucer in accord with modern expectations and did so confident in his great intimacy with the poet's work and language and, indeed, the poet himself.

When Skeat revised some of his thinking in the years after the publication of the Clarendon Chaucer, he continued to base his thinking on an intimacy with Chaucer's intentions. In *The Evolution of the Canterbury Tales,* published by the Chaucer Society in 1907, Skeat makes a series of decisions about the *Tales* on the basis of what was going on in Chaucer's mind. He stated that the order and nature of the manuscripts was: "Hengwrt, an archetype; Petworth, showing the first scheme of arrangement; Corpus and Lansdowne, the second; Harleian, the third; Ellesmere and Cambridge, the fourth and last. In the first three schemes, we find Chaucer himself at work, making various experiments. In the last scheme, we find the work of a careful editor." The Harleian manuscript (7334), therefore, was the "authoritative type" with the tale order as Chaucer left it, though it was not to be considered as final.[57]

On the basis of this ordering, Skeat was then able to conclude such things as Chaucer's intent that the Squire and the Man of Law should "belong to the same group" (12). Later, Chaucer "formed a new intention with regard to the Squire, and proposed to let him follow the Merchant.... After forming this new intention, he had to disconnect what he had at this time connected" (12). Chaucer, Skeat contended, "was not the man to revise his work line by line with anything like careful scrutiny." This, and the fact that he never had the chance to see "a completed set of Tales, accounts for all the difficulties that have so often been noted" (27). It was this, for example, which explained the second Nun's referring to herself as a "son of Eve"; Chaucer would have fixed it, but never got around to it.

Skeat now rejects the Bradshaw Shift and supports the unrealistic order of the journey as it stands without the shift. If the manuscripts bring the pilgrims to Sittingbourne before Rochester, "[t]he simplest, and I believe the only true way, is to admit the fact and leave it. I do not doubt that Chaucer could easily have set it right; but, if we are to go by the evidence, it is obvious that he never even attempted it" (30). The ingeniousness of this solution is that it avoids the necessity for the shift, follows the best manuscripts, but at the same time reaffirms the realist reading, because Chaucer would have fixed the problem if he had wanted to or got around to it. We must consider not "what Chaucer ought to have done, we have rather to consider what he actually did" (31) — a precept that works particularly well when the editor believes he knows the author's mind, perhaps rather better than the author did.

Like Furnivall — if in a less dramatic way — Skeat operated with a sense of moral mission in his literary work. "Knowing" the poet was an aspect of literary scholarship, and literary scholarship was essentially a project of moral renovation. Skeat's particular trajectory heightened the moral aspect of literary work. He had trained in classics and mathematics before entering the church, but was then forced to abandon this career because of a (somewhat mysterious) illness at the age of twenty-eight.[58] He was left, by his own account, with an unfulfilled sense of mission to his "fellow-creatures." His response was to transfer his activities to the secular world, through the agency of the teaching of literature:

I can now believe that I was meant to labour in a different field. Each man has his appointed task; and I have long since loyally accepted the educational duty of endeavouring to instil into the minds of Englishmen the respect in which they ought to hold their noble literature and their noble language, and the desirability of fighting against all the forms of error that beset the study of these invaluable treasures. Every true scholar is in some degree a missionary; he must hold fast to that which is good without wavering, and spare no pains to allure men to the reception of the truth. (xx–xxi)

What Skeat outlines here is something very similar to what Ian Hunter has described as the important transition that takes place in the study of English in the nineteenth century, which is exemplified by the figure of Matthew Arnold. In Hunter's paradigm, Arnold became an *"ethical exemplar,"* that *"embodiment of a special set of personal attributes"* as which the man of letters entered "the social sphere."[59] English education originated, Hunter argues, in what he describes as a minority practice of the self, the practice of an elite caste in the late eighteenth century. With the spread of English education in the nineteenth century, the school inspectorate formed "the initial point of contact" at which the man of letters meets the public, governmentally sanctioned self-cultivation represented in the public education system (106). Skeat and Furnivall, motivated not by aristocratic patronage but by the paternalist philanthropy of the mass education movement, write not out of an evident desire to fashion the self, but to *substitute* Chaucer for themselves, putting him into the role of moral exemplar, and in this respect they mirror the general process described by Hunter. Both, as men of letters, were involved in a moral construction of literature that they brought into the social sphere through the Chaucer Society. Neither entered this sphere through such an official institution as the inspectorate: Furnivall, through his literary entrepreneurism, forced himself on the attention of the educated world and effectively recreated official policy within his private institutions. A teacher in the London Working Men's College and an extension lecturer, Furnivall was a great deal more than the regular schoolteacher, and he was, as Patterson argues, "profoundly committed to the quintessentially liberal and Arnoldian idea that the study of the literature of the English past could serve to recover the organic unity that the class-divided society of the nineteenth century had lost."[60] His efforts were eventually officially recognized when he was rewarded, not (as such earlier scholars as Madden had been) with a knighthood, but with a lifetime civil-list pension, granted by William Gladstone "in acknowledgment of your valuable services to the literature of your country."[61] Skeat, as a professor at Cambridge, did have an official position, but, given the minority status of Anglo-Saxon at Cambridge at the time, his editing work probably had far greater impact.[62]

Late in the nineteenth century, Middle English was beginning to coalesce with the emergent discipline of English studies. The missionary fervor of Furnivall and Skeat was partly responsible. Furnivall was effective in a general way, while Skeat eventually had a more specific role. In the same book in which he described his missionary role, Skeat also described his "chief anxiety . . . the establishment of a University Lectureship in English."[63] He was instrumental in creating this lectureship, first soliciting donations through a letter to the *Times*, which were forthcoming from various individuals, businesses, and the Master of Trinity Hall. An appointment was made in March 1896, remunerated by fifty pounds a year (at a time when the equivalent lecturers in French and German received two hundred).

The entrepreneurial self-confidence that had shaped Middle English was now having the effect of altering the circumstances in which such entrepreneurialism was necessary to the subject. The next generation of scholars, such as Israel Gollancz, increasingly had an academic apparatus to give them their authority, and the highly idiosyncratic statements of authority of the preceding generation became less evident. One of the important works of this period was George Campbell Macaulay's edition of the complete works of John Gower, published in four volumes in 1899–1902, and (unlike the Clarendon Chaucer) never entirely superseded. It too was published by the Clarendon Press, with the English poems co-published by the EETS as part of its selection for 1900. In its own way, this text is no less a monument than Skeat's work, but the tone of Macaulay's scholarship is quite different from Skeat's. Macaulay records that he had begun with the idea of editing *Confessio Amantis*, realizing that this could be effectively done in Oxford, where he was then working. The delegates of Oxford University Press, however, agreed to his proposal only on the condition that he edit everything else of Gower's as well. Macaulay, in his own account, took this task on with diffidence, uncertain of his competency to work with the French texts.

In such moments as these, Macaulay in his own self-representation has none of the supreme confidence of a Skeat or the can-do bluffness of a Furnivall. Despite the fact that some of his work did appear with the EETS, Macaulay was not part of the EETS circle. His stance of critical modesty, his position within the academy, and most aspects of his scholarship produce a *Complete Works of John Gower* that looks forward to twentieth- century academic scholarship rather than back to the utopian-imperialist projects of the 1860s and 1870s. This does not mean that Macaulay shirked the task of coverage or in any way looked back to the more dilettantish antiquarians; his introductory material is highly learned, and his account of the manuscripts of the *Confessio* is exhaustive. The *Confessio* is given in a genuine critical edition, based on the Fairfax manuscript, with extensive recording of manuscript variants at the foot of the page.

Macaulay also practices the belletristic form of literary analysis that would increasingly characterize the literary-critical aspect of academic medieval studies in the early twentieth century. He thought the *Confessio* a successful work, of good "style and poetical qualities," and Gower a good storyteller. The story of Medea, for example, had "[f]orce and picturesqueness . . . with its description of the summer sea glistening in the sun, which blazes down upon the returning hero." We cannot "refuse to recognize," Macaulay continued, "the poetical power of the later phases of the same story, first the midnight rovings of Medea in search of enchantments."[64] At this point, Macaulay quotes from the tale, as he frequently does in illustration of his aesthetic judgments. He acknowledges Gower's debt to Ovid, but feels that the English poet's "descriptions are far more detailed and forcible than the original" (2:xiii). This section of literary criticism then continues with favorable appraisal of the major characters before some discussion of the work's "serious faults" (2:xix).

Through its publication of such works as the Gower edition, Oxford University Press was seriously challenging the EETS as the almost uncontested producer of Middle English. The Press had begun a series of medieval texts in the early 1880s, and they were, according to Peter Sutcliffe, better edited than those of the EETS. The Press was consequently well positioned to answer to an increasing market, with the establishment of "Eng Lit," in the 1890s. By the end of the century, with its flagship Clarendon Chaucer and complete Gower, it rivaled the EETS in a way that signaled the central role the Press would maintain in decades to come. In 1908, Humphrey Milford at the Press took over the running of the EETS, which at that stage had around 250 titles, "most of them so slow-selling that they could be expected to stay in print for the rest of the century."[65] This logical move signals a coming together of two business enterprises, one in the public, one in the academic sphere; it is also a meeting of the canonical and noncanonical, as Oxford's ownership of the major Middle English authors' work put them alongside the more obscure material the EETS had been printing. This beginning of modern academic publishing in the field is one overt facet of the beginning of the modern era of Middle English studies.

1910

Early in 1910, Furnivall was diagnosed with stomach cancer, and his son, a doctor, informed him that he had no more than six months to live.[66] He died on 2 July at the age of eighty-five. Undoubtedly the grand old man of medieval English, in the second half of the nineteenth century he had helped initiate the *OED*, had been director of the Chaucer Society throughout its life, director of the EETS for forty-six years, and a secretary of the Philological Society for sixty-seven years. Of his societies, only the EETS continued, and the directorship was taken up by Israel Gollancz, who held it until his own death in 1930.

Although the university study of English literature and, within it, Middle English was not quite on the footing it would achieve after World War I, this handover of the management of the Early English Text Society effectively signaled the destiny of the discipline. Gollancz was thoroughly a university man, a medievalist who had studied his subject as a university discipline. He had been educated at the City of London School and University College, London before going to Christ's College, Cambridge and taking the Medieval and Modern Languages Tripos, soon after its establishment in 1886. The Tripos, philological in emphasis, was the forerunner of Oxbridge English literary teaching.[67] Gollancz took a second-class degree and lectured for several years at Cambridge and University College, London in English. In 1896, he became the first lecturer in English at Cambridge, occupying the position that Skeat had helped create. In 1903, he took the chair of English language and literature at King's College, London, which he held until his death. As well as transforming English at King's College into an important discipline within the institution, Gollancz was also a prolific scholar and editor. He edited several medieval texts and was in charge of several series: the Temple Shakespeare, the Temple Classics, The King's Library, The King's Novels, and the Medieval Library.[68] Gollancz was thoroughly an academic scholar, and the EETS continued to become under his administration an academic organization.

With the sole exception of the EETS, the function of the publishing societies in Middle English was finished; the function of the nonacademic scholar was finished. The textbooks and editions issuing from Oxford University Press were going to students in universities throughout Britain, America, the colonies, and Australia, not to well-read country vicars. The continuity of English literature was now firmly established on philological principles, as something that developed out of Old English, through Middle English, to Modern. Certainly, there was still division between adherents of the Germanic character of English language and literature and those who wanted to see in English a post-Conquest rejection of the Germanic elements. But the old subject of Anglo-Saxon was now decisively linked to Modern English through a better-understood Middle English. It is easy to forget—most standard accounts of the rise of English do—but Middle English had been instrumental in bringing English studies into the universities. "Middle English," and English proper with it, had come into being.

Conclusion

❖

1999

No doubt the connection between language and thought is a very intimate one, but we are strongly of opinion that in dealing with literature the voyage of the mind should be broken as little as possible by the examination of obstacles and the analysis of the element on which the explorer is floating. This last is a purely scientific study and can be to a great extent separated from the study of the literary art, as the chemical analysis of water can be separated from the observation of the sounds and colours conveyed by it. . . . We believe, therefore, that formal grammar and philology should be recognised as scientific studies, and kept apart (so far as that is possible) from the lessons in which English is treated as an art, a means of creative expression, a record of human experience.

— *The Teaching of English in England,* 1921

Broken-backed from use, its spine faded in the sun, the first paperback edition of *The Riverside Chaucer* sits on my desk. This book, the third edition of F. N. Robinson's *The Works of Geoffrey Chaucer,* was first published in the United States by Houghton Mifflin in 1987 and in an Oxford University Press paperback the following year. On the front of the paperback, various of the Canterbury pilgrims colorfully mill about in an image taken from a Lydgate manuscript, beneath which there is Anthony Burgess's statement that "this is the best edition of Chaucer in existence."

The authority of the edition can scarcely be doubted. It is not just that it proclaims itself a "New Edition" on the cover, and newness, as we have seen, is sometimes taken for authority in itself. It is produced by an impressive group of thirty-three contributors from the United States, Canada, and Britain, working under the general editorship of Larry D. Benson at Harvard University. Burgess's endorsement caps all of this off: the statement is made by a powerful literary authority who is outside academic institutions. The edition is loaded with symbolic capital by Burgess because he is not of the academy that produced it, but is nevertheless a figure of great cultural capital himself.

There could hardly be a clearer example than Burgess's statement of the way in which authority is constructed to erase the past. His endorsement is so massively total and exclusive: it says that nothing that has ever been done in Chaucer studies matches the Riverside. So, while it may not mean to, the statement suggests that *every* piece of Chaucerian editorial scholarship that precedes the Riverside was in some way flawed and incomplete. The entire history of Chaucer editing was leading, therefore, up to this moment of transcendent clarity.

It would be naive, of course, to suggest that this very Wartonian conception of literary history is actually endorsed by the scholars who produced the work. The publisher wants to sell books, and a statement like Burgess's is a godsend. As we have seen, there never was a golden age when people just bought Chaucer because of their appreciation for his genius, without the urging of moneymaking publishers. Nevertheless, it is also wrong to ignore the messages sent out by the framing mechanisms surrounding texts, and the messages delivered here have the effect of erasing a whole history. As Joseph Dane writes in a critique of attitudes to Chaucer editions, "It is a delusion to imagine that the best edition of one culture will be the best for any other, or, less obviously, that the history of editions is progressive, with its *telos* in the most recent edition or editorial project."[1] Books are not socially and ideologically inert, and they cannot simply be taken out of their time.

However, the study of Middle English is frequently based on precisely this assumption: that in order to get at the Middle English text, we must somehow get past the individual printed, textual manifestation in order to reach what Tim William Machan refers to as the "lexical and idealist" original text: "lexical in the sense that words are privileged over their material manifestation and idealist in the sense that the essential intended work has priority over a text that might have appeared at a specific moment in a specific document."[2] Machan's argument is that Middle English editing is based on an inappropriate model originally derived from Renaissance humanism's approach to classical texts, a model that has led to the enshrining of the search for what is in effect a pretextual (and therefore utopian) "true" text. While I think Machan's argument is convincing, I hope I have shown throughout this book that these idealisms often represent a *combination* of such editorial assumptions, with specific and contingent ideologies (such as those which, to take one obvious example, see a Scottish text produced from an English one).

The idealist approach to the text, and its erasure of material textual histories, was consolidated in the document that to a large extent signals the institutionalizing of English studies and the shape medieval studies would have within it. "Books are not things in themselves," the Newbolt Report proposed in 1921, "they are merely the instruments through which we hear the voices of those who have known life better than ourselves."[3] If 1910 be taken as the symbolic date at which the thorough institutionalizing of Middle English can be seen to begin, then 1921 symbolizes the completion of the process and, through the report, the shaping of the discipline and the relation it would have with English overall. In 1910, the figures working in medieval studies are those whose work is still in various ways influential on our own, even where it has been superseded: Skeat, Gollancz, and Macaulay are important in the current formation of Middle English studies in a way that Warton, Scott, and even Madden are not.

The implication of the Newbolt Report in patriotic politics around the time of World War I is well known.[4] Sir Henry Newbolt, chairman of the board of inquiry into English, was also the jingoist poet responsible for exhortations to pay up and play the game.[5] The report takes on an obviously Arnoldian (and no less Furnivallian) mission: English studies, correctly practiced, will be unifying because literature is something all classes can share, and this study is also part of a national mission: "for English children no form of knowledge can take precedence of a knowledge of English, no form of literature can take precedence of English literature: . . . the two are so inextricably connected as to form the only basis possible for a national education" (NR, 14). This represents the triumph of the Arnoldian-Furnivallian vision, now urged as part of an official, national version of what English should be.[6]

At the same time, the report argues *against* a key element of medieval studies, comparative philology. English, the report says, is an art. Philology, by contrast, is a science, and the two must not be confused. The report recommended philology principally as the subject of postgraduate work, and urged that Anglo-Saxon need not be compulsory but could be usefully replaced, as language study, with medieval French or Latin. Although it is nowhere made explicit in the report, it is hard not to see its massive rejection of comparative philology and language study as a reaction to the recent conflict with Germany. English Studies is to be purged of its Germanisms, and to be rendered more purely as an art. It could scarcely be clearer in the report, particularly in the general introduction, that English is being constructed as what we can now call a technique of the self, an officially promoted technique aimed at the shaping of a population.[7] Literature, the report insists, is a practical medium, "the most direct and lasting communication of experience by man to men." Literature must not be thought of as "a mere pastime":

> It is evident that if science and literature can be ably and enthusiastically taught, the child's natural love of goodness will be strongly encouraged and great progress may be made in the strengthening of the will. The vast importance to a nation of moral training would alone make it imperative that education shall be regarded as experience and shall be kept in the closest contact with life and personal relations. (NR, 9)

English is a "fundamental necessity" "for the full development of the mind and character of English children." However, "the use of English does not come to all by nature, but is a fine art, and must be taught as a fine art" (21). English is to shape the moral being of a nation, then, but can only do so in its role as an art, its scientistic branch having been cut off. Sir Walter Raleigh, the Oxford professor of English, stated to the board "that English literature could be the basis of a liberal education, but needed to be freed from slavery to philology and phonology, except so far as these bear on literature" (218).

Comparative philology had been crucial, as studies of the rise of English show, in helping English studies to full academic acceptance, because it had the virtue of seeming to allow something empirical to be said about literature as opposed to "mere chatter," in E. A. Freeman's well-known condemnation.[8] Although medieval studies are relatively neglected by both D. J. Palmer and Chris Baldick in their accounts of English, both Anglo-Saxon and Middle English were prominent in the nineteenth-century versions of academic English. World War I, which, as Chris Baldick argues, provoked a "renaissance" in English literary criticism, changed this.[9] With metaphoric appropriateness, medieval studies became the Middle Ages to criticism's renaissance at this time. Newbolt's committee took evidence from the professors of English, and the repudiation of philology it records among this group was already evident in the universities themselves. It had begun, indeed, well before the war, with a series of paroxysms at Oxford and with a rather simpler process at Cambridge in which a philologically minded professor, H. M. Chadwick, oversaw the secession of his own subject, Anglo-Saxon, to the School of Archaeology and Anthropology. This prepared the way for the establishment of a very "literary" School of English in 1917.

So the moment of acceptance, of triumph, for Middle English, is very nearly the same moment as its downfall, the creation of the marginal status that has been complained about ever since. Under Furnivall, Middle English had invested in patriotism, and this could be seen as the price, when a version of criticism heavily influenced by patriotism became suspicious of foreign critical discourses. Medieval studies was one of the parents of English studies, but the ungrateful child was quick to run away from home. The difference of medieval studies is what makes it easy for its relevance to be questioned. Philology can never be wholly cut out of medieval studies, and so medieval studies comes to be questioned on the grounds that it is not properly literary criticism: science versus art once again. Now that Anglo-Saxon studies has contracted or disappeared in so many places, these problems are particularly those of scholars in Middle English.

The idea of the marginalization of medieval studies is so widespread that it is hardly necessary to go looking for statements about it. Lee Patterson's 1987 statement is something of a classic:

For all its trumpeting of popularity and relevance, Medieval Studies appears to many to be more ghetto than enclave, more prison than prelapsarian garden. To nonmedievalists, it must be admitted, the isolation of medievalism from the mainstream of Anglo-American literary studies is a self-evident fact.... The point is less the resistance of individual medievalists to the winds of change—indeed, one can cite a range of feminist, Marxist, and deconstructionist initiatives now emerging in the field—than the marginalizing of medieval literature as a force within literary studies as a whole.[10]

But a strong statement such as this only gives shape to the overwhelming anecdotal evidence that sums up the mood among practitioners of the subject. In my own institutional context in Australia, it is easy to see how the subject has atrophied in the span of my own career. There were three people teaching medieval studies in a department small by international standards when I studied as an undergraduate; now there is one. The international conferences at Kalamazoo and Leeds appear to beckon, because of sheer weight of numbers, as utopias of medieval studies, but when one arrives the discourse of disgruntled dystopia is everywhere. There are no jobs, the talk runs; student numbers are in decline, funding is down. Morbid rhetoric is pervasive; at the first Leeds conference I stood in a group of people waiting to cross the busy road that lies between the two main conference sites, and remarked, not particularly seriously, that somebody could be killed on this road before the event was over. "Yes," a young woman next to me said with a strange light in her eyes, "and then there'll be a job."

Does Middle English, then, represent an extreme case of the "political suicide" that, Terry Eagleton argues, criticism committed when it academicized itself? Eagleton proposes that by entering the academic institutional context and cutting itself off from any possibility of existence in a public sphere, criticism made itself secure but in the same moment ended its chances of being "a socially active force."[11] The same moment— between the mid-1890s and the immediate postwar period—is, as I have argued, the moment of the triumph and fall of Middle English. Middle English is not just cut off as a potential social force, but marginalized *within* the discipline that houses it, as well. The institutional security accorded the rest of criticism does not extend to medieval studies. In these terms, Middle English not only put the gun to its head but took the poison, too.

Whatever the merits of Eagleton's broader argument, we would have to look more carefully at Middle English and the Habermasian public sphere before drawing this conclusion. Middle English came into being only as the classical public sphere declined, in the late eighteenth century.[12] Given its conservative and very privatized shape in its early phases, the only obvious examples of public-sphere mechanisms in Middle English are the Early English Text Society and the Chaucer Society and the activities surrounding them in the 1860s and 1870s. Anyone who could afford a couple of guineas could belong to the societies and enfranchise themselves in the knowledge on offer. More important, anyone could in theory *edit* for the societies and take charge of critical directions themselves, as Furnivall could hardly have made it clearer that he would have accepted almost any offer.

However, as we have already seen, these possibilities simply were not realized. Early subscriber lists show evidence of the presence of a general, interested public that, in fact, at first outweighed academic interest in the societies. The same subscriber lists show, just as surely, that if academic individuals and institutions had not increasingly interested themselves in the societies through the 1870s, they would have collapsed. Despite everything Furnivall could do, the country vicars and the factory managers fell away, and the academics moved in—even before the subject itself was fully academicized. This "preacademic" phase would seem to signal that the destiny of Middle English was as a highly specialized set of techniques and disciplines even before the institution had set up the environment for such a thing.

I think that we must accept that the country vicars and others who represented an enlightened, educated public sphere were only going to be a significant factor in the societies when they were still a novelty. Much of the literature the early subscribers received under the societies' auspices obviously did not interest them. We have to accept that a great deal of Middle English literature has *never*, in the modern period, been of broad interest. In fact, given that some of the texts we deal with do not seem to have been widely read even in the medieval period, we may have to accept that some of the corpus of Middle English has never, at any point, been widely read or appreciated. What has been constructed as literature in the modern period, and what is now read as literature, renders much of medieval literature alien and difficult, and there is little we can do about that.

This means, in turn, that in Middle English studies we should be suspicious of both the arguments for the importance of the alterity of medieval literature and current arguments about our marginality. It has been argued—most strongly, of course, in the special issue of *New Literary History* devoted to the topic—that the special interest of medieval literature lies or ought to lie in its alterity, its "surprising otherness"—one of the features, as Hans Robert Jauss has argued, that has distinguished medieval studies.[13] That is simply not true, in the subset that is Middle English studies. Middle English has relied not on its special alterity, its *difference*, but its *identity*. As I aimed to show in my genealogy of the subject, it was when the study of Chaucer converged with other Middle English that the discipline was formed, and this was because Chaucer's work allowed critics to approach Middle English in ways that were already familiar from the study of later texts (and also, as Machan argues, from the study of classical texts, given the attempted construction of Chaucer as "Antique auctor"). The centrality of Chaucer that resulted has been a feature of Middle English ever since, with publishing activity focusing on this poet far more extensively than any other. Machan has seen this as built into the assumptions about editing that characterize the study of Middle English: "Modern textual criticism has relied on the priority of its own presumptively transhistorical definitions and has therefore depended unselfconsciously on the authority of vernacular poets. Not coincidentally, *those writers whose aesthetics are the most responsive to modern critical methods or whose sense of authorial identity seems the strongest* — Langland, Chaucer, and Gower in particular — *are the writers on whose works the greatest textual-critical effort has been expended.*"[14]

If Machan is correct here, then Chaucer is still as much the switching device between medieval and modern for us as he was for Warton and earlier scholars. At least as early as Dryden, as Patterson argues, Chaucer is detached from his medieval time to be confirmed as a modern poet. But this is something that has continued to operate under the more self-reflective historicisms that dominate the paradigm of historical criticism today. In a series of trenchant critiques, Patterson and David Aers have attacked the new historicism and cultural materialism of early modern studies because some of the best-known critics at work in that field (such as Stephen Greenblatt, Francis Barker, Catherine Belsey, Jonathan Dollimore, and Terry Eagleton) have simply perpetuated the Burckhardtian notion that subjectivity was an "invention" of the Renaissance. This work, proceeding from avowedly radical critics, serves to perpetuate "the pervasive and apparently ineradicable *grand récit* that organizes Western cultural history, the gigantic master narrative by which modernity identifies itself with the Renaissance and rejects the Middle Ages as by definition premodern."[15]

Both Patterson and Aers use this critique as a point from which to redraw boundaries, in Patterson's case principally to argue for the crucial importance of subjectivity in the work of Chaucer, which is the central thesis of his 1991 book, *Chaucer and the Subject of History*. Aers ranges further, pointing to a concern with interiority in varied texts, including Augustine's *Confessions* and *Piers Plowman*, as well as in Chaucer. Nevertheless, it is Chaucer, inevitably, whose work is the principal textual object to be reconfigured as a result of this critique, as the wide influence of Patterson's book suggests.

What is curious here is the way in which the old way of looking at Chaucer is not only preserved by the new critique, but also enhanced. The argument that Chaucer, before Shakespeare, was the preeminent poet of interiority and subjectivity simply pushes back the boundaries of the modernity that are under dispute — to say, in effect, that Chaucer is more modern than we think. Chaucer, once again, is the poet of modernity because of his concern with the thing that has already been defined as quintessentially modern: a sense of interiority and individualism. This does not really result in any unsettling of the boundaries of disciplines and their periods; it simply says that Middle English literature, apparently so alien, in fact contains within it much that is less alien than is conventionally thought, because of its *identity* with the literature we think of as belonging to modernity. In this respect, we are still answering the question that can be seen as far back as Thomas Percy's time: how do we bring this problematic literature to people's attention without hopelessly marginalizing ourselves? And we are answering it in much the same way as Percy, Warton, and many another, by saying that Middle English literature is particularly worth reading if only we imagine it to be something it is not.

I would like to suggest that we have actually—in as real a sense as we are ever going to—won the battle over marginality, and that, secondly and conversely, there is some ground we need to cede. On the first point, I mean simply that it is difficult to imagine a time when more people have read Chaucer or Langland or the Gawain-poet or Gower. Whether or not we have the best edition of Chaucer in existence is something that will remain the subject of dispute; less open to dispute is the contention that there are more copies of the work of Chaucer in existence than there have ever been, and there are more readers of Chaucer than there have ever been, back to and including the poet's own time. There are more students in universities than there were just a few decades ago; in English-speaking countries there are more students as a proportion of the whole population in the universities, and there are more universities. But Chaucer is available outside the universities, too, in a greater number of volumes than ever before, at a relatively low price. The same is demonstrably true of Langland, who went without any edition of any kind between the mid–sixteenth century and the early nineteenth, while the history of *Sir Gawain and the Green Knight* and *Pearl* is completely confined to the past century and a half. Put simply, more people are reading more Middle English than ever before. If this is marginalization, then we are going to have to work with it.

The second point is the opposite one, that we need to invest more fully in the alien and difficult parts of our subject. This might look like a ceding of territory in that it implies more marginality: students are simply not going to rush to Laȝamon's *Brut* in the way that they do to Chaucer. Such material cannot, therefore, be privileged over the late-fourteenth-century writers for teaching purposes. But it is quite incredible how unavailable much of the more difficult material is, and how expensive it is when it is available. Even Gower is not easily available in complete editions, and it would seem to be a minimal requirement, in a discipline that complains of marginality, that its core texts be available to students and those who want to teach them. Machan argues against those who call for more texts in Middle English, saying that he does "not see that the argument that any edition is better than none at all...is in any way compelling" (192). Nevertheless some of his own arguments more obviously suggest that a better picture of Middle English textuality would only emerge from the wider availability of works currently outside the canon. It is now more than twenty years since Anne Hudson made her call for more editing, particularly in medieval prose works, and there is little to suggest that the situation that she complained of has substantially changed.[16] As Machan remarks, "medieval literature...is caught in a cycle whereby publishers print what will be used in courses and instructors teach from what publishers make available, thereby guaranteeing the production of only those books that are already in use" (189–90). So, for example, the Gawain-poet's works are always in print despite being, as Machan argues, less representative of Middle English than Minot, Lydgate, and Hoccleve. If we do not invest the energy that goes into late-fourteenth-century studies more broadly in Middle English, we run the risk of not teaching "Middle English" at all but, instead, producing something to satisfy modern notions of what medieval textuality ought to be—this, once again, was the project of Percy, Warton, Scott, Ellis, and others.

There is a clear role here for projects in electronic editing and hypertext, as Machan points out. There are projects of this kind already well underway, such as the Labyrinth at Georgetown, which make available texts on Web sites. Hypertext does not necessarily solve the problems of editorial methodology so much as sidestep them, but at least it makes it possible to set up texts in their multiple versions, to create, in effect, "variorum" editions even of such unique texts as *Sir Gawain* (where the editions of 1839 and 1864, for example, could be set up beside a diplomatic transcript and a modern edition). There is now a considerable body of writing on editing in Middle English that makes the persuasive case that it has *always* been a contested zone.[17] Hypertext is a good way of agreeing to disagree. We might have to recognize that what we have, in the case of many texts (including Chaucer), is as good as it is going to get.

There is also, I think, a need to invest in the history of the transmission of Middle English texts via print technology. This would mean more study of the reception, transmission, and use of Middle English texts in order to say, among other things, what people *did* with these texts at different times. Historical literary criticism of Middle English texts is going to be limited otherwise because of the paucity of information about contexts of production as opposed to contexts of reproduction. As it is, historicist work on Chaucer tends to rely on assertions about the nature of this or that manuscript and the order of the *Canterbury Tales*, which can never be finally demonstrated. Much of the most sophisticated critical writing in recent Middle English studies has been on Chaucer, but Middle English will not benefit until writing of similar sophistication is devoted to other writers. We should also encourage consideration of the uses to which writers other than Chaucer have been put in their post-medieval reception.

And we should do all of this not in the gloomy conviction that we are working in a marginalized discipline, but with the sense that however bad things are institutionally, there has never been a time when more people read Middle English texts; there is no golden age behind us when every country vicar read all of Middle English. Our texts *are* often obscure, and, for whatever personal reasons, this is why we read them. We are not going to be able to convey our reasons for this love to all students, or even a majority, but we are *not* in some lapsarian state in this regard. Among the things I hope I have been able to show in this book is that historically, Middle English had a constantly marginal status within English studies by comparison with other areas in the discipline. Baldick demonstrates the way in which the notion of "crisis" in criticism is nothing new; in the same way, the marginality of Middle English has been characteristic of it at all times. It is as well off now, as a field, as it has ever been.

Although this part of the text, the conclusion, is the traditional place where prescriptions for change are made, the point of a genealogy may not necessarily be to change things. The genealogical method presupposes the idea that discursive formations are produced out of certain ideological pressures, and it would be blind indeed to assume that now, in the current formation, I am somehow less ideologically implicated than other, earlier scholars; that I or anyone else is empowered to make broad prescriptions simply because of a demonstrated awareness of the ideologies of the past. This would be not genealogical, but an espousal of the continuist position that proposes the perfectibility of a field of study.

Ultimately, this genealogy has argued for the importance of material histories of texts and disciplines, and perhaps no more than that. I do think that the considerations that arise from such material histories should be worked into teaching and criticism — should, in fact, automatically be a part of teaching. Allen Frantzen's words on a related topic here summarize the situation eloquently: "By examining the interplay between events, actions, and ideas *in* texts and the corresponding events, actions, and ideas *outside* the texts, we can see that the history of Anglo-Saxon studies is not extraneous to the subject of Anglo-Saxon language, literature and history. The ideas and attitudes of readers accumulate around texts; the scholarship of each generation adheres to the subject and becomes *part* of the subject that the next generation then studies."[18] "Middle English" could be substituted for "Anglo-Saxon" in this statement, which is important for the way in which it argues the *centrality* of earlier models of scholarship to later teaching.

I do not, however, in the end share with Frantzen the faith expressed in *Desire for Origins* that such a practice as he proposes will alter the course of a discipline that has come to be perceived as marginalized.[19] Genealogies describe determinant moments in which historical forces shape (in this case) texts, and we have to recognize that we live in a particular moment in which we might equally be caught by historical forces. This might seem a too dismal view in which too much force is ascribed to a blind Power; I do not think this is the case, because we can, of course, bring to bear the lessons revealed by genealogical accounts on the current shape of a discipline. What we cannot do, though, is change the large-scale institutional surrounds. Broad prescriptions for change in the discipline are therefore perhaps less appropriate (and less likely to be realized) than the expression of the wish that others may take something away from a genealogy and that their reading of it might influence their own local and specific practices, and in turn, through their criticism and teaching, influence their students and *their* practices. It is through this means— the circulation of microdiscourses about Middle English at the capillary level rather than that of hegemonic power—that Middle English studies might increase its sense of its own history.

Notes

Preface

1. On English in Australia, see Leigh Dale, *The English Men: Professing Literature in Australian Universities* (Toowoomba, Queensland: Association for the Study of Australian Literature, 1997).

Introduction

1. A prime example is Paul Ruggiers's edited collection, *Editing Chaucer: The Great Tradition* (Norman, Okla: Pilgrim Books, 1984).

2. Norman F. Cantor, *Inventing the Middle Ages: The Lives, Works, and Ideas of the Great Medievalists of the Twentieth Century* (New York: William Morrow, 1991), 29.

3. Charles Dickens, *Dombey and Son*, ed. Alan Horsman (Oxford: Clarendon Press, 1974), 373.

4. Seth Lerer, *Chaucer and His Readers: Imagining the Author in Late-Medieval England* (Princeton, N.J.: Princeton University Press, 1993); the discussion of MS Tanner 346 in chap. 2 is exemplary.

5. Ralph Hanna III, *Pursuing History: Middle English Manuscripts and Their Texts* (Stanford, Calif.: Stanford University Press, 1996).

6. *South Atlantic Quarterly* 91, no. 4 (1992).

7. See Stephen G. Nichols, "Commentary and/as Image," ibid., 965–92, and also Nichols, "Philology and Its Discontents," in *The Future of the Middle Ages: Medieval Literature in the 1990s*, ed. William D. Paden (Gainesville: University Press of Florida, 1994), 118.

8. Nichols, "Philology and Its Discontents," 139 n. 14.

9. Tim William Machan, *Textual Criticism and Middle English Texts* (Charlottesville: University Press of Virginia, 1994), 66.

10. This approach to the printed book is interestingly extended by Joseph A. Dane in the introduction to his *Who Is Buried in Chaucer's Tomb? Studies in the Reception of Chaucer's Book* (East Lansing: Michigan State University Press, 1998). This book appeared too late to be included in the arguments in chapter 7.

11. [Edward V. Utterson], ed., *Kyng Roberd of Cysylle* (London, 1839). BL shelf mark 1077.e.60.

12. Nichols, "Philology and Its Discontents," 118.

13. David F. Hult, "Reading It Right: The Ideology of Text Editing," in *The New Medievalism*, ed. Marina S. Brownlee, Kevin Brownlee, and Stephen G. Nichols (Baltimore, Md.: Johns Hopkins University Press, 1991), 126–27; Hult's essay appears in a section labeled "The New Philology," on which see also Stephen G. Nichols, "Introduction: Philology in a Manuscript Culture," *Speculum* 65 (1990): 1–10.

14. Thomas Warton's considerations of Middle English poems in his *History of English Poetry* form the only extensive critical commentary on Middle English from a university scholar before the 1860s and 1870s, when Walter Skeat began working in the field. Even Skeat, however, was not actually employed to teach and research in Middle English.

15. Chris Baldick, *The Social Mission of English Criticism, 1848–1932* (Oxford: Oxford University Press, 1983); Terry Eagleton, *Literary Theory: An Introduction* (Oxford: Blackwell, 1983), chap. 2, and *The Function of Criticism: From* The Spectator *to Post-Structuralism* (London: Verso, 1984); Allen J. Frantzen, *Desire for Origins: New Language, Old English, and Teaching the Tradition* (New Brunswick, N.J.: Rutgers University Press, 1990); Lee Patterson, *Negotiating the Past: The Historical Understanding of Medieval Literature* (Madison: University of Wisconsin Press, 1987), chap. 1; Theresa Coletti, "Reading REED: History and the Records of Early English Drama," in *Literary Practice and Social Change in Britain, 1380–1530,* ed. Lee Patterson (Berkeley and Los Angeles: University of California Press, 1990), 248–84.

16. Michel Foucault, "Two Lectures," in *Power/Knowledge: Selected Interviews and Other Writings, 1972–1977,* ed. Colin Gordon, trans. Colin Gordon et al. (New York: Harvester Wheatsheaf, 1980), 99.

17. Ian Hunter, *Culture and Government: The Emergence of Literary Education* (Houndmills: Macmillan, 1988), 3.

18. Ian Hunter, "Learning the Literature Lesson: The Limits of the Aesthetic Personality," in *Towards a Critical Sociology of Reading Pedagogy,* ed. Carolyn D. Baker and Allan Luke (Amsterdam: Benjamins, 1991), 72.

19. Michel Foucault, "Technologies of the Self," in *Ethics: Subjectivity and Truth,* ed. Paul Rabinow, trans. Robert Hurley et al., vol. 1 of *The Essential Works of Michel Foucault, 1954–1984,* Paul Rabinow, series ed. (New York: New Press, 1997), 225.

20. Hunter, "Lesson," 72.

21. Foucault himself identified, if only in brief, a shift in the nature of techniques of the self from the eighteenth century, when the Christian "theme of self-renunciation" became less important and the disclosure of self through "verbalization" led to an emphasis on the possibility of constituting new selves, rather than on self-renunciation; "Technologies of the Self," 249.

22. Hunter, "Lesson," 78.

23. On the conservativeness of antiquarianism generally in the period, see Clare A. Simmons, *Reversing the Conquest: History and Myth in Nineteenth-Century British Literature* (New Brunswick, N.J.: Rutgers University Press, 1990), 46.

24. Cited in D. J. Palmer, *The Rise of English Studies: An Account of the Study of the English Language and Literature from Its Origins to the Making of the Oxford English School* (London: Oxford University Press, 1965), 96.

25. "Semi-Saxon, on the other hand, is the name given by scholars to the language because it was almost in the middle, or would have been almost in the middle, between the purer Anglo-Saxon and that English which for our ancestors was native prior to the last 150 years"; George Hickes, *Linguarum Vett. Septentrionalium Thesaurus Grammatico-Criticus et Archaeologicus,* 2 vols. (Oxford, 1703–5), 2:134.

26. John Pinkerton, *Ancient Scotish Poems,* 2 vols. (London: Charles Dilly; Edinburgh: William Creech, 1786), 1:lx, lxi.

27. *Encyclopaedia Britannica,* 3rd ed., 18 vols. (Edinburgh: A. Bell and C. Macfarquhar, 1797), 6:667, col. 2.

28. See A. Campbell, *Old English Grammar* (Oxford: Clarendon Press, 1983), 2 n. 1.

29. Benjamin Thorpe, *Analecta Anglo-Saxonica. A Selection, in Prose and Verse, from Anglo-Saxon Authors of Various Ages; with a Glossary. Designed Chiefly as a first book for students* (London: John and Arthur Arch, 1834), ix.

30. Henry Hallam, *Introduction to the Literature of Europe, in the Fifteenth, Sixteenth, and Seventeenth Centuries,* 4 vols. (London: John Murray, 1837–39), 1:57.

31. R. G. Latham, *The English Language* (London: Taylor and Walton, 1841), 63.

32. *Saturday Review,* 27 March 1869, cited in Philippa Levine, *The Amateur and the Professional: Antiquarians, Historians, and Archaeologists in Victorian England, 1838–1886* (Cambridge: Cambridge University Press, 1986), 79. See the discussion and edition of

the proclamation in Bruce Dickins and R. M. Wilson, eds., *Early Middle English Texts* (London: Bowes & Bowes, 1951), 7–9.

33. Frederic Madden, ed., *Laȝamons Brut, or Chronicle of Britain; a Poetical Semi-Saxon Paraphrase of the Brut of Wace*, 3 vols. (London: Society of Antiquaries, 1847), 1:iv.

34. James Morton, ed., *The Ancren [sic] Riwle; A Treatise on the Rules and Duties of Monastic Life. Edited and Translated from a Semi-Saxon MS of the Thirteenth Century* (London: Camden Society, 1852), xviii.

35. C. Friedrich Koch, *Historische Grammatik der englischen Sprache*, 3 vols. (Weimar: Hermann Böhlau, 1863–68), 1:8.

36. Robert Meadows White, *The Ormulum: Now First Edited from the Original Manuscript in the Bodleian with Notes and a Glossary*, 2 vols. (Oxford: Oxford University Press, 1852).

37. T. L. Kington Oliphant, *The Sources of Standard English* (London: Macmillan, 1873), 35, 182.

38. Henry Sweet, *A History of English Sounds: From the Earliest Period, including an Investigation of the General Laws of Sound Change, and Full Word Lists* (London: English Dialect Society, 1874), 160.

39. Rev. Josiah Forshall and Sir Frederic Madden, eds., *The New Testament in English according to the version by John Wycliffe about A.D. 1380 and revised by John Purvey about A.D. 1388*, with an introduction by Walter Skeat (Oxford: Clarendon Press, 1879), xvi.

40. *Encyclopaedia Britannica*, 9th ed., 24 vols. (Edinburgh: Adam and Charles Black, 1875–89), 8:390, col. 1.

41. Ibid., 391, col. 2.

42. R. G. Latham, *The English Language*, 2nd ed., rev. and enl. (London: Taylor and Walton, 1848), 34.

43. Madden, *Brut*, 1:v.

44. Bosworth to Furnivall, 8 February 1864, HuntL MS FU 45.

45. George L. Craik, *Outlines of the History of the English Language*, 8th ed. (London: Chapman and Hall, 1872), iv.

46. Simmons, *Reversing the Conquest*, 184.

47. Oliphant, *Standard English*, 183.

48. On this see Simmons, *Reversing the Conquest*, 192–99.

49. Bradshaw to Furnivall, 9 January 1868, HuntL MS FU 52.

50. On this see Frantzen, *Desire for Origins*, 35–50; Alice Chandler, *A Dream of Order: The Medieval Ideal in Nineteenth-Century English Literature* (London: Routledge and Kegan Paul, 1971), 13–14. Machan notes that the Reformation, which advanced Old English scholarship, appeared to have had "the opposite effect" in Middle English studies, in which there was little interest after the mid–sixteenth century (*Textual Criticism*, 48); cf. on this Anne Hudson, "Middle English," in *Editing Medieval Texts: English, French, and Latin Written in England*, ed. A. G. Rigg (New York: Garland, 1977), 35.

51. Eagleton, *Function of Criticism*, 65.

1. "Barbarous Productions"

1. The quotation is from the will of James Smithson, in *The Smithsonian Institution: Documents Relative to Its Origin and History*, ed. William J. Rhees (Washington, D.C.: Smithsonian Institution, 1879), 2. Although the baron's title was invented, the surname was that of his stepfather; see Leonard Carmichael and J. C. Long, *James Smithson and the Smithsonian Story* (New York: Putnam, 1965), 132.

2. See, for example, the comments of South Carolina senator William C. Preston in "Congressional Proceedings of the Twenty-Fourth Congress, 1835–37," cited in Rhees, *The Smithsonian Institution*, 141.

3. Smithson's story is most reliably told in Carmichael and Long, *James Smithson*, 45–143. See also *DNB* 53:171–73; this account, however, like that of Rhees, contains errors.

4. From John Quincy Adams's report to the House of Representatives, 19 January 1836, in "Congressional Proceedings of the Twenty-Fourth Congress, 1835–37," cited in Rhees, *The Smithsonian Institution*, 151–52. Adams's internal references are to Addison's writings on the ballad of Chevy Chase in *The Spectator* 70 (21 May 1711) and 74 (25 May 1711); the "bard of our own native land" is Fitz-Greene Halleck, whose poem, "Alnwick Castle," appears in his *Alnwick Castle, with other Poems* (New York: G. & C. Carvill, 1827), 3–9. It is Prince Hal who calls Hotspur "confident against the world in arms" in *1 Henry IV* 5.1.117.

5. On Smithson's republicanism, see Carmichael and Long, *James Smithson*, 88. Despite the great element of luck in the passing of the fortune to Washington, the myth of origins first constructed by Adams is uncritically accepted in standard accounts of the Smithsonian Institution. Cf. Carmichael and Long, *James Smithson*, 269, 143.

6. Ibid., 55. Smithson's certificate of naturalization specifically prohibited him from occupying any public office in Britain.

7. Ibid., 72–73.

8. The notions of "symbolic," "cultural," and "educational" capital in this paragraph I draw from part 1 of Pierre Bourdieu's *Distinction: A Social Critique of the Judgement of Taste*, trans. Richard Nice (Cambridge, Mass.: Harvard University Press, 1984), and from *The Field of Cultural Production: Essays on Art and Literature*, ed. and intro. Randal Johnson (Cambridge: Polity, 1993), 75.

9. *Gentleman's Magazine* 56 (July 1786): 617.

10. Bourdieu, *Distinction*, 24.

11. Ibid., 23.

12. The change of name came in 1756, according to Bertram H. Davis, *Thomas Percy: A Scholar-Cleric in the Age of Johnson* (Philadelphia: University of Pennsylvania Press, 1989), 38; and Nick Groom states that the manuscript was found in 1753, but gives no reference for this; Nick Groom, "The Formation of Percy's *Reliques*," in Thomas Percy, *Reliques of Ancient English Poetry* (London: Routledge/Thoemmes Press, 1996), 1.

13. John Nichols and John Bowyer Nichols, *Illustrations of the Literary History of the Eighteenth Century*, 8 vols. (London: J. B. Nichols and Son, 1817–58), 6:552–53 n. The pedigree can be found in T. Nash, *Collections for the History of Worcestershire*, 2 vols. (London and Oxford, 1781–82), between 2:318 and 319.

14. For a succinct summary of Macpherson, Chatterton, and the import of their historicist inventions, see Marilyn Butler, "Romanticism in England," in *Romanticism in National Context*, ed. Roy Porter and Mikulas Teich (Cambridge: Cambridge University Press, 1988), 37–67, esp. 44–46. John Pinkerton, as an eighteen-year-old, wrote a continuation of the ballad "Hardyknute," which he sent to Percy, claiming to have taken it down as it was told to him by peasants. He later printed the ballad in his own *Scottish Tragic Ballads* (1781). See Bertrand H. Bronson, *Joseph Ritson: Scholar-at-Arms*, 2 vols. (Berkeley and Los Angeles: University of California Press, 1938), 1:114.

15. As Joseph M. P. Donatelli points out in "Old Barons in New Robes: Percy's Use of the Metrical Romances in the *Reliques of Ancient English Poetry*," in *Hermeneutics and Medieval Culture*, ed. Patrick J. Gallacher and Helen Damico (Albany, N.Y.: SUNY Press, 1989), 226.

16. On the influence of Percy's minstrel theory, see Albert B. Friedman, *The Ballad Revival: Studies in the Influence of Popular on Sophisticated Poetry* (Chicago: University of Chicago Press, 1961), 215.

17. Davis, *Thomas Percy*, 155.

18. Allen J. Frantzen, *Desire for Origins: New Language, Old English, and Teaching the Tradition* (New Brunswick, N.J.: Rutgers University Press, 1990), 35–50.

19. Anne Hudson, "Middle English," in *Editing Medieval Texts: English, French, and Latin Written in England*, ed. A. G. Rigg (New York: Garland, 1977), 35.

20. Marilyn Butler, *Romantics, Rebels, and Reactionaries: English Literature and Its Background, 1760–1830* (Oxford: Oxford University Press, 1981), 35.

21. Philippa Levine, *The Amateur and the Professional: Antiquarians, Historians, and Archaeologists in Victorian England, 1838–1886* (Cambridge: Cambridge University Press, 1986), 22.

22. On the early editing of Middle English texts, see A. S. G. Edwards, "Observations on the History of Middle English Editing," in *Manuscripts and Texts: Editorial Problems in Later Middle English Literature*, ed. Derek Pearsall (Cambridge: Brewer, 1987), 34–48.

23. On Warton and Percy in relation to this dilemma, see Lawrence Lipking, *The Ordering of the Arts in Eighteenth-Century England* (Princeton, N.J.: Princeton University Press, 1970), 372; Joseph M. P. Donatelli, "The Medieval Fictions of Thomas Warton and Thomas Percy," *University of Toronto Quarterly* 60 (1991): 435–51, esp. 437. On Warton, see also Clarissa Rinaker, *Thomas Warton: A Biographical and Critical Study* (Urbana: University of Illinois, 1916), esp. 118; on Percy, see Leah Dennis, "Thomas Percy: Antiquarian vs. Man of Taste," *PMLA* 57 (1942): 140–54.

24. See his *Culture and Government: The Emergence of Literary Education* (Houndmills: Macmillan, 1988), esp. 108–53, and "Learning the Literature Lesson: The Limits of the Aesthetic Personality," in *Towards a Critical Sociology of Reading Pedagogy*, ed. Carolyn D. Baker and Allan Luke (Amsterdam: Benjamins, 1991), 49–82.

25. "Percy Ballads," BL Add MS 27879, fol. 1r.

26. For a detailed account of the development of the *Reliques*, see Groom, "Formation."

27. Thomas Warton, *The History of English Poetry*, 3 vols. (London, 1774–81), 2:157; Bronson, *Joseph Ritson*, 1:222.

28. William Shenstone to Thomas Percy, 1 October 1760, in *The Correspondence of Thomas Percy and William Shenstone*, ed. Cleanth Brooks (New Haven, Conn.: Yale University Press, 1977), 72.

29. Ibid., 73.

30. Donatelli, "Old Barons," 228. See also Groom's account of the term in "Formation," 41.

31. Walter Jackson Bate, "Percy's Use of His Folio-Manuscript," *Journal of English and Germanic Philology* 43 (1944): 337–48; see also Donatelli, "Old Barons," 227–28.

32. Donatelli, "Old Barons," 228, 232. See also the similar suggestion made by Brooks, *The Correspondence*, xix. On the influence of the Percyan minstrel figure on ideas about poetic personae later in the eighteenth century, see Kathryn Sutherland, "The Native Poet: The Influence of Percy's Minstrel from Beattie to Wordsworth," *Review of English Studies* 33 (1982): 414–33.

33. See Davis, *Thomas Percy*, 109. On the dedication and its relation to Percy's fortunes, see also Dennis, "Thomas Percy," 152–53 (she misdates Percy's contact with the countess to June 1764).

34. Thomas Percy, *Reliques of Ancient English Poetry*, 3 vols. (London: Dodsley, 1765), 3:9. On the changes made, see Davis, *Thomas Percy*, 111–12. Subsequent references to the first edition of the *Reliques*, using the abbreviation *R* where necessary, appear parenthetically in the text.

35. Davis, *Thomas Percy*, 91.

36. John W. Hales and Frederick J. Furnivall, eds., *Bishop Percy's Folio Manuscript. Ballads and Romances*, 3 vols. (London, 1867–68), 2:210, lines 6, 7. Manuscript versions are quoted from this text; subsequent references appear parenthetically in the text with the abbreviation *BPFM* where necessary.

37. Groom ("Formation," 36, 38) records that Percy had at one stage planned to dedicate the work to the earl, but does not say why the plan was changed.

38. Tim William Machan, *Textual Criticism and Middle English Texts* (Charlottesville: University Press of Virginia, 1994), 47.

39. Lipking, *Ordering*, 361.

40. Ronald Paulson, *The Beautiful, Novel, and Strange: Aesthetics and Heterodoxy* (Baltimore, Md.: Johns Hopkins University Press, 1996), 67.

41. Warburton to Thomas Warton, 5 December 1770, in *The Correspondence of Thomas Percy and Thomas Warton*, ed. M. G. Robinson and Leah Dennis ([Baton Rouge?]: Louisiana State University Press, 1951), 170; Lipking, *Ordering*, 360.

42. Arthur Johnston, *Enchanted Ground: The Study of Medieval Romance in the Eighteenth Century* (London: Athlone, 1964), 9.

43. [Richard Hurd], *Letters on Chivalry and Romance* (London and Cambridge, 1762), 24. On Hurd's debt to French writers, see Johnston, *Enchanted Ground*, 60–61.

44. Johnston, *Enchanted Ground*, 60.

45. Hurd, *Letters on Chivalry and Romance*, 6–7. Further references appear parenthetically in the text.

46. Percy, "On the Ancient Metrical Romances," *R*, 3:ii.

47. On the notion of the supposed descent of minstrels from the ancient bards in the period, see Sutherland, "The Native Poet."

48. [Thomas Percy], "An Essay on the Ancient English Minstrels," in *Four Essays, As Improved and Enlarged in the Second Edition of the Reliques of Ancient English Poetry* (London: Dodsley, 1767), 3.

49. On Pegge's critique, see Davis, *Thomas Percy*, 153–54; see also Friedman, *Ballad Revival*, 202–16.

50. "The nobility of Percy's family would require very strong proof to any one knowing his inventive talents....I expect that he treated his pedigree as he did his ballads; filled up the gaps, and made it go smoothly. Had it been necessary to carry it back to Adam, it would have gone there without a check, under the Bishop's hands, we may be sure"; *BPFM*, 1:lix n. 1.

51. The Rev. Edward Blakeway to Percy, 4 July 1765, in *Illustrations of the Literary History of the Eighteenth Century*, ed. Nichols and Nichols, 5:644.

52. [Thomas Percy], *The Hermit of Warkworth: A Northumberland Ballad* (London, 1771), 5. Further references parenthetically in the text are to page numbers.

53. Christopher Smart was another; neither his dedication nor his poem match Percy's in rhetorical skill. See Christopher Smart, *Ode to the Right Honourable Earl of Northumberland, On his being appointed Lord Lieutenant of Ireland* (London, 1764).

54. He claimed as much in a letter to John Pinkerton in that year. See Percy to Pinkerton, 20 July 1778, in *The Correspondence of Thomas Percy and John Pinkerton*, ed. Harriet Harvey Wood (New Haven, Conn.: Yale University Press, 1985), 10.

55. See George Birkbeck Hill, ed., *Boswell's Life of Johnson*, rev. and enl. L. F. Powell, 6 vols. (Oxford: Clarendon Press, 1934–50), 3:271, 271 n. 5; cf. 3:520–21.

56. Joseph Ritson, ed., *Ancient Engleish Metrical Romanceës*, 3 vols. (London, 1802), 1:cix.

2. Turning the World Upside Down

1. Bertrand H. Bronson, *Joseph Ritson: Scholar-at-Arms*, 2 vols. (Berkeley and Los Angeles: University of California Press, 1938), 1:287. Further references appear parenthetically in the text, with the abbreviation *JR* where necessary.

2. "My complaint is neither a fever nor a consumption:" he wrote to his nephew in 1798, "but it renders my existence miserable....indeed, it is a subject upon which I do not like to explain myself; and wish nobody to enquire after. I am apprehensive of an entire loss of memory"; Ritson to [Joseph Frank], 5 April 1798, in *The Letters of Joseph Ritson...*, [ed. J. Frank], 2 vols. (London, 1833), 2:165–66.

3. Douce to John Pinkerton, 18 December 1823, in "Letters of Douce to Pinkerton & Palgrave 1818–183-", Bod Lib MS Douce d. 2, fol. 47r. Douce said that the story was told him by someone about to publish a biography of Ritson. This was almost certainly Joseph Haslewood, author of *Some Account of the Life & Publications of the late Joseph Ritson, Esq.* (London, 1824).

4. See John Nichols and John Bowyer Nichols, *Illustrations of the Literary History of the Eighteenth Century*, 8 vols. (London: J. B. Nichols and Son, 1817–58), 7:139.

5. R. H. Cromek, ed., *Select Scotish Songs, Ancient and Modern . . .* , 2 vols. (London, 1810), 1:224.

6. As Arthur Johnston writes, "The infirmity of Ritson's temper is not an irrelevance in a study of this kind. The desire not to rouse his ire must have had an effect on the quality of medieval scholarship"; *Enchanted Ground: The Study of Medieval Romance in the Eighteenth Century* (London: Athlone, 1964), 127.

7. Cf. Harris Nicolas, "Memoir of Joseph Ritson," in *Letters*, [ed. Frank], 1:i, and Bronson's retort, *JR*, 1:8.

8. In his early poem, "Verses to the Ladies of Stockton," he wrote of "Brave Percy," saying of Stockton, "Her valiant deeds let History proclaim, / And Cheviot hills record the fatal name." See *Letters*, [ed. Frank], 2:246 for an expression of antipathy.

9. "Alphabetical Collections for an Athenae Cantab.," vol. R, BL Add MS 5879, fol. 148v; attributed by Bronson to a Rev. W. Cole; *JR*, 1:70 n. 43.

10. *JR*, 1:222; Johnston, *Enchanted Ground*, 139.

11. Michel Foucault, *The Order of Things: An Archaeology of the Human Sciences* (New York: Vintage Books, 1973), 168.

12. B. A. Windeatt, "Thomas Tyrwhitt," in *Editing Chaucer: The Great Tradition*, ed. Paul Ruggiers (Norman, Okla.: Pilgrim Books, 1984), 119.

13. *HEP*, 1:i. On the influence of the belief in progress and perfectibility in eighteenth-century England, see David Spadafora, *The Idea of Progress in Eighteenth-Century Britain* (New Haven, Conn.: Yale University Press, 1990), esp. chap. 6.

14. Clarissa Rinaker, *Thomas Warton: A Biographical and Critical Study* (Urbana: University of Illinois, 1916), 23.

15. Percy was one who thought this; see ibid., 112.

16. Joseph M. P. Donatelli, "The Medieval Fictions of Thomas Warton and Thomas Percy," *University of Toronto Quarterly* 60 (1991): 445.

17. Johnston, *Enchanted Ground*, 19.

18. Ibid., 23.

19. *HEP*, Dissertation 1, 1:e4v–f1r, g2.

20. [Joseph Ritson], *Observations on the Three First Volumes of The History of English Poetry. In a Familiar Letter to Their Author* (London, 1782), 23–24.

21. The attack on Steevens and Johnson was *Remarks, Critical and Illustrative, on the Text and Notes of the Last Edition of Shakspeare* (London, 1783); remarks on Percy are made in both the preface and introductory essay to [Joseph Ritson, ed.], *A Select Collection of English Songs*, 3 vols. (London, 1783).

22. Ritson to Harrison, 8 October 1782, in *Letters*, [ed. Frank], 1:61.

23. [Ritson], *Observations*, title-page verso.

24. Ibid., 12.

25. Ibid., 47.

26. Robert Surtees, *The History and Antiquities of the County Palatine Durham . . .* , 4 vols. (London and Durham, 1816–40), 3:193; Haslewood, *Some Account*, 7; Nicolas, "Memoir," 1:xviii.

27. [Ritson], *Select Collection*, 1:x n.

28. Ibid., 1:lii.

29. Cf. *JR*, 2:545. In 1809, Francis Douce wrote to a correspondent: "I had the pleasure of a slight acquaintance with [Thomas Percy] before he left us to go to Ireland; & when I

reported to Ritson the reality of the Bishop's famous manuscript, he said, 'then I fear I must believe in it'"; Douce to J. Cooper Walker, 1 March 1809, Bod Lib MS Douce d 17, fol. 73v. Percy went to Ireland in 1782.

30. [Joseph Ritson, ed.], *Ancient Songs, From the Time of King Henry the Third, to the Revolution* (London, 1790), vii, x. Despite the date, the work was not actually published until 1792; see *JR*, 2:549.

31. [Ritson], *Ancient Songs*, xxi.

32. See [Ritson], *Select Collection*, 1:x.

33. A. S. G. Edwards, "Observations on the History of Middle English Editing," in *Manuscripts and Texts: Editorial Problems in Later Middle English Literature*, ed. Derek Pearsall (Cambridge: Brewer, 1987), 41–42.

34. Tim William Machan, *Textual Criticism and Middle English Texts* (Charlottesville: University Press of Virginia, 1994), 48.

35. Edwards, "Observations," 43.

36. Albert B. Friedman, *The Ballad Revival: Studies in the Influence of Popular on Sophisticated Poetry* (Chicago: University of Chicago Press, 1961), 209.

37. As is also noted by Frederick Christopher Porcheddu, "Editing the Auchinleck: Textual Criticism and the Reconstruction of a Medieval Manuscript" (Ph.D. diss., Ohio State University, 1994), 59. Porcheddu tries to overemphasize Ritson's similarity to the other antiquarians by insisting that he had barely looked at the Auchinleck manuscript and so, like them, was reliant on transcripts. But Ritson had undoubtedly studied the manuscript at length. See *JR*, 1:47–48, 250.

38. [Walter Scott], "Romance," *Supplement to the Fourth, Fifth, and Sixth Editions of the Encyclopaedia Britannica* (Edinburgh and London, 1824), 6:441. See further Johnston, *Enchanted Ground*, 96–99.

39. William Godwin, *Life of Geoffrey Chaucer*, 2 vols. (London, 1803).

40. [Joseph Ritson, ed.], *Robin Hood: A Collection of all the Ancient Poems, Songs, and Ballads, now Extant, Relative to that Celebrated English Outlaw: To Which Are Prefixed Historical Anecdotes of His Life*, 2 vols. (London, 1795), 1:xi–xii.

41. Stephen Knight, *Robin Hood: A Complete Study of the English Outlaw* (Oxford: Blackwell, 1994), 51; on the politics of Ritson's version of Robin Hood, see also 154–58.

42. [Joseph Ritson, ed.], *Poems on Interesting Events in the Reign of King Edward III. Written, in the Year MCCCLII. By Laurence Minot* (London, 1795), xxxviii.

43. [Ritson], *Robin Hood*, 1:xxxvii.

44. [Joseph Ritson], *Bibliographia Poetica: A Catalogue of Engleish Poets, of the Twelfth, Thirteenth, Fourteenth, Fifteenth, and Sixteenth Centurys, with a short account of their works* (London, 1802), 87, 88.

45. Johnston, *Enchanted Ground*, 125.

46. Edwards, "Observations," 41.

47. Johnston, *Enchanted Ground*, 140. Johnston lists here some of Ritson's characteristic errors as a transcriber.

48. [Joseph Ritson, ed.], *Pieces of Ancient Popular Poetry: From Authentic Manuscripts and Old Printed Copies* (London, 1791), xiii; cf. [Ritson], *Select Collection* 1:x n. Despite his words, Ritson's use of single quotation marks to highlight words that have been emended is not consistent in *Pieces of Ancient Popular Poetry*.

49. [Ritson], *Ancient Songs*, unpaginated "advertisement."

50. Ibid., unpaginated "advertisement."

51. Anon. rev. of *Ancient Songs, Critical Review*, new arr., 6 (1792): 289.

52. [Ritson], *Poems on Interesting Events*, xv.

53. Joseph Ritson, ed., *Ancient Engleish Metrical Romanceës*, 3 vols. (London, 1802), 1:iv.

54. Joseph Ritson, *The Life of King Arthur: From Ancient Historians and Authentic Documents* (London, 1825), 133.

55. Edwards, "Observations," 44.

56. [Ritson], *Pieces of Ancient Popular Poetry*, xiii–xiv.

57. [Walter Scott], rev. of George Ellis, *Specimens of Early English Metrical Romances*, and Joseph Ritson, *Ancient Engleish Metrical Romanceës*, *Edinburgh Review* 7 (1806): 387–413, at 392.

3. The Last Minstrel

1. Walter Scott, *The Monastery* (Edinburgh: Adam and Charles Black, 1853), 218. Hereafter cited by page number in the text.

2. Walter Scott, *Memoirs*, in *Scott on Himself: A Selection of the Autobiographical Writings of Sir Walter Scott*, ed. David Hewitt (Edinburgh: Scottish Academic Press, 1981), 1.

3. Ibid., 2.

4. Walter Scott, Introduction to *Chronicles of the Canongate* (1827), in *The Prefaces to the Waverley Novels*, ed. Mark A. Weinstein (Lincoln: University of Nebraska Press, 1978), 78.

5. Scott, *Memoirs*, 2.

6. Walter Scott, "General Preface to the Waverley Novels," in *Scott on Himself*, ed. Hewitt, 244.

7. John Sutherland, *The Life of Walter Scott: A Critical Biography* (Oxford: Blackwell, 1995), 172. Hereafter cited parenthetically with the abbreviation *LWS* where necessary.

8. Scott, "General Preface," 253.

9. J. G. Lockhart, *Memoirs of the Life of Sir Walter Scott, Bart.*, 7 vols. (Edinburgh: Robert Cadell; London: John Murray and Whitaker and Co., 1837–38), 1:340.

10. Sutherland: "famously insanitary"; Buchan: "reached by a foul common stair, and the narrow windows looked out upon wynds where refuse rotted in heaps, and pigs roamed as in a farmyard"; Quayle: a "perpetually dirty little court"; Johnson: off a "dismal lane." Sutherland, *LWS*, 11; John Buchan, *Sir Walter Scott* (New York: A. L. Burt, 1932), 24; Eric Quayle, *The Ruin of Sir Walter Scott* (London: Rupert Hart-Davis, 1968), 18; Edgar Johnson, *Sir Walter Scott: The Great Unknown*, 2 vols. (London: Hamish Hamilton, 1970), 1:3.

11. Alice Chandler, *A Dream of Order: The Medieval Ideal in Nineteenth-Century English Literature* (London: Routledge & Kegan Paul, 1971), chap. 1; Mark Girouard, *The Return to Camelot: Chivalry and the English Gentleman* (New Haven, Conn.: Yale University Press, 1981), esp. chap. 3.

12. Johnson, *Walter Scott*, 1:222; Arthur Johnston, *Enchanted Ground: The Study of Medieval Romance in the Eighteenth Century* (London: Athlone, 1964), 187. See also Cedric E. Pickford, "*Sir Tristrem*, Sir Walter Scott, and Thomas," in *Studies in Medieval Literature and Languages in Memory of Frederick Whitehead*, ed. W. Rothwell, W. R. J Barron, David Blamires, and Lewis Thorpe (Manchester: Manchester University Press, 1973), 219–28.

13. Jane Millgate, *Walter Scott: The Making of the Novelist* (Edinburgh: Edinburgh University Press, 1984), 10. Hereafter cited parenthetically in the text, with the abbreviation *WS* where necessary.

14. Lockhart, *Memoirs*, 1:38. See also Chandler, *Dream of Order*, 26–27.

15. Scott became sheriff-depute of Selkirkshire in 1799, a position with a salary of £250, later £300, as a result "of patronage, pure and simple" (*LWS*, 71).

16. Walter Scott, *The Lay of the Last Minstrel* (London: Longman, Hurst, Rees, and Orme; Edinburgh: A. Constable and Co., 1805), unpaginated prefatory material. Further references appear parenthetically by page number.

17. Ibid., 3–4.

18. Sutherland notes, in addition, how the figure of the wizard Michael Scott in the *Lay* "is a version of the poet" (*LWS*, 103).

19. J. G. L[ockhart], ed., *The Poetical Works of Sir Walter Scott, Bart.*, 12 vols. (Edinburgh: Robert Cadell; London: Whitaker and Co., 1833–34), 6:22.

20. Cf. *WS*, 16, and Nancy Moore Goslee, *Scott the Rhymer* (Lexington: University Press of Kentucky, 1988), 22. Millgate points out that this story was in existence, pri-

vately, soon after the poem's publication, when Scott told a similar tale in a letter to Anna Seward (*WS*, 15).

21. "I see that no one recites the songs and spoken tales by Erceldoune and Kendal as they wrote them; in the reciting they seem worthless; you can hear this in *Sir Tristrem*, which is esteemed above all stories, all that are or were, if men recite it the way Thomas wrote it; but I hear no man recite it without parts of some of the couplets missing"; Frederick J. Furnivall, ed., *The Story of England of Robert Manning of Brunne, A.D. 1338*, 2 vols. (London: HMSO, 1887), 1:3–4, lines 93–102.

22. John Pinkerton, *Ancient Scotish Poems...*, 2 vols. (London: Charles Dilly; Edinburgh: William Creech, 1786), 1:lix. See also 1:lxix.

23. See ibid., 1:lxxvi.

24. See *The Auchinleck Manuscript: National Library of Advocates' MS.19.2.1*, intro. by Derek Pearsall and I. C. Cunningham (London: Scolar Press, 1977), fol. 281r.

25. See Walter Scott, ed., *Sir Tristrem; a Metrical Romance of the Thirteenth Century; by Thomas of Ercildoune [sic], called The Rhymer* (Edinburgh: Archibald Constable; London: Longman and Rees, 1804), lxxxii. Hereafter cited parenthetically in the text, abbreviated as *ST* where necessary.

26. See Scott to Ellis, 24 September 1801, in *The Letters of Sir Walter Scott*, ed. H. J. C. Grierson, 12 vols. (London: Constable & Co., 1932–37), 12:194–95; cf. Bertrand H. Bronson, *Joseph Ritson: Scholar-at-Arms*, 2 vols. (Berkeley and Los Angeles: University of California Press, 1938), 1:250.

27. Scott's letter to Ellis of the previous note confirms that the Border ballads and the Auchinleck manuscript, at least, were discussed.

28. Scott to Ellis, [19 March 1804], in *Letters*, ed. Grierson, 1:214–15.

29. *WS*, 13. Sutherland's view is that the delay in the publication of *Sir Tristrem* occurred because Scott was strengthening his case (*LWS*, 92). This seems to be confirmed by the Scottish antiquary Robert Anderson in a letter to Thomas Percy in 1803, who noted that although *Sir Tristrem* had been printed two years before, it remained unpublished because of the lack of introduction and glossary and its editor's "great difficulties in ascribing it to Learmont"; Anderson to Percy, 14 October 1803, in *Illustrations of the Literary History of the Eighteenth Century*, ed. John Nichols and John Bowyer Nichols, 8 vols. (London: J. B. Nichols and Son, 1817–58), 7:121.

30. Walter Scott, *Minstrelsy of the Scottish Border: Consisting of Historical and Romantic Ballads, etc.*, 2 vols. (Kelso, London, and Edinburgh, 1802), 2:250.

31. Ibid., 2:287.

32. Pinkerton, *Ancient Scotish Poems*, 1:lxii.

33. Ibid., 1:lxvi.

34. Ibid., 1:xvii.

35. Scott to Ellis, [25 August–8 September 1801], in *Letters*, ed. Grierson, 12:191.

36. Robert Crawford, *Devolving English Literature* (Oxford: Clarendon Press, 1992), 18.

37. *LWS*, 91; cf. *Letters*, ed. Grierson, 12:174 n. 2, where Leyden is quoted as having stopped after one thousand lines because the poem became too "free and easy." One cut was made to the published text, which Scott often referred to as a "castration" (e.g., Scott to Douce, 7 May 1804, in *Letters*, ed. Grierson, 1:221).

38. Scott to Ellis, 1 July [1807], in *Letters*, ed. Grierson 12:293.

39. See Price's "Note on the Romance of Sir Tristram," in his *The History of English Poetry...by Thomas Warton...A New Edition Carefully Revised...*, 4 vols. (London: Thomas Tegg, 1824), 1:181–98.

40. Richard Taylor, ed., *The History of English Poetry...*, 3 vols. (London: Thomas Tegg, 1840); note by R. G. (i.e., Richard Garnett), 1:109–12; note by W. (i.e., Wright), 1:109 n.

41. L[ockhart], ed., *Poetical Works*, 5:v–vi.

42. George McNeill, ed., *Sir Tristrem* (Edinburgh and London: Scottish Text Society, 1886); John MacQueen and Tom Scott, eds., *The Oxford Book of Scottish Verse* (Oxford: Clarendon Press, 1966). See also David Irving, *The History of Scotish Poetry*, ed. John Aitken

Carlyle (Edinburgh: Edmonston and Douglas, 1861), 51–78, and George Eyre-Todd, ed., *Early Scottish Poetry*... (Glasgow: William Hodge & Co., 1891). I have discussed the Scottish "afterlife" of the poem at greater length in my " 'Quaint Inglis': Walter Scott and the Rise of Middle English Studies," *Studies in Medievalism* 7 (1995): 33–48.

43. Cf. Scott to [Ellis], 21 Aug 1801, in *Letters*, ed. Grierson, 12:187. Edgar Johnson records (*Sir Walter Scott*, 1:180) that George Ellis sent Scott a transcription of "the ending of a French metrical version" of Tristram and this, combined with a suggestion from Ritson, suggested to Scott that he complete the poem.

44. Johnston, *Enchanted Ground*, 178–79.

45. John M. Ganim, "The Myth of Medieval Romance," in *Medievalism and the Modernist Temper*, ed. Stephen G. Nichols and R. Howard Bloch (Baltimore, Md.: Johns Hopkins University Press, 1996), 152.

46. George Ellis, *Specimens of the Early English Poets* (London, 1790), i.

47. George Ellis, *Specimens of the Early English Poets, to which is prefixed an Historical Sketch of the Rise and Progress of the English Poetry and Language*, 3 vols. (London, 1801), 1:viii. Hereafter cited parenthetically in the text, abbreviated as *SP* where necessary.

48. George Ellis, *Specimens of Early English Metrical Romances, chiefly written during the early part of the fourteenth century*..., 3 vols. (London: Longman, Hurst, Rees, & Co.; Edinburgh: A. Constable & Co., 1805), 2:95.

49. Johnston, *Enchanted Ground*, 33.

50. Scott to [Ellis], 21 August 1801, in *Letters*, ed. Grierson, 12:186.

51. Ibid., 187.

52. Ellis, *Specimens of Early English Poets* (1801), 1:127.

53. Ellis, *Metrical Romances*, 1:7, 9 n.

54. Kurt Gamerschlag, "Henry Weber: Medieval Scholar, Poet, and Secretary to Walter Scott," *Studies in Scottish Literature* 25 (1990): 212.

55. Henry Weber, *Metrical Romances of the Thirteenth, Fourteenth, and Fifteenth Centuries: Published from Ancient Manuscripts*..., 3 vols. (Edinburgh: Archibald Constable & Co.; London: John Murray, and Constable, Hunter, Park and Hunter, 1810), 1:xi.

56. Gamerschlag, "Henry Weber," 213.

57. Weber, *Metrical Romances*, 1:xxxviii; hereafter cited in the text.

58. Lockhart, *Memoirs*, 2:168.

59. When Scott first heard of Ellis's plans for his work on the metrical romances, he wrote to Richard Heber that he would "think myself very happy in assisting him from our invaluable folio Ms which is once more snug in my possession. I intend shortly to transmit you a brief of its contents — I believe we will try one or two here for the honor of Scotland: at least I wish Sir Tristram [*sic*] to make his appearance first in Edinr."; Scott to Richard Heber, 10 March 1801, in *Letters*, ed. Grierson, 12:174. Further letters, to Ellis (e.g., *Letters*, 12:200), confirm that the promised aid, in the form of transcriptions, was forthcoming.

60. The account of Weber's life is based on Gamerschlag, "Henry Weber."

61. *DNB* 33:146–48; see also James Loch, *Memoir of George Granville, late Duke of Sutherland, K.G.* (London, 1834), esp. 7, 10–11.

62. Scott to Ellis, [8 October 1808], *Letters*, ed. Grierson, 2:93.

63. Gamerschlag, "Henry Weber," 204–5.

64. Lockhart, *Memoirs*, 3:110.

65. Gamerschlag, "Henry Weber," 216.

66. Lockhart, *Memoirs*, 2:331.

67. Gamerschlag, "Henry Weber," 215.

4. Turtle Soup and Texts

1. T. F. Dibdin, *The Bibliographical Decameron*, 3 vols. (London, 1817), 3:52, 3:49 n, 3:65 n; ellipses in final quotation in original.

2. John Hill Burton, *The Book-Hunter, etc.* (Edinburgh and London: William Blackwood and Sons, 1862), 245.

3. Dibdin, *Bibliographical Decameron,* 3:72 n.

4. Lieut.-Col. the Hon. Clive Bigham, *The Roxburghe Club: Its History and Its Members, 1812–1927* (Oxford: Oxford University Press, 1928), 4–6, quotation at 6.

5. "Rules and Regulations," 1, in *Chronological List of Members; Catalogue of Books; Rules and Regulations,* Roxburghe Club (London, 1850).

6. *DNB* 15:7.

7. Bigham, *Roxburghe Club,* 13.

8. On this see Linda Colley, *Britons: Forging the Nation, 1707–1837* (New Haven, Conn.: Yale University Press, 1992), chap. 4.

9. Bigham, *Roxburghe Club,* 7.

10. David Laing, ed., *The Bannatyne Club. Lists of Members and the Rules, with a Catalogue of the Books Printed for the Bannatyne Club Since its Institution in 1823* (Edinburgh, 1867), 8.

11. Maitland Club, *Rules of The Maitland Club. Instituted March, M.DCCC.XXVIII* (n.p., [1828]), 3.

12. Abbotsford Club, *Rules of the Abbotsford Club, July IX., M.DCCC.XXXVI* (n.p., [1836]), 1.

13. Thomas Dunham Whitaker, ed., *Visio Willī de Petro Plouhman...The Vision of William concerning Peirs Plouhman...ascribed to Robert Langland...* (London: John Murray, 1813), v–vi.

14. Charlotte Brewer, *Editing* Piers Plowman: *The Evolution of the Text* (Cambridge: Cambridge University Press, 1996), 39.

15. Whitaker, *Visio,* ii.

16. Brewer, *Editing* Piers, 45.

17. Robert Southey, *The Byrth, Lyf, and Actes of Kyng Arthur; of His Noble Knyghtes of the Rounde Table...and in the End Le Morte Darthur...,* 2 vols. (London: Longman, Hurst, Rees, Orme, and Brown, 1817). The 1816 editions were *La Mort D'Arthur: The Most Ancient and Famous History of the Renowned Prince Arthur, and the Knights of the Round Table. by Sir Tho⁵. Malory, Knᵗ.* 3 vols. (London: R. Wilks, 1816), and *The History of the Renowned Prince Arthur, and His Knights of the Round Table,* 2 vols. (London: J. Walker & Co, 1816). Neither names an editor.

18. Southey, *Kyng Arthur,* 1:xxxi.

19. [William B. D. D. Turnbull], ed., *The Romances of Sir Guy of Warwick, and Rembrun His Son...* (Edinburgh: Abbotsford Club, 1840), ix.

20. James Heywood Markland, *Chester Mysteries: De Deluvio Noe. De Occisione Innocentium* (London: Roxburghe Club, 1818).

21. Thomas Ponton, ed., *Le Morte Arthur: The Adventures of Sir Launcelot Du Lake* (London: Roxburghe Club, 1819), unpaginated preface.

22. William B. D. D. Turnbull, ed., *Sir Beves of Hamtoun: A Metrical Romance. Now First Edited From the Auchinleck MS* (Edinburgh: [Maitland Club], 1838), xii.

23. *DNB* 11:401–2.

24. *DNB* 58:73–74.

25. [David Laing], ed., *Select Remains of the Ancient Popular Poetry of Scotland* (Edinburgh: Privately printed, 1822), 6.

26. J. G. L[ockhart], ed., *The Poetical Works of Sir Walter Scott, Bart.,* 12 vols. (Edinburgh: Robert Cadell; London: Whitaker and Co., 1833–34), 4:117 n.

27. Cf. the minutes of the meeting of 7 May 1856, in "Abbotsford Club" (circular), 2. Bound as part of BL Ac. 8247/34.

28. E. V. U[tterson], ed., *Select Pieces of Early Popular Poetry: Re-Published Principally from Early Printed Copies, in the Black Letter,* 2 vols. (London: Longman, Hurst, Rees, Orme, and Brown, 1817), 1:xvi–xvii.

29. Harrison Ross Steeves, *Learned Societies and English Literary Scholarship in Great Britain and the United States* (New York: Columbia University Press, 1913), 102.

30. Pierre Bourdieu, *Distinction: A Social Critique of the Judgement of Taste,* trans. Richard Nice (Cambridge, Mass.: Harvard University Press, 1984), 23.

31. [James Maidment], ed., *Notices Relative to the Bannatyne Club* (Edinburgh: Printed for private circulation, 1836), 275.

32. Bourdieu, *Distinction,* 53.

33. Ibid., 53–54.

34. See Colley, *Forging the Nation,* 155–77; on education, see 167.

35. Bigham, *Roxburghe Club,* 35.

36. *DNB* 55:257.

37. Bigham, *Roxburghe Club,* 22. The internal quotation is not referenced, and I have not been able to find its source. Colley's remarks on the rise of foxhunting in this period as another marker of the new class are pertinent; see *Forging the Nation,* 170–72.

38. Bourdieu, *Distinction,* 71–72.

39. Madden to Earl Powis, 17 June 1845, BL Eg MS 2844, fol. 61v.

40. John Gough Nichols, *A Descriptive Catalogue of the Works of the Camden Society* (Westminster: J. B. Nichols and Sons, 1862), iv.

41. *Gentleman's Magazine* 83 (September 1813): 211; "Remarks Upon the Bannatyne Club," *The New Scots Magazine,* April 1829, 58.

42. Nichols, *Descriptive Catalogue,* ix–xiv.

43. Philippa Levine, *The Amateur and the Professional: Antiquarians, Historians, and Archaeologists in Victorian England, 1838–1886* (Cambridge: Cambridge University Press, 1986), 164.

44. Thomas Wright, ed., *Alliterative Poem on the Deposition of King Richard II. Ricardi Maydiston De Concordia Inter Ric. II. Et Civitatem London* (London: Camden Society, 1838), v, vi, vii; emphases mine.

45. *DNB* 63:130–33.

46. [Richard Garnett], "Antiquarian Club Books," *Quarterly Review* 82 (1847–48): 309–42, at 319.

47. Hans Aarsleff, *The Study of Language in England, 1780–1860* (London: Athlone; Minneapolis: University of Minnesota Press, 1983), 166.

48. See Allen Frantzen, *Desire for Origins: New Language, Old English, and Teaching the Tradition* (New Brunswick, N.J.: Rutgers University Press, 1990), chap. 2.

5. "The Deadly Poison of Democracy"

1. "Chartism," in *Thomas Carlyle: Selected Writings,* ed. Alan Shelston (London: Penguin, 1971), 151.

2. *Gentleman's Magazine,* n.s., 12 (August 1839): 191–92.

3. Ian Anstruther, *The Knight and the Umbrella: An Account of The Eglinton Tournament, 1839* (London: Geoffrey Bles, 1963), 193.

4. *Gentleman's Magazine,* n.s., 12 (October 1839): 414.

5. See the illustrations in Mark Girouard, *The Return to Camelot: Chivalry and the English Gentleman* (New Haven, Conn.: Yale University Press, 1981), 103.

6. Anstruther, *Knight and Umbrella,* 59–60. On Disraeli, Young England, and medievalism, see Alice Chandler, *A Dream of Order: The Medieval Ideal in Nineteenth-Century Literature* (London: Routledge & Kegan Paul, 1971), chap. 5.

7. Cited in Anstruther, *Knight and Umbrella,* 172.

8. Sir Frederic Madden, ed., *Syr Gawayne: A Collection of Ancient Romance-Poems, by Scotish and English Authors, Relating to that Celebrated Knight of the Round Table* ([Edinburgh]: Bannatyne Club, 1839). Hereafter cited in the text with the abbreviation *SG* as necessary.

9. Represented by A. C. Spearing's opinion, on the one hand, that the courtiers' laughter at Gawain's shame should guide our response and, on the other, Edward Wilson's belief that the court's adoption of the green lace, Gawain's "sign of infamy," was "the deepest irony"; see Spearing, *The Gawain-Poet: A Critical Study* (Cambridge: Cambridge University Press, 1970), 230; and Wilson, *The Gawain-Poet* (Leiden: Brill, 1976), 130.

10. "It was a strange action for the Birmingham authorities to have taken against meetings which were neither riotous nor threatening, and it is not surprising that the Chartist leaders interpreted it as the long-anticipated attack on the Convention"; Dorothy Thompson, *The Chartists* (London: Temple Smith, 1984), 69.

11. Girouard, *Return to Camelot*, esp. chap. 1.

12. John Ganim, "The Myth of Medieval Romance," in *Medievalism and the Modernist Temper*, ed. R. Howard Bloch and Stephen G. Nichols (Baltimore, Md.: Johns Hopkins University Press, 1996), 148–66, at 149.

13. On medievalism in this role, see Chandler, *Dream of Order*, 1–11.

14. Carlyle, "Chartism," 193. On Carlyle's medievalism, see Chandler, *Dream of Order*, 122–51.

15. Phillipps to FM, 22 May 1839, BL Eg MS 2842, fol. 44r.

16. BL Add MS 63652, vol. 1, fol. 125r.

17. Anstruther, *Knight and Umbrella*, 234.

18. The figure is based on information drawn from treasurer's reports of the Bannatyne Club, bound together as volume 4 of the club's records in the British Library, shelf mark G.285.

19. Michel Foucault, "Two Lectures," in *Power/Knowledge: Selected Interviews and Other Writings, 1972–1977*, ed. Colin Gordon, trans. Colin Gordon et al. (New York: Harvester Wheatsheaf, 1980), 99.

20. Hans Aarsleff, *The Study of Language in England, 1780–1860* (London: Athlone; Minneapolis: University of Minnesota Press, 1983), 202.

21. Robert W. Ackerman and Gretchen Ackerman, *Sir Frederic Madden: A Biographical Sketch and Bibliography* (New York: Garland, 1979), ix, hereafter abbreviated *FM* (see also Robert W. Ackerman, "Sir Frederic Madden and Medieval Scholarship," *Neuphilologische Mitteilungen* 73 [1972], 1, where almost identical phrasing is used); Robert W. Ackerman, "Madden's Gawain Anthology," in *Medieval Studies in Honor of Lillian Herlands Hornstein*, ed. Jess B. Bessinger Jr. and Robert R. Raymo (New York: New York University Press, 1976), 8–9, 9; A. S. G. Edwards, "Observations on the History of Middle English Editing," in *Manuscripts and Texts: Editorial Problems in Later Middle English Literature*, ed. Derek Pearsall (Cambridge: Brewer, 1987), 44, 45. Edwards does note the textual-critical conservatism of Madden's approach.

22. *The Diary of Sir Frederic Madden*, 12 August 1825, Bod Lib MS Eng. Hist. c. 146, 282. Hereafter referenced as *Diary*, with the relevant shelf mark given; unless otherwise noted, references are to page numbers. Parts of the diary are foliated, and some parts have both pagination and foliation, which is indicated when it occurs.

23. J. J. Conybeare, *Illustrations of Anglo-Saxon Poetry*, ed. William Daniel Conybeare (London, 1826), lxxviii; noted in *Diary*, 29 July 1826, Bod Lib MS Eng. Hist. c. 146, 460.

24. *Diary*, 19 December 1826, Bod Lib MS Eng. Hist. c. 146, 511.

25. FM to Spencer, 3 December 1827, BL Eg MS 2837, fols. 244r–244v.

26. FM to Spencer, 4 December 1827, BL Eg MS 2837, fol. 246r.

27. Spencer to FM, 5 December 1827, BL Eg MS 2837, fol. 247r.

28. In a letter to Walter Scott, 19 October 1829, BL Eg MS 2838, fol. 70r.

29. Walter W. Skeat, ed., *The Lay of Havelok the Dane*, EETS, e.s., 4 (London: EETS, 1868), ii.

30. Frederick Madden, ed., *The Ancient English Romance of Havelok the Dane; Accompanied by the French Text: With an Introduction, Notes, and a Glossary* (London: Roxburghe Club, 1828), 213. Hereafter abbreviated *H*.

31. James Orchard Halliwell, ed., *The Thornton Romances. The Early English Metrical Romances of Perceval, Isumbras, Eglamour, and Degrevant. Selected from Manuscripts at Lincoln and Cambridge* (London: Camden Society, 1844), 307.

32. "The colour of her cheek is like the rose on the rosebush when it is newly opened out in the bright, warm sun"; the quotation is from *Havelok*, lines 2918–21, in his own edition; he quotes from *The Complaint of the Black Knight* on li; emphases in original.

33. T. G. Repp, rev. of *The Ancient English Romance of Havelok the Dane*, reprinted in [James Maidment], ed., *Notices Relative to the Bannatyne Club...* (Edinburgh: Printed for private circulation, 1836), 48–56, quotation at 50.

34. Anon. rev. of *Havelok*, ed. Madden, *The Oxford Literary Gazette*, no. 1 (March 11, 1829): 2–4; continued in no. 4 (April 22, 1829): 54–56, quotations at 2 and 56. Attributed by Madden to Arthur Johnson, Rawlinson and Bosworth professor of Anglo-Saxon, Oxford University, 1827–29; see Houghton MS Eng 566F, fol. 27.

35. Singer's pamphlet was titled *Remarks on the Glossary to the Antient Metrical Romance of Havelok the Dane, in a letter to Francis Douce, Esq. F.A.S.* (London, [1829]); Madden's was titled *Examination of the "Remarks on the Glossary to the Antient Metrical Romance of Havelok the Dane..." Addressed to Henry Petrie, Esq. Keeper of his Majesty's Records in the Tower of London* (London, 1829). On the distribution of Madden's pamphlet, see W. Nicol to FM, 13 November 1829, Houghton Library MS Eng 566F, fol. 45. It was thought at the time that the whole affair had been provoked by the Roxburghe Club's Joseph Haslewood, who got Singer to write his remarks out of pique at not having been asked to edit the romance himself by the club; see Harrison Ross Steeves, *Learned Societies and English Literary Scholarship in Great Britain and the United States* (New York: Columbia University Press), 104–5. There is a great deal of material, particularly correspondence, concerning the edition in the Houghton Library under the title *Havelock the Dane: Correspondence of Sir F. Madden.*

36. I[ohn] M[itchell] K[emble], "On English Praeterites," *The Philological Museum* 2 (Cambridge: Deightons; London: Rivingtons; Oxford: Parker, 1833): 373–88, quotation at 381 n. 3.

37. FM to Bliss, 27 March 1829, BL Eg MS 2838, fol. 21r.

38. Aarsleff, *Study of Language*, 185–89.

39. Frederick Madden, ed., *The Ancient English Romance of William and the Werwolf; Edited from an Unique Copy in King's College Library, Cambridge; with an Introduction and Glossary* (London: Roxburghe Club, 1832), xv.

40. *DNB* 26:168.

41. Madden, *William*, 5–6.

42. Madden did produce another black-letter edition, in a small book containing the late poem *How the Goode Wif thaught hir Doughter* (London, 1838). Signed only "F.M.," printed in a run of fifty copies and containing very little scholarly material, this very much resembles some of the club books or Edward Utterson's private printings.

43. *SG*, xlv. See Edwards, "Observations," 44.

44. Edwards, "Observations," 45.

45. On Madden's role in the controversy over new philology, see Aarsleff, *Study of Language*, 199–201.

46. Did the greatest expert on Middle English of his age really imagine the poem to be Scottish, or did he somewhat cynically push the poem across the border, Tristrem-like, to give it more appeal to the Bannatyne Club? Of course *Sir Gawain*, given a northern dialect that must have looked very peculiar to readers of the 1830s, is more easily mistakable than *Sir Tristrem* as a Scottish production. Nevertheless it is difficult not to suspect Madden of making the poem more attractive to Scott and to the Bannatyne Club, which was formed with the purpose of printing "ancient manuscripts, books, or tracts, connected with *Scottish* literature" (*Rules of the Bannatyne Club: Instituted February 1823* [Edin-

burgh, 1823], rule no. 7; emphasis added). In Madden's defense is the fact that from the moment he saw the poem, he noted that it was in the "same stanza & probably by the same person, as Gawan & Golagros, and Gawan & Galaron," both of which he thought to be Scottish. The latter—later renamed by Madden *The Awntyrs of Arthur*—had been edited by Pinkerton in his *Scotish Poems* (1792). *Diary*, 8–9 July 1829, Bod Lib MS Eng. Hist. c. 147, Madden fol. 30v/Bodleian fol. 123v.

47. Arthur Johnston, *Enchanted Ground: The Study of Medieval Romance in the Eighteenth Century* (London: Athlone, 1964), 25.

48. Once again, the influence of Scott might have been at work here; Scott had referred to the way in which Malory's account of Tristram "misrepresents the adventures, and traduces the character of Sir Gawain, and other renowned Knights of the Round Table"; Walter Scott, ed., *Sir Tristrem* (Edinburgh: Archibald Constable; London: Longman and Rees, 1804), lxxx.

49. The notion of power in "its more regional and local forms"—at which it is "capillary"—is Foucault's; see "Two Lectures," 96.

50. To these can be added others among the prolific Halliwell's editions: *The Harrowing of Hell, A Miracle-Play Written in the Reign of Edward the Second* (London: John Russel Smith, 1840); *A Selection from the Minor Poems of Dan John Lydgate*, Early English Poetry, Ballads, and Popular Literature of the Middle Ages series, vol. 2 (London: Percy Society, 1840); and *Morte Arthure. The Alliterative Romance of the Death of King Arthur. Now First Printed from a Manuscript in Lincoln Cathedral* (Brixton Hill: Privately printed, 1847). But Halliwell's trajectory was the reverse of the general trend toward accessibility. His later, privately printed editions tended to recall the ways of the book clubs: *Morte Arthure*, for example, was printed in a run of seventy-five copies in quarto, twenty-five of them on thick paper.

51. Karl Marx, *The Revolutions of 1848: Political Writings, Volume 1*, ed. and intro. David Fernbach (London: Penguin, 1993), 101.

52. *Diary*, 31 December 1837, Bod Lib MS Eng. Hist. 151, Madden 134/Bodleian fol. 237v.

53. Ian Hunter, *Culture and Government: The Emergence of Literary Education* (Houndmills: Macmillan, 1988), 3.

54. Steeves, *Learned Societies*, 109.

6. "Go-a-head-itiveness"

1. *The Diary of Sir Frederic Madden*, 23 July 1866, Bod Lib MS Eng. Hist. c. 179, 202. On the disturbances at Hyde Park and their context, see E. L. Woodward, *The Age of Reform, 1815–1870* (Oxford: Clarendon Press, 1954), 177–78.

2. *Diary*, 18 August 1867, Bod Lib MS Eng. Hist. c. 180, 165.

3. W. C. Hazlitt, *Hand-Book to the Popular, Poetical, and Dramatic Literature of Great Britain From the Invention of Printing to the Restoration* (London: John Russell Smith, 1867); as the full title suggests, this book was chiefly of use to the medievalist in its descriptions of incunables and other early prints; Richard Morris, *Specimens of Early English Selected from the Chief English Authors A.D. 1250–A.D.1400* (Oxford: Clarendon Press, 1867). Bradshaw, typically, did not publish his work until 1871; see G. W. Prothero, *A Memoir of Henry Bradshaw* (London: Kegan Paul, Trench & Co., 1888), 213–14, 221.

4. See *Diary*, 3 November 1831, Bod Lib MS Eng. Hist. c. 148, 63, and MS note of sometime after October 1865, 64. Cf. Robert W. Ackerman, "Madden's Gawain Anthology," in *Medieval Studies in Honor of Lillian Herlands Hornstein*, ed. Jess B. Bessinger Jr. and Robert R. Raymo (New York: New York University Press, 1976), 14. See also John Edward Martin to Frederic Madden, 17 October 1865, Thomas Fisher Rare Book Library, University of Toronto. This is a letter of introduction for Edward Meade, a grandson of Percy's.

5. Frederick Furnivall, *Bishop Percy's Ballad Manuscript: Proposal for Its Publication* (London, 1866), 1.

6. John W. Hales and Frederick J. Furnivall, eds., *Bishop Percy's Folio Manuscript*, 3 vols. (London, 1867–68), 1:xvi, xvii.

7. As Charlotte Brewer notes, "it is virtually impossible—or at least so I have found—to turn up any explicit statement by Furnivall of his views on editing that fully acknowledges his position relative to those of others"; *Editing* Piers Plowman: *The Evolution of the Text* (Cambridge: Cambridge University Press, 1996), 88.

8. William Benzie, *Dr. F. J. Furnivall: Victorian Scholar Adventurer* (Norman, Okla.: Pilgrim Books, 1983), 78, 73, 74. Hereafter cited parenthetically in the text, with the abbreviation *FJF* where necessary. For a more skeptical account of Furnivall, see Derek Pearsall, "Frederick James Furnivall," in *Medieval Scholarship: Biographical Studies on the Formation of a Discipline*, ed. Helen Damico, with Donald Fennema and Karmen Lenz, vol. 2: *Literature and Philology*, Garland Reference Library of the Humanities 2071 (New York: Garland, 1998), 125–38.

9. On Furnivall's politics in relation to his literary activities, see Peter Faulkner, "'The Paths of Virtue and Early English': F. J. Furnivall and Victorian Medievalism," in *From Medieval to Medievalism*, ed. John Simons (Houndmills: Macmillan, 1992), 144–58. Faulkner sees medieval studies as having lost the "political edge" (157) that Furnivall had given it when it entered the academy; in this and the next chapter I take a different view of the political character of Middle English under Furnivall.

10. Peter Sutcliffe, *The Oxford University Press: An Informal History* (Oxford: Oxford University Press, 1978), 54.

11. Skeat to Furnivall, 22 January 1866, Furnivall Papers, King's College, London, 1/1/1.

12. John Gross, *The Rise and Fall of the Man of Letters: Aspects of English Literary Life since 1800* (London: Penguin, 1991), 184.

13. John Munro, ed., *Frederick James Furnivall: A Volume of Personal Record* (London: Oxford University Press, 1911), xliii. Brandl's comment is on 11. Hereafter cited parenthetically in the text, with the abbreviation *VPR* where necessary.

14. Hans Aarsleff, *The Study of Language in England, 1780–1860* (London: Athlone; Minneapolis: University of Minnesota Press, 1983), 221.

15. Alfred Tennyson, "The Epic," in *Poems*, 2 vols. (London: Edward Moxon, 1842), 2:1.

16. The revised poem in the larger scheme of the *Idylls*, "The Passing of Arthur," is located in a contemporary context with a prefaced dedicatory poem lamenting the death of Prince Albert. In the somewhat less optimistic ending of this version, it seems that Arthur arrives at an afterlife, perhaps as a militant Christ-figure ("a king returning from his wars"), but there is no sense that he will come back. He is, in Patrick Brantlinger's words, though "noble and blameless," "a failed reformer." In the temporal world of Bedivere, there is only "the new sun" rising, "bringing the new year." The dying Arthur now seems intended, additionally, as a recollection of Albert. Alfred Tennyson, *Idylls of the King* (London, 1869), 404, 405; Patrick Brantlinger, *The Spirit of Reform: British Literature and Politics, 1832–1867* (Cambridge, Mass.: Harvard University Press, 1977), 187.

17. For an account of Trench and his work see Aarsleff, *Study of Language*, 230–63. Hereafter cited parenthetically in the text.

18. Richard Chenevix Trench, *On the Study of Words: Five Lectures* (London: John W. Parker and Son, 1851), 49.

19. Aarsleff, for whom Trench is the hero of the last part of his book as William Jones is for the first, gives the dean the credit (*Study of Language*, 258–63); Benzie claims much of it back for Furnivall (*FJF*, 86). K. M. Elisabeth Murray's account shows it to have been a more collective affair; see her *Caught in the Web of Words: James Murray and the Oxford English Dictionary* (Oxford: Oxford University Press, 1979).

20. *VPR*, xxxii. Munro implies that Furnivall's loss of faith was a gradual process in the late 1850s and 1860s; that idea is preferable to Benzie's view that he "converted" to agnosticism in 1858 (*FJF*, 22, 277), partly because of the anachronism of using the term for that date and partly because some comments of Furnivall's in his 1862 edition of *Hand-*

lyng Synne suggest only a rational rejection of a literal reading of the Bible, not a rejection of religious belief: "if any doubt the effect of our author's Marvels on the minds of the hearers of this time, let such doubter [*sic*] think of the effect produced on the minds of most people now by the account of the Creation of the World in six of our days; the absurdity of it glides off them like water off a duck's back, and they only receive an impression of the power of the Almighty, which reminds them that He is near to help in their time of need"; Frederick J. Furnivall, ed., *Roberd of Brunnè's Handlyng Synne* (London: Roxburghe Club, 1862), xxv–xxvi.

21. Furnivall to Madden, 31 January 1859, BL Eg MS 2847, fol. 32r; Madden to Furnivall, 2 February 1859, HuntL MS FU 534. Madden had an interest in Mannyng going back to the 1830s; he had transcribed a large part of the *Chronicle* in 1834, but the focus in the transcript on Arthurian material probably suggests that the work can be related to the Gawain edition rather than taken as evidence of a projected edition of the *Chronicle* itself. The transcript is in F. Madden, "Manuscripts and Notices of MS.S. xi–xiv cent. Old English Poetry and Prose," Houghton Library MS Eng 526F, vol. 4.

22. *Transactions of the Philological Society 1858* (Berlin: A. Asher & Co., [1862]).

23. Cf. Sutcliffe, *Oxford University Press*, 54.

24. Circular on the founding of the EETS, preserved as item 4c in the Furnivall Papers, King's College, London.

25. [Frederick Furnivall], "Fifth Report of the Committee [of the EETS], January, 1869," 22. Reports of the EETS can be read in the British Library (Early English Text Society, *Third Annual Report...*, shelf mark Ac. 9925/50) and in King's College, London (Furnivall Papers, item 4c). Neither has a complete run. The third, seventh, ninth, and eleventh reports are in the British Library, along with the unnumbered circulars that appear from 1905. The second, fourth, and fifth reports can be read in King's College. The "Committee" frequently referred to in these reports and attributed with their authorship shows no signs of consisting of anyone other than Furnivall himself.

26. [Frederick Furnivall], "Seventh Report of the Committee, February, 1871," 1–2; the internal quotation is slightly misquoted from J. R. Seeley, "English in Schools," *Macmillan's Magazine*, no. 97 (November 1867): 75–86, quotation on 84; emphasis and ellipses are Furnivall's.

27. [Frederick Furnivall], "Ninth Report of the Committee, January, 1873," 15–16.

28. [Frederick Furnivall], "Eleventh Report of the Committee, September, 1879," 24.

29. [Furnivall], "Seventh Report," 14–15.

30. Ibid., 6.

31. See "Fifth Report of the Committee, January, 1869," 22.

32. Ibid., 15.

33. Skeat himself credited Bradshaw with this, in a letter of 1878 to Bradshaw, printed in Prothero, *Memoir*, 358–59.

34. *Diary*, 12 March 1864, Bod Lib MS Eng. Hist. c. 177, 59.

35. J. Rawson Lumby, ed., *King Horn, with Fragments of Floriz and Blauncheflur, and of the Assumption of our Lady*, EETS, o.s., 14 (London: EETS, 1866); George G. Perry, ed., *Morte Arthure*, EETS, o.s., 8 (London: EETS, 1865); W. W. Skeat, ed., *Lancelot of the Laik*, EETS, o.s., 6 (London: EETS, 1865).

36. Lumby, *King Horn*, x–xii.

37. Ibid., v.

38. Skeat, *Lancelot*, vi; Perry, *Morte*, xii.

39. Nevertheless, Richard Morris began the preface to his edition of *Genesis and Exodus* by saying that he would, as editor, "no doubt, both astonish and alarm his readers by informing them that he has never seen the manuscript from which the work he professes to edit has been transcribed." He goes on to explain that the transcription was done by Furnivall, the proofs read with the manuscript by Skeat, and part of the text collated by Lumby; Richard Morris, ed., *The Story of Genesis and Exodus, An Early English Song*, EETS, o.s., 7 (London: EETS, 1865), v.

40. On this in relation to the *Piers Plowman* editions, see Brewer, *Editing* Piers, 134.

41. Quoted in Morris, ed., *Early English Alliterative Poems in the West-Midland Dialect of the Fourteenth Century*, EETS, o.s., 1 (London: EETS, 1864), xvii, from Frederic Madden, ed., *Syr Gawayne* (Edinburgh: Bannatyne Club, 1839), 302. Emphasis is Morris's.

42. Morris, *Genesis and Exodus*, xii.

43. [Frederick Furnivall], "Early English Text Society: [Fourth] Report of the Committee, January, 1868," 1.

44. *Diary*, 25 March 1868, Bod Lib MS Eng. Hist c. 180, 294.

45. *Diary*, 12 February 1864, Bod Lib MS Eng. Hist. c. 177, 37.

46. Richard Morris, ed., *Sir Gawayne and the Green Knight: An Alliterative Romance-Poem*, EETS, o.s., 4 (London: EETS, 1864), viii.

47. It is notable, though, that Morris ascribed *Sir Gawain* to 1320–30, while Madden had always recognized it as a late-fourteenth-century poem.

48. Gross, *Man of Letters*, 186.

49. Michel Foucault, *The Order of Things: An Archaeology of the Human Sciences* (New York: Vintage Books, 1973), 252.

50. As he makes clear in the "Eleventh Report of the Committee, September, 1879," 1.

51. Figures are based on the list of subscribers in "Third Annual Report of the Committee. January, 1867," 9–14; it is difficult to be exact, as some of the addresses are incomplete and some subscribers have addresses in two places.

52. Based on the subscriber lists in the "Eleventh Annual Report of the Committee, September, 1879," 17–27, and Early English Text Society, Circular [London, 1905], 3–8.

53. Circular [1905], 2. Furnivall's authorship is less clear in this circular; by 1905, the full reports of earlier years had been replaced by a standard-format flyer, which can often be found at the front of EETS editions of the period. The spelling "Shakspere" probably points to the hand of Furnivall.

7. "Wise and Gentle Speech"

1. Frederick J. Furnivall, ed., *The Regement of Princes*, part 3 of *Hoccleve's Works*, ed. Furnivall, EETS, e.s., 72 (London: EETS, 1897), lines 4992–98.

2. M. H. Spielmann, *The Portraits of Geoffrey Chaucer* (London: Chaucer Society, 1900), 6.

3. William Godwin, *Life of Geoffrey Chaucer, The Early English Poet...*, 2 vols. (London: Richard Phillips, 1803), 2:582–83.

4. David R. Carlson, "Thomas Hoccleve and the Chaucer Portrait," *Huntington Library Quarterly* 54 (1991): 283–300; see 289. On this portrait in relation to literary authority, see also Tim William Machan, *Textual Criticism and Middle English Texts* (Charlottesville: University Press of Virginia, 1994), 121.

5. Seth Lerer, *Chaucer and His Readers: Imagining the Author in Late-Medieval England* (Princeton, N.J.: Princeton University Press, 1993), 18–19.

6. Robert Southey, *Specimens of the Later English Poets...*, 3 vols. (London, 1807), 1:xvii.

7. William Wordsworth, "Preface to the Second Edition... of 'Lyrical Ballads,'" in *Wordsworth: Poetical Works*, ed. Thomas Hutchinson, rev. Ernest de Selincourt (London: Oxford University Press, 1969), 735 n. 1.

8. On this construction of Chaucer, see also Machan, *Textual Criticism*, 88–92.

9. William Thynne, ed., *The Workes of Geffray Chaucer newly printed / with dyuers workes whiche were neuer in print before: As in the table more playnly dothe appere* (London, 1532), A2v.

10. [George Puttenham], *The Arte of English Poesie* (London, 1589), 48.

11. Richard Baker, *A Chronicle of the Kings of England. From the Time of the Romans Goverment, unto the Raigne of our Soveraigne Lord King Charles* (London, 1643), Z1r.

12. [John Dart], "The Life of Geoffrey Chaucer," in *The Works of Geoffrey Chaucer, Compared with the Former Editions, and many valuable MSS*, ed. John Urry (London: Bernard Lintot, 1721), E2v.

13. Ibid., F1r.

14. Lee Patterson, *Chaucer and the Subject of History* (Madison: University of Wisconsin Press, 1991), 15.

15. Philip Sidney, "An Apology for Poetry," in *English Critical Texts: Sixteenth Century to Twentieth Century*, ed. D. J. Enright and Ernst de Chickera (Oxford: Clarendon Press, 1962), 40.

16. As did Francis Beaumont, for example, in the prefatory letter in Thomas Speght, *The Workes of our Antient and lerned English Poet, Geffrey Chavcer, newly Printed* (London, 1598).

17. Godwin, *Life of Chaucer*, 2:581.

18. Robert Southey, *Select Works of the British Poets, From Chaucer to Jonson, with Biographical Sketches* (London: Longman, Rees, Orme, Brown, and Green, 1831), 1.

19. FM to Child, 16 November 1855, Houghton Library bMS Am 1922 (185).

20. On Tyrwhitt and his edition, see B. A. Windeatt, "Thomas Tyrwhitt," in *Editing Chaucer: The Great Tradition*, ed. Paul G. Ruggiers (Norman, Okla.: Pilgrim Books, 1984), 117–43.

21. Ibid., 119.

22. Lerer, *Chaucer and His Readers*, 28.

23. Robert Anderson, *A Complete Edition of the Poets of Great Britain*, 13 vols. (London: John and Arthur Arch; Edinburgh: Bell & Bradshute & I. Mundell, 1792–95), 1:vi.

24. On this see Joseph A. Dane, "The Reception of Chaucer's Eighteenth-Century Editors," *Text* 4 (1988): 217–36.

25. S. W. Singer, ed., *The Poems of Geoffrey Chaucer*, 6 vols. (London: C. Whittingham, 1822).

26. Richard Morris, ed., *The Poetical Works of Geoffrey Chaucer: With Memoir by Sir Harris Nicolas*, vols. 1–6, The Aldine Edition of the British Poets (London: Bell and Daldy, 1866).

27. Ralph Hanna III, *Pursuing History: Middle English Manuscripts and Their Texts* (Stanford, Calif.: Stanford University Press, 1996), 5.

28. Eleanor Hammond, *Chaucer: A Bibliographical Manual* (New York: Macmillan, 1908), 40.

29. Thomas Wright, ed., *The Canterbury Tales of Geoffrey Chaucer: A New Text with Illustrative Notes*, vols. 24–26, Early English Poetry, Ballads, and Popular Literature of the Middle Ages series (London: Percy Society, 1847–51).

30. Thomas Ross, "Thomas Wright," in *Editing Chaucer*, ed. Ruggiers, 145. On Child's adoption of Wright, see 154. Wright's edition was reissued in one volume in 1853 and as part of Cooke's Universal Library in 1867.

31. As Madden suggested, a long and careful collation would be needed to establish Wright's debt to Tyrwhitt, and I have not carried this out. However, following a suggestion for which I am greatly indebted to Stephen Knight, I have compared Wright's use of punctuation with Tyrwhitt's. Even where Wright's text varies quite markedly, orthographically, from Tyrwhitt's, there is a high coincidence in punctuation. Collating 400 lines of the *Miller's Tale*, for example, I count 470 instances where Wright and Tyrwhitt share the same punctuation in the same place; 42 instances where they both punctuate, but use different forms; 19 instances where Wright uses punctuation that Tyrwhitt does not, and 12 where Tyrwhitt punctuates and Wright does not. (I ignored quotation marks, which Tyrwhitt does not use, and counted each parenthesis as a single mark of punctuation, as Wright generally has one or two commas where Tyrwhitt has brackets.) A less charitable construction of Wright's practice than the proto-best-text argument is that he selected a good manuscript that differed from Tyrwhitt's text and then saved much of the editing labor by copying Tyrwhitt's punctuation into his base text. The result was the easiest way of producing what looked like a substantially new text.

32. William Benzie, *Dr. F. J. Furnivall: Victorian Scholar Adventurer* (Norman, Okla.: Pilgrim Books, 1983), 254 n. Early pamphlets show that it was not planned, as John Munro seems to have thought, to have separate Lydgate and Hoccleve societies. Cf. John Munro, ed., *Frederick James Furnivall: A Volume of Personal Record* (London: Oxford University Press, 1911), lii n.

33. W. W. Skeat, "The Language of Chaucer," lecture, King's College, London, Skeat-Furnivall Papers, Skeat 3/5 (1875), 28. Furnivall's comments were made in his unsuccessful application for the secretaryship of the Royal Academy in 1873; quoted in Munro, *Furnivall*, l.

34. Walter W. Skeat, ed., *The Complete Works of Geoffrey Chaucer: Edited from Numerous Manuscripts*, 7 vols. (Oxford: Clarendon Press, 1894–97), 1:vii; hereafter abbreviated *CC*.

35. See Donald C. Baker, "Frederick Furnivall," in *Editing Chaucer*, ed. Ruggiers, 158.

36. G. W. Prothero, *A Memoir of Henry Bradshaw* (London: Kegan Paul, Trench & Co., 1888), 223.

37. A. S. G. Edwards, "Walter Skeat," in *Editing Chaucer*, ed. Ruggiers, 173.

38. Bartholomew Price to Bradshaw, 9 November 1870, Camb UL Add 2592, Bradshaw Papers, item 243. Subsequent letters from this discussion are referenced by the abbreviation *BP* and item number. Note that most of the letters written by Bradshaw in this collection are copies or drafts of the letters actually sent.

39. Bradshaw to Price, 10 November 1870, *BP*, item 244.

40. Price to Bradshaw, 30 November 1870, *BP*, item 250.

41. Bradshaw to Macmillan, 6 December 1870, *BP*, item 251; Bradshaw to Price, 17 December 1870, item 253.

42. Furnivall to Bradshaw, 20 December 1870, *BP*, item 254. This is Furnivall's response to Bradshaw's acceptance; the letter of acceptance is not in this collection but it becomes clear in later letters that it is the Minor Poems project that is referred to.

43. Furnivall to Bradshaw, 20 November 1874, *BP*, item 387, where Furnivall mentions his contact with Price, and Price to Furnivall, 21 December 1874, item 389, in which Price tells Furnivall of the rejection.

44. Plans for the project are detailed in *BP*, items 528, 530, 532, 533, and 534. The quotation is from the last of these, Bradshaw to Furnivall, 25 August 1879.

45. See Furnivall to Bradshaw, 19 August 1879, *BP*, item 533.

46. Prothero, writing in 1888, did not think that the project had been "revived... during Bradshaw's lifetime" (*Bradshaw*, 225). Edwards was not able to determine the date ("Skeat," 173, 281 n. 21) and found that some of the Oxford University Press correspondence on the topic was missing. On 13 March 1871 (*BP*, item 273), Furnivall asked Bradshaw if he had heard that the Press had given up its edition of Chaucer—he was obviously unaware that they had in fact done so partly on Bradshaw's advice (see Price to Bradshaw, 3 March 1871, *BP*, item 270; Bradshaw to Price, 9 March 1871, item 271; Price to Bradshaw, 15 March 1871, item 274). A revived Clarendon Chaucer very late in the 1880s would tally with Prothero's statement and the fact that Oxford's medieval series was commenced in that decade. Yet early in 1890, Skeat wrote to Macmillan to decline a suggestion that he edit a complete Chaucer, on the grounds that there would be too much work in it: "it is too laborious a matter to undertake." In this letter, Skeat makes it clear that he has a proposal with Oxford University Press to produce what he says would be "a working text, with notes, &c. of the Canterbury Tales only" (Skeat to Macmillan, 3 February 1890, BL Add MS 55016, fol. 21). A letter to Macmillan a day later points out that "A complete edition is still wanted," and editions such as those of Bell and Morris's Aldine edition "are all, in various ways, quite unsatisfactory" (Skeat to Macmillan, 4 February 1890, BL Add MS 55016, fol. 23). All of this suggests that unless he was engaging in some uncharacteristic chicanery, Skeat was not at work on the Clarendon Chaucer at the time. Given the demands of the edition, though, he must surely have begun on it not very long after February 1890, perhaps expanding his original *Canterbury Tales* project into a complete works edition.

47. Edwards, "Skeat," 171.

48. Robert Bell, ed., *Poetical Works of Geoffrey Chaucer*, vols. 1–8, The Annotated Edition of the English Poets (London: John W. Parker and Son, 1854–56), 1:38.

49. Frederick J. Furnivall, *Trial-Forewords to my "Parallel-Text Edition of Chaucer's Minor Poems" for the Chaucer Society (with a try to set Chaucer's works in their right order of time)* (London: Chaucer Society, 1871), 28.

50. Furnivall to James Russell Lowell, 4 December 1873, Houghton Library bMS Am 765 (338).

51. Furnivall to Bradshaw, 23 June 1873, *BP*, item 331.

52. Walter W. Skeat, *A Student's Pastime: Being a Select Series of Articles Reprinted From "Notes and Queries"* (Oxford: Clarendon Press, 1896), xxvii.

53. Edwards, "Skeat," 182–83.

54. Ibid., 185. Charlotte Brewer, referring to Skeat's editing of *Piers Plowman*, notes the same "breezy self-confidence, coupled with a sure sense of what his audience wanted to read"; Charlotte Brewer, *Editing* Piers Plowman: *The Evolution of the Text* (Cambridge: Cambridge University Press, 1996), 90.

55. Hammond, *Chaucer: A Bibliographical Manual*, 146.

56. Edwards, "Skeat," 186.

57. Walter W. Skeat, *The Evolution of the Canterbury Tales* (London: Kegan Paul, Trench, Trübner & Co., for the Chaucer Society, 1907), 9.

58. See Skeat, *Student's Pastime*, xx; hereafter referenced parenthetically in the text. Brewer plausibly suggests that Skeat's illness was possibly "of psychosomatic origin." It was certainly convenient, removing Skeat from a country parish and leading him "to a leisurely life in Cambridge"; Brewer, *Editing* Piers, 95.

59. Ian Hunter, *Culture and Government: The Emergence of Literary Education* (Houndmills: Macmillan, 1988), 100.

60. Lee Patterson, *Negotiating the Past: The Historical Understanding of Medieval Literature* (Madison: University of Wisconsin Press, 1987), 13.

61. Gladstone to Furnivall, 20 January 1884, HuntL MS FU 326.

62. On Skeat as a lecturer, see Brewer, *Editing* Piers, 102–3.

63. Skeat, *Student's Pastime*, lvii.

64. G. C. Macaulay, ed., *The Complete Works of John Gower*, 4 vols. (Oxford: Clarendon Press, 1899–1902), 2:xiii.

65. Peter Sutcliffe, *The Oxford University Press: An Informal History* (Oxford: Oxford University Press, 1978), 168. See, for an example of thorough scholarship in the OUP series (and a rare contribution from a woman in the male world of Middle English), Lucy Toulmin Smith, ed., *York Plays: The Plays Performed by the Crafts or Mysteries of York...* (Oxford: Clarendon Press, 1885). Lucy Toulmin Smith entered the world of scholarship when her father drowned before seeing his work on guilds through the press for the EETS; see Toulmin Smith, ed., with an introduction and glossary by Lucy Toulmin Smith, *English Gilds...*, EETS, o.s., 40 (London: EETS, 1870).

66. Benzie, *Furnivall*, 38.

67. See D. J. Palmer, *The Rise of English Studies: An Account of the Study of the English Language and Literature from Its Origins to the Making of the Oxford English School* (London: Oxford University Press, 1965), 80.

68. J. R. H. Weaver, ed., *The Dictionary of National Biography, 1922–1930* (London: Oxford University Press, 1937), 351–52.

Conclusion

1. Joseph A. Dane, "The Reception of Chaucer's Eighteenth-Century Editors," *Text* 4 (1988): 217–36, at 218.

2. Tim William Machan, *Textual Criticism and Middle English Texts* (Charlottesville: University Press of Virginia, 1994), 12.

3. *The Teaching of English in England* (the Newbolt Report) (1921; London: HMSO, 1938), 17. Hereafter cited in the text as NR.

4. See Chris Baldick, *The Social Mission of English Criticism, 1848–1932* (Oxford: Oxford University Press, 1983), 92–107.

5. "Play up! play up! and play the game!" Henry Newbolt, "Vitaï Lampada," in *Collected Poems, 1897–1907* (London: Thomas Nelson, n.d.), 131–33.

6. For a different account of the report, one that deemphasizes the role of Arnold's thinking, see Ian Hunter, *Culture and Government: The Emergence of Literary Education* (Houndmills: Macmillan, 1988), 108–11.

7. See ibid., 120–32.

8. See, for example, D. J. Palmer, *The Rise of English Studies: An Account of the Study of the English Language and Literature from Its Origins to the Making of the Oxford English School* (London: Oxford University Press, 1965), chap. 7. Freeman's comment is recorded on 96.

9. On this see Baldick, *Social Mission*, 86.

10. Lee Patterson, *Negotiating the Past: The Historical Understanding of Medieval Literature* (Madison: University of Wisconsin Press, 1987), 38.

11. Terry Eagleton, *The Function of Criticism from* The Spectator *to Post-Structuralism* (London: Verso, 1984), 65.

12. See Jürgen Habermas, *The Structural Transformation of the Public Sphere: An Inquiry into a Category of Bourgeois Society,* trans. Thomas Burger, with the assistance of Frederick Lawrence (Cambridge, Mass.: MIT Press, 1989), esp. chap. 1.

13. Hans Robert Jauss, "The Alterity and Modernity of Medieval Literature," *New Literary History* 10 (1979): 181–227, at 182.

14. Machan, *Textual Criticism*, 43, 134; emphasis added.

15. Lee Patterson, "On the Margin: Postmodernism, Ironic History, and Medieval Studies," *Speculum* 65 (1990): 92. See also his "Introduction: Critical Historicism and Medieval Studies," in *Literary Practice and Social Change in Britain, 1380–1530,* ed. Lee Patterson (Berkeley and Los Angeles: University of California Press, 1990), 1–14, and David Aers, "A Whisper in the Ear of Early Modernists; or, Reflections on Literary Critics Writing the 'History of the Subject,'" in *Culture and History, 1350–1600,* ed. David Aers (New York: Harvester Wheatsheaf, 1990), 177–202.

16. Anne Hudson, "Middle English," in *Editing Medieval Texts: English, French, and Latin Written in England,* ed. A. G. Rigg (New York: Garland, 1977), 49.

17. In addition to Machan's *Textual Criticism* and Brewer's *Editing* Piers Plowman, already discussed here, see Derek Pearsall, "Editing Medieval Texts: Some Developments and Some Problems," in *Textual Criticism and Literary Interpretation,* ed. Jerome McGann (Chicago: University of Chicago Press, 1985), 92–106.

18. Allen J. Frantzen, *Desire for Origins: New Language, Old English, and Teaching the Tradition* (New Brunswick, N.J.: Rutgers University Press, 1990), 125.

19. On this point see Peter Richardson, "The Consolation of Philology," *Modern Philology* 92 (1994): 1–13. Richardson sees the demise of Anglo-Saxon as the result "of important political shifts both inside and outside the academy" (5).

Index

Aarsleff, Hans, 107, 117, 125, 135, 145, 158
Abbotsford Club, 89–90, 94, 97, 107
Ackerman, Gretchen, 118, 120, 125
Ackerman, Robert, 118, 120, 125
Adams, John Quincy, 3, 4
Addison, Joseph, 4, 14
Advocates' Library, 28, 60
Aers, David, 193
Aldine Edition of the British Poets, 170
Aldis Wright, William, 174–75
alliterative revival, 72
allotexts, xix, xxi
Amis and Amiloun, 73, 77–78, 81
Analecta Anglo-Saxonica (Thorpe), xxviii
Ancient Engleish Metrical Romanceës (Ritson), xxx, 25, 40, 45, 51, 77, 80, 131; character of textual editing of, 46–50; reviewed by Scott, 52–53
Ancient English Romance of Havelok the Dane (Madden), xiv, xxx, 88–89, 99, 104, 107, 119, 120–26, 128, 130; glossary of, 121–22, 125; reviews of, 124–25
Ancient Scotish Poems (Pinkerton), 131
Ancient Songs (Ritson), 38, 40–41, 45, 46
Ancrene Riwle (Morton), xxx, 107–8, 134
Anderson, Robert, 170
Anglo-Saxon studies, 108, 135, 190, 196
antiquarianism: amateurism of, 7–8; conservatism of, xxiv–xxv, 117; provincial character of, 7. *See also* taste and antiquarianism
Apostles, The (Society), 145
Arnold, Matthew, 183
Arthour and Merlin, 81; edited by Turnbull, 90, 94–95
Auchinleck manuscript, 28, 57, 60, 69, 153, 206 n. 37; Laing's use of, 96; Scott's possession of, 61, 81, 209 n. 59; Turnbull's use of, 90; Weber's use of, 78, 81
Awntyrs of Arthur, 65, 96, 214 n. 46
Ayenbite of Inwyt, 156

Baldick, Chris, xxi, xxii, 136, 190, 196
Ballad Society, 140
Ballantyne, James, 89
Bandinel, Bulkeley, 118
Bannatyne Club, 90, 107, 114, 117, 124, 136; purpose of, 89; and *Syr Gawayne*, 125
Bannatyne manuscript, 96
Barbour, John, 63, 71, 73, 156
Barker, Francis, 193
Bate, Walter Jackson, 10
"Battle of Otterbourne, The" (ballad), 11
Bell, Robert, 169, 170, 171, 175, 177
Belsey, Catherine, 193
Benzie, William, 141, 144, 151, 153, 154
Berners, Juliana, 71
Berthelette, Thomas, xv
Bevis of Hampton, 73–74; edited by Turnbull, 90, 95, 100
Bibliographia Poetica (Ritson), 41, 43–44
bibliomania, 85, 87, 103, 105, 150
Blair, Hugh, 170
Blakeway, Edward, 19
Blandford, marquis of, 85
Bliss, Philip, xx, 118, 119, 125
Book of the Duchess, The (Chaucer), 180
Book of the Knight of La Tour-Landry, The (Wright), 153
Boswell, James, 22, 60
Bosworth, Joseph, xxxii, 141, 157
Bourdieu, Pierre, 5, 103; notion of "aesthetic disposition," 102
Bradshaw, Henry, xxvi, 164, 177, 180; becomes Cambridge librarian, 139; Bradshaw Shift, 173, 182; constructs canon of Middle English literature, xxxiii; influences Skeat, 151; proposes edition of Chaucer's minor poems, 174; role in Clarendon Chaucer of, 174, 175; "Skeleton of Canterbury Tales," 139
Brandl, Alois, 142, 159
Brewer, Charlotte, 91
Brewer, John, 157

Bronson, Bertrand, 10, 27, 28, 29, 37, 43
Brut (Laȝamon), 194; edited by Madden, xv, xxx, 107, 108, 125, 130, 134; thought to be Semi-Saxon, xxviii, xxix, xxx, 125
Brydges, Samuel Egerton, 86, 103
Buccleuch, duchess of, 60
Buccleuch, duke of, 58–59
Burgess, Anthony, 187–88
Butler, Marilyn, 7

Camden Society, xxv, xxx, 104–9, 121, 134, 149, 157
Campbell, John, earl of Cawdor, 126, 127
Canterbury Tales, The, 168, 173, 195; edited by Skeat, 181–82; edited by Tyrwhitt, 168–70; edited by Wright, xxv, 168, 170–72; printed by Caxton, 165
Cantor, Norman, xvi, xvii
capital: cultural, 5, 102, 103, 150, 187; symbolic, 5, 6, 8, 9, 171
Carlson, David, 164
Carlyle, Thomas, 113, 116
Caxton, William, 92, 165
Certaine Bokes of Virgiles Aeneais (Surrey), 86, 94
Chadwick, H. M., 190
Chandler, Alice, 57
Chartism, 113, 115, 116, 134, 212 n. 10
Chatterton, Thomas, 6, 9, 11, 40
Chaucer and the Subject of History (Patterson), 193
Chaucer, Geoffrey, xvii, xxix, xxxiv, 7, 13, 31, 39, 43–44, 65, 71, 90, 123, 195; "bad" work of, 177–79; compared with other poets, 168, 173; Ellis on, 73; father of English poetry, 167; Hoccleve portrait of, 162–63, 165, 175–77, 179, 180; literary value and, 124, 173; moral exemplar, 179–80, 183; nineteenth-century editions of, 168–75; proposed Globe edition of, 174–75; realism of, 167; reception of, 165–71; seen as improving English language, 34, 76, 163; status as *auctor,* 165, 193; supposed character of, 163, 175–81; supposed modernity of, 164, 166–68, 170, 193. *See also* Clarendon Chaucer
Chaucer Society, xxv, xxxiii, 140, 159, 162, 171–72, 174, 183; and Hoccleve portrait, 177, 180; and public sphere, 192; role in Clarendon Chaucer of, 173
Chaucer studies, xxv, 30, 91, 162, 168, 188
Chester Mysteries (Markland), 94, 98, 99
Chevalere Assigne, 156; edited by Utterson, 88, 98, 121

"Chevy Chace" (ballad), 4, 11, 21
Child, Francis, xiv, 157, 171, 173; plans to write on Chaucer and Gower, 168–69
Chronicle (Mannyng), 60–61
Churl and The Bird, The (Lydgate), 88
Clarendon Chaucer, The (Skeat), 173–75, 177, 179, 181, 184, 185, 219 n. 46
Cleanness, 116, 149, 156
Coletti, Theresa, xxi
Colley, Linda, 103
Commission of Historical Record, 118
comparative philology. *See* philology
Complaint of the Black Knight, The (Lydgate), 123–24
Complete Edition of the Poets of Great Britain, A (Anderson), 170
Complete Works of John Gower (Macaulay), 184–85
Confessio Amantis (Gower), xv, 72–73, 184–85
Constable, Archibald, 67, 77, 89
Conybeare, J. J., 119
Copland, William, 99
Crawford, Robert, 66
Critical Review, 45
Cromek, Robert, 26, 27

Dalkeith, countess of. *See* Buccleuch, duchess of
Dalkeith, earl of. *See* Buccleuch, duke of
Dane, Joseph, 188
Dart, John, 167
Davie, Adam, 71
de Brunne, Robert. *See* Mannyng, Robert
de la Batut, Baron Eunice. *See* Hungerford, Henry James
Desire for Origins (Frantzen), 196
Devonshire, duke of, 86, 103
de Worde, Wynkyn, 97, 99
Dibdin, Thomas Frognall, 85–86, 87, 100, 102
Dickens, Charles, xvii
Dickinson, Henry James. *See* Hungerford, Henry James
Dodsley, J., 7
Dollimore, Jonathan, 193
Dombey and Son (Dickens), xvii
Donatelli, Joseph, 10, 31
Douce, Francis, 26, 64, 78, 118, 124
Dryden, John, 167, 193
Dyboski, Roman, 146

Eagleton, Terry, xxi, xxii, xxxv, 191, 193
Earle, John, 174

Early English Alliterative Poems (Morris),
152–53, 156
Early English Poems and Lives of Saints
(Furnivall), 147
Early English Text Society, xiv, xv, xxii,
xxv, xxvi, 58, 107, 134, 173, 184; and
Arthurian literature, 147, 157; character
of texts produced by, 141, 151–56; and
Chaucer, 172; Extra Series of, 139, 140;
founding of, 140, 147; influences on,
157; and Madden, 135, 147, 155–56; and
patriotism, 147–48; promotes study of
Middle English in schools, 157; and
public sphere, 192; role of Bradshaw in,
xxxiii; subscriber base of, xxxiv, 148–
50, 159–61; taken over by Oxford Uni-
versity Press, 185; and textual editing,
150–51
Early Metrical Tales (Laing), 97
Edinburgh Review, 52
editing, textual. *See under* individual
editors; *see also* Early English Text
Society; Machan, Tim William; Middle
English studies
Edwards, A. S. G., 39; on Madden, 118,
128, 212 n. 21; on Ritson, 44, 47; on
Skeat, 175, 181
EETS. *See* Early English Text Society
Eger and Grime, 65
Eglamour of Artois, 73
Eglinton Tournament, 113–14, 115, 117
"Elegy on Henry, fourth Earl of
Northumberland" (Skelton), 11
Ellesmere manuscript, 173, 177, 181, 182
Ellis, Alexander, 141, 156
Ellis, George, 7, 52–53, 80, 93, 97, 123; on
Chaucer, 73; correspondence with Scott
of, 62, 66, 67; indolent and cursory
reader of, 71, 73; influenced by Scott,
71, 78, 81; on minstrels, 76; works of,
70–77
Ellis, Henry, 119, 135
Encyclopaedia Britannica, xxvii, xxxi
Engels, Friedrich, 134
English, rise of, xxi, xxii
English Historical Review, 105
English Language, The (Latham), xxix–xxx
English Past and Present (Trench), 145
Erceldoune, Thomas of, xxv, 67–69, 172;
supposed authorship of *Sir Tristrem* of,
60–66; construction as minstrel of,
62–63
Evolution of the Canterbury Tales (Skeat),
182

Florice and Blaunchefour, 73, 81, 151
Forme of Cury, The (Pegge), 44
Forshall, Josiah, 119, 120, 134
Fortescue Aland, John, 44
Foucault, Michel, on *episteme*, 29, 158–59;
on power, xxii, 117; on techniques of the
self, xxiii, 200 n. 21
Frantzen, Allen J., xxi, 7, 196
*Frederick James Furnivall: A Volume of
Personal Record* (Munro), 142–43
Freeman, E. A., xxxii, 190
Friedman, Albert B., 40
Furnivall, Frederick, xiv, xvii, xxv, xxxiii,
19, 22–23, 137, 164, 177, 184, 192;
argument with Swinburne, 142; awarded
pension by Gladstone, 183; begins career
in editing, 89, 146–47; begins Extra
Series of EETS, 139; and Chaucer
Society, 162, 172–75; death of, 185;
directorships of, 186; early life and
career, 141–43; edition of Percy Folio,
139–40; editorial theory of, 140–41, 150,
152, 215 n. 7; edits *Handlyng Synne*,
146, 154; edits Lovelich, 146, 154; and
EETS, 147–50, 216 n. 25; influence of
Arthurian romance on, 142; lectures of,
146; patriotism of, 46, 155, 190; and
philology, 143–44, 159; politics of,
142–43; proposes Lydgate and Occleve
Society, 172, 219 n. 32; relations with
Madden, 147, 155; relations with Skeat,
141, 142; religious belief, xxiv, 141–42,
145, 146, 215–16 n. 20; role in Clarendon
Chaucer, 174–75; view of Chaucer, 173,
179–81; view of Ritson and Percy, 140

*Galoran of Galloway. See Awntyrs of
Arthur*
Gamerschlag, Kurt, 78, 82
Ganim, John, 70, 82, 116
Garnett, Richard, 67, 141; critique of
Wright, 106–7
Gawain (character), 114–15, 118, 132–34
Gawain-poet, 194, 195
Gawan and Gologras, 65
Genesis and Exodus (Morris), 154
Gentleman's Magazine, 37, 105, 113, 114,
115, 117
Gentlemen of the Privy Chamber, 116–17
Gest Historiale of the Destruction of Troy,
156
Girouard, Mark, 57, 115
Gladstone, William, 183–84
Gloucester, Robert of, 71, 72, 126

Index

Godwin, William, 28, 42, 164, 167–68
Gollancz, Israel, xxvi, 184, 186, 189
Gower, John, xxxiv, 18, 71, 72, 78, 88, 167, 194; seen as improving English language, 34, 76
Greenblatt, Stephen, 193
Grimm, Jacob, xxviii, xxix, 131, 145
Grundtvig, N. F. S., 107, 108, 119, 125
Guy of Warwick, 73, 79; edited by Turnbull, 90, 93

Hales, John W., 23, 139
Hali Meidenhad, 156
Hallam, Henry, xxviii, xxix
Halliwell, James Orchard, 107–8, 121, 134, 151, 214 n. 50; implicated in theft of manuscripts, 104, 106
Hammond, Eleanor, 170, 181
Hand-Book to the Popular, Poetical, and Dramatic Literature of Great Britain (Hazlitt), 139
Handlyng Synne (Mannyng), xxxi, xxxii; edited by Furnivall, 146–47
Hanna, Ralph, xviii, 170
Haslewood, Joseph, 37, 100, 102, 213 n. 35
Havelok the Dane, xiii, xiv, xv, xx, 88–89, 99, 104, 107, 128, 130; discovery of, 118–19; edited by Madden, 120–26; edited by Skeat, 139, 156
Hazlitt, W. Carew, 31, 138
Hearne, Thomas, 8, 32, 44, 47, 165
Heber, Richard, 70, 86, 91, 92
Hengwrt manuscript, 173, 182
Henry III, proclamation of, xxix
Henryson, Robert, 96
Herbert, Algernon, 126–27
Hermit of Warkworth, The (Percy), 19–22
Hickes, George, xxvii, xxviii, 91
History of English Poetry, The (Warton), xvi, 7, 28, 29, 40, 41, 58, 71; Anglo-Saxon excluded from, 30–31; attacked by Ritson, 36–37; discussion of language in, xxvii, 34; incompletion of, 31; minstrels in, 33; notion of modernity in, 35–36; notion of progress in, 30, 31–32; revisions of, 31, 67, 138; view of Chatterton in, 9–10; view of fifteenth-century literature in, 35; view of Langland's meter in, 72; view of romance origins in, 32–34
History of the Holy Grail (Lovelich), 156
Hoccleve, Thomas, 39, 73, 78, 195; memorializes Chaucer, 162–63, 164, 177; seen as improving English language, 34
Holcroft, Thomas, 28

Huchowne of the Awle Ryal, 65, 156, 172
Hudson, Anne, 7, 195
Hult, David F., xxi
Hungerford, Henry James, 3, 5
Hunter, Ian: on English as technology of the self, xxii, xxiii, xxiv, 8; on origins of English study, xxiii, 136, 183
Huntyng of the Hare, The, 77
Hurd, Richard, 14, 32, 33, 41, 82; theory of romance of, 15–16
Hutcheon of the Awle Royal. *See* Huchowne of the Awle Ryal
hypertext, 195

Idylls of the King (Tennyson), 143–44, 149, 215 n. 16
Illustrations of Anglo-Saxon Poetry (Conybeare), 119
Illustrations of the Literary History of the Eighteenth Century (Nichols), 6
Ingram, John K., 157
Introduction to the Literature of Europe (Hallam), xxviii
Inventing the Middle Ages (Cantor), xvii
Irving, David, 89
Isted, George, 86
Ivanhoe (Scott), 115

Jackson, Andrew (U. S. President), 3
Jamieson, John, 96
Jauss, Hans Robert, 192
Johnson, Arthur, 213 n. 34
Johnson, Edgar, 57
Johnson, Samuel, 12, 19, 36, 75
Johnston, Arthur, 33, 132; on Ritson, 29, 44; on romance 15, 74; on Scott's *Sir Tristrem*, 57–58

Kalamazoo, international congress at, 191
Kemble, John Mitchell, 125, 141
Kendal, Thomas, 61, 65
King Horn, 46, 62, 65, 123; edited by Lumby, 151–52
King's College, London, 136
Knight of Courtesy, 46
Knight, Stephen, 42, 218 n. 31
Koch, C. Friedrich, xxx
Kyng Alisaunder, 77–78, 79, 80
Kyng Roberd of Cysylle (Utterson), xx, 99

Lai d'Havelok le Danois (Michel), xiv
Laing, David, 99, 106, 131; and Abbotsford Club, 90, 94; and Bannatyne Club, 89; career and publications of, 95–97

Lancelot of the Laik (Skeat), 152, 181
Land of Cokaygne, The, 72, 73, 146
Langland, William, 43, 71, 72, 90–91, 123, 173, 194
Latham, R. G., xxix–xxx, xxxii, 144
Launfal, 46
Laȝamon, 71, 72
Lay le Freine, 77, 81
Lay of Havelok the Dane (Skeat), xiii, xiv, xvii, 120, 139, 156
Lay of the Last Minstrel (Scott), 58–60, 67, 68, 70
Leeds, international congress at, 191
Lerer, Seth, xvii, 164–65, 170
Lermont, Thomas. *See* Erceldoune, Thomas of
Letters on Chivalry and Romance (Hurd), 14, 15
Leveson Gower, George Granville, 82, 85, 88
Levine, Philippa, 7–8, 105
Leyden, John, 67
Life of Geoffrey Chaucer (Godwin), 42, 164, 167–68
Life of Johnson (Boswell), 22
Lipking, Lawrence, 13–14
Littledale, Joseph, 103
Lockhart, J. G., 56, 67, 83, 89, 96
Lodge, David, 173
London Working Men's College, 146, 183
Lowell, James Russell, 157
Ludlow, John Malcolm, 142, 146
Lumby, J. Rawson, 151–52
Lybeaus Desconus, 46
Lydgate, John, 18, 35, 39, 43, 71, 73, 78, 195; seen as improving English language, 76
Lyfe of Ipomydon, The, 77

Macaulay, G. C., 184–85, 189
Machan, Tim William, xix, 188; on construction of Chaucer as auctor, 13, 193; on textual editing in Middle English, 14–15, 39, 194–95
Macie, Elizabeth, 3, 6
Macie, Jacques Louis. *See* Smithson, James
Macmillan, Alexander, 174–75
Macpherson, James, 6, 9, 11
Madden, Frederic, xiii, xiv–xv, xviii, xx, xxv, xxx, xxxii, 23, 24, 88–89, 99, 102, 107, 108–9, 114–15, 146, 151, 171, 189; becomes keeper of manuscripts, 120; character of textual editing of, 127–30; conservatism, 116–17, 131, 137, 138–39,

212 n. 21; critique of earlier editors, 129; critique of by Kemble, 125; early career, 117–20; editions of, 120–32; enemy of Wright and Halliwell, 104, 106; interest in Mannyng, 216 n. 21; knighthood, 132; later career, 134–35; literary criticism of, 124, 154; membership in Gentlemen of Privy Chamber, 116–17; and professional medieval studies, 120; relations with Furnivall, 147, 155; relations with Scott, 119, 125; relations with Skeat, 138, 155; relations with Spencer, 119, 125, 128, 132; role in Middle English studies, 116, 117–18, 136; similarities to Scott and Percy, 118; view of Chaucer editions, 168–69; view of romances, 122–23. *See also Syr Gawayne*
Maitland Club, 89–90, 94, 107, 152
Malory, Thomas, 92–93
Mandeville, John, xxix
Mannyng, Robert, 71, 72, 126, 146; claimed as originator of English, xxxi, xxxii–xxxiii; mentions Thomas of Erceldoune, 60–61, 63, 67; seen as improving English language, 34
Markland, James Heywood, 94, 98, 99
Marx, Karl, 134
Masson, David, 157
Maurice, F. D., 141, 146
McGann, Jerome, xviii
Merlin (Lovelich), 146
Metrical Romances (Weber), 26, 77–83
Michel, Francisque, xiv
Middle English language: belief in poets as improvers of, 34, 76, 163; development of terminology of, xxvii–xxxiii, 172; perceived barbarism of, xxvii, 164, 166; uncertainty of category of, xxxiv
Middle English literature: belief in historical value of, 13, 14, 122; belief in philological value of, 93, 99, 154, 156, 166; depiction of manners and customs in, xxv, 32, 42, 73, 74, 75, 77, 78, 80, 93, 96, 97, 99, 122, 123, 124, 132, 157, 173, 179; difference and identity in, xxv, 165–66, 192–93, 194; negative impact of Reformation on, 201 n. 50; perceived barbarism of, xxv, 13, 14, 15, 32, 34, 35, 43, 70, 146, 165, 168
Middle English studies: aristocratic patronage in, xxiii, xxv, 58, 68, 83, 118, 158, 183; coalesces with English studies, xxii, 136, 184, 186; dominance of romance in, xxv, 90, 115, 137, 138;

Middle English studies *(continued):*
emerges as scholarly topic, xxii, xxvi, 7;
export of, 157; marginality of, 190–92,
194, 196; merges with Chaucer studies,
xxv, 168, 171, 192; nationalism in, xxiv,
xxv, xxxiv; political character of, xxiv,
23–24, 117; possible existence in public
sphere of, xxxiv, 8, 23–24, 157–61, 185,
191–92; role of EETS in, 157; role of
Madden in, 117–18, 120; study of
relative to Anglo-Saxon, xxii, xxxiv, 7,
108; as technology of the self, xxiii, xxiv,
8, 9, 23, 70, 109, 158; textual editing in,
39, 128, 195; use of type facsimiles in,
45, 46, 127, 128, 150, 152
Millgate, Jane, 58–59, 62, 68
Minot, Laurence, 40, 43, 45–47, 51, 72,
126, 195
minstrels, 22, 47, 48, 52, 72, 79, 98, 172;
Percy's conception of, 13, 16–19, 21,
59–60; Scott's conception of, 59–60, 65,
69, 75–76, Warton's conception of, 33
Minstrelsy of the Scottish Border (Scott),
58–59, 62, 63, 67, 68–69, 70, 131
modernity, constructions of, 35, 40, 130,
164, 166–68, 194
Molbech, Christian, 119
Monastery, The (Scott), 54–55
Morley, Henry, 157
Morris, Richard, xviii, xix, 141, 152–53;
edits Chaucer, 170; and literary value,
154; reedits *Syr Gawayne,* 155–56;
textual editing of, 151, 153
Morte Arthure, alliterative, 149; edited by
Perry, 152–54
Morte Arthure, stanzaic, 37, 88, 94
Morte D'Arthur (Malory), 37, 92–93
Morte d'Arthur (Tennyson), 142–44
Morton, James, xxx, 107–8, 134
MS Cotton Nero A.x (manuscript), xviii,
xxi, 116, 131, 134, 151, 156
MS Laud Misc. 108 (manuscript), xiii, 152
Munro, John, 142–43, 146, 147
Murray, James, xxxi–xxxii

Napier, A. S., 160
nationalism, xxiv, xxv, xxvii, xxxiii, 66–67,
133, 146, 147–48, 189
Newbolt, Henry, 189
Newbolt Report, 187, 188–90
*New English Dictionary. See Oxford
English Dictionary*
Nichols, John, 6
Nichols, John Gough, 105

Nichols, Stephen G., xxi; and
"supplementation," xviii–xix
Nicolas, Harris, 37, 169, 170
"Northumberland Betrayed by Douglas"
(ballad), 11

*Observations on the Faerie Queene of
Spenser* (Warton), 36
*Observations on the Three First Volumes
of the History of English Poetry* (Ritson),
28, 36–38
Octavian, 77
Oliphant, T. L. Kington, xxx–xxxi,
xxxii–xxxiii
On the Study of Words (Trench), 145
Ormulum, The, xxvii, xxviii, xxix, xxx, 72,
73
Ossian, 9
Otuel a Knight, 81; edited by Turnbull, 90
Owl and The Nightingale, The, 88–89
Oxford Book of Scottish Verse (MacQueen
and Scott), 68
Oxford English Dictionary, 145, 147, 186,
215 n. 19
Oxford Literary Gazette, 124
Oxford University Press, medieval texts of,
185

Palgrave, Francis, 118, 119
Palmer, D. J., 190
Panizzi, Antonio, 135, 138
Patience, 116, 149, 155
Patterson, Lee, xviii, 183, 190–91; on
Chaucer, 167, 193
Paulson, Ronald, 14
Pearl, 116, 149, 153, 155, 194
Pegge, Samuel, 19, 44
Percy, Elizabeth, countess, later duchess of
Northumberland, 3, 11, 13, 22, 23
Percy Folio (BL Add MS 27879), 6, 10, 14,
22, 38, 81, 202 n. 12, 205–6 n. 29; Hales
and Furnivall's edition of, 139–41
Percy, Hugh, earl, later duke of
Northumberland, 3, 5, 6, 11, 12, 22
Percy, Thomas, xxiv, xxx, 41, 50, 71, 75,
84, 86, 87, 93, 97, 102, 194; adopts
Percy name, 6, 202 n. 12; attacks by
Ritson on, 36, 38–39, 46–47, 52; com-
parison with Ritson, 28, 32, 43, 44;
comparison with Scott, 67, 68, 69;
distances himself from *Reliques,* 22;
early life of, 6; editing of *Reliques* by,
8–12, 40; essay on ancient English
minstrels, 7, 18, 23, 31, 122;

Percy, Thomas *(continued)*, essay on
Langland, 72, 91; essay on metrical
romances, 7, 16–18, 23; influence on
nineteenth-century scholars, 107, 139–
40; influence on Scott, 58–60; invented
genealogy of, 6, 22, 117, 204 n. 50; later
career, 13, 22; rewrites ballad of "Sir
Cauline," 10; role in Middle English, 7,
22; self-construction as minstrel, 22;
spreads story of Ritson's death, 26–27;
theory of minstrels, 16–19, 21, 22, 23,
26, 38, 76; theory of romance, 15–18, 79
Perry, George, 152–53
Peterborough Chronicle, xxix
Petrarch, 34
Petrie, Henry, 118, 124
Phillipps, Thomas, 116
Philological Museum, The, 125
Philological Society, 109, 141, 143, 145,
147, 149, 157; *Transactions* of, 147
philology, 136, 144–45; comparative, xiv,
xxv, xxvii, xxx, xxxii, 40, 83, 107, 108,
130, 135, 164; "material," xxi; new, xxi,
107, 125, 141, 143, 158; rejected in
Newbolt Report, 189–90
Pickering, William, 169, 170
Pieces of Ancient Popular Poetry (Ritson),
40, 44, 45, 51
Pierce the Ploughman's Crede (Whitaker),
91
Piercy, Thomas. *See* Percy, Thomas
Piers Plowman (Langland), xv, 43, 106,
193; edited by Whitaker, 90–91;
Furnivall lectures on, 146; printed by
EETS, 149, 156
Pinkerton, John, xxvii, 6–7, 11, 50, 69, 71,
131; and *Sir Tristrem*, 60–61, 64;
"Hardyknute" forgery of, 40, 202 n. 14;
theory of Scottish language of, 65–66
Pistel of Swete Susan, The, 96
Planta, Joseph, 119
Poems on Interesting Events (Ritson),
46–50
Poetical Works of Geoffrey Chaucer
(Skeat), 174–75
Poetical Works of Sir Walter Scott
(Lockhart), 67
Political Songs (Wright), 134
Ponton, Thomas, 88, 94
Porcheddu, Frederick, 206 n. 37
Portraits of Geoffrey Chaucer, The
(Spielmann), 162
Powis, Earl (Edward Herbert, Lord Clive),
86, 104

Price, Bartholomew, 174
Price, Richard, 31, 67
public sphere. *See* Chaucer Society; Early
English Text Society; Middle English
studies
Pursuing History (Hanna), xviii
Puttenham, George, 166–67

Raleigh, Walter, 160, 190
Rask, Rasmus, xxix, 107, 144
Reform Bill, second, 138
Regement of Princes, The (Hoccleve), 162,
164
Reliques of Ancient English Poetry, The
(Percy), xvii, xxiv, xxx, 6, 7, 21, 38–40,
44–45, 58, 67, 101, 131; compared with
Folio manuscript, 11; dedication of, 11,
12, 13, 18, 203 n. 37; first edition, 10;
fourth edition, 22; influence of, 23,
139–40; principle of order in, 154; second
edition, 7, 19; Shenstone's role in, 9–10;
third edition, 30
Repp, T. G., 124
Richard Coer de Lyon, 73, 77
Richard the Redeless (Wright), 106, 134,
171
Rime of the Ancient Mariner, The
(Coleridge), 40
"Rising in the North, The" (ballad), 11–12
Ritson, Joseph, xxiv, xxx, 7, 10, 23, 62, 64,
71, 77, 87, 93, 96, 97, 102, 123; admires
Tyrwhitt, 30; aesthetics and criticism of,
42–43; attacks Percy, 36, 38–39, 46, 52;
attacks minstrel theory, 38, 41; attacks
Steevens and Johnson, 36; attacks
Warton, 31, 36–37; dedicates works to
the public, 51–52, 101; discovers *Sir
Tristrem*, 28, 60; insists on fidelity to
manuscripts, 9, 40, 44, 46, 128, 130; last
illness and death, 25–26, 204 n. 2; life
and career, 27–28; meets Scott, 28, 61;
notions of medieval and modern, 41;
politics of, 28, 43, 51, 70; scholarship
and textual editing of, 29, 44–52; view of
Lydgate, 43–44
Riverside Chaucer, The (Benson), 187–88
Robert of Gloucester's *Chronicle*, 32–33,
147
Robin Hood (Ritson), 40–41, 42, 43, 51
Robinson, Lucius Hooke, 117
Robson, John, 107, 134
Roland and Vernagu, 81; edited by
Turnbull, 90
Rolle, Richard, 72, 79, 126, 156

Ross, Thomas, 171
Rowley, Thomas, 9, 40
Roxburghe Club, xiii, xiv, xx, xxv, 82, 89,
  98, 101, 119, 157; character of editions
  of, 88, 94, 99, 104, 107, 120–21; character
  of members, 88, 99–100, 103; founding,
  86; later history, 146, 149, 150, 158;
  Madden's editions for, 88, 107, 120–21,
  124–27; purpose of, 86; rules of, 87
Roxburghe, duke of, 67, 85

Sainte-Palaye, J. B. de la Curne, 15, 33
Saint Marharete, 72
Saintsbury, George, 160
Scalachronicon, 63
Scotish Song (Ritson), 40
Scott, Walter, xxiv, xxv, 7, 41, 54, 59, 75,
  76, 93, 102, 115, 123, 189; early writings,
  58; founds Bannatyne Club, 89;
  genealogy and early life, 57; influence of
  Reliques on, 23, 24, 58, 75; influences
  Ellis, 71; invented ending to *Sir Tristrem*,
  40, 69, 75, 209 n. 43; involvement with
  Weber, 77–84; joins Roxburghe Club, 86;
  meets Ritson, 28, 61; nationalism of,
  66–67, 69; relations with Madden, 119,
  125; reviews Ritson's *Metrical
  Romanceës*, 52–53; and the Rhymer's
  Glen, 96; and Thomas of Erceldoune,
  60–69; view of his own character, 55–56
Select Collection of English Songs, A
  (Ritson), 38–39, 40, 44, 45
Select Pieces of Early Popular Poetry
  (Utterson), 97, 100
*Select Remains of the Ancient Popular
  Poetry of Scotland* (Laing), 96–97, 99
Select Scotish Songs (Cromek), 26
Semi-Saxon, xxvii–xxviii, xxix–xxxi, xxxii,
  72, 200 n. 25
Seven Sages of Rome, The, 73, 77–78, 81
Sharpe, Charles Kirkpatrick, 94
Shenstone, William, 9–10, 11
Sidney, Philip, 167
Simmons, Clare A., xxxii
Singer, S. W., 124, 125, 170, 213 n. 35
Sir Amadas, 77
"Sir Cauline," (ballad). *See* Percy, Thomas
Sir Cleges, 77
Sir Degaré, 81, 97
Sir Gawain and the Green Knight, xviii,
  xxi, 89, 114, 116, 118, 128–34, 135, 149,
  155–56, 194, 195; supposed Scottishness
  of, 131, 146, 213 n. 46
Sir Isumbras, 73

Sir Orfeo, 46, 96
Sir Tristrem, 79, 81, 123; authorship of,
  xxv, 60–66; censorship of, 67, 208 n. 37;
  discovery of, 28, 60; Scott's edition,
  57–58, 60, 62–66, 75–76, 70; Scott's
  invented conclusion to, 40, 69, 75, 209 n.
  43; supposed Scottishness of, xxv, 62,
  67–68, 131
Skeat, Walter William, xiii, xiv–xv, xvii,
  xxvi, 125, 164, 189; beginnings of work
  in Middle English of, 151, 152; career,
  182–83; and Chaucer, 153, 172–75, 177,
  179, 181–82; edits Langland, 153; helps
  establish English lectureship, 184, 186;
  illness, 220 n. 58; on language, xxxi;
  relations with Furnivall, 141, 174;
  relations with Madden, xv, 120, 138; role
  in establishing Middle English studies,
  xxxiii, xxxiv; textual editing of, 153,
  181–82
Skelton, John, 11
Smart, Christopher, 204 n. 53
Smith, Robert, 25–26
Smithson, Hugh. *See* Percy, Hugh, earl,
  later duke of Northumberland
Smithson, James, 3–6
Smithsonian Institution, 4, 5, 202 n. 5
Society of Antiquaries of Scotland, 96
Society of Antiquaries, 19, 96, 108, 125
Sources of Standard English, The
  (Oliphant), xxx–xxxi
Southey, Robert, 165–66, 168; edits
  Malory, 92–93
Specimens of Early English (Morris), 139,
  149, 156–57
*Specimens of Early English Metrical
  Romances* (Ellis), 70, 71, 73–77, 80,
  81–82; reviewed by Scott, 52–53
Specimens of the Early English Poets
  (Ellis), 70–73, 75, 77
Speght, Thomas, 169
Spencer, George John, second earl, 85–86,
  88, 103, 121; library of, 87, 92, 103, 136;
  relations with Madden, xiv, xx, 119, 125,
  128, 132
Spenser, Edmund, xxx, 7, 34
Spielmann, M. H., 162
Squyr of Lowe Degre, 46
Stansby, William, 92
Steeves, Harrison, 99
Stevenson, Joseph, 88, 152
Surtees, Robert, 37
Surtees Society, 104–5
Sutcliffe, Peter, 185

Sutherland, countess of, 82
Sutherland, John, 56, 57, 59, 67
Sweet, Henry, xxxi, 141
Sykes, Mark Masterman, 86, 88, 101, 103
Sykes, Tatton, 103
Syr Gawayne (Madden), xix, 114–15, 116, 125, 135, 152, 156; costs of, 117; character of textual editing and scholarship in, 128–34; principle of order in, 154

Taill of Rauf Coilyear, The, 96
taste and antiquarianism; dichotomy of, 8, 87, 99; in *History of English Poetry, The*, 32; in work of Ritson, 38, 42, 47, 51, 53
Taylor, Richard, 31
Teaching of English in England, The. See Newbolt Report
ten Brink, Bernhard, 173
Tennyson, Alfred, 141, 142–44
Thelwall, John, 28
Thesaurus (Hickes), xxvii, 91
Thomas of Erceldoune. *See* Erceldoune, Thomas of
Thomas of Ersyldoune, 96–97
Thomas the Rhymer. *See* Erceldoune, Thomas of
Thornton Romances (Halliwell), 107, 134, 151
Thorpe, Benjamin, xxviii, xxix, 107, 108, 141
Three Early English Metrical Romances (Robson), 107
Thynne, William, 166
Toulmin Smith, Lucy, 220 n. 65
treason trial of 1794, 28, 43
Trench, R. C., 141, 145
Tristan (von Strassburg), 67, 82
Troilus and Criseyde (Chaucer), 180
Turnbull, William B. D. D., 89–90, 93–94, 95, 97, 100, 106
Tyrwhitt, Thomas, 7, 34, 64, 71, 107, 123, 165, 171, 181; admired by Ritson, 30; importance of Chaucer edition of, 168–70

University College, London, 136, 141
Urry, John, 167, 169

Utterson, Edward V., xx, 88, 95–96, 97–99, 100, 103, 121

Valdarfer Boccaccio, sale of, 85
Visio Will;ami de Petro Plouhman (Whitaker), 90–92

Wade, 65
Wallace (Blind Harry), 63
Warburton, William, 13, 14
Warton, Thomas, xvi, xxvii, 7, 8, 13, 40, 41, 64, 84, 95, 97, 123, 189, 193, 194; on Chaucer and Gower, 168; influence on nineteenth-century scholars, 107. *See also History of English Poetry*
Weber, Henry, 86, 122, 124; attitude to Ritson, 78; attitude to romances, 78–80; critiques Gower, Hoccleve, and Lydgate, 78; discusses origin and decline of romance, 79; involvement with Scott, 67, 77–83; life of, 82; literary appreciation of, 80–81; madness and death of, 83; textual editing of, 77–78
Wheatley, Henry Benjamin, 141, 151
Whitaker, Thomas Dunham, 90–92
White, Robert Meadows, xxx
William and the Werwolf (Madden), 125–28, 130, 135. *See also William of Palerne*
William of Palerne, 88, 125–28, 130, 135; edited by Skeat, 139, 156
Wolfgram, William, xiii
Wordsworth, William, 91, 140; on Chaucer, 165
Works of Geoffrey Chaucer, The (Robinson), 187
Wright, Thomas, 104, 108, 134; Chaucer edition of, xxv, 168, 169, 170–72; critiqued by Garnett, 106–7; debt to Tyrwhitt, 218 n. 31; nature of scholarship of, 106, 153; textual editing of, 171; on Thomas of Erceldoune, 67
Wycliffe, John, 134
Wyntoun, Andrew, 63, 71, 73

Yorkshire Garland, The (Ritson), 40
Ywain and Gawain, 46, 50, 51, 79

MEDIEVAL CULTURES

VOLUME 10
Claire Sponsler
*Drama and Resistance: Bodies, Goods, and Theatricality in
Late Medieval England*

VOLUME 9
Edited by Barbara A. Hanawalt and David Wallace
*Bodies and Disciplines: Intersections of Literature and
History in Fifteenth-Century England*

VOLUME 8
Marilynn Desmond
Reading Dido: Gender, Textuality, and the Medieval "Aeneid"

VOLUME 7
Edited by Clare A. Lees
Medieval Masculinities: Regarding Men in the Middle Ages

VOLUME 6
Edited by Barbara A. Hanawalt and Kathryn L. Reyerson
City and Spectacle in Medieval Europe

VOLUME 5
Edited by Calvin B. Kendall and Peter S. Wells
Voyage to the Other World: The Legacy of Sutton Hoo

VOLUME 4
Edited by Barbara A. Hanawalt
Chaucer's England: Literature in Historical Context

VOLUME 3
Edited by Marilyn J. Chiat and Kathryn L. Reyerson
The Medieval Mediterranean: Cross-Cultural Contacts

VOLUME 2
Edited by Andrew MacLeish
The Medieval Monastery

VOLUME 1
Edited by Kathryn Reyerson and Faye Powe
The Medieval Castle

David Matthews is a lecturer in the Department of English at the University of Newcastle, Australia. He is the author of several articles on Middle English and Old French, and the coauthor (with Murray Bramwell) of *Wanted for Questioning: Interviews with Australian Comic Artists and Writers.*